New Inside Out

Sue Kay, Vaughan Jones,

Helena Gomm, Peter Maggs,

Caroline Brown & Chris Dawson

Elementary

Teacher's Book

MACMILLAN

Macmillan Education
Between Towns Road, Oxford OX4 3PP
A division of Macmillan Publishers Limited
Companies and representatives throughout the world

ISBN 978-1-4050-8601-1

Text © Sue Kay and Vaughan Jones 2007
Text by Helena Gomm
Photocopiable resource materials by Peter Maggs, with Sue Kay, Jon Hird,
Carmen Santos Maldonado, Nicholas Sheard, Philip Borrell, Elisa Jiménez Lazcano
and Fernando Alba
Design and illustration © Macmillan Publishers Limited 2007

First published 2007

Note to Teachers

Designed by 320 Design Limited
Page layout by Carolyn Gibson
Illustrated by Phil Garner, Peter Harper, Ben Hasler and Ed McLachlan
Cover design by Andrew Oliver

The authors and publishers would like to thank the following for permission to
reproduce their material: Quotation from *Language and Problems of Knowledge* by Noam
Chomsky copyright © Noam Chomsky 1988 Massachusetts Institute of Technology,
reprinted by permission of The MIT Press, Cambridge, Massachusetts. Quotation from
Understanding Second Language Acquisition by Rod Ellis copyright © Rod Ellis 1985,
reproduced by permission of Oxford University Press. *I Like The Way* lyrics by Dylan
Burns copyright © BMG Music Publishing Limited/Sony/ATV Music Publishing (UK)
Limited 2005, reprinted by permission of the publishers. All Rights Reserved; *Don't Worry
Be Happy* Words and Music by Bobby McFerrin copyright © Prob Noblem Music/BMG
Music Publishing Ltd, Bedford House, 69–79 Fulham High Street, London, SW6 1994,
reprinted by permission of the publisher; *Sailing* Words and Music by Gavin Sutherland
copyright © Island Music Limited/Universal Music Limited 1972, reprinted by
permission of Music Sales Limited. All Rights Reserved. International Copyright Secured;
Get Here Words and Music by Brenda Russell copyright © Rutland Road Music 1988,
reprinted by permission of Warner/Chappell Music Ltd, London, W6 8BS.

These materials may contain links for third party websites. We have no control over, and
are not responsible for, the contents of such third party websites. Please use care when
accessing them.

Although we have tried to trace and contact copyright holders before publication, in
some cases this has not been possible. If contacted, we will be pleased to rectify any
errors or omissions at the earliest opportunity.

Printed and bound in Spain by Edelvives

2011 2010 2009 2008 2007
10 9 8 7 6 5 4 3 2

Contents

Student's Book contents map

Units & topics	Speaking & Writing	Reading & Listening texts	Grammar, Vocabulary & Pronunciation
1 Airport **Introductions** **Air travel** **Nationalities** page 4	Introducing yourself and saying where you are from Exchanging names and numbers Identifying objects **WB** **W** Punctuation (1). Form filling	Meeting on a plane Going through customs Airline phone numbers Exchanging contact details **Useful phrases:** Asking for clarification	**G** *be*: present simple affirmative. Nouns. *a/an. this/these* **V** Countries. Nationalities. Languages. Common objects. Numbers *0–10* **Focus on:** instructions **P** Sounds of the alphabet
2 People **Favourite things** **Jobs** **Personal details** page 10	**S** Favourite things **S** Discussing ages **S** Jobs **W** Questions to find out personal details **WB** **W** Punctuation (2). Personal description	**R** Brad Pitt's favourite things In the world today … **R** The percentage of women in certain jobs in the UK **Useful phrases:** Greetings and introductions	**G** Possessive determiners. *be*: present simple **V** Favourite things. Numbers *11–999*. Jobs **P** *a/an*
3 Family **Family** **Lifestyle** page 16	**S** Families **S** Lifestyle **Anecdote:** Your favourite relative **W** Sentences about your family **WB** **W** Punctuation (3). Description of a family	**R** Meet the Collisters **R** Who is it? **R** *Wife Exchange* Sophie's favourite relative **Useful phrases:** Advice and warnings	**G** Possessive '*s/s*'. Present simple affirmative **V** Family **P** 3rd person endings /s/, /z/, /ɪz/
4 Different **Men & women** **Likes & dislikes** page 22	**S** Differences between men and women **S** Likes and dislikes **W** A short personal message **WB** **W** Punctuation (4). Email to a new friend	**R** He or She? **R** How are men and women different? Jack and Layla's likes and dislikes **Useful phrases:** Expressing opinions	**G** Present simple. Object pronouns **V** *like / don't like + ing* **Focus on:** instructions **P** *ing* sound
Review A page 28	**Pages 28, 29: Grammar / Vocabulary / Pronunciation review** **Pages 30, 31: Reading & Listening. Writing (web profile) & Speaking • Song:** *I Like The Way …*		
5 Days **Daily routine** **Going out** page 32	**S** Daily routines **S** The weekend **W** A perfect weekend **WB** **W** Sequencing: *then, after (that)*. Description of a perfect day	**R** Seven perfect daily moments Interview with three people **R** Ms Dynamite's perfect weekend **Useful phrases:** Ordering and paying	**G** Present simple: daily routine. Telling the time **V** Days of the week. Verb phrases: *have* and *go* **P** Long vowel sounds: /iː/, /ɜː/, /ɔː/
6 Living **Habits** **Special days** page 38	**S** Habits and frequency **S** Special days **Anecdote:** Your favourite festival / party **WB** **W** Paragraph organisation	**R** Little and Large **R** The top three world festivals Conor's favourite festival **Useful phrases:** Asking about opening and closing times	**G** Present simple with adverbs of frequency. Prepositions of time **V** Verb phrases: *make* and *do*. Months. Ordinal numbers. Dates **Focus on:** *go* **P** Ordinal numbers
7 Sea **Water sports** **Holidays** page 44	**S** Water sports **W** A simple narrative **WB** **W** Time expressions. Telling a story	Two interviews about water sports **R** It's always warm on the inside **R** Shark attack! **Useful phrases:** Talking about the weather	**G** Past simple: regular and irregular verbs **V** Water sports. Time expressions. *ago*. Time linkers **Focus on:** *make* and *do* **P** *ed* endings
8 Alone **Feelings** **Experiences** page 50	**S** Feelings **W** A retired person **Anecdote:** Your last summer holiday **WB** **W** Description of a holiday	**R** Alone at sea Interview about Debra Veal Lottie's last summer holiday **R** I want to be alone **Useful phrases:** Complaints and suggestions	**G** Past simple: affirmative, negative and question forms **V** Feelings. Adjectives **P** Vowel sounds: irregular past simple forms
Review B page 56	**Pages 56, 57: Grammar / Vocabulary / Pronunciation review** **Pages 58, 59: Reading & Listening. Writing (a memorable day) & Speaking • Song:** *Don't Worry, Be Happy*		

WB = **Workbook**. Each unit of the Workbook contains a one-page section which develops practical writing skills.

Introduction

Welcome to *New Inside Out!*

New Inside Out is the fruit of many years teaching, writing and developing material. Everything we write is informed by the reactions we get from our students. Our aim is simply to produce a set of materials that will help you create optimum conditions in your classroom for learning to take place.

Sue Kay   *Vaughan Jones*

Engaging content

The American linguist and philosopher Noam Chomsky once said:

'The truth of the matter is that about 99% of teaching is making the students feel interested in the material. Then the other 1% has to do with your methods.'

While we might want to quibble with the percentages, we would nevertheless agree whole-heartedly with the central message in Professor Chomsky's assertion: namely, students learn best when they're interested in the material. It's as simple as that. A text might contain six beautifully-crafted examples of the past simple, a good spread of high frequency lexical items and exemplify some useful functional language, but if it doesn't engage the students, if they can't relate to it, if it feels alien to them, then the most important ingredient for successful learning is missing.

In *New Inside Out*, we've drawn on our own classroom experience, and that of our colleagues around the world, to select topics, texts and tasks that engage students both emotionally and intellectually. Students are our richest resource. They come to class with their own knowledge of the world, their own tastes, feelings and opinions. It's up to us to exploit this rich resource by organising learning around topics that they can relate to – topics that are part of their life experience.

Structured support

We all know that learning a language is a messy, non-linear business. We're dismayed when there seems to be little correlation between what is taught and what is learned! However, there is plenty of evidence to suggest that 'instructed' learners (those who attend classes or follow a course of study) learn faster, and ultimately attain a higher level of proficiency than 'non-instructed' learners.

In *New Inside Out*, new language input is carefully controlled: we aim to maximise exposure to high frequency language appropriate to this level. Students are encouraged to notice new grammar and new vocabulary in contexts where the meaning is clear. They are then given opportunities to manipulate the new language and try it out in different situations. They discover why using one particular form rather than another one actually matters: not just because it's right or wrong, but because it does or doesn't communicate a meaning successfully. The emphasis is always on what students can do with the language rather than what they know about the language. The new language is systematically reviewed and recycled until finally the students feel confident enough to use it to make their own meanings. It becomes part of their available repertoire. It has been 'learned'.

Real world tasks

We're strong believers in the old adage: 'practice makes perfect'. *New Inside Out* emphasises output, particularly speaking, and there are a huge number of tasks that are designed to develop fluency. Students practise functional language in sections entitled *Useful phrases*. But for the most part, the speaking tasks simply encourage the students to talk about things that actually matter to them, rather than playing roles or exchanging invented information. One of our main objectives is to ensure that the language our students spend time rehearsing in the classroom is transferable to the real world. By orchestrating tasks that require the students to use grammar and vocabulary to make meaningful utterances, this objective becomes obtainable. As the linguist and academic Rod Ellis reminds us:

'It is the need to get meanings across and the pleasure experienced when this is achieved that motivates second language acquisition.'

www.insideout.net
'the art of communication'

Components of the course

Student's materials

- Student's Book *see page viii–x*
- CD-ROM *see page xi*
- Workbook and Audio CD
  see page xi

Teacher's materials

- Teacher's Book
  see page xii
- Class Audio CDs
  see page xii
- Test CD *see page xii*
- DVD *see page xiii*
- DVD Teacher's Book
  see page xiii
- Website *see page xiii*

Student's materials A typical Student's Book unit (Unit 4)

A language menu at the beginning of each unit summarises the main teaching point.

Headings throughout the units provide clear information about what the students are studying.

Motivating reading texts have been adapted and graded to suit the Elementary level student. They have been selected not only for their language content, but also for their interest and appropriacy.

Readings are supported by recordings.

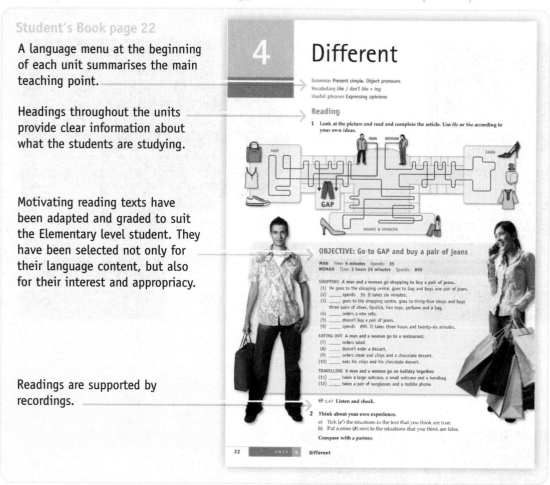

New Inside Out Elementary includes an average of two grammar sections in every unit. Typically, these follow a five-stage approach.

1 New grammar is presented in a realistic context, usually a dialogue or a short text.

2 Students listen to the sentences and do choral repetition of the new language.

3 Students focus on the way the new language works.

4 The practice stage is designed to be realistic and meaningful.

5 Students use the target sentences for controlled, personalised practice.

Additional support is provided in the margin.

In addition, students are referred to the *Grammar Extra* at the back of the Student's Book for extended explanations and further practice.

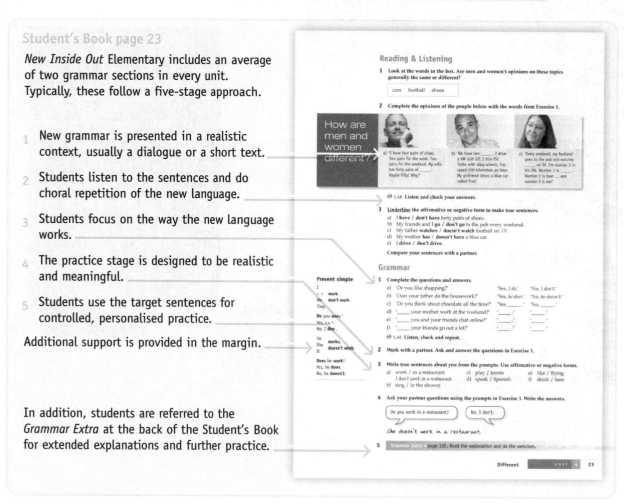

Here is another example of a typical grammar section.

Motivating writing practice is provided in a task where students follow a model. There is also a comprehensive writing course which runs throughout the Workbook.

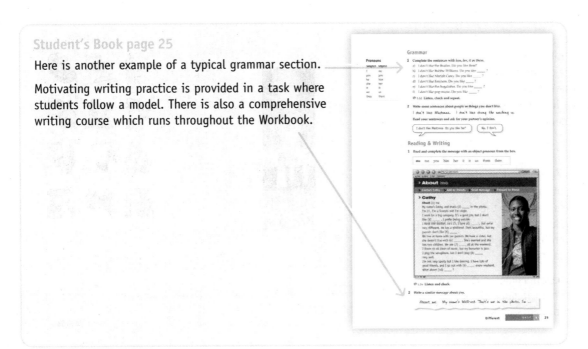

Vocabulary is presented in context and is related to the themes and topics in the unit.

The pages are designed to feel airy and spacious.

There is one pairwork for every unit which offers further speaking practice. These are clearly labelled for the student.

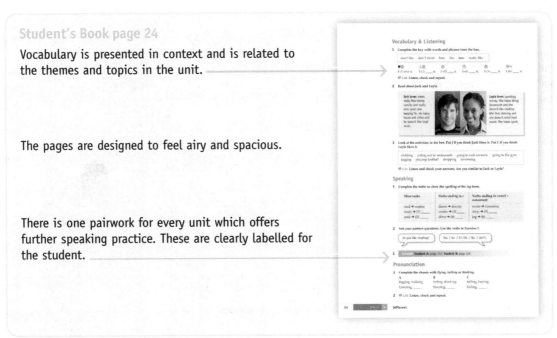

The listenings include texts specially written for language learning. There are dialogues, conversations and monologues. There is a variety of English accents and the tasks are designed to develop real-life listening skills.

Pronunciation work on particular areas of sound, stress and intonation is integrated into every unit.

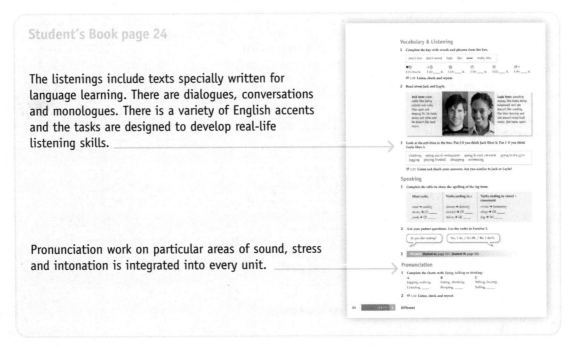

Useful phrases gives students a portable toolkit of functional language. These sections are designed to be fun and engaging and the phrases are recorded on the Audio CD.

The *Vocabulary Extra* pages at the end of every unit recycle the key vocabulary items taught in the unit. This provides students with an activated wordlist and a useful bank of vocabulary.

The *Focus on* section singles out a specific area of high frequency vocabulary and provides extra practice.

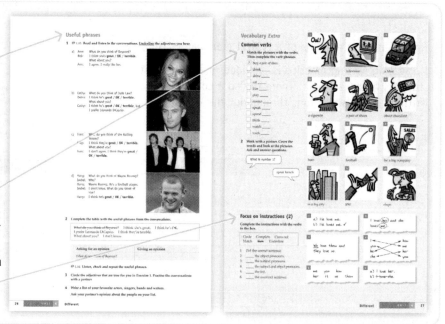

There are four Review units in *New Inside Out* Elementary Student's Book. Each Review unit revises the new structures taught in the previous four teaching units.

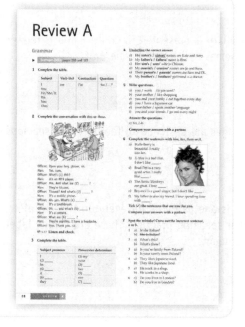

The *Grammar Extra* pages at the back of the Student's Book provide a summary of the new grammatical structures as well as extra practice.

CD-ROM

The CD-ROM in the back of every Student's Book provides a wealth of interactive practice activities along with integrated listening material and video clips contextualising the *Useful phrases*.

Workbook pages 16 and 17

The Workbook provides revision of all the main points in the Student's Book, plus extra listening practice, pronunciation work and a complete self-contained writing course. There are with and without key versions, and a story is included in the back of the Workbook.

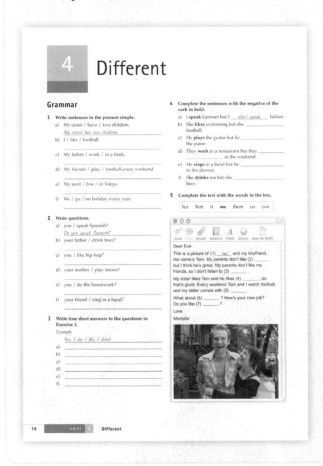

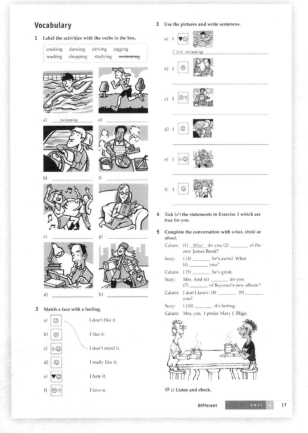

Teacher's materials

Teacher's Book

The 6-in-1 Teacher's Book contains:

- an Introduction
- Practical methodology
- Council of Europe (CEF) checklists
- complete teaching notes with answer keys
- a bank of extra photocopiable grammar, vocabulary and communicative activities
- a Test CD with word files that you can edit and the recordings of the listening test activities

Class CD set

The Class CDs contain:

- the dialogues and listening activities from the Student's Book
- recordings of the songs
- recordings of the reading texts

DVD and DVD Teacher's Book

The DVD contains programmes which complement the topics in the Student's Book. There is a wide variety of formats including interviews, profiles, documentaries and video diaries. The DVD Teacher's Book contains related teaching notes and photocopiable worksheets.

Website

www.insideout.net

Visit www.insideout.net to find out more details about the course and its authors. The new magazine-style website provides downloadable resources and more information about *New Inside Out*.

Practical methodology

Teaching elementary students

Students find themselves in an elementary class for all sorts of different reasons. Many will have spent some time being taught (but not learning!) English at secondary school. Others will be moving up from a beginner level. Some may still be genuine beginners but will join the class because it is the lowest level available at the school. For *New Inside Out* Elementary we drew on our own experience of teaching elementary students, and talked to many other colleagues teaching at this level. We decided that it was best to assume that students have at least some prior knowledge of the language, but that this knowledge was quite sketchy and incomplete. We opted for a building block approach – low and slow – where the content of each unit builds on the previous one, and where the grammar and vocabulary is frequently and systematically reviewed and recycled.

Right from the start

Every teacher has their own way of setting up their classroom, interacting with their students and conducting their lessons. Here are a few things we've found useful to bear in mind.

The right atmosphere

It's important to do everything you can to create a supportive learning environment. Start by memorising every student's name and learn as much information as you can about them.

Elementary students are often shy about speaking in English. As anyone who has learnt a foreign language will know, in the very early stages it takes a great deal of courage to open your mouth and say something. Yet we know that the sooner you start, the more practice you get, the more confident you feel and the easier it becomes.

In *New Inside Out* Elementary we've used a number of strategies to help build up the students' confidence. Students aren't required to use new language before they've had a chance to listen and repeat words and phrases chorally. 'Drilling' is the technique most teachers use to help their students get their tongues around new language. However, when you're focusing on form, it doesn't follow that you have to abandon meaning. In *New Inside Out* language practice, however controlled, is always meaningful.

- Instructions are simple and the same ones are repeated throughout the course.

- Activity-types are repeated, especially in the grammar sections, so that the students get used to what is expected of them.

- Students are encouraged to work in pairs and groups, so that they can rehearse the language 'in private' rather than be immediately required to speak in the more intimidating arena of the class.

Elementary students may need more time to think. It's perfectly normal to have moments of silence while students absorb and process new information, write down new vocabulary from the board, or think about their answers. Don't be afraid of the 'pregnant pause'!

The right environment

Your classroom might be the only exposure to English that students get. Make that exposure as rich as you can by decorating the walls with maps and posters. Here are some further ideas.

- Stick up useful formulaic phrases. For example, phrases from Unit 1 *Useful phrases: How you spell it?, Can you repeat that please?,* or Unit 5 *Useful phrases: How much is it?, Can I have the bill please?,* etc.

- Keep a 'wordbox' on your table, where words or phrases that come up in the lesson are recorded on strips of paper and put in the box. Alternatively, you could institute the 'class scribe' idea. One student in the class is given the role of recording any new language that comes up during the lesson that isn't necessarily the target language of that lesson. This record is then photocopied for everyone in the class, including the teacher who can use the data for revision activities. The role of class scribe is rotated.

- Introduce your students to simplified graded readers. Many of them now come as 'talking books' with CDs. This is invaluable input. Get your students hooked on books!

- Use English in the classroom. It's very tempting to slip into the students' language – particularly if you're teaching elementary students in a monolingual situation. Try to use the L1 only for an occasional quick translation or brief explanation.

The right learning skills

Elementary students may need some help with learning strategies. Here are some thoughts.

- Spend time encouraging students to experiment with how they record words and phrases from the lesson. Get them to draw the word rather than translate it. They're then associating the word with the concept rather than with another word. Make sure they note the part of speech – verb, noun, adjective, etc. Tell them to find a way of noting the pronunciation of the word, either using phonemic script (in the back of the Student's Book), or by developing their own system. Ask them to write complete personalised sentences putting the new word or phrase in a real context and thereby making it more memorable.

- A dictionary is a very important language learning tool and most students will buy one. Elementary students prefer a bilingual dictionary as this provides them with a quick translation of the word they need. Although at elementary level most of the vocabulary they need is straightforward, it's important to begin teaching them good dictionary skills.

The right amount of practice

In our experience of teaching elementary students, the most successful lessons consist of a manageable amount of new input, and then a lot of meaningful practice. For this reason, we've tried to provide maximum practice activities in *New Inside Out*, both in the Student's Book and in the other supporting components.

The top 10 activities for elementary students

These tried and trusted activities can be used as lead-ins, warmers, fillers, pair-forming activities, or for revision and recycling. Most of them require very little or no preparation and can be adapted to cover a wide variety of different language points. You may be familiar with some of the ideas and others may be new. In any event, we hope they provide a useful extension to your teaching repertoire. They certainly get used and re-used in our own classrooms!

It is always useful to have a stock of small white cards and access to a stock of pictures. Magazine pictures are ideal, and can be filed in alphabetical order according to topics.

Alternatively, use the pictures in the *Vocabulary Extra* section at the end of each unit in *New Inside Out* Elementary Student's Book.

1 Board bingo

Aim

This activity is good for revising any type of vocabulary.

Preparation

Write down twelve to fifteen words you want to revise on the board.

Procedure

- Ask the students to choose five of the words and write them down. When they've done that, tell the students that you're going to read out words in random order and that they should cross out one of their words if they hear it. When they've crossed out all five words, they shout *Bingo!* Make sure you keep a record of the words you call out so that you can check the students' answers.

- You can make this more challenging by reading out dictionary definitions of the words rather than the words themselves. (Or if you teach a monolingual class, then you could read out a translation of each word). Alternatively, you can turn it into a listening exercise and choose words that are phonetically similar, i.e. *work* /wɜːk/, *walk* /wɑːk/ and *woke* /wəʊk/, etc.

- At the beginning of the course, you could simplify the activity by writing up single letters (especially the vowels) or numbers (or a mixture of cardinal and ordinal numbers).

2 Standing in line

Aim

This is a great way to review names after Unit 1.

Preparation

None.

Procedure

- Ask all the students to stand up and then line up in alphabetical order according to the first letter of their first name. Show the class where the line should begin. Encourage them to ask one another *What's your first name?* so that they can put themselves in order.

- Once they've lined up, check that they're in the correct order by asking them to take it in turns down the line to say *My name's …*

- Here are some more ideas for line-ups.

  1 Use middle names, surnames, or their mother's or father's first name, etc.

  2 To recycle numbers: hand out cards with different numbers on them. Ask them to repeat their number out loud till they can organise themselves in numerical order.

  3 To practise dates and months: line up in order of the date and month of birth.

  4 To practise saying times: hand out a clock face with a different time on it to each student in the class. Ask them to line up in chronological order by saying the time on their clock.

  5 To recycle vocabulary: hand out one picture card to each student. Ask them to line up according to the first letter of the word it represents by saying their word out aloud.

  6 To recycle vocabulary: divide the class into groups, mix up the letters of a word and give one letter to each student in the group. Call out the complete word and ask them to get into the correct order to spell the word.

  7 To revise word order: mix up the words of a sentence and give one word to each student in the group. Ask them to arrange themselves in the correct order to make a sentence by saying their word out aloud.

Follow-up

Once the students have completed a line-up activity, you can divide them into pairs or small groups before they sit down by asking them to work with the student(s) they're standing next to. This works well in a class where students always tend to sit in the same place.

3 Battleships

Aim

To practise the alphabet and revise vocabulary.

Preparation

Each student will need a grid of roughly ten to twelve squares across and down (see below). Graph paper is ideal for this activity.

Procedure

- Demonstrate the activity by drawing a blank grid on the board. Think of a word or words you want to revise and write them onto a different grid on a piece of paper, but don't tell the students what they are yet. You should write the words horizontally, one letter per square, as shown below.

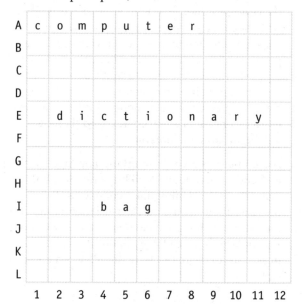

- Now tell the students that there are some words hidden in the grid. Explain that they need to find the squares with letters in them. Tell them to guess squares by giving letter and number references. For example, C–2, F–12, J–4, etc. When a student guesses a square with a letter in, write it in the square. Continue like this until they've found all the words.

- Now ask the students to work in pairs. First, they should draw two grids. One of them should remain blank, and on the other they need to write words, but without showing their partner. Either you can let the students choose their own words, or else you can give them a topic. For example, write three countries / nationalities / jobs / classroom objects / names.

- When they've written their words, tell the students to take it in turns to name a square on their partner's grid. If there's a letter in the square, their partner should say what the letter is and they should write it in the blank grid.

- As soon as they think they know their partner's word, they can guess. If it's wrong, they miss a turn.

4 Category dictation

Aim

This activity can be adapted to review almost any vocabulary. It can also be used to review certain pronunciation and grammar points.

Preparation

Choose the language you want to review and devise a way of categorising it into two or more categories.

Procedure

- Write the category headings on the board and ask the students to copy them onto a piece of paper. Two simple categories is usually best. More than three can get complicated. Then dictate the words (ten–twelve maximum) slowly and clearly, and ask the students to write them down in the correct category.

  For example, you want to revise jobs from Unit 2. Your categories might be jobs you do inside and jobs you do outside. So, write the following on the board and ask the students to copy it down.

Inside	Outside

- Then dictate the words: e.g. *a doctor, a hairdresser, a lawyer, a taxi driver*, etc. The students write down the words in the correct category. When you've dictated ten or twelve words, ask the students to compare their lists. When they've done this, ask them to call out their answers and write them on the board in the correct category, so that they can check the spelling. Alternatively, you could ask the students to take it in turns to write the answers on the board.

- Here are some more ideas for categories:

  1 Revise numbers. (Unit 2)
    Suggested categories: *11 to 999; Even numbers* and *Odd numbers*.

  2 Revise furniture. (Unit 9)
    Suggested categories: *Usually in a living room* and *Not usually in a living room; Cost under £100* and *Cost over £100*.

  3 Revise food and drink. (Unit 10)
    Suggested categories: *Proteins and carbohydrates; Singular and plural; Countable and uncountable*.

5 Mill drills

Aim

To provide controlled practice of new language in a drill-like way, and to give students the opportunity to repeat the same language with several different partners.

Preparation

Organise your classroom so that the students can move around and speak to one another. Prepare one prompt card for each student in the class. The prompts will depend on the language you want to practise. See below for examples of cue cards.

Procedure

- Tell the students that they're going to spend 10 to 15 minutes practising the new language, and that you're going to demonstrate this.

- Give one card to each student in the class, and keep one for yourself. Write a sample dialogue on the board. Point to the part of the dialogue to be supplied by the picture or word prompts on the card. For example:

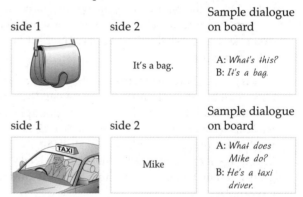

side 1	side 2	Sample dialogue on board
	It's a bag.	A: *What's this?* B: *It's a bag.*

side 1	side 2	Sample dialogue on board
	Mike	A: *What does Mike do?* B: *He's a taxi driver.*

- Explain that the language will change according to the prompt on the card. Show the students how to hold their cards. This is important because cards must be held in such a way that when the students are talking to a partner, they're both able to see each other's cards.

- Choose a confident student to demonstrate the activity with you. Then ask two or three pairs of students to demonstrate the dialogue.

- Ask all the students to stand up and to go round the class or group, repeating the dialogue with as many different partners as possible, and using their cards as prompts.

- Stop the activity after a few moments, and ask the students to either exchange cards with another student or turn their card around so that the students get the opportunity to make new responses.

6 Chain memorisation

Aim

This memory activity can be used to review vocabulary or a grammatical structure. It's also very useful for elementary students, because it gives them an opportunity to get their tongues around longer utterances.

Preparation

Some simple prompt cards can be helpful, but they aren't essential.

Procedure

- If you have a very large group, it's better to split the group into two or three smaller groups, so that everyone has the opportunity to speak before the sentences get too long!

- First, demonstrate how the game will work before you split the group. For example, to practise *There's / There are* and the vocabulary from Unit 9, prepare prompt cards based on the vocabulary of the lesson, in this case, features of a home or a hotel. Model the phrase *In my living room, there's a ...*, turn over a card and add the relevant word, for example, *a sofa*. Ask the first student to repeat *In my home, there's a sofa.*

- As they finish, add the words *and there ...*, and turn over another card indicating that you want the next student to add this to the sentence. For example, *In my home there's a sofa and there are some cushions.* Repeat this procedure with several students. Encourage them to memorise the sentence as it grows. If they falter, you can show them the card as a prompt.

- When they've understood how the activity works, split the class into groups and if necessary, give a set of prompt cards to each group. Alternatively, the students can choose the words to add sentence themselves.

- Alternative chain sentences at this level include:
  Last weekend, I played/went ... + water sport. (Unit 7)
  I went to market and I bought ... + food. (Unit 10)
  Today, I'm wearing ... + clothes. (Unit 11)

7 Crosswords

Aim

This activity is good for revising lexical sets and can help with spelling.

Preparation

Choose a lexical set you want to revise. For example, *countries* or *nationalities* (Unit 1), *jobs* (Unit 2), *food* (Unit 10), *clothes* (Unit 11), etc.

Procedure

- Students work in pairs. They'll need a piece of paper, preferably graph paper with squares on.

- Choose a topic, for example, *nationalities.*

- Student A writes 'Across' words, and Student B writes 'Down' words.

- It's a good idea to provide the first word across, and make sure that it's a long one. Student B then adds another nationality down the paper from top to bottom. This word must intersect with the nationality word written across the page.

- Student A then writes another nationality across that intersects with the nationality Student B has written down. Students continue taking it in turns to write in their words.

- The students build up a crossword until they can't think of any more nationalities. (You could make it into a game by saying that the last person to write a nationality is a winner.) Note that the students must leave one square empty between each word – this is why it's better and clearer to use squared paper.

8 Odd one out

Aim

This activity can be used to revise almost any language.

Preparation

Think of the vocabulary, pronunciation or grammar point you want to revise.

Procedure

- Write five words on the board and ask the students which one is the odd one out. The students then explain why, either in the L1 or in the L2. This usually relates to the meaning of the word.

blue	dog	pink	red	yellow

  Here *dog* is the odd one out because it's an animal. The other words are colours.

- Note that it doesn't matter if the students can't explain in perfect English why *dog* is the odd one out. The important thing is that they're looking at and thinking about the words you want to revise.

- You can use this format to practise and revise all sorts of things. Here are some examples.

  1 For meaning:
  sister / grandfather / daughter / wife / mother
  grandfather is the odd one out because he's a man. The other words describe women.

  2 For spelling:
  pen / book / bag / phone / diary
  diary is the odd one out because you spell the plural *ies*. The other words you just add *s*.

  3 For pronunciation: sounds
  A / I / H / J / K
  I is the odd one out because the vowel sound is different.

  4 For pronunciation: stress
  hospital / banana / potato / Italian / computer
  hospital is the odd one out because the stress is on the first syllable. The other words have the stress on the second syllable.

  5 For collocation:
  boat / bus / foot / train / car
  foot is the odd one out because you say *on foot*. For the other words you use *by*.

  6 For grammar:
  work / go / see / take / swim
  work is the odd one out because it's regular. The other verbs are irregular.

- You should tell the students what the criteria is, for example 'think about meaning' or 'think about the sounds'. To make the activity a little more challenging, instead of writing the words on the board you can dictate them. As a follow-up, ask the students to write their own odd ones out.

9 Making sentences

Aim

This activity is good for revising any type of vocabulary. It works best if the words are a fairly random selection and not part of a tight lexical set.

Preparation

Choose 12 words you want to revise and write them in a circle (like a clockface) on the board.

Procedure

- Students work in pairs. They choose two or more of the words and try to make a sentence with them.

  Example sentences:
  My brother plays *tennis* in his *bedroom*.
  The *farmer* eats *cakes* on *Friday*.
  I sailed a *blue boat* on the *river*.

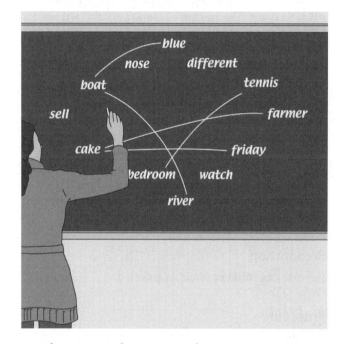

- The students then read out their sentences and you connect the words they've used on the board. You can correct the grammar as necessary (or you can make it more difficult for the students by only accepting grammatically correct sentences). It doesn't matter how bizarre the sentences are, the important thing is that students spend time looking at and remembering the vocabulary.

- If you write the words and draw the connecting lines on an OHP transparency, you can show it to the students a few weeks later and see if they remember the sentences they wrote.

10 TPR (Total Physical Response)

Aim

To give students the opportunity to show that they understand language without having to respond orally.

Note: TPR is a language teaching method developed in the early 1970s by James J. Asher, a professor of psychology at San Jose State University, California. It's based on the idea that learning a foreign language – certainly in the initial stages – can parallel the way a child learns their native tongue. Asher claims that most of the language directed at young children consists of commands: *Pick up the teddy, Give Mummy the book, Hold Daddy's hand*, etc. Children show that they've understood by responding physically to these instructions; a verbal response isn't necessary. Asher suggests that this process can be mirrored in the language classroom. Students are exposed to new language input through a series of commands that require a physical response: *Stand up, Look left, Look right, Sit down*. The teacher demonstrates the actions and then the students act them out. TPR can be described as a 'comprehension approach'. There is no pressure for the students to produce the language until they're ready.

At an elementary level, where there's still a lot of basic vocabulary to be learned, you can use TPR techniques very effectively. Linking the learning of new language with different physical actions creates strong memory associations. It really helps students to remember. Using TPR can also provide a welcome change of pace and focus in your lesson. It's worth experimenting. Here are three simple ideas.

Preparation

Provide cue cards or realia as required.

Procedure

- Minimal pairs for pronunciation practice:
  For each student, prepare a set of pairs of words that students often confuse e.g. *hat* and *hot*, *here* and *hair*, *know* and *now*, etc. Hand out a set to each student. Read out a word and ask the students to hold up the word they hear. This also works well with numbers *13/30*, *14/40*, etc.

- Stand up / Sit down to show comprehension:
  In a listening activity, ask different students to listen out for different words. Ask them to stand up when they hear their word, and sit down when they hear it again. Useful for pop song activities.

- Follow instructions:
  To practise prepositions of place, and recycle fruit and vegetable vocabulary, bring a bag of fruit and vegetables to the class. Ask students to arrange the fruit according to your instructions. For example: *Put the banana next to the apple. Hide the strawberry behind the orange*, etc.

Anecdote tasks

New Inside Out Elementary includes a number of extended speaking tasks, where students tackle a longer piece of discourse. We've called these 'Anecdotes'. They are based on personal issues, for instance, memories, stories, people you know. When you learn a musical instrument, you can't spend all your time playing scales and exercises: you also need to learn whole pieces in order to see how music is organised. Anecdotes give students a chance to get to grips with how discourse is organised. We've found the following strategies helpful in getting our students to tell their Anecdotes.

1 Choose global topics that everybody can relate to

One of the main objectives of an Anecdote is to encourage students to experiment with and hopefully grow more competent at using language at the more demanding end of their range. It therefore seems only fair to ask them to talk about subjects they know something about. With familiar subject matter students can concentrate on *how* they are speaking as well as *what* they are speaking about. The six Anecdote topics in *New Inside Out* Elementary have been carefully selected to appeal to the widest range of students, whilst at the same time, fitting in to the context of the unit.

Unit 3	Your favourite relative
Unit 6	Your favourite festival/party
Unit 8	Your last summer holiday
Unit 10	Your last delicious meal
Unit 14	Your favourite TV programme
Unit 15	An old school friend

As soon as you have got to know your students well enough, you'll be able to choose other Anecdote topics suited to their particular interests and experiences.

2 Allow sufficient preparation time

Students need time to assemble their thoughts and think about the language they'll need. The Anecdotes are set up through evocative questions. Students read or listen to a planned series of questions and choose what specifically they'll talk about; shyer students can avoid matters they feel are too personal. This student preparation is a key stage and should not be rushed. Research, by Peter Skehan and Pauline Foster among others, has shown that learners who plan for tasks attempt more ambitious and complex language, hesitate less and make fewer basic errors.

The simplest way to prepare students for an Anecdote is to ask them to read the list of questions in the book and decide which ones they want to talk about. This could be done during class time or as homework preparation for the following lesson. Ask them to think about the language they'll need. Sentence beginnings are provided in the Student's Book to give the students some extra help. Encourage them to use dictionaries and make notes – but not to write out what they'll actually say. Finally, put them into pairs to exchange Anecdotes.

A variation is to ask the students to read the questions in the book while, at the same time, listening to you read them aloud. Then ask them to prepare in detail for the task, as above.

Alternatively, ask the students to close their books – and then to close their eyes. Ask them to listen to the questions as you read them aloud and think about what they evoke. Some classes will find this a more involving process. It also allows you to adapt the questions to your class: adding new ones or missing out ones you think inappropriate. After the reading, give them enough time to finalise their preparation before starting the speaking task.

3   Monitor students and give feedback

It's important for students to feel that their efforts are being monitored by the teacher. Realistically, it's probably only possible for a teacher to monitor and give feedback to one or two pairs of students during each Anecdote activity. It's therefore vital that the teacher adopts a strict rota system, and makes sure that everyone in the class is monitored over the course of a term. Constructive feedback helps students improve their delivery.

4   Provide a 'model anecdote'

It's always useful for the students to hear a model Anecdote at some stage during the Anecdote task cycle. The most obvious model is you, the teacher. Alternatively you might ask a teaching colleague or friend to talk to the students. For every Anecdote activity in *New Inside Out* Elementary there's a model listening on the CD with an accompanying task in the Student's Book. You may wish to let the students listen to a model anecdote earlier in the task cycle – before they have prepared their own anecdotes.

5   Repeat the same anecdote with a new partner at regular intervals

Consider going back to Anecdotes and repeating them in later classes. Let the students know that you're going to do this. This will reassure them that you're doing it on purpose, but more importantly, it will mean that they'll be more motivated to dedicate some time and thought to preparation. When you repeat the task, mix the class so that each student works with a new partner, i.e. one who has not previously heard the Anecdote.

In our experience, most students are happy to listen to their partner's Anecdotes. If, however, any of your students are reluctant listeners, you might think about giving them some sort of 'listening task'. Here are three examples:

- Ask the listener to tick the prompt questions that the 'Anecdote teller' answers while telling the Anecdote.

- Ask the listener to time the 'Anecdote teller'. In *Teaching Collocations* (page 91) Michael Lewis suggests reducing the time allowed to deliver the Anecdote each time it's repeated: for example, in the first instance the student has five minutes; for the second telling they have four minutes; and the third three minutes.

- Ask the listener to take brief notes about the Anecdote and write them up as a summary for homework. Then give the summary to the 'Anecdote teller' to check.

The pedagogic value of getting students to re-tell Anecdotes – repeat a 'big chunk' of spoken discourse – cannot be over-stated. Repeating complex tasks reflects real interactions. We all have our set pieces: jokes, stories. And we tend to refine and improve them as we retell them. Many students will appreciate the opportunity to do the same thing in their second language. Research by Martin Bygate among others has shown that given this opportunity students become more adventurous and at the same time more precise in the language they use.

You can also use the Anecdotes to test oral proficiency and thereby add a speaking component to accompany the tests in the Teacher's Book.

Key concepts in *New Inside Out*

The following excerpts are from *An A–Z of ELT* by Scott Thornbury (Macmillan Books for Teachers, 2006). They give clear authoritive definitions and explanations of some of the most important concepts in *New Inside Out*.

Scott Thornbury

Contents

- classroom interaction
- collocation
- communicative activity
- context
- drill
- dynamics: group, classroom
- fluency
- focus on form
- function
- grammar teaching
- learner-centred instruction, learner-centredness
- learner style
- listening
- motivation
- noticing
- personalization
- practice
- pronunciation teaching
- reading
- speaking
- task
- vocabulary teaching
- writing

Note: SLA = Second Language Acquisition

classroom interaction METHODOLOGY

Classroom interaction is the general term for what goes on between the people in the classroom, particularly when it involves language. In traditional classrooms, most interaction is initiated by the teacher, and learners either respond individually, or in unison. Teacher-centred interaction of this kind is associated with *transmissive* teaching, such as a lecture or presentation, where the teacher *transmits* the content of the lesson to the learners. In order to increase the amount of student involvement and interaction, teacher–learner interaction is often combined with **pairwork** and **groupwork**, where learners interact among themselves in pairs or small groups. Other kinds of interaction include *mingling* or *milling*. Pairwork and groupwork are associated with a more **learner-centred** approach. Rather than passively receiving the lesson content, the learners are actively engaged in using language and discovering things for themselves. The value of pairwork and groupwork has been reinforced by the belief that **interaction** facilitates language learning. Some would go as far as to say that it is *all* that is required.

The potential for classroom interaction is obviously constrained by such factors as the number of students, the size of the room, the furniture, and the purpose or type of activity. Not all activities lend themselves to pairwork or groupwork. Some activities, such as reading, are best done as *individual work*. On the other hand, listening activities (such as listening to an audio recording, or to the teacher) favour a *whole class* format, as do grammar presentations. The whole class is also an appropriate form of organization when reviewing the results of an activity, as, for example, when spokespersons from each group are reporting on the results of a discussion or survey.

The success of any classroom interaction will also depend on the extent to which the learners know what they are meant to be doing and why, which in turn depends on how clearly and efficiently the interaction has been set up. Pair- and groupwork can be a complete waste of time if learners are neither properly prepared for it, nor sure of its purpose or outcome.

Finally, the success of pair- and groupwork will depend on the kind of group **dynamics** that have been established. Do the students know one another? Are they happy working together? Do they mind working without constant teacher supervision? Establishing a productive classroom dynamic may involve making decisions as to who works with whom. It may also mean deliberately staging the introduction of different kinds of interactions, starting off with the more controlled, teacher-led interactions before, over time, allowing learners to work in pairs and finally in groups.

collocation VOCABULARY

If two words *collocate*, they frequently occur together. The relation between the words may be grammatical, as when certain verbs collocate with particular prepositions, such as *depend on, account for, abstain from*, or when a verb, like *make, take*, or *do*, collocates with a noun, as in *make an arrangement, take advantage, do the shopping*. The collocation may also be lexical, as when two **content words** regularly co-occur, as in *a broad hint, a narrow escape* (but not *a wide hint* or *a tight escape*). The strength of the collocation can vary: *a broad street* or *a narrow path* are weak collocations, since both elements can co-occur with lots of other words: *a broad river, a busy street*, etc. *Broad hint* and *narrow escape* are stronger. Stronger still are combinations where one element rarely occurs without the other, as in *moot point, slim pickings* and *scot free*. Strongest of all are those where both elements never or rarely occur without the other, such as *dire straits* and *spick and span*. These have acquired the frozen status of *fixed expressions*.

Unsurprisingly, learners lack intuitions as to which words go with which, and this accounts for many errors, such as *You can <u>completely</u> enjoy it* (instead of *thoroughly*), *On Saturday we <u>made</u> shopping* (instead of *went*), and *We went the <u>incorrect</u> way* (for *wrong*). Using texts to highlight particular collocations, and teaching new words in association with their most frequent collocations are two ways of approaching the problem. Nowadays learners' dictionaries also include useful collocational information, such as this entry from the *Macmillan English Dictionary for Advanced Learners*:

communicative activity METHODOLOGY

A communicative activity is one in which real communication occurs. Communicative activities belong to that generation of classroom **activities** that emerged in response to the need for a more **communicative approach** in the teaching of second languages. (In their more evolved form as **tasks**, communicative activities are central to **task-based learning**). They attempt to import into a practice activity the key features of 'real-life' communication. These are

- *purposefulness*: speakers are motivated by a communicative goal (such as getting information, making a request, giving instructions) and not simply by the need to display the correct use of language for its own sake
- *reciprocity*: to achieve a purpose, speakers need to interact, and there is as much need to listen as to speak

- *negotiation*: following from the above, they may need to check and **repair** the communication in order to be understood by each other
- *unpredictability*: neither the process, nor the outcome, nor the language used in the exchange, is entirely predictable
- *heterogeneity*: participants can use any communicative means at their disposal; in other words, they are not restricted to the use of a pre-specified grammar item.

And, in the case of spoken language in particular:

- *synchronicity*: the exchange takes place in real time

The best known communicative activity is the *information gap* activity. Here, the information necessary to complete the task is either in the possession of just one of the participants, or distributed among them. In order to achieve the goal of the task, therefore, the learners have to share the information that they have. For example, in a *describe-and-draw* activity, one student has a picture which is hidden from his or her partner. The task is for that student to describe the picture so that the partner can accurately draw it. In a *spot-the-difference* task, both students of a pair have pictures (or texts) that are the same apart from some minor details. The goal is to identify these differences. In a *jigsaw activity*, each member of a group has different information. One might have a bus timetable, another a map, and another a list of hotels. They have to share this information in order to plan a weekend break together.

Information gap activities have been criticized on the grounds that they lack **authenticity**. Nor are information gap activities always as productive as might be wished: unsupervised, learners may resort to **communication strategies** in order to simplify the task. A more exploitable information gap, arguably, is the one that exists between the learners themselves, ie, what they don't know – but might like to know – about one another (→ **personalization**).

context LINGUISTICS

The context of a language item is its adjacent language items. In the absence of context, it is often impossible to assign exact meaning to an item. A sentence like *Ben takes the bus to work*, for example, could have past, present, or future reference, depending on the context:

> I know this chap called Ben. One day *Ben takes the bus to work*, and just as …
> Most days *Ben takes the bus to work*, but sometimes he rides his bike …
> If *Ben takes the bus to work* tomorrow, he'll be late, because there's a strike …

Likewise, a sentence like *You use it like this* is meaningless in the absence of a context. By the same token, a word or sentence in one context can have a very different meaning in another. The sign *NO BICYCLES* in a public park means something different to *NO BICYCLES* outside a bicycle rental shop. It is sometimes necessary to distinguish between different kinds of context. On the one hand, there is the context of the accompanying **text**, sometimes called the *co-text*. The co-text of this sentence, for example, includes the sentences that precede and follow it, as well as the paragraph of which it forms a part. It is the co-text that offers clues as to the meaning of unfamiliar vocabulary in a text. The *situational* context (also *context of situation*, *context of use*), on the other hand, is the physical and temporal setting in which an instance of language use occurs. The typical context for the spoken question *Are you being served?* is in a shop, for example. Both co-text and context influence the production and interpretation of language. **Discourse analysis** studies the relationship between language and co-text, including the way that sentences or utterances are connected. **Pragmatics** studies the relationship between language and its contexts of use, including the way meaning can be inferred by reference to context factors.

Various theories have been proposed in order to account for the ways that language choices are determined by contextual factors. One of the best known of these is Michael Halliday's **systemic functional linguistics**. Halliday distinguishes three variables in any context that systematically impact on language choices and which, together, determine a text's **register**:

- the *field*: what the language is being used to talk about, and for what purposes
- the *tenor*: the participants in the language event, and their relationship
- the *mode*: how language is being used in the exchange, eg is it written or spoken?

For example, this short text shows the influence of all three factors:

> Do u fancy film either 2nite or 2moro? Call me.

The field is 'making arrangements about leisure activities', hence the use of words like *film*, *2nite* (*tonight*), *2moro* (*tomorrow*). The tenor is one of familiarity and equality (accounting for the informal *fancy* and the imperative: *call me*); and the mode is that of a written text message, which explains its brevity, its use of abbreviated forms (*u*, *2nite*) and the absence of salutations. A change in any of these contextual factors is likely to have a significant effect on the text.

Language learners, it is argued, need to know how these contextual factors correlate with language choices in order to produce language that is appropriate to the context. One way of doing this is to ask them to make changes to a text (such as the text message above) that take into account adjustments to the field, tenor, or mode.

drill METHODOLOGY

A drill is repetitive oral practice of a language item, whether a sound, a word, a phrase or a sentence structure. Drills that are targeted at sentence structures are sometimes called *pattern practice drills*.

Drills follow a prompt–response sequence, where the prompt usually comes from the teacher, and the students respond, either in chorus (a *choral drill*) or individually. An *imitation drill* simply involves repeating the prompt, as in:

Teacher	They have been watching TV.
Student	They have been watching TV.

A *substitution drill* requires the students to substitute one element of the pattern with the prompt, making any necessary adjustments:

Teacher	They have been watching TV.
Student	They have been watching TV.
Teacher	She
Student	She has been watching TV.
Teacher	I
Student	I have been watching TV.

etc.

A *variable substitution drill* is the same, but the prompts are not restricted to one element of the pattern:

Teacher	They have been watching TV.
Student	They have been watching TV.
Teacher	She
Student	She has been watching TV.
Teacher	radio
Student	She has been listening to the radio.
Teacher	We
Student	We have been listening to the radio.

etc.

Drills were a defining feature of the **audiolingual** method, and were designed to reinforce good language 'habits'. The invention of language laboratories allowed sustained drilling without the need for a teacher to supply the prompts. With the demise of audiolingualism, drilling fell from favour. However, many teachers – even those who subscribe to a **communicative approach** – feel the need for some form of repetition practice of the kind that drills provide. This may be for the purpose of developing **accuracy**, or as a form of **fluency** training, ie, in order to develop **automaticity**. Hence, communicative drills were developed. A communicative drill is still essentially repetitive, and focuses on a particular structure or pattern, but it has an *information gap* element built in. Learners can perform the drill in pairs, or as a *milling activity* (→ **classroom interaction**) and they are required to attend to what they hear as much as what they say. The milling activity popularly known as *Find someone who …* is one such activity. Students are set the task of finding other students in the class who, for example, can ride a horse, can speak French, can play the guitar, etc. They mill around, asking questions of the type *Can you …?* until they have asked all the other students their questions, and then they report their findings.

dynamics: group, classroom METHODOLOGY

Dynamics are the actions and interactions, both conscious and unconscious, that take place between members of a group, whether the whole class or subgroups. Group dynamics are instrumental in forging a productive and motivating classroom environment. They are determined by such factors as: the composition of the group (including the age, sex, and relative status of the members, as well as their different attitudes, beliefs, learning styles and abilities); the patterns of relationships between members of the group, including how well they know each other, and the roles they each assume, such as group leader, spokesperson, etc; physical factors such as the size of the group and the way it is seated; and the tasks that the group are set, eg: Does the task require everyone to contribute? Does it encourage co-operation or competition? Are the goals of the task clear to the group members?

Ways that the teacher can promote a positive group (and class) dynamic include:

- ensuring all class or group members can see and hear one another, and that they know (and use) each other's names
- keeping groups from getting too big – three to six members is optimal
- setting – or negotiating – clear rules for groupwork, such as using only the target language, giving everyone a turn to speak, allowing individuals to 'pass' if they don't want to say anything too personal
- using 'ice-breaking' activities to encourage interaction, laughter, and relaxation
- ensuring that group tasks are purposeful, interactive, and collaborative
- personalizing tasks, ie, setting tasks that involve the sharing of personal experiences and opinions
- defining the roles and responsibilities within the group, and varying these regularly, eg by appointing a different spokesperson each time
- monitoring groupwork in progress, and being alert to any possible conflicts or tensions between members, and reconstituting groups, if necessary
- discussing the importance of groupwork with learners, and getting feedback on group processes

fluency SLA

If someone is said to be fluent in a language, or to speak a language fluently, it is generally understood that they are able to speak the language idiomatically and accurately, without undue pausing, without an intrusive accent, and in a manner appropriate to the context. In fact, research into listeners' perceptions of fluency suggests that fluency is primarily the ability to produce and maintain speech in *real time*. To do this, fluent speakers are capable of:

- appropriate pausing, ie:
  - their pauses may be long but are not frequent
  - their pauses are usually filled, eg with **pause fillers** like *erm, you know, sort of*
  - their pauses occur at meaningful transition points, eg at the intersections of clauses or phrases, rather than midway in a phrase
- long runs, ie, there are many syllables and words between pauses

All of the above factors depend on the speaker having a well-developed grammar, an extensive vocabulary, and, crucially, a store of memorized *chunks*. Being able to draw on this store of chunks means not having to depend on grammar to construct each utterance from scratch. This allows the speaker to devote **attention** to other aspects of the interaction, such as planning ahead. Speakers also use a number of 'tricks' or *production strategies* to convey the illusion of fluency. One such strategy is disguising pauses by filling them, or by repeating a word or phrase.

Some proponents of the **communicative approach** re-defined fluency so as to distinguish it from **accuracy**. Fluency came to mean 'communicative effectiveness', regardless of formal accuracy or speed of delivery. Activities that are communicative, such as information-gap activities, are said to be *fluency-focused*. This is the case even for activities that produce short, halting utterances. Separating accuracy and fluency, and defining the latter as *communicative* language use, is misleading, though. There are many speech events whose communicativeness depends on their accuracy. Air traffic control talk is just one. Moreover, many learners aspire to being more than merely communicative.

Classroom activities that target fluency need to prepare the learner for real-time speech production. Learning and memorizing lexical chunks, including useful conversational gambits, is one approach. **Drills** may help here, as will some types of **communicative activity** that involve repetition. Research has also shown that fluency improves the more times a **task** is repeated. Fluency may also benefit from activities that manage to distract learners' attention away from formal accuracy so that they are not tempted to slow down. (This has been called 'parking their attention'). Some interactive and competitive language **games** have this effect. **Drama** activities, such as roleplays, recreate conditions of real-time language use, and are therefore good for developing fluency. Finally, learners can achieve greater fluency from learning a repertoire of **communication strategies**, ie, techniques for getting around potential problems caused by a lack of the relevant words or structures.

focus on form SLA

When learners focus on form, they direct conscious attention to some formal feature of the language **input**. The feature may be the fact that the past of *has* is *had*, or that *enjoy* is followed by verb forms ending in *-ing*, or that adjectives do not have plural forms in English. The learners' attention may be self-directed, or it may be directed by the teacher or by another learner. Either way, it has been argued that a focus on **form** is a necessary condition for language learning. Simply focusing on the **meaning** of the input is not enough. Focusing on form is, of course, not a new idea: most teaching methods devote a great deal of time to the forms of the language, eg when new grammar items are presented. But the term *focus on form* captures the fact that this focus can, theoretically, occur at any stage in classroom instruction. Thus, **correction**, especially in the form of negative **feedback**, is a kind of focus on form. In fact, some researchers argue that the most effective form focus is that which arises incidentally, in the context of communication, as when the teacher quickly elicits a correction during a classroom discussion. This incidental approach contrasts with the more traditional and deliberate approach, where teaching is based on a **syllabus** of graded structures (or *forms*), and these are pre-taught in advance of activities designed to practise them. This traditional approach is called – by some researchers – a *focus on formS*.

function LINGUISTICS

The function of a language item is its communicative purpose. Language is more than simply **forms** and their associated meanings (ie, **usage**). It is also the communicative **uses** to which these forms and meanings are put. These two sentences, for example, share the same forms, but function quite differently:

[in an email] *Thank you for sending me the disk.*
[a notice in a taxi] *Thank you for not smoking.*

The function of the first is *expressing thanks*, while the second is more like a *prohibition*. Likewise, the same function can be expressed by different forms:

[a notice in a taxi] *Thank you for not smoking.*
[a sign in a classroom] *No smoking.*

Thus, there is no one-to-one match between form and function. Assigning a function to a text or an utterance usually requires knowledge of the **context** in which the text is used. The study of how context and function are interrelated is called **pragmatics**.

Communicative functions can be categorized very broadly and also at increasing levels of detail. The 'big' functions, or macrofunctions, describe the way language is used in very general terms. These include the use of language for *expressive* purposes (eg poetry), for *regulatory* purposes (eg for getting people to do things), for *interpersonal* purposes (eg for socializing), and for *representational* purposes (eg to inform). More useful, from the point of view of designing language syllabuses, are microfunctions. These are usually expressed as **speech acts**, such as *agreeing and disagreeing, reporting, warning, apologizing, thanking, greeting,* etc. Such categories form the basis of **functional syllabuses**, a development associated with the **communicative approach**. They often appear as one strand of a coursebook **syllabus**. Functions differ from notions in that the latter describe areas of meaning – such as *ability, duration, quantity, frequency,* etc – rather than the uses to which these meanings are put.

One way to teach functions is to adopt a 'phrasebook' approach, and teach useful ways of expressing common functions (what are called *functional exponents*), such as *Would you like …?* (*inviting*) and *Could you …, please?* (*requesting*). More memorable, though, is to teach these expressions in the contexts of **dialogues**, so that the functional exponents are associated not only with common situations in which they are used, but with related functions (such as *accepting* and *refusing*). The term *function*, in contrast to **form**, is also used in linguistics, specifically with regard to the functions of the different elements of a **clause** (such as subject and object).

grammar teaching METHODOLOGY

Like the word **grammar** itself, the topic of grammar teaching is a controversial one, and teachers often take opposing views. Historically, language teaching methods have positioned themselves along a scale from 'zero grammar' to 'total grammar', according to their approach to grammar teaching. Proponents of *natural methods*, who model their approach to teaching second languages on the way that first languages are acquired, reject any explicit teaching of grammar at all. (They may, however, teach according to a grammar **syllabus**, even if no mention of grammar as such is made in the classroom). This implicit approach is common both to the **direct method** and to **audiolingualism**. Through exposure to demonstrations, situations or examples, learners are expected to pick up the rules of grammar by **inductive learning**. At the other end of the spectrum, there are approaches, such as **grammar-translation**, that adopt an explicit and **deductive learning** approach. From the outset, learners are presented with rules which they study and then practise. Occupying a midway point between zero grammar and total grammar is the approach called **consciousness-raising**. Instead of being given rules, learners are presented with language data which challenge them to re-think (and *restructure*) their existing mental grammar. This data might take the form of **input** that has been manipulated in some way. For example, pairs of sentences, such as the following, have to be matched to pictures, forcing learners to discriminate between them, and, in theory, **notice** the difference (→ **noticing**):

The Queen drove to the airport.
The Queen was driven to the airport.

(This is sometimes called a *grammar interpretation task*, or *structured input*.) In order to do the task, learners have to process not just the individual words, but also their grammatical form. That is why this approach to teaching grammar is sometimes called *processing instruction*. There are other researchers who argue that it is by means of manipulating the learner's output, eg through productive practice, that mental restructuring is best effected.

The **communicative approach** accommodates different approaches to grammar teaching. Proponents of **task-based learning**, for example, argue that, if the learner is engaged in solving problems using language, then the mental grammar will develop of its own accord. However, advocates of the weaker version of the communicative approach (and the version that is most widespread) justify a role for the pre-teaching of grammar in advance of production. This view finds support in **cognitive learning theory**, which suggests that conscious attention to grammatical form (called **focus on form**) speeds up language learning, and is a necessary corrective against premature **fossilization**. There is some debate, though, as to whether this form focus should be planned or incidental. Incidental grammar teaching occurs when the teacher deals with grammar issues as and when they come up, eg in the form of **correction**, or task **feedback**. In this way (it is argued) grammar teaching follows the learners' own 'syllabus'. Such an approach attempts to address one of the dilemmas of grammar teaching: the fact that the learner's mental grammar, and the way it develops, bears only an accidental relation to a formal grammar syllabus.

Nevertheless, the research into these different choices is still inconclusive. It may be the case that some items of grammar respond better to explicit teaching, while others are more easily picked up through exposure. There are also different learner types: some prefer learning and applying rules, while others are happier with a more 'deep-end' approach (→ **learning style**). Most current teaching materials hedge their bets on these issues. They offer both deductive and inductive grammar presentations, and opportunities for incidental as well as for planned learning.

learner-centred instruction, learner-centredness
METHODOLOGY

Learner-centred instruction aims to give learners more say in areas that are traditionally considered the domain of the teacher or of the institution. Learner-centred instruction is true to the spirit of progressive education, including the movement towards providing learners with greater **autonomy**. For example, a learner-centred **curriculum** would involve learners in negotiating decisions relating to the choice of syllabus content, of materials, of activity-types, and of assessment procedures. Learner-centredness also describes ways of organizing **classroom interaction** so that the focus is directed away from the teacher, and on to the learners, who perform tasks in pairs or small groups. This contrasts with traditional, teacher-centred, classroom interaction. Some writers believe that the dichotomy between learner-centred (= good) and teacher-centred (= bad) is a false one. It might be more useful to talk about *learning-centred instruction*, ie, instruction which prioritizes sound learning principles. In a learning-centred approach there would be room for both learner-centred *and* teacher-centred interactions.

learning style PSYCHOLOGY

Your learning style is your preferred way of learning. This style may be influenced by biographical factors (such as how you were taught as a child) or by innately endowed factors (such as whether you have a 'good ear' for different sounds). Types of learning style are often presented in the form of polarities (some of which may overlap), such as:

- analytic versus global (or holistic) thinkers, ie, learners who tend to focus on the details, versus learners who tend to see 'the big picture'
- rule-users versus data-gatherers, ie, learners who learn and apply rules, versus those who prefer exposure to lots of examples
- reflective versus impulsive learners
- group-oriented versus solitary learners
- extrovert versus introverted learners
- verbal versus visual learners
- passive versus active learners

Attempts have been made to group these polarities and relate them to brain lateralization. So, a bias towards left-brain processing correlates with analytic, rule-forming and verbal learners, while a bias towards right-brain processing correlates with their opposite. A less binary view of learning style is that proposed by the psychologist Howard Gardner. He identified at least seven distinct intelligences that all individuals possess but to different degrees. These include the *logical/mathematical*, the *verbal/linguistic*, and the *visual/spatial*. Similarly, proponents of **neuro-linguistic programming** distinguish between different sensory orientations, including the *visual*, *aural* and *kinesthetic* (ie, related to movement, touch). So far, though, there is no convincing evidence that any of these dispositions correlates with specific learning behaviours. Nor has it been shown that a preference in one area predicts success in language learning. In fact, it is very difficult to separate learning style from other potentially influential factors, such as personality, intelligence, and previous learning experience. Nor is it clear to what extent learning style can be manipulated, eg through **learner training**. The best that can be said is that, if the learner's preferred learning style is out of synch with the type of instruction on offer, then success is much less likely than if the two are well matched. This supports the case for an **eclectic** approach, on the one hand, and the individualization of learning, on the other.

listening METHODOLOGY

Listening is the skill of understanding spoken language. It is also the name given to classroom activities that are designed to develop this skill – what are also called *listening comprehension* activities – as in 'today we're going to do a listening'. Listening is one of the four language **skills**, and, along with **reading**, was once thought of as being a 'passive' skill. In fact, although receptive, listening is anything but passive. It is a goal-oriented activity, involving not only processing of the incoming speech signals (called *bottom-up processing*) but also the use of prior knowledge, contextual clues, and expectations (*top-down processing*) in order to create meaning. Among the sub-skills of listening are:

- perceiving and discriminating individual sounds
- segmenting the stream of speech into recognizable units such as words and phrases

- using **stress** and **intonation** cues to distinguish given information from new information
- attending to **discourse markers** and using these to predict changes in the direction of the talk
- guessing the meaning of unfamiliar words
- using clues in the text (such as vocabulary) and context clues to predict what is coming
- making inferences about what is not stated
- selecting key information relevant to the purpose for listening
- integrating incoming information into the mental 'picture' (or **schema**) of the speech event so far

Also, since listening is normally interactive, listeners need to be capable of:

- recognizing when speakers have finished their turns, or when it is appropriate to interrupt
- providing ongoing signals of understanding, interest, etc. (*backchannelling*)
- asking for clarification, asking someone to repeat what they have just said, and repairing misunderstandings

These sub-skills exist across languages, so, in theory, learners should be able to transfer them from their first language into their second. In fact, there are a number of reasons why this does not always happen. One is that speakers of different languages process speech signals differently, depending on the phonetic characteristics of the language they are used to. This means that speakers of some languages will find it harder than others to match the spoken word to the way that the word is represented in their mind. They simply do not recognize the word. Another problem is lack of sufficient L2 knowledge, such as vocabulary or grammar. A third problem is that learners may lack the means (and the confidence) to negotiate breakdowns in understanding. Finally, many learners simply lack exposure to spoken language, and therefore have not had sufficient opportunities to experience listening. These problems can be compounded in classrooms because:

- Listening to audio recordings deprives the learners of useful visual information, and allows the learners no opportunity to interact and repair misunderstandings.
- Classroom acoustics are seldom ideal.
- If learners do not know what they are listening for (in the absence, for example, of some pre-set listening task) they may try to process as much information as possible, rather than being selective in their listening. This can lead to listening overload, which in turn can cause inhibiting anxiety.
- Listening texts that have been specially written for classroom use are often simplified. But if this simplification means eliminating a lot of redundant language, such as speaker repetitions, pause fillers and vague language, the density of information that results may make it harder – not easier – to process.

For this reason, the use of audio recordings to develop listening skills needs to be balanced against the advantages of using other media, such as video, and face-to-face interaction with the teacher or another speaker.

Nevertheless, the use of audio recordings is an established part of classroom practice, so it is important to know how to use them to best advantage. The following approach is one that is often recommended:

- Provide some minimum contextual information, eg who is talking to whom about what, and why. This helps to compensate for lack of visual information, and allows learners to activate the relevant mental **schema**, which in turn helps top-down processing, including the sub-skill of prediction.
- Pre-teach key vocabulary: this helps with bottom-up processing, although too much help may mean that learners don't get sufficient practice in guessing from context.
- Set some 'while-listening' questions. Initially, these should focus on the overall *gist* of the text. For example: true / false questions, selecting, ordering or matching pictures, ticking items on a list, following a map
- Play a small section of the recording first, to give learners an opportunity to familiarize themselves with the different voices, and to trigger accurate expectations as to what they will hear.
- Play the recording right through, and then allow learners to consult on the answers to the pre-set task. Check these answers. If necessary, re-play the recording until satisfied that learners have 'got the gist'.
- Set a more demanding task, requiring more intensive listening, such as listening for detail, or inferring speakers' attitudes, intentions, etc. If the recording is a long one, it may pay to stage the intensive listening in sections. Again, allow learners to consult in pairs, before checking the task in open class.
- On the basis of the learners' success with these tasks, identify problem sections of the recording and return to these, playing and re-playing them, and perhaps eliciting a word-by-word transcription and writing this on the board.
- Distribute copies of the transcript of the recording (if available) and re-play the recording while learners read the transcript. This allows the learners to clear up any remaining problems, and also to match what they hear to what they see.

The above approach can be adapted to suit different kinds of recorded texts and different classroom needs. For higher level learners, for example, it may be counter-productive to make listening *too* easy. The approach can also be adapted to the use of video, and even to *live listenings*, such as listening to the teacher or a guest.

motivation PSYCHOLOGY

Motivation is what drives learners to achieve a goal, and is a key factor determining success or failure in language learning. The learner's goal may be a short-term one, such as successfully performing a classroom task, or a long-term one, such as achieving native-like proficiency in the language. With regard to long-term goals, a distinction is often made between *instrumental motivation* and *integrative motivation*. Instrumental motivation is when the learner has a functional objective, such as passing an exam or getting a job. Integrative motivation, on the other hand, is when the learner wants to be identified with the target language community. Intersecting with these two motivational *orientations* are two different *sources* of motivation: *intrinsic* (eg the pleasure of doing a task for its own sake) and *extrinsic* (eg the 'carrot and stick' approach). Another motivational source that has been identified is success: experience of succeeding can result in increased motivation (called *resultative motivation*), which raises the question as to whether motivation is as much a result as a cause of learning.

Various theories of motivation have been proposed. Most of these identify a variety of factors that, in combination, contribute to overall motivation, such as:

- *attitudes*, eg to the target language and to speakers of the language
- *goals*, both long-term and short-term, and the learners' *orientation* to these goals
- how much *value* the learner attaches to achieving the goals, especially as weighed against *expectancy of success*; expectancy of success may come from the learner's assessment of their own abilities, and how they account for previous successes or failures
- *self-esteem*, and the need to achieve and maintain it
- *intrinsic interest*, *pleasure*, *relevance* or *challenge* of the task
- *group dynamic*: is it competitive, collaborative, or individualistic?
- *teacher's attitudes*, eg what expectations does the teacher project about the learners' likelihood of success?

As the last point suggests, teachers can play a key role in motivating learners, not just in terms of choosing activities that are intrinsically motivating, but in the attitudes they project. Two researchers on motivation offer the following advice for teachers:

Ten commandments for motivating language learners

1. Set a personal example with your own behaviour
2. Create a pleasant, relaxed atmosphere in the classroom.
3. Present the tasks properly.
4. Develop a good relationship with the learners.
5. Increase the learner's linguistic self-confidence.
6. Make the language classes interesting.
7. Promote learner autonomy.
8. Personalise the learning process.
9. Increase the learners' goal-orientedness.
10. Familiarise learners with the target language culture.

noticing SLA

If you notice a feature of the language that you are exposed to, it attracts your attention and you make a mental note of it. For example, a learner might notice (without necessarily understanding) the sign *Mind the gap*, repeated several times on a railway station platform. That same day, the learner hears the teacher say *would you mind* in the context of making a request in class. A day or two later, the same learner hears someone else say *I don't mind*. Each successive 'noticing' both primes the learner to notice new occurrences of *mind*, and at the same time contributes to a growing understanding of the use and meaning of *mind*. Proponents of **cognitive learning theory** believe that noticing is a prerequisite for learning: without it input would remain as mere 'noise'. The *noticing hypothesis*, then, claims that noticing is a necessary condition for acquisition, although not the only one. Some kind of mental processing of what has been noticed is also necessary before the **input** becomes *intake*, ie before it is moved into long-term **memory**.

Teachers obviously play an important role in helping learners to notice features of the language. They do this when they repeat words or structures, write them on the board, or even drill them. One way of increasing the chance of learners' noticing an item is to include it lots of times in a text, a technique called *input flood*. For example, learners read a text with the word *mind* included several times. They then categorize these examples according to their meaning. A set of **concordance** lines for a particular word can be used in the same way.

There is another type of noticing, called *noticing the gap*. This is when learners are made aware of a gap in their language knowledge. This might happen when they do a **dictation**, for example. When they compare their version with the correct version, they may notice certain differences, such as the lack of past tense endings, that represent a gap in their **interlanguage**. It has been argued that noticing the gap can trigger the **restructuring** of interlanguage. That is, 'minding the gap' leads learners to 'fill the gap'.

personalization METHODOLOGY

When you personalize language you use it to talk about your knowledge, experience and feelings. Personalization of the type *Now write five true sentences about yourself using 'used to'* is often motivated by the need to provide further practice of pre-taught grammar structures. But it is also good preparation for the kinds of situations of genuine language use that learners might encounter outside the classroom. These advantages are lost, though, if the teacher's response is to treat the exercise as *only* an exercise, and correct the learners' errors without responding to the content. The influence of **humanistic approaches** has given a fresh impetus to personalization, both in terms of providing a more coherent rationale and suggesting a broader range of activity types. For a start (it is argued), personalization creates better classroom **dynamics**. This is because groups are more likely to form and bond if the individuals in them know more about one another. And the mental and emotional effort that is involved in finding personal associations with a language item is likely to make that item more memorable. This quality is called cognitive and affective *depth*. Finally, lessons are likely to be more interesting, and hence more motivating, if at least some of the content concerns the people in the room, rather than the characters in coursebooks. On these grounds, some writers have suggested that personalization should not be considered simply as an 'add-on', but should be the principle on which most, if not all, classroom content should be based. One teaching approach that is committed to this view is **community language learning**. In this approach, all the content of the lesson comes from the learners themselves. Personalization is not without risks, though. Teachers need to be sensitive to learner resistance: learners should have the right to 'pass' on questions that they consider too intrusive. And teachers should be authentic in the way that they respond to learners' personalizations. This means that they should respond to *what* their learners are saying, not just how they say it.

practice METHODOLOGY

If you practise a skill, you experience doing it a number of times in order to gain control of it. The idea that 'practice makes perfect' is fundamental to **cognitive learning theory**. It is through practice that the skill becomes automatic. **Sociocultural learning theory** finds room for practice too. Performing a skill with the assistance of someone who is good at it can help in the **appropriation** of the skill. At issue, then, is not so much whether practice is beneficial, but what form it should take, when, and how much of it is necessary. In addressing these questions, it is customary to distinguish between different kinds of practice, such as *controlled practice* vs *free practice*, *mechanical practice* vs *meaningful/communicative practice*, and *receptive practice* vs *productive practice*.

Controlled practice is associated with the second P of the **PPP** instructional model. Practice can be controlled in at least two senses: *language control* and *interactional control*. In the first, the language that is being practised is restricted to what has just been presented (hence it is also called *restricted practice*). For example, if the first **conditional** has been presented, learners practise this, and only this, structure, and in a repetitive way, eg through a sequence of **drills**. Practice is also said to be controlled if the learners' participation is overtly managed and monitored by the teacher, such as in open-class work, as opposed to closed **pairwork** or **groupwork**. One reason for this degree of control is

that it maintains a focus on accuracy, and pre-empts or corrects errors. *Free practice*, on the other hand, allows learners a measure of creativity, and the opportunity to integrate the new item into their existing language 'pool'. It is also less controlled in terms of the interactions, with pairwork and groupwork being favoured. Typical free practice activities might be **games**, **discussions** or **drama**-based activities.

Mechanical practice is a form of controlled practice, where the focus is less on the meaning of an item than on manipulating its component parts. Mechanical practice can be either oral or written: many traditional **exercises** are mechanical in this sense, such as when learners transform sentences from active into passive, or from direct speech into reported speech. The arguments in favour of controlled and mechanical practice have lost their force since the decline of **behaviourism** and its belief that learning is simply habit-formation.

Meaningful practice requires learners to display some understanding of what the item that they are practising actually means. One way of doing this is through **personalization**. *Communicative practice* involves the learners interacting in order to complete some kind of task, such as in an *information gap* activity (→ **communicative activity**). Proponents of a communicative approach argue that it is only this kind of practice that is truly effective. This is because learners are not simply practising language, but are practising the behaviours associated with the language, and this is a pre-condition for long-term behavioural change.

Finally, some practice activities are purely *receptive*. They involve the learners in identifying, selecting, or discriminating between language items, but not actually producing them. Many **consciousness-raising** activities are receptive, on the grounds that learners first need to understand a new structure before they can properly internalize it. Receptive practice is also associated with comprehension-based approaches to teaching. *Productive practice*, on the other hand, requires learners to produce the targeted items (either orally or in writing), and is associated with output-based models of learning.

There is fairly general agreement nowadays that the most effective practice activity combines at least some of the following features:

- It is meaningful, which may mean that is personalized.
- It is communicative, thus it will require learners to interact.
- It involves a degree of repetition – not of the mindless type associated with imitation drills, but of the type associated with many games.
- It is language-rich, ie, learners have to interpret or produce a lot of language.
- Learners can be creative and take risks, but support is at hand if they need it.
- Learners are pushed, at least some of the time, to the limits of their competence
- Learners get **feedback**.

pronunciation teaching PHONOLOGY

Pronunciation is the general term for that part of language classes and courses that deals with aspects of the **phonology** of English. This includes the individual sounds (**phonemes**) of English, sounds in **connected speech**, word and sentence **stress**, **rhythm** and **intonation**. These components are customarily divided into two groups: the *segmental* features of pronunciation, ie, the individual sounds and the way they combine, and the *suprasegmental* features, ie, stress, rhythm and intonation. **Paralinguistic** features of speech production such as voice quality, tempo and loudness, are also classed as suprasegmental.

Effective pronunciation teaching needs to consider what goals, course design and methodology are most appropriate for the learners in question. The goal of acquiring a native-like **accent** is generally thought to be unachievable for most learners (and perhaps even undesirable). Instead, the goal of **intelligibility** is nowadays considered more realistic, if less easily measurable. It is often claimed that suprasegmental features play a greater role in intelligibility than do segmental ones. Unfortunately, however, some of these suprasegmental features, such as intonation, are considered by many teachers to be unteachable. Moreover, learners intending to interact with native speakers may need to set different goals from those learners whose purpose is to learn **English as an international language (EIL)**. For this latter group, the so-called **phonological core** is a checklist of those pronunciation features considered critical for intelligibility in EIL.

In terms of the design of course content, a basic choice is whether the pronunciation focus is *integrated* or *segregated*. In an integrated approach, pronunciation is dealt with as part of the teaching of grammar and vocabulary, or of speaking and listening. In a segregated approach it is treated in isolation. A classical segregated exercise is the **minimal pairs** task, in which learners are taught to discriminate and produce two contrasted phonemes (as in *hit* and *heat*). There are doubts as to whether this item-by-item approach to pronunciation reflects the way that the features of pronunciation are interconnected. Nor does it reflect the way that they jointly emerge over time ('as a photo emerges in the darkroom'). A related issue is whether pronunciation teaching should be *pre-emptive* or *reactive*. That is to say, should pronunciation teaching be planned around a syllabus of pre-selected items, or should the focus on pronunciation emerge *out of* practice activities, in the form, for example, of **correction**? There is evidence that the latter approach is more effective than the former.

In 1964 the writer (and former language teacher) Anthony Burgess wrote, 'Nothing is more important than to acquire a set of foreign phonemes that shall be entirely acceptable to your hosts'. However, there is generally less emphasis given to pronunciation teaching nowadays. Indeed, some teachers are sceptical as to the value of teaching pronunciation at all. This view is reinforced by research that suggests that the best predictors of intelligible pronunciation are 'having a good ear' and prolonged residence in an English-speaking country. On the other hand, faulty pronunciation is one of the most common causes of misunderstandings. This is an argument for demanding higher standards than the learners can realistically achieve, in the hope that they will meet you 'halfway'.

reading METHODOLOGY

Reading is a receptive **skill**. But the fact that it is receptive does not mean that it is passive: reading is an active, even interactive, process. Readers bring their own questions to the text, which are based on their background knowledge, and they use these to interrogate the text, modifying their questions and coming up with new ones according to the answers they get. In order to do this, they draw on a range of knowledge bases. They need to be able to decode the letters, words and grammatical structures of the individual sentences – what is called *bottom-up processing*. But they also enlist *top-down processes*, such as drawing on **discourse** and schematic knowledge, as well as on immediate contextual information. Discourse knowledge is knowing how different text-types – such as news reports, recipes or academic papers – are organized. Schematic knowledge is the reader's existing knowledge of the topic. Reading involves an interaction between these different 'levels' of knowledge, where knowledge at one 'level' can compensate for lack of knowledge at another.

Readers also bring their own *purposes* to texts, and these in turn determine the way they go about reading a text. The two main purposes for reading are for *information* (such as when consulting a directory), and for *pleasure* (such as when reading a novel), although these purposes may overlap. Different ways of reading include:

- *skimming* (*skim-reading, reading for gist*): rapidly reading a text in order to get the *gist*, or the main ideas or sense of a text. For example, a reader might skim a film review in order to see if the reviewer liked the film or not.
- *scanning*: reading a text in search of specific information, and ignoring everything else, such as when consulting a bus timetable for a particular time and destination.
- *detailed reading*: reading a text in order to extract the maximum detail from it, such as when following the instructions for installing a household appliance.
- *reading aloud*: such as when reading a prepared speech or lecture, or reading a story aloud, or an extract from the newspaper.

A reader's purpose usually matches the writer's intentions for the text. Readers seldom read telephone books from cover to cover, for example. Nor do they normally skim through a novel looking for names beginning with *Vron* .... In classrooms, however, texts are frequently used for purposes other than those for which they were originally intended. They are often used not so much as vehicles of information or of pleasure, but as 'linguistic objects', that is, as contexts for the study of features of the language. A distinction needs to be made, therefore, between two types of classroom reading: reading as *skills development*, and reading as *language study*. There is no reason why the same text cannot be used for both purposes.

Another distinction that is often made is between *intensive reading* and *extensive reading*. The former applies to the way short texts are subject to close and detailed classroom study. Extensive reading, on the other hand, means the more leisurely reading of longer texts, primarily for pleasure, or in order to accumulate vocabulary, or simply to develop sound habits of reading. This is typically done outside class, using graded **readers**, authentic texts, or literary texts.

A third important distinction is between testing reading and teaching reading. Traditional reading tasks usually involve reading a text and then answering **comprehension questions** about it. This is the testing approach. A teaching approach, on the other hand, aims to help learners to become more effective readers by training them in the *sub-skills* of reading, and by teaching them *reading strategies*. Some of the sub-skills of reading are:

- understanding words and identifying their grammatical function
- recognizing grammar features, such as word endings, and 'unpacking' (or **parsing**) the syntax of sentences
- identifying the topic of the text, and recognizing topic changes
- identifying text-type, text purpose, and text organization, and identifying and understanding **discourse markers** and other cohesive devices
- distinguishing key information from less important information
- identifying and understanding the gist
- inferring the writer's attitude
- following the development of an argument
- following the sequence of a narrative
- paraphrasing the text

Activities designed to develop these sub-skills include: underlining topic-related words; contrasting different text-types; comparing different examples of the same text type and identifying *generic* features; circling and categorizing discourse markers; identifying what the pronouns refer to; predicting the direction the text will take at each discourse marker; choosing the best summary of a text; putting a set of pictures in order; extracting key information on to a grid, writing a summary of the text, etc. *Strategy training* involves training learners in ways of overcoming problems when they are reading. Some useful strategies include:

- using contextual and extra-linguistic information (such as pictures, layout, headlines) to make predictions regarding what the text is about

- brainstorming background (or schematic) knowledge in advance of reading
- skimming a text in advance of a more detailed reading
- keeping the purpose of the text in mind
- guessing the meaning of words from context
- **dictionary** use

There is some argument, however, as to the value of a 'skills and strategies' approach to teaching reading. Most adult learners of English come to English texts with already well-developed reading skills in their own language. They already know how to skim, scan, use context clues, enlist background knowledge, and so on. Theoretically, at least, these skills are transferable. What makes reading difficult is not so much lack of reading skills as lack of *language knowledge*. That is, learners lack sufficient vocabulary and grammar to unpack sentences, and they cannot easily identify the ways that sentences are connected. This can result in 'tunnel vision', with readers becoming distracted by unfamiliar words, at the expense of working out meaning from context. On the other hand, it can also result in an over-reliance on guesswork, and on superficial 'text attack' strategies such as skimming. This suggests that texts needs to be chosen that do not over-stretch learners' ability to read them fluently. At the same time, texts should not be so easy that learners can process them simply by skimming. It also means that tasks need to be chosen that both match the original purpose of the text, and that encourage learners to transfer their first language reading skills. Such tasks are likely to be those that motivate learners to *want* to read the text. This might mean activating interest in the topic of the text, through, for example, a pre-reading quiz. At the same time, classroom reading texts should be exploited, not just for their potential in developing reading skills, but as sources of language input. This will involve, at some point, detailed study of the text's formal features, such as its linking devices, its collocations or its grammar.

speaking METHODOLOGY

Speaking is generally thought to be the most important of the four **skills**. The ability to speak a second language is often equated with proficiency in the language, as in *She speaks excellent French*. Indeed, one frustration commonly voiced by learners is that they have spent years studying English, but still can't speak it. One of the main difficulties, of course, is that speaking usually takes place spontaneously and in real time, which means that planning and production overlap. If too much **attention** is paid to planning, production suffers, and the effect is a loss of **fluency**. On the other hand, if the speaker's attention is directed solely on production, it is likely that **accuracy** will suffer, which could prejudice **intelligibility**. In order to free up attention, therefore, the speaker needs to have achieved a degree of **automaticity** in both planning and production. One way of doing this is to use memorized routines, such as **formulaic language**. Another is to use *production strategies*, such as the use of **pause fillers**, in order to 'buy' planning time. The situation is complicated by the fact that most speaking is interactive. Speakers are jointly having to manage the flow of talk. The management of interaction involves *turn-taking skills*, such as knowing how and when to take, keep, and relinquish speaker turns, and also knowing how to repair misunderstandings.

For language learners these processing demands are magnified through lack of basic knowledge of grammar and vocabulary. For the purposes of most day-to-day talk, however, the grammar that is required is not as complex nor need be as accurate as the grammar that is required for writing. Nor do speakers need an enormous vocabulary, especially if they have developed some **communication strategies** for getting round gaps in their knowledge. A core vocabulary of 1000–1500 high-frequency words and expressions will provide most learners with a solid basis for speaking.

Activating this knowledge, though, requires **practice**. This in turn suggests that the more speaking practice opportunities that learners are given, and the sooner, the easier speaking will become. Speaking practice means more than simply answering the teacher's questions, or repeating sentences, as in grammar practice activities. It means interacting with other speakers, sustaining long turns of talk, speaking spontaneously, and speaking about topics of the learners' choice.

Approaches to teaching speaking vary. Traditionally, speaking was considered to be a by-product of teaching grammar and vocabulary, reinforced with work on **pronunciation**. This view has been replaced by approaches that treat speaking as a skill in its own right. One such approach is to break down the speaking skill into a number of discrete sub-skills, such as *opening and closing conversations, turn-taking, repairing, paraphrasing, interrupting*, etc. Another approach is to focus on the different *purposes* of speaking and their associated **genres**, such as *narrating, obtaining service, giving a presentation, making small talk*, etc. This approach is particularly well suited to learners who have a specific purpose for learning English. A third is to adopt a topic-based approach, where learners are encouraged to speak freely on a range of topics, at least some of which they have chosen themselves. This is the format used in many conversation classes. Typical activity types for the teaching of speaking include: **dialogues**, **drama** activities (including *roleplays* and *simulations*), many **games**, **discussions** and debates, as well as informal classroom chat.

task METHODOLOGY

A task is a classroom activity whose focus is on communicating meaning. The objective of a task may be to reach some consensus on an issue, to solve a problem, to draft a plan, to design something, or to persuade someone to do something. In contrast, practising a pre-selected item of language (such as the present perfect) for its own sake would not be a valid task objective. In the performance of the task, learners are expected to make use of their own language resources. In theory, tasks may be receptive or productive, and may be done individually or in pairs or small groups. However, in practice, most activities that are labelled 'tasks' in coursebooks involve production (either speaking or writing, or both) and require learners to interact with one another.

Tasks are the organizing principle in **task-based learning**. In order to devise a syllabus of tasks it is necessary both to classify tasks, and to identify the factors that make one task more difficult than another. Different criteria for classifying tasks have been suggested. For example, tasks can be *open-ended* or *closed*. An open-ended task is one in which learners know there is no predetermined solution. It might be planning an excursion, or debating a topical issue. A closed task, on the other hand, requires learners to discover the solution to a problem, such as identifying the differences in a *spot-the-difference* task (→ **communicative activity**). Tasks can also be classified according to the kinds of operations they involve, such as *ranking, selecting, sorting, comparing, surveying* and *problem-solving*.

Factors which influence the degree of difficulty of the task, and hence which affect the grading of tasks, include:

- *linguistic factors*: How complex is the language that learners will need to draw on, in order to do the task? How much help, either before, or during the task, will they get with their language needs?
- *cognitive factors*: Does the task require the processing of complex data? Is the task type familiar to learners?
- *performance factors*: Do the learners have to interact in real time in order to do the task? Do they have time to rehearse? Do they have to 'go public'?

The term *task* is now widely accepted as a useful way of labelling certain types of classroom activity, including many which have a thinly disguised grammar agenda. But the concept of task is not without its critics. Some writers feel that the associations of task with 'work' undervalues the more playful – and possibly less authentic or communicative – types of classroom activity, such as games, songs and drama.

vocabulary teaching METHODOLOGY

Vocabulary describes that area of language learning that is concerned with word knowledge. Vocabulary learning is a major goal in most teaching programmes. It hasn't always been so. In methods such as **audiolingualism**, vocabulary was subordinated to the teaching of grammar structures. Words were simply there to fill the slots in the sentence patterns. The move towards *semantic* (ie, meaning-based) **syllabuses** in the 1970s, along with the use of **authentic** materials, saw a revival of interest in vocabulary teaching. Subsequently, developments in **corpus** linguistics and **discourse analysis** started to blur the distinction between vocabulary and grammar. In the 1990s the **lexical**

approach ushered in a major re-think regarding the role of vocabulary. This concerned both the *selection* of items (**frequency** being a deciding factor) and the *type* of items: **formulaic language** (or lexical chunks) were recognized as being essential for both **fluency** and **idiomaticity**. These developments have influenced the design of teaching materials. Most contemporary coursebooks incorporate a lexical syllabus alongside the grammar one. Recent developments in lexicography have complemented this trend. There is now a wide range of **dictionaries** available for learners, many of which come with sophisticated software for accessing databases of examples and collocations.

It is now generally agreed that, in terms of goals, learners need a receptive vocabulary of around 3000 high-frequency words (or, better, **word families**) in order to achieve independent user status. This will give them around ninety per cent coverage of normal text. For a productive vocabulary, especially for speaking, they may only need half this number.

Classroom approaches to achieving these goals include dedicated vocabulary lessons. Typically these take the form of teaching *lexical sets* of words (ie, groups of thematically linked words) using a variety of means, including visual **aids**, demonstration, situations, texts and dictionary work. As well as the **meaning** of the items, the **form**, both spoken (ie, **pronunciation**) and written (ie, **spelling**), needs to be dealt with, especially if the words are being taught for productive use. Other aspects of word knowledge that may need to be highlighted include **connotation** and **style**, **collocation**, derived forms, and grammatical features, such as the word's **word class**. Vocabulary is also taught as preparation for listening or reading (*pre-teaching vocabulary*) or as a by-product of these skills.

It would be impossible, in class, to teach all the words that learners need. Learners therefore need opportunities for *incidental* learning, eg through *extensive reading*. They may also benefit from training in how to make the most of these opportunities, eg by means of dictionary use, note-keeping, etc. Some strategies for deducing the meaning of unfamiliar words will also help.

Amassing a fully-functioning vocabulary is essentially a **memory** task, and techniques to help in the memorizing of words can be usefully taught, too. It also helps to provide learners with repeated encounters with new words, eg through the re-reading of texts, or by reading several texts about the same topic. Constant recycling of newly learned words is essential. One simple way of doing this is to have a *word box* (or word bag) in the classroom. New words are written on to small cards and added to the word box. At the beginning of the next lesson, these words can be used as the basis for a review activity. For example, the teacher can take words out of the box and ask learners to define them, provide a translation or put them into a sentence. The words can also form the basis for peer-testing activities, in which learners take a number of word cards and test each other in pairs or small groups.

writing METHODOLOGY

Like speaking, writing is a productive **skill**, and, like other skills, writing involves a hierarchy of *sub-skills*. These range from the most mechanical (such as handwriting or typing legibly) through to the ability to organize the written text and lay it out according to the conventions of the particular text type. Along the way, writers also need to be able to:

- produce grammatically accurate sentences
- connect and punctuate these sentences
- select and maintain an appropriate style
- signal the direction that the message is taking
- anticipate the reader's likely questions so as to be able to structure the message accordingly

In order to enable these skills, writers need an extensive knowledge base, not only at the level of vocabulary and grammar, but at the level of connected discourse. This includes familiarity with a range of different text types, such as *informal letters*, *instructions*, *product descriptions*, etc. It follows that if classroom writing is mainly spelling- or grammar-focused, many of the sub-skills of writing will be neglected.

Nevertheless, the teaching of writing has tended to focus on the 'lower-level' features of the skill, such as being able to write sentences that are both accurate and complex, that demonstrate internal cohesion, and that are connected to the sentences next to them. This language-based approach is justified on the grounds that stricter standards of accuracy are usually required in writing than in speaking. Also, writing demands a greater degree of explicitness than speaking, since writers and their readers are separated in time and space. They therefore can't rely on immediate feedback in order to clear up mis-understandings.

By contrast, a text-based approach to teaching writing takes a more 'top-down' view. This approach finds support in **discourse analysis**, which shows that a **text** is more than a series of sentences, however neatly linked. Instead, texts are organized according to larger *macrostructures*, such as problem-solution, or definition-examples. Hence, learners need explicit guidance in how texts are structured. This typically involves analysing and imitating models of particular text types. For example, a business letter might be analysed in terms of its overall layout, the purpose of each of its paragraphs, the grammatical and lexical choices within each paragraph, and the punctuation. Each of these features is then practised in isolation. They are then recombined in tasks aimed first at reproducing the original text and then at producing similar texts incorporating different content.

This approach is called a *product approach* to the teaching of writing, since the focus is exclusively on producing a text (the product) that reproduces the model. By contrast, a *process approach* argues that writers do not in fact start with a clear idea of the finished product. Rather, the text emerges out of a creative process. This process includes: *planning* (*generating ideas, goal setting* and *organizing*), *drafting* and *re-drafting; reviewing*, including *editing* and *proofreading*, and, finally, '*publishing*'. Advocates of a process approach argue for a more organic sequence of classroom activities, beginning with the brainstorming of ideas, writing preliminary drafts, comparing drafts, re-drafting, and *conferencing*, that is, talking through their draft with the teacher, in order to fine-tune their ideas.

The process approach to writing has a lot in common with the **communicative approach** to language teaching, and each has drawn support from the other. The communicative approach views writing as an act of communication in which the writer interacts with a reader or readers for a particular purpose. The purpose might be to ask for information about a language course, to relay personal news, to complain about being overcharged at a hotel, or simply to entertain and amuse. Thus, advocates of a communicative approach argue that classroom writing tasks should be motivated by a clear purpose and that writers should have their reader(s) in mind at all stages of the writing process. Such principles are now reflected in the design of writing tasks in public examinations, such as this one, from the Cambridge ESOL First Certificate in English (FCE) paper:

> The school where you learn English has decided to buy some videos in English. You have been asked to write a report to the Principal, suggesting what kinds of videos the school should buy. In your report you should also explain why students at the school will like these videos.
>
> Write your report.

The social purposes of writing are also foregrounded by proponents of a *genre-based approach*. **Genre** analysis attempts to show how the structure of particular text-types are shaped by the purposes they serve in specific social and cultural contexts. Put simply, a business letter is the way it is because of what it does. Advocates of genre-based teaching reject a process approach to teaching writing. They argue that to emphasize self-expression at the expense of teaching the generic structures of texts may in fact disempower learners. Many learners, especially those who are learning English as a *second* language, need a command of those genres – such as writing a CV, or requesting a bank loan – that permit access to the host community. A genre approach to teaching writing is not unlike a product approach, therefore. It starts with model texts that are subjected to analysis and replication. The difference is that these models are closely associated with their contexts of use, and they are analysed in functional terms as much as in linguistic ones. The genre approach has been particularly influential in the teaching of academic writing.

In reality, none of these approaches is entirely incompatible with any other. Resourceful teachers tend to blend elements of each. For example, they may encourage learners to 'discover' what they want to write, using a process approach. They may then give them a model text, both as a source of useful language items, and as a template for the final product. They may also provide exercises in specific sub-skills, such as linking sentences, or using a formal style.

The Common European Framework and *New Inside Out*

The Common European Framework for language learning

Introduction

The Common European Framework (CEF) is a widely used standard created by the Council of Europe. In the classroom, familiarity with the CEF can be of great help to any teacher in identifying students' actual progress and helping them to set their learning priorities.

Students can use the descriptors (description of competences) at any point to get a detailed, articulated, and personal picture of their own individual progress. This is important, as no two language learners progress in the same way, and consequently it's always rather artificial to apply a 'framework level' to a class as a whole, or to a course or coursebook.

The European Language Portfolio is another Council of Europe project, designed to give every learner a structure for keeping a record of their language learning experiences and their progress as described in the CEF. Up-to-date information about developments with the CEF and Portfolio can be found on www.coe.int/portfolio.

The Swiss-based Eurocentres Foundation played a major role in the development of the levels and the descriptors for the CEF and the prototype Portfolio. The CEF descriptors, developed in a Swiss National Research Foundation project, were presented in clearer, simpler, self-assessment form in the prototype (Swiss) Portfolio. There are now dozens of different national versions of the Portfolio for different educational sectors, but the only version for adults is that developed from the Swiss version by EAQUALS (European Association for Quality Language Services) in collaboration with ALTE. The descriptors used in this guide are taken from the EAQUALS/ALTE Portfolio. An electronic version that can be completed on-line can be downloaded in English or French from www.eelp.org. The EAQUALS/ALTE portfolio descriptors have been used in this guide, as they're more concrete and practical than the original CEFR descriptors.

New Inside Out CEF checklists

New Inside Out Elementary is appropriate for students who have had no previous contact with the language, or whose knowledge of the language is very sketchy. By the end of *New Inside Out* Elementary, if the students have had access to English outside the classroom, and have had the opportunity to practise, they should be able to do most of the things described at the A2 level.

In order to help the teacher and student assess their progress, we've provided a list of the A2 descriptors for each unit of *New Inside Out* Elementary. So, for example, in Unit 1 nearly all of the descriptors listed are things that the students certainly won't feel confident about doing yet. However, with a lot of help and support from the teacher, many of the students should be feeling that they can try to do a range of things in English by the end of the unit. Once they've studied more units, they should begin to feel more confident about certain aspects of the language. The descriptors in these charts allow the teacher to see a typical pattern of language acquisition.

At elementary level, students will need the help of the teacher if they're to use the self-assessment at all, since they won't be able to understand the descriptors. The descriptors may be of use to the teacher; not in formally assessing the students, but in gauging their progress through the course across the whole range of language abilities. This will help clarify for the teacher which students are making quicker or slower progress in the different areas, and will assist them in planning the focus of future lessons.

New Inside Out offers a wide range of teaching materials in its various components, which together give teachers the opportunity to develop all aspects of their students' language ability. The CEF can be used to follow their progress. By checking whether the students' confidence is at an appropriate level across the whole range of language skills at any point in the course, the teacher can decide if there is an area that requires more practice. Suggested targets for the checklist are provided on pages xlv and xlvi of the Teacher's Book, on the website www.insideout.net and on the Test CD at the back of the Teacher's Book.

---

1 Schneider, Günther, & North, Brian (2000): "Fremdsprachen können – was heisst das?" Zürich, Rüegger
North, Brian (2000): "The Development of a Common Framework Scale of Language Proficiency", New York, Peter Lang

2 EAQUALS is a pan-European language school accreditation body with over 100 full members. ALTE is an association dedicated to raising standards in language testing and encompasses the major European examination providers. Eurocentres provides high quality language teaching in countries where the language concerned is spoken. EAQUALS, ALTE and Eurocentres are the three NGOS advisers for language learning to the Council of Europe and all three implement the CEFR.

CEF Student checklists

Unit 1

Complete the checklist.

1 = I can do this with a lot of help from my teacher
2 = I can do this with a little help
3 = I can do this fairly well
4 = I can do this really well
5 = I can do this almost perfectly

Competences	Page	Your score				
I can understand what is said clearly, slowly and directly to me in simple everyday conversation; it is possible to make me understand, if the speaker can take the trouble.	4, 6, 8	1	2	3	4	5
I have a sufficient vocabulary for coping with simple everyday situations.	5, 6, 7	1	2	3	4	5

Unit 2

Complete the checklist.

1 = I can do this with a lot of help from my teacher
2 = I can do this with a little help
3 = I can do this fairly well
4 = I can do this really well
5 = I can do this almost perfectly

Competences	Page	Your score				
I can use some simple structures correctly.	11, 13	1	2	3	4	5
I have a sufficient vocabulary for coping with simple everyday situations.	10, 11, 12	1	2	3	4	5
I can make and accept apologies.	14	1	2	3	4	5
I can say what I like and dislike.	10	1	2	3	4	5
I can describe my educational background, my present or most recent job.	12	1	2	3	4	5

Unit 3

Complete the checklist.

1 = I can do this with a lot of help from my teacher
2 = I can do this with a little help
3 = I can do this fairly well
4 = I can do this really well
5 = I can do this almost perfectly

Competences	Page	Your score
I can use some simple structures correctly.	17, 19	1 2 3 4 5
I can make myself understood using memorised phrases and single expressions.	17, 20	1 2 3 4 5
I can describe myself, my family and other people.	16, 19	1 2 3 4 5
I can identify important information in news summaries or simple newspaper articles in which numbers and names play an important role and which are clearly structured and illustrated.	16, 17, 18	1 2 3 4 5
I can write about aspects of my everyday life in simple phrases and sentences (people, places, job, school, family, hobbies).	17	1 2 3 4 5

Unit 4

Complete the checklist.

1 = I can do this with a lot of help from my teacher
2 = I can do this with a little help
3 = I can do this fairly well
4 = I can do this really well
5 = I can do this almost perfectly

Competences	Page	Your score
I can understand what is said clearly, slowly and directly to me in simple everyday conversation; it is possible to make me understand, if the speaker can take the trouble.	23	1 2 3 4 5
I can say what I like and dislike.	24, 26	1 2 3 4 5
I can understand a simple personal letter in which the writer tells or asks me about aspects of everyday life.	23, 25	1 2 3 4 5
I can describe my hobbies and interests in a simple way.	24, 26	1 2 3 4 5
I can briefly introduce myself in a letter with simple phrases and sentences (family, school, job, hobbies).	25	1 2 3 4 5

Unit 5

Complete the checklist.

1 = I can do this with a lot of help from my teacher
2 = I can do this with a little help
3 = I can do this fairly well
4 = I can do this really well
5 = I can do this almost perfectly

Competences	Page	Your score
I can generally identify the topic of discussion around me when people speak slowly and clearly.	30	1 2 3 4 5
I can understand the essential information in short recorded passages dealing with predictable everyday matters which are spoken slowly and clearly.	34	1 2 3 4 5
I can find the most important information on leisure time activities, exhibitions etc. in information leaflets.	32, 35	1 2 3 4 5
I can use public transport: buses, trains and taxis, ask for basic information and buy tickets.	36	1 2 3 4 5
I have a sufficient vocabulary for coping with simple everyday situations.	33, 34	1 2 3 4 5

Unit 6

Complete the checklist.

1 = I can do this with a lot of help from my teacher
2 = I can do this with a little help
3 = I can do this fairly well
4 = I can do this really well
5 = I can do this almost perfectly

Competences	Page	Your score
I can write about aspects of my everyday life in simple phrases and sentences (people, places, job, school, family, hobbies).	38	1 2 3 4 5
I can understand the essential information in short recorded passages dealing with predictable everyday matters which are spoken slowly and clearly.	41	1 2 3 4 5
I can make and accept apologies.	42	1 2 3 4 5
I can understand short narratives about everyday things dealing with topics which are familiar to me if the text is written in simple language.	38, 41	1 2 3 4 5
I can give short, basic descriptions of events.	41	1 2 3 4 5

Unit 7

Complete the checklist.

1 = I can do this with a lot of help from my teacher
2 = I can do this with a little help
3 = I can do this fairly well
4 = I can do this really well
5 = I can do this almost perfectly

Competences	Page	Your score				
I can use some simple structures correctly.	45, 46	1	2	3	4	5
I can understand short narratives about everyday things dealing with topics which are familiar to me if the text is written in simple language.	45, 47	1	2	3	4	5
I can identify the main point of TV news items reporting events, accidents etc. when the visual supports the commentary.	44	1	2	3	4	5
I can describe past experiences and personal experiences (e.g. the last weekend, my last holiday).	46	1	2	3	4	5
I can use the most important connecting words to indicate the chronological order of events (first, then, after, later).	47	1	2	3	4	5

Unit 8

Complete the checklist.

1 = I can do this with a lot of help from my teacher
2 = I can do this with a little help
3 = I can do this fairly well
4 = I can do this really well
5 = I can do this almost perfectly

Competences	Page	Your score				
I can ask how people are and react to news.	54	1	2	3	4	5
I can understand short narratives about everyday things dealing with topics which are familiar to me if the text is written in simple language.	51, 52	1	2	3	4	5
I can say what I like and dislike.	50, 54	1	2	3	4	5
I can identify important information in news summaries or simple newspaper articles in which numbers and names play an important role and which are clearly structured and illustrated.	51, 52	1	2	3	4	5
I can describe an event in simple sentences and report what happened when and where (for example a party or an accident).	51, 52	1	2	3	4	5

 New Inside Out **Elementary Teacher's Book**

Unit 9

Complete the checklist.

1 = I can do this with a lot of help from my teacher
2 = I can do this with a little help
3 = I can do this fairly well
4 = I can do this really well
5 = I can do this almost perfectly

Competences	Page	Your score
I have a sufficient vocabulary for coping with simple everyday situations.	61, 62, 63	1 2 3 4 5
I can ask for attention.	64	1 2 3 4 5
I can give short, basic descriptions of events.	64	1 2 3 4 5
I can make and accept apologies.	64	1 2 3 4 5
I can skim a small advertisement in newspapers, locate the heading or column I want and identify the most important pieces of information (price and size of apartments, cars, computers).	60	1 2 3 4 5

Unit 10

Complete the checklist.

1 = I can do this with a lot of help from my teacher
2 = I can do this with a little help
3 = I can do this fairly well
4 = I can do this really well
5 = I can do this almost perfectly

Competences	Page	Your score
I can make simple purchases by stating what I want and asking the price.	70	1 2 3 4 5
I can describe past experiences and personal experiences (e.g. the last weekend, my last holiday).	69	1 2 3 4 5
I can make simple transactions in shops, post offices or banks.	69, 70	1 2 3 4 5
I can understand the essential information in short recorded passages dealing with predictable everyday matters which are spoken slowly and clearly.	68	1 2 3 4 5
I can write short, simple notes and messages.	68	1 2 3 4 5

Unit 11

Complete the checklist.

1 = I can do this with a lot of help from my teacher
2 = I can do this with a little help
3 = I can do this fairly well
4 = I can do this really well
5 = I can do this almost perfectly

Competences	Page	Your score				
I can understand phrases, words and expressions related to areas of most immediate priority (e.g. very basic personal and family information, shopping, local area, employment).	73	1	2	3	4	5
I can identify the main point of TV news items reporting events, accidents etc. when the visual supports the commentary.	75	1	2	3	4	5
I can make simple transactions in shops, post offices or banks.	73, 76	1	2	3	4	5
I can describe myself, my family and other people.	72, 73	1	2	3	4	5
I can use some simple structures correctly.	75	1	2	3	4	5

Unit 12

Complete the checklist.

1 = I can do this with a lot of help from my teacher
2 = I can do this with a little help
3 = I can do this fairly well
4 = I can do this really well
5 = I can do this almost perfectly

Competences	Page	Your score				
I can identify important information in news summaries or simple newspaper articles in which numbers and names play an important role and which are clearly structured and illustrated.	78, 81	1	2	3	4	5
I have a sufficient vocabulary for coping with simple everyday situations.	79, 80	1	2	3	4	5
I can use some simple structures correctly.	79, 81	1	2	3	4	5
I can describe my hobbies and interests in a simple way.	80	1	2	3	4	5
I can make myself understood using memorised phrases and single expressions.	80	1	2	3	4	5

Complete the checklist.

1 = I can do this with a lot of help from my teacher
2 = I can do this with a little help
3 = I can do this fairly well
4 = I can do this really well
5 = I can do this almost perfectly

Competences	Page	Your score				
I can make myself understood using memorised phrases and single expressions.	89	1	2	3	4	5
I can discuss with other people what to do, where to go, and make arrangements to meet.	92	1	2	3	4	5
I can make and accept apologies.	92	1	2	3	4	5
I can make and respond to invitations.	92	1	2	3	4	5
I can identify important information in news summaries or simple newspaper articles in which numbers and names play an important role and which are clearly structured and illustrated.	90	1	2	3	4	5

Complete the checklist.

1 = I can do this with a lot of help from my teacher
2 = I can do this with a little help
3 = I can do this fairly well
4 = I can do this really well
5 = I can do this almost perfectly

Competences	Page	Your score				
I can discuss with other people what to do, where to go, and make arrangements to meet.	97, 98	1	2	3	4	5
I can ask people questions about what they do at work and in free time, and answer such questions addressed to me.	94, 97	1	2	3	4	5
I can describe my hobbies and interests in a simple way.	97	1	2	3	4	5
I can identify the main point of TV news items reporting events, accidents etc. when the visual supports the commentary.	94, 96	1	2	3	4	5
I can say what I like and dislike	94, 98	1	2	3	4	5

Unit 15

Complete the checklist.

1 = I can do this with a lot of help from my teacher
2 = I can do this with a little help
3 = I can do this fairly well
4 = I can do this really well
5 = I can do this almost perfectly

Competences	Page	Your score				
I can find the most important information on leisure time activities, exhibitions etc. in information leaflets.	100, 102	1	2	3	4	5
I can describe myself, my family and other people.	103	1	2	3	4	5
I can order something to eat or drink.	104	1	2	3	4	5
I can generally identify the topic of discussion around me when people speak slowly and clearly.	100, 102	1	2	3	4	5
I can understand the essential information in short recorded passages dealing with predictable everyday matters which are spoken slowly and clearly.	100, 102	1	2	3	4	5

Unit 16

Complete the checklist.

1 = I can do this with a lot of help from my teacher
2 = I can do this with a little help
3 = I can do this fairly well
4 = I can do this really well
5 = I can do this almost perfectly

Competences	Page	Your score				
I can ask for and give directions referring to a map or plan.	107, 110	1	2	3	4	5
I can understand the essential information in short recorded passages dealing with predictable everyday matters which are spoken slowly and clearly.	108	1	2	3	4	5
I can identify important information in news summaries or simple newspaper articles in which numbers and names play an important role and which are clearly structured and illustrated.	106, 108	1	2	3	4	5
I can describe past experiences and personal experiences (e.g. the last weekend, my last holiday).	109	1	2	3	4	5
I can make myself understood using memorised phrases and single expressions.	107	1	2	3	4	5

 New Inside Out Elementary Teacher's Book   © Macmillan Publishers Limited 2007

CEF Student checklists: Answer key

Unit 1

Competences	Page	Your score
I can understand what is said clearly, slowly and directly to me in simple everyday conversation; it is possible to make me understand, if the speaker can take the trouble.	4, 6, 8	**1** 2 3 4 5
I have a sufficient vocabulary for coping with simple everyday situations.	5, 6, 7	1 **2** 3 4 5

Unit 2

Competences	Page	Your score
I can use some simple structures correctly.	11, 13	1 **2** 3 4 5
I have a sufficient vocabulary for coping with simple everyday situations.	10, 11, 12	1 **2** 3 4 5
I can make and accept apologies.	14	**1** 2 3 4 5
I can say what I like and dislike.	10	**1** 2 3 4 5
I can describe my educational background, my present or most recent job.	12	**1** 2 3 4 5

Unit 3

Competences	Page	Your score
I can use some simple structures correctly.	17, 19	1 **2** 3 4 5
I can make myself understood using memorised phrases and single expressions.	17, 20	**1** 2 3 4 5
I can describe myself, my family and other people.	16, 19	**1** 2 3 4 5
I can identify important information in news summaries or simple newspaper articles in which numbers and names play an important role and which are clearly structured and illustrated.	16, 17, 18	**1** 2 3 4 5
I can write about aspects of my everyday life in simple phrases and sentences (people, places, job, school, family, hobbies).	17	**1** 2 3 4 5

Unit 4

Competences	Page	Your score
I can understand what is said clearly, slowly and directly to me in simple everyday conversation; it is possible to make me understand, if the speaker can take the trouble.	23	**1** 2 3 4 5
I can say what I like and dislike.	24, 26	**1** 2 3 4 5
I can understand a simple personal letter in which the writer tells or asks me about aspects of everyday life.	23, 25	**1** 2 3 4 5
I can describe my hobbies and interests in a simple way.	24, 26	**1** 2 3 4 5
I can briefly introduce myself in a letter with simple phrases and sentences (family, school, job, hobbies).	25	**1** 2 3 4 5

Unit 5

Competences	Page	Your score
I can generally identify the topic of discussion around me when people speak slowly and clearly.	30	**1** 2 3 4 5
I can understand the essential information in short recorded passages dealing with predictable everyday matters which are spoken slowly and clearly.	34	**1** 2 3 4 5
I can find the most important information on leisure time activities, exhibitions etc. in information leaflets.	32, 35	**1** 2 3 4 5
I can use public transport: buses, trains and taxis, ask for basic information and buy tickets.	36	**1** 2 3 4 5
I have a sufficient vocabulary for coping with simple everyday situations.	33, 34	1 2 **3** 4 5

Unit 6

Competences	Page	Your score
I can write about aspects of my everyday life in simple phrases and sentences (people, places, job, school, family, hobbies).	38	1 **2** 3 4 5
I can understand the essential information in short recorded passages dealing with predictable everyday matters which are spoken slowly and clearly.	41	1 **2** 3 4 5
I can make and accept apologies.	42	1 **2** 3 4 5
I can understand short narratives about everyday things dealing with topics which are familiar to me if the text is written in simple language.	38, 41	1 **2** 3 4 5
I can give short, basic descriptions of events.	41	**1** 2 3 4 5

Unit 7

Competences	Page	Your score
I can use some simple structures correctly.	45, 46	1 2 **3** 4 5
I can understand short narratives about everyday things dealing with topics which are familiar to me if the text is written in simple language.	45, 47	1 **2** 3 4 5
I can identify the main point of TV news items reporting events, accidents etc. when the visual supports the commentary.	44	**1** 2 3 4 5
I can describe past experiences and personal experiences (e.g. the last weekend, my last holiday).	46	**1** 2 3 4 5
I can use the most important connecting words to indicate the chronological order of events (first, then, after, later).	47	**1** 2 3 4 5

Unit 8

Competences	Page	Your score
I can ask how people are and react to news.	54	1 2 **3** 4 5
I can understand short narratives about everyday things dealing with topics which are familiar to me if the text is written in simple language.	51, 52	1 2 **3** 4 5
I can say what I like and dislike.	50, 54	1 2 **3** 4 5
I can identify important information in news summaries or simple newspaper articles in which numbers and names play an important role and which are clearly structured and illustrated.	51, 52	1 **2** 3 4 5
I can describe an event in simple sentences and report what happened when and where (for example a party or an accident).	51, 52	**1** 2 3 4 5

Unit 9

Competences	Page	Your score
I have a sufficient vocabulary for coping with simple everyday situations.	61, 62, 63	1 2 3 **4** 5
I can ask for attention.	64	1 2 **3** 4 5
I can give short, basic descriptions of events.	64	1 2 **3** 4 5
I can make and accept apologies.	64	1 2 **3** 4 5
I can skim a small advertisement in newspapers, locate the heading or column I want and identify the most important pieces of information (price and size of apartments, cars, computers).	60	**1** 2 3 4 5

Unit 10

Competences	Page	Your score
I can make simple purchases by stating what I want and asking the price.	70	1 **2** 3 4 5
I can describe past experiences and personal experiences (e.g. the last weekend, my last holiday).	69	1 2 **3** 4 5
I can make simple transactions in shops, post offices or banks.	69, 70	1 **2** 3 4 5
I can understand the essential information in short recorded passages dealing with predictable everyday matters which are spoken slowly and clearly.	68	1 2 **3** 4 5
I can write short, simple notes and messages.	68	1 2 **3** 4 5

Unit 11

Competences	Page	Your score
I can understand phrases, words and expressions related to areas of most immediate priority (e.g. very basic personal and family information, shopping, local area, employment).	73	1 ② 3 4 5
I can identify the main point of TV news items reporting events, accidents etc. when the visual supports the commentary.	75	1 ② 3 4 5
I can make simple transactions in shops, post offices or banks.	73, 76	1 2 ③ 4 5
I can describe myself, my family and other people.	72, 73	1 2 ③ 4 5
I can use some simple structures correctly.	75	1 2 3 ④ 5

Unit 12

Competences	Page	Your score
I can identify important information in news summaries or simple newspaper articles in which numbers and names play an important role and which are clearly structured and illustrated.	78, 81	1 2 3 4 5
I have a sufficient vocabulary for coping with simple everyday situations.	79, 80	1 2 3 4 ⑤
I can use some simple structures correctly.	79, 81	1 2 3 4 ⑤
I can describe my hobbies and interests in a simple way.	80	1 2 ③ 4 5
I can make myself understood using memorised phrases and single expressions.	80	1 2 ③ 4 5

Unit 13

Competences	Page	Your score
I can make myself understood using memorised phrases and single expressions.	89	1 2 ③ 4 5
I can discuss with other people what to do, where to go, and make arrangements to meet.	92	1 ② 3 4 5
I can make and accept apologies.	92	1 2 3 ④ 5
I can make and respond to invitations.	92	1 ② 3 4 5
I can identify important information in news summaries or simple newspaper articles in which numbers and names play an important role and which are clearly structured and illustrated.	90	1 2 3 ④ 5

Unit 14

Competences	Page	Your score
I can discuss with other people what to do, where to go, and make arrangements to meet.	97, 98	1 2 3 ④ 5
I can ask people questions about what they do at work and in free time, and answer such questions addressed to me.	94, 97	1 ② 3 4 5
I can describe my hobbies and interests in a simple way.	97	1 2 3 ④ 5
I can identify the main point of TV news items reporting events, accidents etc. when the visual supports the commentary.	94, 96	1 2 ③ 4 5
I can say what I like and dislike	94, 98	1 2 3 4 5

Unit 15

Competences	Page	Your score
I can find the most important information on leisure time activities, exhibitions etc. in information leaflets.	100, 102	1 2 ③ 4 5
I can describe myself, my family and other people.	103	1 2 3 4 5
I can order something to eat or drink.	104	1 2 ③ 4 5
I can generally identify the topic of discussion around me when people speak slowly and clearly.	100, 102	1 2 ③ 4 5
I can understand the essential information in short recorded passages dealing with predictable everyday matters which are spoken slowly and clearly.	100, 102	1 2 3 ④ 5

Unit 16

Competences	Page	Your score
I can ask for and give directions referring to a map or plan.	107, 110	1 2 3 ④ 5
I can understand the essential information in short recorded passages dealing with predictable everyday matters which are spoken slowly and clearly.	108	1 2 3 4 ⑤
I can identify important information in news summaries or simple newspaper articles in which numbers and names play an important role and which are clearly structured and illustrated.	106, 108	1 2 3 4 ⑤
I can describe past experiences and personal experiences (e.g. the last weekend, my last holiday).	109	1 2 3 4 5
I can make myself understood using memorised phrases and single expressions	107	1 2 3 4 ⑤

1 Airport *Overview*

Section	Aims	What the students are doing
Listening **SB page 4**	*Listening skills*: listening for specific information	• Listening to people introducing themselves. • Identifying names and places from the dialogues.
Speaking **SB page 4**	*Conversation skills*: introductions	• Introducing themselves to classmates.
Vocabulary **SB page 5**	*Vocabulary*: country, nationality and language words	• Listening and repeating words for countries, nationalities and languages. • Listening and identifying languages. • Practising country, nationality and language words.
Grammar **SB page 5**	*Grammar*: *be* present simple	• Completing questions and answers.
Vocabulary & Listening **SB page 6**	*Vocabulary*: common objects *Listening skills*: listening for specific information	• Listening and repeating the names of common objects. • Listening to conversations at an airport and identifying people's bags.
Grammar **SB page 6**	*Grammar*: articles *a* and *an*; *this* and *these*	• Completing a table with *a* or *an*. • Writing questions and answers with *this / it* and *these / they*.
Pronunciation **SB page 7**	*Pronunciation*: the alphabet	• Listening and repeating the letters of the alphabet. • Differentiating between the vowels.
Vocabulary **SB page 7**	*Vocabulary*: numbers 0–10	• Listening and repeating numbers. • Listening and repeating phone numbers. • Practising saying and identifying phone numbers.
Listening & Speaking **SB page 7**	*Listening skills*: listening for specific information *Conversation skills*: exchanging personal information	• Listening to and completing a conversation. • Practising a conversation. Asking other people the same questions.
Useful phrases **SB page 8**	*Vocabulary*: useful conversational phrases – asking for repetition and spelling	• Listening to and completing conversations. • Listening to and repeating useful phrases. • Writing and practising new conversations.
Vocabulary *Extra* **SB page 9**	*Vocabulary*: revision of words from the unit: common nouns. Focus on instructions (1)	• Matching pictures with words.
Writing **WB page 7**	Using capital letters and full stops Completing a form with personal information	

1 Airport *Teacher's notes*

Warm-up

Introduce yourself around the class with a simple friendly greeting such as *Hello, I'm (name). What's your name?* Encourage individual students to respond with *Hello, I'm (Marta)* and then follow up with *Nice to meet you* before moving on to the next student.

Listening (SB page 4)

1 🌐 1.01

- Focus the students' attention on the photo. Tell the students that the two people are sitting next to each other on a plane and that they've never met before. Then focus their attention on the questions. Hold up the book and point to the man as you ask *What's his name?* (emphasising the pronoun *his*). Point to the woman and ask *What's her name?* (emphasising the pronoun *her*). Ask the students to listen to the recording and read the conversation below the photo as they listen. Then ask them to answer the questions.

- Finally, play the recording again and ask the student to repeat the lines of the conversation after the speakers. Focus their attention to the contractions *I'm* and *What's* and the useful phrase *Nice to meet you*, which completes the introduction.

- You could then ask several pairs of students to role-play the conversation. If your classroom set-up allows, you could add a degree of reality to this by putting two chairs side by side at the front of the class and asking students to come out and sit in them as they do the role-play.

> a) Mike.   b) Helen.

Language notes

Vocabulary: *name*

- The response to the question *What's your name?* could be the full name, surname or first name depending on the context. Here, because Mike only gives his first name before asking the question, the most appropriate reply is also just the first name.

- In more formal situations, you'd give both your first name and your surname. *What's your surname?* is practised on page 7.

Grammar: contractions

- Remind the students that it's more common to use contracted forms than full forms in conversation.

2 🌐 1.02

- Again, focus the students' attention on the photo. Point to Helen and Mike in turn and ask the questions. Emphasise the pronouns *she* and *he*. Students listen to the recording and read the conversation as they listen. They then answer the questions.

- Pairwork. Play the recording again and ask the students to repeat. Then ask them to work in pairs and role-play the meeting between Mike and Helen.

> a) London.   b) New York.

Language note

Vocabulary: *British*

A *British* person could be English, Scottish, Welsh or Northern Irish.

Speaking (SB page 4)

- Read out the conversation in the speech bubbles to the class. Then choose a confident student and demonstrate the conversation using your own names.

- Put the students in pairs and ask them to practise the conversation using their own names. When they've finished, they can mingle around the class introducing themselves to other students. Monitor and help where necessary.

Vocabulary (SB page 5)

1 🌐 1.03

- Remind the students that Mike asked Helen *Are you American?* and she replied *No, I'm English* in the conversation on page 4. Point out that the words for countries and nationalities are different. Explain that someone who is *American* comes from *America*, and someone who is *English* comes from *England*.

- Focus attention on the first two columns of the table and point out the formulae *I'm from + name of country* and *I'm + nationality*. Explain that the underlining in the first few words of the table shows which syllables of the words are stressed. Play the recording for students to listen to and repeat the country and nationality words. Play it a second time and ask them to underline the stressed syllables in the other words in columns 1 and 2. Allow them to compare results in pairs before checking with the whole class.

- Finally, ask for individual repetition of the words and check that the students are putting the stress on the right syllables.

Brazil, Brazilian	Poland, Polish
Germany, German	Spain, Spanish
Italy, Italian	China, Chinese
Russia, Russian	Japan, Japanese

Language note
Pronunciation: word stress

You can check the stress of any word by looking in your dictionary. Dictionaries usually mark the stress of a word as well as giving the phonetic script, i.e. *Brazil* /brəˈzɪl/. In *New Inside Out* the stressed syllable is always underlined.

2 🌐 **1.04**

- Focus attention on the third column of the table. Remind the students that the word for the language spoken by people of various nationalities is sometimes different from the nationality word (as with *Brazilian* and *Portuguese*), and sometimes it's the same (as with *German* and *German*).
- Tell the students that they're now going to listen to similar greetings said in six different languages. (They are all greetings you might hear when you arrive by plane in various airports around the world.) They have to listen and decide which language is being spoken each time. Point out that the first speaker is speaking Spanish so a number 1 has been put in the box next to *Spanish*. Play the recording more than once if students need to hear it again to make their choices. Allow them to compare notes in pairs or groups before checking with the class.

1 Spanish	2 Italian	3 Polish	4 Chinese
5 Russian	6 Japanese		

3 🌐 **1.05**

Focus attention on the third column of the table again. Ask the students to complete it with the language words from Exercise 2 and to underline the stressed syllables. They shouldn't find this too difficult as the stressed syllables in these words are the same as they are for the nationality words. Play the recording for them to listen, check their answers and repeat the words.

1 Portuguese	2 German	3 Italian
4 Russian	5 Polish	6 Spanish	7 Chinese
8 Japanese		

4

- Pairwork. Focus attention on the speech bubbles. Explain the activity and demonstrate it with a confident student by saying *China,* and encouraging the student to respond with *Chinese, Chinese.* Choose another country word and get another student to respond with the correct nationality and language words.
- Then put the students into pairs and ask them to take turns being the person who gives the country name, and the one who responds with the nationality and language. As they do this, go round monitoring and checking that everyone is stressing the correct syllables.

Grammar (SB page 5)

be

1

- Point out the table in the margin which shows the present simple affirmative of *be*, and the contracted forms that are commonly used in speaking. Remind the students that Mike and Helen on page 4 used *I'm* when they introduced themselves. Go through the question and answer forms in the margin as well. Then focus the students' attention on the example and the picture of the pilot labelled (a). Explain that you don't use contractions in affirmative short answers to questions, so the correct answer to *Is he Chinese?* is *Yes, he is,* not *Yes, he's.* (Students will encounter contractions in negative short answers in Unit 2.)
- Ask the students to complete the exercise. Go round monitoring and giving help if required. Allow them to compare answers in pairs.

a) 'Is he Chinese?'
   'Yes, he is.'
	d) 'Is she Russian?'
	   'Yes, she is.'

b) 'Are they Spanish?'
   'Yes, they are.'
	e) 'Is it Polish?'
	   'Yes, it is.'

c) 'Is it Japanese?'
   'Yes, it is.'
	f) 'Are they British?'
	   'Yes, they are.'

2 🌐 **1.06**

Play the recording for the students to check their answers. Play it again and ask them to repeat the sentences after the speakers.

Vocabulary & Listening (SB page 6)

1 🌐 **1.07**

This exercise introduces the students to some more vocabulary: common objects. Focus the students' attention on the two bags and the labelled objects. Give them a minute or two to identify the different objects before you play the recording and ask them to repeat the words. Encourage them to point to the items as they hear them.

Vocabulary: *mobile phone, mobile number*

Mobile phone and *mobile number* are British English terms. In American English they are *cellphone* and *cell number* respectively.

2 🌐 1.08

Tell the students that one bag belongs to Mike and one to Helen, and explain that they've been opened by a customs official at the airport. Ask them if they can predict which bag is which, but don't spend too much time on this. Play the recording and ask the students to listen and read the two conversations. Then ask them to identify which is Mike's bag and which is Helen's.

Mike's bag is bag B. Helen's bag is bag A.

3

- Go through anything in the conversations that the students don't understand. Point out that the customs official addresses Mike as *sir* and Helen as *madam*, and explain that these are formal and polite ways to address men and women whose names you don't know.

- Pairwork. Put the students into pairs and ask them to practise the conversations, taking turns to be the customs official, Mike and Helen. Go round, offering help and encouragement. Take a note of any pronunciation problems which can be addressed with the whole class when the pairs have finished.

Grammar (SB page 6)

Nouns – singular/plural

1 🌐 1.09

- Focus the students' attention on the conversations in the last section, and point out the customs official's two questions *What's this?* and *What are these?* Explain that you use *What's this?* for one object (*an apple, a magazine*, etc), and *What are these?* when there's more than one object (*aspirins, tissues*, etc). Tell the students that single objects can usually be made plural by adding an *s* at the end. Ask them to practise saying *this* and *these*, making sure they differentiate between the short /ɪ/ sound of *this* and the longer /iː/ sound of *these*. Also check that they can pronounce *they're* /ðeə/ correctly, and that they understand that *are* is the plural form of *is*.

- Now focus the students' attention on the information in the margin. Go through the first question (*What's this?*) with the class and point out that you use *a* with words that start with a consonant (*a book, a camera, a diary*, etc), but you use *an* with words that start with the vowels *a, e, i, o* and *u* (*an apple, an umbrella*, etc).

- Then go through the second question (*What are these?*). Remind the students that you use this question to ask about plural objects. Point out that you don't use *a* or *an* with plurals.

- Ask the students to look at the table in Exercise 1 and complete it. Allow them to compare notes in pairs or small groups before you play the recording for them to check their answers.

- Point out that the plural of *diary* is *diaries* not *diarys*. Explain that some words that end with a *y* lose the *y* and take *ies* to form the plural (e.g. *party – parties*). Also point out that words ending in *sh* (like *toothbrush*) take *es* in the plural (*toothbrushes*). Play the recording again for the students to repeat.

> 1 aspirins 2 an apple 3 a diary
> 4 a toothbrush

2 🌐 1.10

- Focus the students' attention on the pictures. Then go through the example question and answer with them. Point out that picture a) shows only one diary, so the question is *What's this?* and the answer *It's a diary*. Do b) with the whole class as a further example if they are still having difficulties.

- Ask the students to complete the exercise in pairs. Then play the recording for them to listen and check their answers. Play it a second time for them to repeat the questions and answers. Point out the plural of *watch* (*watches*).

> 1 What's this? It's a diary.
> 2 What are these? They're pens.
> 3 What are these? They're keys.
> 4 What are these? They're coins.
> 5 What's this? It's a bag.
> 6 What are these? They're watches.

Grammar: euro coins

- *Money* is uncountable, *coins* are countable. So it's possible to say both *What's this?* (when referring to the money) – *It's money* or *It's cash*, and *What are these?* (when referring to the euro coins) – *They're euros* or *They're coins*.

- Although most elementary learners will have already met the concept of countable and uncountable nouns, *money* is always difficult for them as it seems to be countable when in fact it's *euros, dollars* or *pounds* which are countable.

- Take some of the items in Exercise 1 from your own bag or pocket. Make sure you include both singular and plural items. Ask students to identify them.

- Put the things in a box at the front of the class and allow students to come up, put their hand in the box and pull out an item for the rest of the class to identify.

3 *Grammar Extra* 1

Ask the students to turn to *Grammar Extra* 1 on page 126 of the Student's Book. Here they'll find an explanation of the grammar they've been studying and further exercises to practise it.

1

1   1 a pen   2 an exercise   3 people   4 babies
    5 a child   6 buses   7 an apple

2   3
a) It's a book.   a) They're books.
b) It's an aspirin.   b) They're aspirins.
c) It's a woman.   c) They're women.
d) It's a watch.   d) They're watches.
e) It's an umbrella.   e) They're umbrellas.
f) It's a man.   f) They're men.

Pronunciation (SB page 7)

The alphabet

1 🌐 1.11

- Focus the students' attention on the information in the margin about the pronunciation of the letters of the alphabet. Explain that the symbols in the *Sound* column are in phonemic script, which shows how words are pronounced. Point out that the letters of the alphabet are grouped according to their vowel sound, so *A*, *H*, *J* and *K*, for example, all have the vowel sound /eɪ/. If students are worried about phonemic script, reassure them that it may look complicated, but they'll soon get used to it, and it's extremely useful for finding out how unknown words are pronounced. At this point, you might like to show them a dictionary with phonemic script to demonstrate how useful it can be.

- Explain that the alphabet is divided into vowels and consonants. Play the recording for the students to listen and repeat the vowels. Ask them to find the vowels in the chart in the margin, and to see which consonants have the same sound.

2 🌐 1.12

Play the recording for the students to repeat the letters of the alphabet. Encourage them to read the letters in the table in the margin as they listen and repeat. Note that in British English the letter *z* is pronounced /zed/, and in American English it's pronounced /ziː/.

3 🌐 1.13

Ask the students to practise saying the groups of vowels in pairs before you play the recording. Point out that the number 1 next to group c) indicates that this is the first group they'll hear. Ask them to number the others from 2 to 5.

---

c) 1   e) 2   b) 3   a) 4   d) 5

Extra activity

- Do an alphabet dictation, spelling out words that the students have already seen in the unit. For example, *favourite*, *Polish*, *Japanese*, *language*, *nationality*, *city*.

- As you dictate, get the students to write down the letters. They should then call out the word. Finally, ask them to find examples of this word in the book.

Vocabulary (SB page 7)

Numbers *0–10*

1 🌐 1.14

Focus the students' attention on the numbers *oh* to *ten* in the margin. Play the recording for them to listen and repeat. When they've finished, ask for individual repetition.

Language note

Vocabulary: *oh* and *zero*

Oh is often pronounced like the letter 'O' when saying numbers one figure at a time – for example, in a reference number or telephone number. Note that *0h* can also be pronounced *zero*.

2 🌐 1.15

- Focus the students' attention on the margin notes again and go through the pronunciation of the telephone number with them. Point out that *oh* is usually used for the pronunciation of *0* in telephone numbers in British English, and when the same number occurs twice in a row, you tend to say *double six*, *double three*, etc, rather than *six six* or *three three*. Ask the student to repeat the telephone number in the margin before moving on to the exercise.

- Explain that these are all the names of airlines, and that the students have to listen to the recording and complete the London telephone numbers for them. Point out that the first one has been done for them.

- You could revise nationality words by asking the students to identify the nationalities of the airlines before you play the recording – do the first one for them as *French* was not one of the nationalities taught earlier (a) French, b) British, c) German, d) American, e) Chinese, f) Japanese).

- Play the recording for the students to complete the numbers. You may need to play it more than once. Allow the students to compare notes in pairs before checking answers with the class.

---

a) 0870 142 4343   d) 020 7365 0777
b) 0870 850 9850   e) 020 8745 4624
c) 0870 837 7747   f) 020 8990 6010

1.15

a) The number for Air France is oh eight seven oh, one four two, four three four three.

b) The number for British Airways is oh eight seven oh, eight five oh, nine eight five oh.

c) The number for Lufthansa is oh eight seven oh, eight three seven, double seven four seven.

d) The number for American Airlines is zero two zero, seven three six five, zero seven double seven.

e) The number for China Airlines is zero two zero, eight seven four five, four six two four.

f) And the number for Japan Airlines is oh two oh, eight double nine oh, six oh one oh. I'll repeat that: oh two oh, eight double nine oh, six oh one oh.

3 Pairwork

- The pairwork exercise for this unit is on pages 116 and 121 of the Student's Book. Put the students in pairs and tell them who will be Student A, and who will be Student B.

- You might find it useful to preteach the pronunciation of the city names:

  Milan, /mɪˈlæn/, New York /njuː ˈjɔːk/, Rome /rəʊm/, Moscow /ˈmɒskəʊ/, Seville /seˈvɪl/, Paris /ˈpærɪs/.

- While they're doing the exercise, go round monitoring and giving help. Take note of any errors which may need particular attention later, and also any examples of good language use which you can praise. Check answers with the class.

> Student A: 1 BA561   2 AZ200   3 IB4144
> Student B: 1 AA132   2 SU243   3 AF1370

Listening & Speaking (SB p 7)

1 1.16

- Focus the students' attention on the photo. Tell the students that Mike and Helen from the Vocabulary & Listening section are leaving the airport. Mike is getting Helen's contact details because he wants to see her again.

- Ask the students to look at the conversation. Point out the gaps for them to complete with the information in the box. Ask them to read the conversation and decide which information goes in which gap.

- Play the recording for the students to listen and check. Then play it a second time for them to repeat after the speakers.

- Put the students in pairs to practise the conversation. They can use their own name and contact details.

> 1 Taylor. T-A-Y-L-O-R   2 020 7653 2001
> 3 It's helen21@hotpost.com

2

Make sure the students realise that the three questions are *What's your surname?* *What's your phone number?* and *What's your address?* Ask them to mingle and ask three other people these questions. When they've finished, ask them to report back to the class. Remind them to use the pronouns *his* and *her*.

Useful phrases (SB page 8)

1 1.17

- Focus the students' attention on the illustration, which shows two students and a teacher in a language school. One of the students is asking the teacher a question. Give students time to look at the illustration. Make sure the students understand *say*, *spell* and *repeat*.

- Play the recording for the students to listen and complete the conversation. You may need to play it more than once.

- Check answers with the class.

> 1 say   2 spell   3 say   4 spell   5 say
> 6 spell   7 repeat

Language notes

Grammar: *Sorry? Can you …?*

- *Sorry?* in this context is an informal request for someone to repeat what they've just said. Note that the more formal *Can you repeat that, please?* also occurs in this conversation. In this context, *Can you …?* is a polite request.

- Note that *can* for ability will be taught in Unit 13.

Grammar: *spell, say, repeat*

- The structure of the verbs *spell*, *repeat* and *say* are all followed by an object. You say *Can you spell that?*, or *Can you spell your name?*, not ~~*Can you spell?*~~ or ~~*Can you spell me*~~.

2 1.18

Play the recording. The students repeat the phrases after the speaker. Make sure that they match the speaker's intonation. Ask several students to repeat the phrases individually.

3 1.19

- Play the recording for the students to listen and repeat the words in the table.

- Ask the students to translate the words into their own language(s). In monolingual classes, they can work in pairs to do this. If you have a mixture of nationalities in your class, encourage them to form pairs with someone else who speaks their language.

4

- Pairwork. This will work best if both students speak the same language. In monolingual classes this is no problem, but in classes with mixed nationalities it will be necessary for pairs to tell each other their translations of the words. They prepare conversations similar to that in Exercise 1, but using the words from Exercise 3.
- While they're practising their conversations, go round monitoring and giving help. Take note of any errors which may need attention later, and also any examples of good language use which you can praise.

Vocabulary *Extra* (SB page 9)

Common nouns

1

- Focus the students' attention on the list of words and point out that they're all common nouns. Point out that the underlining indicates the syllable of the word that has the strongest stress. Check that the students can pronounce the words correctly.
- Ask the students to look at the pictures and match each one with one of the words. Point out that the first two have been done for them.

```
10  an aspirin – aspirins
 1  a bag – bags
13  a child – children
 7  a diary – diaries
 3  an MP3 player – MP3 players
 2  a key – keys
 9  a magazine – magazines
 4  a man – men
 8  a mobile phone – mobile phones
11  a person – people
12  a  sweet – sweets
14  a tissue – tissues
16  a toothbrush – toothbrushes
 6  an umbrella – umbrellas
15  a watch – watches
 5  a woman – women
```

2

Ask students to work individually and complete the list with the missing singular or plural forms.

```
See answers in Exercise 1.
```

3

Pairwork. Demonstrate the activity with a confident student. Cover the words, point to one of the pictures and ask *What's this?* Elicit the answer. Then put the students into pairs to continue the activity. Go round, checking that everyone is pronouncing the words correctly and using *It's* and *They're* appropriately.

1

- Focus the students' attention on the list of phrases and point out that they're all common phrases that are used in the classroom. Check that the students can pronounce the phrases correctly.
- Ask the students to look at the pictures and match each one with one of the phrases. Point out that the first one has been done for them.

```
3  Listen to the conversation.
2  Look at the board.
5  Read the text.
1  Work with a partner.
4  Write your name on a piece of paper.
6  Use a dictionary.
```

2

Ask the students to work individually and complete the instructions with the verbs from Exercise 1. Point out that the first one has been done for them.

```
a) Read    b) Look    c) Use    d) Listen
e) Work    f) Write
```

Further practice material

Need more writing practice?

→ Workbook page 7
- Using capital letters with full stops
- Completing a form with personal information

Need more classroom practice activities?

→ Photocopiable resource materials pages 151 to 153
  Grammar: *Landing card*
  Vocabulary: *Common objects*
  Communication: *Where in the world?*
→ Top 10 activities pages xv to xx

Need progress tests?

→ Test CD – *Test Unit 1*

Need more on important teaching concepts?

→ Key concepts in *New Inside Out* pages xxii to xxxv

Need student self-study practice?

→ CD-ROM – Unit 1: *Airport*

Need student CEF self-evaluation?

→ CEF Checklists pages xxxvii to xliv

Need more information and more ideas?

→ www.insideout.net

2 People *Overview*

Section	Aims	What the students are doing
Vocabulary **SB page 10**	*Vocabulary*: favourite things	• Completing a table of favourite things. • Categorising words under headings.
Speaking **SB page 10**	*Conversation skills*: favourite things	• Asking and answering questions about favourite things with *Who ...?* and *What ...?*
Grammar **SB page 11**	*Grammar*: possessive determiners	• Completing sentence with possessive determiners.
Vocabulary **SB page 11**	*Vocabulary*: numbers from *11 to 100*	• Listening and repeating numbers from *11 to 100*. • Listening and circling the numbers they hear. • Using numbers to complete a text.
Speaking **SB page 11**	*Conversation skills*: ages	• Matching people with ages. • Writing ages in words.
Vocabulary **SB page 12**	*Vocabulary*: jobs	• Matching jobs with photos. • Writing sentences about people's jobs. • Completing a table with percentages.
Pronunciation **SB page 12**	*Pronunciation*: jobs with *a* and *an*	• Completing a table with jobs. • Practising saying job titles with *a* and *an*.
Grammar **SB page 13**	*Grammar*: *be* present simple affirmative, negative and questions	• Completing sentences. • Completing questions and answers. • Asking and answering questions.
Writing & Speaking **SB page 13**	*Writing skills*: writing questions *Conversation skills*: asking questions about personal information	• Writing questions about personal information. • Matching answers to questions.
Useful phrases **SB page 14**	*Vocabulary*: useful conversational phrases for greeting people and introducing yourself	• Reading and completing conversations with greetings. • Categorising useful phrases for greetings. • Listening to and repeating useful phrases. • Practising conversations.
Vocabulary *Extra* **SB page 15**	*Vocabulary*: revision of words from the unit: jobs. Focus on countries and nationalities	• Matching pictures with words.
Writing **WB page 11**	Using punctuation Writing about yourself	

Quick revision

Revise greetings from the previous unit by saying to your students *Hello, I'm* (name). Encourage several of them to respond as before with their names. Follow-up by saying *Nice to meet you* before moving on to the next student.

Vocabulary (SB page 10)

1 🌐 1.20

- Focus the students' attention on the photo of Brad Pitt. Ask the students if they know who he is (a famous Hollywood actor). Find out if they've seen any films that he has been in. This can all be done in the students' L1 if necessary.
- Explain the meaning of *favourite things*. Give some examples of your own favourite things: your favourite actor, your favourite film, etc, but don't go on for too long as students will have the opportunity later to discuss their own favourites.
- Focus the students' attention on the list of Brad Pitt's favourite things, and the categories in the box. Explain that they have to complete the table with the headings from the box. Go through the headings and make sure that the students understand them. Point out that the first one has been done for them as an example: Dianne Wiest is Brad Pitt's favourite actor. If students ask, you may like to point out that *actress* is the feminine form of *actor*, but recently it has become customary to use the term *actor* for both men and women.
- Ask the students to complete the table. Then play the recording for them to listen and check their answers. Go through the vocabulary at the end to make sure there are no unknown items. Then play the recording again for the students to repeat.

a) Actor	b) Singer	c) Film	d) Writer
e) Food	f) Drink	g) Sport	h) Animal

Cultural notes

Brad Pitt (born 1963)
American actor who shot to fame in 1991 in the film *Thelma and Louise*. Other films he's starred in include *Seven*, *Fight Club* and *Ocean's Eleven*. He was married to the actress Jennifer Aniston (2000–2005). He's currently married to Angelina Jolie.

Dianne Wiest (born 1948)
American actress who has been in several films directed by Woody Allen, including *Hannah and Her Sisters* (1988), and *Bullets Over Broadway* (1994) in which she won Academy Awards. She also acted in the film *Edward Scissorhands* (1990).

Jimi Hendrix (1942–1970)
Jimi Hendrix was an American rock guitarist and an icon of the 60s. Among his hit records were *Purple Haze* and *All Along the Watchtower*. He died in 1970 at the age of 27, and is considered to be the greatest rock guitarist ever.

Bob Marley (1945–1981)
Jamaican singer, songwriter and guitarist who made reggae music famous around the world. In the 1960s, he formed the band The Wailers with Bunny Livingstone and Peter Tosh. Although the Wailers broke up in 1975, he continued to record as Bob Marley and the Wailers. His songs included *Get Up, Stand Up*; *Jamming*; *I Shot the Sheriff* and *No Woman, No Cry*. He died of cancer at the age of 36.

Planet of the Apes
Originally a 1968 science fiction film, it was remade in 2001 and directed by Tim Burton. The film is set in the year 2029. In the film, an astronaut finds himself on a strange planet, where talking apes rule the human race.

Saturday Night Fever
This 1977 film about an uneducated teenager from Brooklyn who likes dancing made John Travolta a household name, and disco music and the Bee Gees very popular.

Cormac McCarthy (born 1933)
American novelist who became famous when he won the US National Book Award in 1992 with *All the Pretty Horses*, which was made into a film in 2000.

2

- You could put the headings on the board and ask individual students to come to the front and write up the various things under the correct headings.
- Finally, ask students to decide what their own favourite things are, and to add them to the lists.

Actor: Gwyneth Paltrow, Johnny Depp
Singer: Christina Aguilera, Louis Armstrong
Film: *Mission Impossible, Star Wars*
Writer: Dan Brown, JK Rowling
Food: pasta, steak
Drink: Coke, tea
Sport: football, swimming
Animal: cats, horses

Cultural notes

Dan Brown (born 1964)
American author famous for his controversial book *The Da Vinci Code* in 2003, which quickly became an international best seller. Dan Brown is especially interested in cryptography (the study of hidden messages and codes), which is a recurring theme in his books.

Frank Sinatra (1915–1998)
American singer said to be one of the most popular and influential in the 20th century. His best-known songs include *Strangers in the Night, My Way*, and *New York, New York*. He also acted in several films including *High Society* (1956) with Bing Crosby and Grace Kelly, and won an Academy Award for best supporting actor in *From Here to Eternity* (1953).

JK Rowling (born 1965)
British fiction writer who became famous as the author of the *Harry Potter* series.

Johnny Depp (born 1963)
Johnny Depp's film debut was in *Nightmare On Elm Street* (1984). He then acted in the popular TV series *21 Jump Street*, before starring in the film *Edward Scissorhands* (1990), directed by Tim Burton. His most popular film to date is probably acting as Jack Sparrow in the *Pirates of the Caribbean* trilogy.

Louis Armstrong (1901–1971)
Louis Armstrong was born in New Orleans. He was one of the most famous jazz musicians of the 20th century and had a great influence on the history of jazz music. He played the trumpet, but is also well known as a jazz singer.

Mission Impossible
Series of three action films starring Tom Cruise based on a 1960s TV series about American secret agents employed by the United States government.

Star Wars
Star Wars is a series of six science fantasy films. The original *Star Wars* film, directed by George Lucas, was released in 1977 and starred Mark Hamill, Harrison Ford and Carrie Fisher. It became a huge pop culture phenomenon with TV series, books, comics and video games.

Speaking (SB page 10)

- Pairwork. With the whole class, focus the students' attention on the speech bubbles and read out the questions and answers. Point out that you use *Who ...?* to ask about people and *What ...?* to ask about things. Demonstrate the activity with a couple of confident students, asking the two questions and eliciting their own replies.

- Ask the students to work in pairs, and to take turns asking and answering about their favourite things. Go round monitoring and giving help with vocabulary where necessary. Make a note of any problems which you can deal with later with the whole class.

Grammar (SB page 11)

Possessive determiners

1 🌐 1.21

- Focus the students' attention on the table in the margin, which shows the subject pronouns and corresponding possessive determiners. Make sure everyone understands the function of these before you move on. Remind them of the three they've already seen on page 10, in the question *Who's your favourite singer?* and the instruction *Ask your partner about his or her favourite things.*

- Go through the example with the class and explain that the first sentence, *I'm an actor*, tells you who is speaking, so that you know the correct possessive determiner is *my*.

- Ask the students to complete the sentences. Allow them to work in pairs if they wish, and to compare their results before you play the recording for them to check.

a) My	b) His	c) Her	d) Our	e) Their

Language notes

Grammar: *his/her*

- The possessive determiners *my, your, his, her, its, our* and *their* are sometimes called 'possessive adjectives' in older grammars and dictionaries.

- The possessive determiners *his* and *her* can be confusing for students. You use *his* to refer to something a man possesses. You use *her* to refer to something a woman possesses.

  *Bill and **his** daughter.*

  *Mary and **her** husband.*

- Note that in some languages the possessive determiner agrees with the gender of the noun, i.e. masculine, feminine or plural. This doesn't happen in English.

Jimi Hendrix (1942–1970)
(See notes about Jimi Hendrix on page 9.)

Bob Marley (1945–1981)
(See notes about Bob Marley on page 9.)

Lara Croft
Lara Croft is an English video game character and the heroine of the *Tomb Raider* series of video games, films and comic books, who races against time and villains to recover ancient artifacts. Angelina Jolie starred in the 2001 film *Lara Croft: Tomb Raider*.

Mr & Mrs Smith
2005 comedy film starring Brad Pitt and Angelina Jolie. They play a married couple who have kept a secret from each other – they're both professional assassins, until one day, their employers tell them to go after and kill the same person.

2

Pairwork. Ask the students to work in pairs and to try and identify the people in Exercise 1. Check answers with the class.

---

a) Brad Pitt
b) Prince Charles
c) Angelina Jolie
d) Bill and Hillary Clinton
e) Julio and Enrique Iglesias

Cultural notes

Brad Pitt (born 1963)
(See notes about Brad Pitt on page 9.)

Prince Charles (born 1948)
Prince Charles is the eldest son of Queen Elizabeth II and Prince Philip. He was married to Lady Diana Spencer, who was killed in a car crash in Paris in 1997. They had two sons, William and Harry. Prince Charles is now married to Camilla Parker-Bowles.

Angelina Jolie (born 1975)
Angelina Jolie is the daughter of actor John Voight. Among the films she's appeared in are *The Bone Collector* (1999), *Lara Croft: Tomb Raider* (2001), and *Mr & Mrs Smith* (2005). She's married to actor Brad Pitt and spends much of her time doing humanitarian work.

Bill Clinton (born 1945) and **Hillary Clinton** (born 1947)
Democratic politician Bill Clinton was the President of the United States of America from 1993 to 2001. His wife, Hillary was elected the United States Senator for New York in November 2000, the first woman elected to national office.

Julio Iglesias (born 1943) and **Enrique Iglesias** (born 1975)
Spanish singer Julio Iglesias was popular in the 1970s and 1980s. He was one of the most successful recording artists of all time, and has sold albums in seven languages. His first English language hit song was *Begin The Beguine* in 1982.

Enrique Iglesias, like his father Julio, is an internationally famous singer, and has recorded songs in four languages. He now lives in America.

Vocabulary (SB page 11)

Numbers *11–100*

1 🔊 1.22

- Focus the students' attention on the numbers shown in the margin. Remind them that the underlining shows which syllable carries the main stress. Draw their attention to the group of words that end in *teen* and those that end in *ty*. Some nationalities find it difficult to tell the difference between numbers that end in *teen* and those that end in *ty*. Point out that it's important to pronounce the ends of all these words clearly, so that they make a difference between them. Also point out how the position of the stressed syllable changes in, for example, *thir<u>teen</u>* and *<u>thir</u>ty*. Emphasise that it's important to make a distinction.

- Play the recording and ask the students to repeat the numbers. When they've done this chorally, ask individual students to pronounce the words.

2 🔊 1.23

Before you play the recording, ask several confident students to read out the pairs of numbers, being careful to make a distinction between them. Then play the recording and ask them to circle the numbers they hear. When you've checked answers with the class, play the recording again for them to repeat.

---

a) 13   b) 14   c) 50   d) 16   e) 70   f) 80
g) 19

Extra activity

To make sure that the students focus on the endings *teen* and *ty* when listening and speaking, tell them that you are going to call out some numbers. If the number ends in *teen*, they should stand up, but if it ends in *ty*, they should remain seated. Call out some different numbers at random. When they've got the hang of this, invite several students to come to the front of the class and call out numbers for the others to react to.

3 🔊 1.24

Remind students that numbers can be written either in words or in numerals. Focus attention on the example, and then ask the students to work individually to write the remaining numerals next to the words. Check answers with the class, then play the recording for them to listen and repeat the numbers. Point out that *110* can be said as *one hundred and ten* or *a hundred and ten*.

> a) 7   b) 28   c) 47   d) 65   e) 110   f) 245

4 🔊 1.25

Pairwork. In this exercise, students get the opportunity to use the numbers in a real-world context. Go through the information with the class and then ask the students to discuss in pairs what numbers they think should go in the gaps. Tell them that all the numbers they need are in Exercise 3. Play the recording for them to check their answers. Ask for some kind of personal reaction from the students. Are they surprised by any of the statistics?

> a) 28%   b) 65%   c) 7%   d) 47%   e) 245
> f) 110

Extra activity

- Play the game *Secret number* to practise the numbers the students have learnt in Unit 1 and this unit. Write a number on the board and get the students to say what it is. Repeat this a few times until they seem quite confident.
- Write a number on a piece of paper hiding the paper in an exaggerated way, so that the students can't see the number. Then write a big question mark in the centre of the board and ask *What's the number?* Keep pointing at the question mark until a student calls out a number. Write the number on the board. Gesture that it's incorrect but with a big smile on your face, and indicate with your hands whether it's higher or lower than the secret number. If it's higher, write the number above the question mark. If it's lower, write it below.
- Encourage the students to suggest other numbers until they find the correct number.
- Repeat this game two or three times.

Speaking (SB page 11)

1

Focus attention on the photos. Point to the people in them and ask some of the students to guess how old they are. Then point out that the actual ages are amongst those in the box in Exercise 1, and ask the students to match the ages with the people. Allow them to discuss this in pairs or small groups if they wish. Don't tell them the answers at this stage.

Language note

Vocabulary: talking about age

When you talk about a person's age, you can say *She's twenty*, or *She's twenty years old*. However, you can't say ~~She's twenty years~~.

2 🔊 1.26

Remind the students that in the previous section they were given numbers in words and had to write the correct numerals. Now they have to do the reverse. They are given the numerals and have to write the words. Focus attention on the example and point out that numbers such as *twenty-nine* are hyphenated.

Play the recording for the students to find out if their answers to Exercise 1 were correct. Ask them if they find the actual ages of the people in the photos surprising.

> a) She's nineteen.
> b) He's sixty-four.
> c) She's forty-one.
> d) He's seven.

Vocabulary (SB page 12)

Jobs

1 🔊 1.27

- Focus the students' attention on the photos. Read aloud the list of jobs in the box, and ask the students to work in pairs and try to match them to the photos. Go round giving help and assistance. Check answers before moving on to the next stage of the exercise. Point out the use of indefinite articles with jobs.
- Next, focus the students' attention on the sentences under the photos. Ask three confident students to read them aloud. Then ask the students to write sentences for the other photos.
- Play the recording for the students to check their answers. Then play it again for them to listen and repeat the sentences. Make sure they can pronounce all the words correctly. They may have difficulty with *lawyer* /ˈlɔɪə/, *technician* /tekˈnɪʃən/ and *nurses* /nɜːsɪz/.

> | a) a lawyer | a) He's a lawyer. |
> |---|---|
> | b) a hairdresser | b) She's a hairdresser. |
> | c) shop assistants | c) They're shop assistants. |
> | d) an IT technician | d) He's an IT technician. |
> | e) a doctor | e) He's a doctor. |
> | f) a taxi driver | f) He's a taxi driver. |
> | g) a sales manager | g) He's a sales manager. |
> | h) nurses | h) They're nurses. |

Extra activity

If your students have jobs, find out what they are and if they know the English words for them.

2 🔊 1.28

- Focus attention on the table and explain what it shows (the percentage of people in various jobs in the UK who are women). Ask the students to work in pairs and to decide where the percentages in the box should go in the table. Emphasise that they are not expected to know the correct answers, but should discuss with their partner what they think may be right. Allow them to compare notes with another pair.

- Play the recording for the students to listen and see how accurately they guessed the percentages. Allow time for them to discuss their answers, before asking them if they have any idea what the percentages would be for their own country or countries. Again, emphasise that they are not expected to know exact figures.

a) 25%	b) 39%	c) 89%	d) 42%
e) 32%	f) 83%	g) 73%	h) 8%

Pronunciation (SB page 12)

1

In Unit 1, the students learnt that you use *a* with singular nouns that begin with a consonant, and *an* with those that begin with a vowel. Remind them of this and ask them to complete the table with the jobs. Encourage them to say the words aloud as they do this. Allow them to compare notes in pairs.

2 🔊 1.29

Play the recording for the students to check their answers. Then play it a second time for them to listen and repeat. Ask for individual repetition of the jobs around the class. Be careful with *university professor*. Although the letter that begins *university* is a vowel, it begins with a consonant sound /juː/ and is pronounced /juːnɪˈvɜːrsəti/, so it takes *a* rather than *an*.

A: *an* with vowel sounds – an actor, an English teacher, an IT technician
B: *a* with consonant sounds – a doctor, a singer, a student, a university professor, a writer

Grammar (SB page 13)

be: present simple affirmative, negative and questions

1 🔊 1.30

- Focus the students' attention on the first table in the margin, which shows the affirmative and negative forms of the present simple of *be*. Point out that the table shows the contracted forms which are normally used in speech. The full forms of *aren't* and *isn't* are shown under the table.

- Pairwork. Focus the students' attention on the example. Read it aloud to the class, emphasising the affirmative and negative forms *is* and *isn't*. Then ask the students to work in pairs and complete the rest of the exercise. They'll have to rely on general knowledge to determine which gaps should be completed with the affirmative, and which with the negative. Allow the pairs to compare notes with others before playing the recording for them to check their answers.

a) is; isn't	d) isn't; 's
b) aren't; 're	e) are; aren't
c) isn't; 's	f) is, isn't

Language note

Grammar: contractions – *be*

- In the negative, there are two ways of contracting the verb *be*. For example *No, he isn't* (contracting *not*) or *No, he's not* (contracting *is*). In *New Inside Out* only *isn't* and *aren't* are used, but accept both forms from your students as both are correct. Note that with *I* only *No, I'm not* is correct.

- Remember that you don't use the contractions in affirmative short answers. You say *Yes, she is*. Not ~~Yes, she's~~.

Cultural notes

George W Bush (born 1946)
George W Bush is the 43rd President of the United States. He first became president on 20th January 2001, and was re-elected on 2nd November 2004. His family have a long history in Republican Party and US politics, and he's the eldest son of the 41st US President, George H.W. Bush.

Domenico Dolce and **and Stefano Gabbana**
Italian fashion designers based in Milan. Their clothes are very popular among Hollywood actors and they've designed clothes for stars such as Madonna, Isabella Rosselini and Kylie Minogue.

Isabel Allende (born 1942)
Chilean writer and niece of Salvador Allende, President of Chile (1970–1973), who was removed from power and killed in General Pinochet's military coup. Isabel Allende's novels have been translated into more than 27 languages, and are popular throughout the world. Her first novel *The House of the Spirits* was made into a film starring Jeremy Irons, and Meryl Streep.

The White House

The White House is the official residence and principal workplace of the US President and is situated in the centre of Washington DC. There are six floors and 132 rooms. Every US president has lived there since the building was completed in 1800.

The Petronas Towers

The Petronas Towers are in Kuala Lumpur, Malaysia. They were designed by architect Cesar Pelli, and on the date of their completion in 1998 became the tallest buildings in the world until 2004. The twin tower spires rise to a height of 452 metres and have 88 floors. A skybridge links the two towers on the 41st and 42nd floors.

2 🌐 1.31

- Focus attention on the second table in the margin, which shows the question form, and affirmative and negative short answers. Read these aloud to the class. Remind the students that you don't use contractions in affirmative short answers, but point out that you do in negative short answers.

- Focus the students' attention on the example in the exercise, and ask three confident students to read it out: one reading the question, one the affirmative answer and one the negative. Then ask the students to complete the rest of the exercise. Go round giving help with vocabulary if necessary.

- Play the recording for the students to check their answers. Play it a second time for them to listen and repeat.

---

a) 'Are you a university student?'
   'Yes, I am.' 'No, I'm not.'
b) 'Are you 21?'
   'Yes, I am.' 'No, I'm not.'
c) 'Is your mother a taxi driver?'
   'Yes, she is.' 'No, she isn't.'
d) 'Is your father over 65 years old?'
   'Yes, he is.' 'No, he isn't.'
e) 'Is your favourite drink Coke?'
   'Yes, it is.' 'No, it isn't.'
f) 'Are your grandparents from here?'
   'Yes, they are.' 'No, they aren't.'

3

Pairwork. Put the students into pairs, and ask them to take turns asking and answering the questions. Tell them to give true information in their answers.

4 *Grammar Extra* 2

Ask students to turn to *Grammar Extra* 2 on page 126 of the Student's Book. Here they'll find an explanation of the grammar they've been studying and further exercises to practise it.

---

1 a) I'm not from China.
   b) I'm not twenty-five years old.
   c) My watch isn't Japanese.
   d) Our teacher isn't English.
   e) My parents aren't on holiday.
   f) The Pyramids aren't in Tunisia.
2 a) Is your mobile phone new?
   b) Is your name Maria?
   c) Is your computer an Apple?
   d) Are you at home?
   e) Is your favourite band U2?
   f) Are all your friends students?

Writing & Speaking (SB page 13)

1 🌐 1.32

- Focus the students' attention on the example. Tell the students once again that contractions are usually used in speech. Ask them to write the remaining questions in the correct order, and then to rewrite each one using contractions if possible.

- Play the recording for the students to check their answers. Then play it a second time for them to listen and repeat. Go through any difficult vocabulary with the class, and point out that you don't normally use the contracted form with *Where are …?*, though it's possible to do so.

---

a) What's your surname?
b) How old are you?
c) What's your email address?
d) What's your first name?
e) What's your mobile number?
f) What's your home phone number?
g) Where are you from?
h) What's your job?

2

- Explain that Dateline is an agency that matches men and women who are looking for partners. A *profile* is a list of personal details about someone. If the students are familiar with the American sitcom *Friends*, they may recognise the character of Rachel Green, played by Jennifer Anniston.

- Go through the examples and make sure the students know that they have to match the information on the profile with the questions in the previous exercise. Ask them to work in pairs to do this, then check answers with the class.

1 d) 2 a) 3 g) 4 b) 5 h) 6 c)
7 f) 8 e)

3 Pairwork

- The pairwork exercise for this unit is on pages 116 and 121 of the Student's Book. Put the students in pairs and tell them who will be Student A, and who will be Student B.

- While they are doing the exercise, go round monitoring and giving help. Take note of any errors which may need particular attention later, and also any examples of good language use which you can praise.

Useful phrases (SB page 14)

1 🌐 1.33

- These short conversations will help students to greet people whom they already know as well as to greet strangers. Go through the items in the box with the class and make sure that they understand them. Then ask the students to read each of the conversations and decide which items they should use to fill the gaps. Go round, giving help and encouragement.

- Play the recording for them to listen and check their answers.

1 I'm very well	4 Good morning
2 how are you?	5 Nice to meet you
3 Fine	6 Goodbye

Language notes

Vocabulary: *addressing people*

The people in these conversations use several different forms of address.

- In the first conversation, the younger woman addresses the older woman in the shop as *Mrs Jones*. She uses her surname and title rather than her first name as a mark of respect. Mrs Jones calls the younger woman *dear*, an informal term of endearment.

- In the second conversation, two friends are greeting each other. They don't use names and the conversation is quite informal.

- In the third conversation, two people of roughly the same age and status are meeting for the first time in a business setting. The first one to speak introduces himself using his full name (note that you don't use titles when you introduce yourself). After that, they both use first names, although the conversation is reasonably formal.

- In the fourth conversation, which also takes place in a shop, the newsagent calls the customer *sir*. She doesn't know his name and uses *sir* as a term of respect. The conversation is quite formal. The correct neutral term for a woman in this context is *madam*.

2 🌐 1.34

- Go through the first column of the table with the class and encourage the students to read the different ways of saying *hello* aloud. Tell them that *Good morning* and *Good afternoon* are more formal than *Hi!* and *Hello*, which are more likely to be used with friends. *Hi!* is the most informal greeting of the four. Ask them to find examples in the conversations where all these greetings are used.

- Focus attention on the second column of the table. Ask the students to read through the items and decide what heading from the box the column should have. Check answers and again point out that the final item in the column is more formal than the others. Ask them to find places in the conversations where each of these was used.

- Repeat the same procedure with the third and fourth columns.

- Play the recording for the students to check their answers. Then play it again for them to listen and repeat the useful phrases. Ask several students to repeat the phrases individually.

1 Saying hello	3 Introducing people
2 Greeting people	4 Saying goodbye

Language notes

Vocabulary: *greetings*

You can also say *Good evening* as a formal way of saying *hello* in the evening. However, you say *Good night* to say goodbye at the end of the evening, or when someone goes to bed.

Vocabulary: *See you!*

See you is an expression which means the same as *See you later*, or *See you soon!*

3

Pairwork. Ask the students to practise the conversations, taking turns to be each of the people. Go round, monitoring and giving help where necessary. Ask a few confident pairs to perform their conversations for the class.

Vocabulary *Extra* (SB page 15)

Jobs

1

- Focus the students' attention on the list of words and point out that they're all to do with jobs. Remind students that the underlining indicates the syllable of the word that has the strongest stress. Check that the students can pronounce the words correctly.

- Ask the students to look at the pictures and match each one with one of the jobs. Point out that the first one has been done for them.

10	an actor	12	a sales manager
8	a doctor	4	a shop assistant
6	a hairdresser	1	a singer
3	an IT technician	7	a taxi driver
9	a lawyer	11	a waiter
2	a nurse	5	a writer

2

Pairwork. Demonstrate the activity with a confident student. Cover the words, point to one of the pictures and ask *What does he/she do?* Elicit the answer. Then put the students into pairs to continue the activity. Go round, checking that everyone is pronouncing the jobs correctly.

3

Ask students think of their family and friends and write down the names of their jobs.

Focus on countries and nationalities

1

- Focus the students' attention on the example in the table. Point out that *Brazil* is the name of the country, *Brazilian* is the nationality word and *Portuguese* is the language they speak in that country. Remind students that the underlining indicates the syllable of the word that has the strongest stress.

- Ask the students to work individually and complete the table with the missing words and to underline the stressed syllable for each one.

- Allow students to compare answers in pairs before checking with the class. Ask for choral and individual repetition to check that they're pronouncing the words correctly.

Country	Nationality	Language
Brazil	(1) Bra<u>zil</u>ian	Portu<u>gu</u>ese
(2) <u>Chi</u>na	Chi<u>nese</u>	(3) Chi<u>nese</u>
Germany	(4) <u>Ger</u>man	(5) <u>Ger</u>man
(6) <u>I</u>taly	I<u>ta</u>lian	(7) I<u>ta</u>lian
(8) Ja<u>pan</u>	(9) Japa<u>nese</u>	Japa<u>nese</u>
Poland	(10) <u>Po</u>lish	(11) <u>Po</u>lish
(12) <u>Ru</u>ssia	<u>Ru</u>ssian	(13) <u>Ru</u>ssian
Spain	(14) <u>Spa</u>nish	(15) <u>Spa</u>nish
The UK	<u>Bri</u>tish	(16) <u>Eng</u>lish
The USA	(17) A<u>me</u>rican	(18) <u>Eng</u>lish

2

Ask the students to write down three more countries that they know, with their nationalities and languages, and add them to the table. Go round, checking that everyone is pronouncing the country, nationality and language correctly.

Further practice material

Need more writing practice?

→ Workbook page 11
- Using punctuation
- Writing about yourself

Need more classroom practice activities?

→ Photocopiable resource materials pages 154 to 156
   Grammar: *True or false?*
   Vocabulary: *What's the job?*
   Communication: *Match the numbers*
→ TOP 10 activities pages xv to xx

Need DVD material?

→ DVD – Programme 1: *Favourite things*

Need progress tests?

→ Test CD – *Test Unit 2*

Need more on important teaching concepts?

→ Key concepts in *New Inside Out* pages xxii to xxxv

Need student self-study practice?

→ CD-ROM – Unit 2: *People*

Need student CEF self-evaluation?

→ CEF Checklists pages xxxvii to xliv

Need more information and more ideas?

→ www.insideout.net

Before the next lesson ...

Find some family photos to bring to class for the Warm-up activity in Unit 3, and encourage your students to do the same.

3 Family *Overview*

Section	Aims	What the students are doing
Reading **SB page 16**	*Reading skills*: reading for specific information	• Reading and listening to a description of a family and matching names to people. • Talking about twins.
Vocabulary **SB page 16**	*Vocabulary*: family	• Matching names to family words. • Listening and repeating family words.
Reading **SB page 17**	*Reading skills*: reading for specific information	• Reading descriptions of members of a family and identifying them. • Drawing family trees and talking about members of their family.
Grammar **SB page 17**	*Grammar*: possession	• Matching sentences with names.
Writing **SB page 17**	*Writing skills*: family sentences	• Writing sentences about their family.
Reading **SB page 18**	*Reading skills*: reading for detail	• Underlining the correct names in sentences. • Using possessive forms to replace pronouns in sentences.
Grammar **SB page 19**	*Grammar*: present simple – affirmative forms	• Writing out third person singular forms of verbs. • Completing sentences. • Writing sentences about their family.
Pronunciation **SB page 19**	*Pronunciation*: /s/, /z/ and /ɪz/ verb endings	• Circling the correct ending sound in third person singular verbs.
Speaking: anecdote **SB page 19**	*Conversation skills*: fluency practice	• Listening to a description about someone and underlining the correct information. • Talking about a favourite relative.
Useful phrases **SB page 20**	*Vocabulary*: advice and warnings	• Completing conversational phrases. • Listening to and repeating useful phrases. • Deleting *don't* where necessary in a conversation. • Practising conversations.
Vocabulary *Extra* **SB page 21**	*Vocabulary*: revision of words from the unit: family. Focus on numbers	• Matching pictures with words.
Writing **WB page 15**	Using apostrophes Writing about a family	

3 Family *Teacher's notes*

Warm-up

- Use photos of your own family to introduce the theme of the unit and pre-teach some of the vocabulary the students will need. Show the photos to the class and point to the members saying, for example, *This is my father. This is my mother*, etc.

- If any students have brought their own family photos to class, encourage them to identify the family members in the photos.

Reading (SB page 16)

1 ⊕ 1.35

- Focus the students' attention on the photo. Ask them what they notice about Peter and John (they are identical twins so they look very similar). Allow them to use their mother tongue for this. Then explain that Peter and John are identical twins.

- Play the recording and ask the students to read the text as they listen. Point out that not only are Peter and John identical twins, but their wives are sisters (though not twins). Go through any difficult vocabulary with the class. Then ask them to work in pairs and to name the people in the photograph. Point out that the first one has been done for them as an example. Check answers with the class.

> a) Joe   b) Jack   c) Tom   d) Pauline
> e) Pat   f) Jennifer   g) Kitty

2

- Remind the students that Peter and John are identical twins. Point out that there are two types of twins: identical (the same sex and look the same) and non-identical (fraternal – can be of different sexes, and don't necessarily look alike).

- Pairwork. Put the students into pairs and ask them to tell their partners if they know any twin brothers or sisters. If they don't, encourage them to tell each other about any famous twins they know about. Students may know that the President George W Bush has twin daughters: Barbara and Jenna. Also in politics, Lech and Jaroslaw Kaczynski are President and Prime Minister of Poland. Kofi Annan, Secretary General of the United Nations had a twin sister. In entertainment, James and Oliver Phelps are twins who play George and Fred Weasley in the *Harry Potter* films.

Vocabulary (SB page 16)

Family

1

- Go through the family words in the table with the class. Make sure they can pronounce all the words correctly. Pay particular attention to the pronunciation of *daughter* /ˈdɔːtə/, *niece* /niːs/ and *cousin* /ˈkʌzən/, which can cause problems for some students. Point out that some family words are used exclusively with male family members (*husband, father, son, brother, uncle, nephew, brother-in-law*), some with female members only (*wife, mother, daughter, sister, aunt, niece, sister-in-law*) and some with both (*cousin, parent*).

- Go through the examples with the class and then ask them to complete the table with the other names. Allow them to compare notes in pairs.

Language note

Vocabulary: *in-law*

The expression *in-law* can be added to parents, mother, father, daughter, son, sister and brother, to refer to people related by marriage.

2 ⊕ 1.36

Play the recording for the students to listen and check their answers to Exercise 1. Then play it again for them to repeat. Ask for individual repetition of the family words.

> a) Pauline   b) Tom   c) Kitty   d) Joe
> e) John   f) Pat   g) Jennifer   h) Peter

Reading (SB page 17)

1 ⊕ 1.37

- Read out the first description to the class. Ask the students to decide who is speaking.

- Now put the students in pairs. Ask them to take turns reading out the other descriptions and identifying the speakers. Go round monitoring and giving help.

- Play the recording for the students to check their answers.

```
a) I'm Kitty.        d) They're Tom and Jack.
b) She's Pat.        e) They're John and Pat.
c) He's Peter.
```

2 Pairwork

- The pairwork exercise for this unit is on pages 116 and 121 of the Student's Book. Put the students in pairs and tell them who will be Student A, and who will be Student B.

- While they're doing the exercise, go round monitoring and giving help. Take note of any errors which may need particular attention later, and also any examples of good language use which you can praise.

3

- Remind the students that a family tree shows the members of a family and their relationships to each other. Explain that an equals sign (=) in a family tree means *is married to*. Draw your own family tree on the board, and then ask the students to work individually to draw their family trees. Go round monitoring and giving help.

- When the students have finished their trees, focus their attention on the speech bubble and read it aloud. Point to your own father on your family tree on the board. Make similar sentences about him.

- Put the students in pairs and ask them to talk to each other about the different people in their family trees.

Language note

Vocabulary: additional vocabulary

Depending on their family situation, students may want to express other relationships not covered by the vocabulary taught. If necessary, give them extra vocabulary, such as: *stepmother*, *partner*, *ex-wife*, *girlfriend*, *half-brother*, etc.

Grammar (SB page 17)

1 ⊕ 1.38

- This exercise focuses on the possessive '*s/s*'. Go through the information in the margin, making sure everyone understands that *father's* is singular and *brothers'* is plural. Practise the pronunciation, making sure that the students realise that the possessive '*s* in *father's* and *brothers'* has a /z/ sound. You might like to read out the first line of the exercise, *My wife's name is Pauline*, to demonstrate that the possessive '*s* sometimes also has an /s/ sound.

- Go through the example with the class. Students then work in pairs to match the sentences with the names.

- Play the recording for the students to check their answers, then play it again for them to repeat.

Language notes

Grammar: possessive '*s*

- It isn't usual to say *the name of my wife*. Most native speakers would say *my wife's name*.

- To make the possessive form, for a singular noun, you add an apostrophe and *s*, (e.g. *my brother's name*.).

- The possessive '*s* is pronounced like a plural ending, (e.g. *brother's*, *brothers'*).

- If the singular noun ends in an *s* (e.g. *James*), you usually add an apostrophe after the *s* to make the possessive (e.g. *James' brother*). This is pronounced /ˈdʒeɪmzɪz/. It's also possible to write *James's*, which is pronounced the same.

- The apostrophe *s* can be confusing for students as it's used for different purposes:
  Contraction of *is*, for example, *He's British. Where's John?*
  The possessive form, for example, *Pauline's sister. Pat's husband.*
  Point out to the students that it's the same form used for different meanings.

```
a) Peter    b) Pauline    c) Joe    d) Pat
e) Kitty    f) John and Pat
```

2 *Grammar Extra* 3

Ask students to turn to *Grammar Extra* 3 on page 126 of the Student's Book. Here they'll find an explanation of the grammar they've been studying and further exercises to practise it.

```
1  1 My    2 My    3 our    4 our    5 Their
   6 His    7 Her    8 her    9 your

2  a) parents'    b) parents'    c) mother's
   d) mother's    e) father's    f) father's
```

Writing (SB page 17)

Go through the examples with the class and then ask the students to work on their own on their five sentences. Go round, monitoring and giving help where necessary. Then ask the students to compare their sentences with a partner.

Reading (SB page 18)

1 ⊕ 1.39

- Focus the students' attention on the photos of the two families, and tell them that they are of two families who took part in a reality TV show called *Wife Exchange*. Explain briefly that on the show two wives leave their own homes and families and go and live with the other wife's family for two weeks. They then talk about their experiences.

- Go through the eight sentences with the class. Then play the recording and ask the students to read the two texts as they listen. When they've finished, ask them to underline either *Margaret* or *Caroline* in the sentences. Tell them not to worry about the tick and cross in the texts at this stage. Check answers with the class. Go through the texts, answering any questions about vocabulary.

> a) Margaret b) Margaret c) Margaret
> d) Margaret e) Caroline f) Caroline
> g) Caroline h) Caroline

2 🌐 1.40

Tell the students that they're going to hear first an interview with Caroline saying what she thinks is bad and good about Margaret's family, and then an interview with Margaret talking about Caroline's family. Before you play the recording, go through the sentences with the class. As the students listen to the interviews, they put ticks or crosses in the boxes according to whether the sentences describe good things or bad things about the families. Play the recording a second time for them to check their answers. Don't discuss the answers at this stage.

> 🌐 1.40 (I = Interviewer; C = Caroline; M = Margaret)
>
> I: *Hello, Caroline. What's bad about Margaret's family?*
>
> C: *The pets live in the house – ugh! Oh, and Andy and Margaret smoke in the house. That's horrible. Um, the children go to bed very late.*
>
> I: *Hmm. What's good about Margaret's family?*
>
> C: *Well, they do everything together. They eat meals together in the kitchen. They talk and play games together and they go out together at the weekends.*
>
> I: *Thank you, Caroline. … Now, Margaret. What's bad about Caroline's family?*
>
> M: *Well, Paul and Caroline work at the weekends. So the children watch TV and DVDs in their bedrooms. Ahh. And … they eat meals on the sofa in front of the TV.*
>
> I: *Oh dear. What's good about Caroline's family?*
>
> M: *Paul buys flowers for Caroline. That's nice. And the children go to bed early. And … the cleaner does the housework. That's very good.*

3

Ask the students to compare their answers to Exercise 2. Then check with the whole class. Ask them if they agree with Caroline and Margaret's opinions of the two families.

> Margaret's family
> - The pets live in the house. ☒
> - The family eat meals together in the kitchen. ☑
> - They talk and play games together. ☑
> - Andy and Margaret smoke in the house. ☒
> - The children go to bed very late. ☒
> - They go out together at the weekends. ☑

> Caroline's family
> - Paul and Caroline work at the weekends. ☒
> - The children watch TV and DVDs in their bedrooms. ☒
> - Paul buys flowers for his wife. ☑
> - The children go to bed early. ☑
> - They eat meals on the sofa in front of the TV. ☒
> - The cleaner does the housework. ☑

Grammar (SB page 19)

Present simple: affirmative forms

1 🌐 1.41

- Go through the information in the margin, pointing out that you use the same present simple form for *I, you, we* and *they*, but that for *he, she* and *it*, the verb takes an *s*. Ask the students to write the *he, she, it* forms of the verbs in the exercise. Go round, monitoring and giving help.

- Play the recording for the students to listen and check their answers. Focus their attention on the irregular verb *have – has*, and to the fact that *do* and *go* add an *e* as well as an *s*. Explain that sometimes the *s* is pronounced /s/, sometimes /z/ and sometimes /ɪz/, but don't spend too long on this as they'll get an opportunity to practise pronunciation of third person singular endings later. Play the recording again for them to repeat the verbs.

> a) has b) goes c) does d) eats
> e) lives f) plays g) buys h) watches

Language notes

Grammar: *have*

- There are two possible ways of expressing possession in British English – *have/has* or *have got/has got*. In *New Inside Out* Elementary, only *have/has* is introduced, as this form works in all contexts, i.e. as a main verb to express possession: *I have two brothers*, and as a de-lexicalised verb in expressions such as *He has lunch at 1.00 p.m.* This form also has the added advantage of conjugating with *do/does* in the present simple and behaving exactly the same way as all other verbs (apart from *be* and modal verbs).

Grammar: third person *s*

- Studies of native speakers show that the third person *s* is one of the last items of language to be assimilated correctly by some young native speaker learners.

- Some of your students may need a great deal of practice before they can produce this form without error.

- Note that the omission of the third person *s* rarely leads to a breakdown of communication.

2 💿 1.42

- Focus the students' attention on the example. Point out that *parents* is plural, so the present simple form is *live*, not *lives*. Ask the students to work in pairs to complete the remaining sentences. Go round, monitoring and giving help. Allow them to compare notes with other pairs before you check answers.

- Play the recording for students to check their answers. Then play it a second time for them to repeat the sentences.

- Ask the students to work on their own to write their sentences. Then put them in pairs to compare what they've written. Ask some pairs to read out their sentences to the class.

> a) live   b) goes   c) buys   d) have
> e) plays   f) watches   g) eat   h) does

Pronunciation (SB page 19)

1 💿 1.43

- Read the three pronunciations of the *s* ending aloud to the class and make sure everyone can hear the difference. Explain that in each group of words the *s* is pronounced in the same way. They have to decide whether it is /s/, /z/ or /ɪz/.

- Play the recording and ask the students to circle the correct symbol for each chant. Check answers with the class.

> A: /s/   B: /z/   C: /ɪz/

2

Play the recording again for the students to listen and practise the chants.

Speaking: anecdote (SB page 19)

Anecdotes are features that occur regularly in the other levels of this series. They are extended speaking tasks, where students tackle a longer piece of discourse on a personal topic. This is the first anecdote to occur in this level, and the students should have learnt enough language to give an account of their favourite relative. There are questions to guide them and a model to listen to. For more information about how to set up, monitor and repeat anecdotes, see Practical methodology, page xx in the Introduction.

1 💿 1.44

- Focus the students' attention on the photo of Sophie. Explain that they're going to hear her talking about her favourite relative. Check that they understand *relative* and remind them of the work they did on *favourite things* in the previous unit.

- Go through the sentences and the choices with the class. Explain any unknown vocabulary.

- Play the recording and ask the students to listen and underline the correct information. Then check answers with the class.

> a) cousin   b) Daniel   c) 34
> d) Los Angeles   e) single
> f) Champagne and Caviar   g) photographer
> h) *People* magazine

2

- Give the students a minute or two to decide who their favourite relative is. Then ask them to write similar sentences about him or her. Tell them that they can use Sophie's sentences as a model, and just replace her information with theirs. Go round, monitoring and giving help.

- Pairwork. Put the students in pairs and ask them to take turns to tell their partner about their favourite relative. Encourage them to ask each other questions to get further information.

- Ask some pairs to report back to the class about what they found out.

Useful phrases (SB page 20)

1 💿 1.45

- Focus attention on the pictures. Go through the verbs in the box and look at the example. Tell the students that in the first picture, the father is telling his daughter to do one thing (drive carefully) and not to do something else. Ask them what they think this something else might be (be late).

- Ask the students to read the other phrases and decide how they should be completed. When they've finished, ask them to compare their results in pairs.

- Play the recording for the students to check their answers. Then play it again for them to listen and repeat. Ask several students for individual repetition of the phrases.

> a) Drive; be   b) Smile   c) worry
> d) Have; Call

Language notes

Grammar: imperatives

- You use imperatives to tell people what to do, how to do it, to advise and encourage.

- To make imperatives, you use the infinitive without *to*, e.g. *Drive carefully*. To make the negative, you use *Do not/Don't*, e.g. *Don't forget*.

2 💿 1.46

- Focus attention on the picture and tell the students that the girl is going to drive to Paris for the weekend. Her parents are worried. Ask them to read the dialogue in pairs and decide where the word *Don't* isn't needed.

- Play the recording for the students to check their answers. Then play it again for them to listen and repeat.
- Groupwork. Put the students in groups of three and ask them to take one role each and practise the conversation. Go round, monitoring and giving help. Then ask several groups to perform the conversation at the front of the class.

1 ~~Don't~~ drive carefully.	4 Don't forget
2 Don't worry	5 ~~Don't~~ call us.
3 ~~Don't~~ have a good time	6 ~~Don't~~ take care.

Vocabulary *Extra* (SB page 21)
Family

1
- Go through the words in the box with the class, asking for choral and individual repetition. Check that the students can pronounce all of them correctly.
- Ask the students to look at the family tree and complete the sentences with the words from the box.

a) father	b) brother	c) son
d) brother-in-law	e) nephew	f) uncle
g) husband	h) cousin	i) grandson
j) mother	k) sister	l) daughter
m) sister-in-law	n) niece	o) aunt
p) wife	q) cousin	r) granddaughter

2
Ask the students to write sentences about their families, using the family words from the box in Exercise 1.

Focus on numbers

1
Ask the students to write the words for the numbers. Allow them to compare their answers in pairs.

11 = eleven	20 = twenty
12 = twelve	30 = thirty
13 = thirteen	40 = forty
14 = fourteen	50 = fifty
15 = fifteen	60 = sixty
16 = sixteen	70 = seventy
17 = seventeen	80 = eighty
18 = eighteen	90 = ninety
19 = nineteen	100 = one hundred

121 = one hundred and twenty-one
257 = two hundred and fifty-seven
376 = three hundred and seventy-six
492 = four hundred and ninety-two
533 = five hundred and thirty-three
648 = six hundred and forty-eight
764 = seven hundred and sixty-four
805 = eight hundred and five
999 = nine hundred and ninety-nine

2
The students work in pairs to dictate numbers to each other. Demonstrate the activity with a confident student, making sure everyone understands that they have to write the words for the numbers rather than the figures. Then put the students into pairs to continue the activity. Go round, offering help and encouragement.

Further practice material

Need more writing practice?
→ Workbook page 15
- Using apostrophes
- Writing about a family

Need more classroom practice activities?
→ Photocopiable resource materials pages 157 to 159
  Grammar: *Who's who?*
  Vocabulary: *Family photos*
  Communication: *Am I right?*
→ TOP 10 activities pages xv to xx

Need progress tests?
→ Test CD – *Test Unit 3*

Need more on important teaching concepts?
→ Key concepts in *New Inside Out* pages xxii to xxxv

Need student self-study practice?
→ CD-ROM – Unit 3: *Family*

Need student CEF self-evaluation?
→ CEF Checklists pages xxxvii to xliv

Need more information and more ideas?
→ www.insideout.net

Before the next lesson ...
For the revision activity at the beginning of the next unit, cut out some pictures of famous people that students are likely to recognise from newspapers or magazines and take them to class. Students are likely to recognise.

4 Different *Overview*

Section	Aims	What the students are doing
Reading **SB page 22**	*Reading skills*: reading for detail	• Reading a text and completing it with pronouns. • Talking about the ideas in a text.
Reading & Listening **SB page 23**	*Reading skills*: reading for detail	• Completing texts and listening to check. • Making true sentences.
Grammar **SB page 23**	*Grammar*: present simple	• Completing questions and answers. • Writing true sentences from prompts. • Asking and answering questions.
Vocabulary & Listening **SB page 24**	*Vocabulary*: like + ing	• Putting words for liking and disliking in sequence. • Predicting whether two people will like or dislike certain things.
Speaking **SB page 24**	*Conversation skills*: asking about likes and dislikes	• Completing a table with *ing* forms. • Asking and answering questions about likes and dislikes.
Pronunciation **SB page 24**	*Pronunciation*: *ing* forms	• Completing chants with *ing* forms.
Grammar **SB page 25**	*Grammar*: object pronouns	• Completing sentences with object pronouns. • Writing sentences. • Talking about likes and dislikes.
Reading & Writing **SB page 25**	*Reading skills*: reading for detail	• Completing a text with object pronouns. • Writing a web page giving personal information.
Useful phrases **SB page 26**	*Vocabulary*: expressing an opinion	• Completing conversations with the correct options. • Completing a table with phrases for asking and giving an opinion. • Practising conversations with a partner. • Asking a partner's opinion about favourite things.
Vocabulary *Extra* **SB page 27**	*Vocabulary*: revision of words from the unit: common verbs. Focus on instructions (2)	• Matching pictures with words.
Writing **WB page 19**	Punctuation review Writing an email to a new friend	

4 Different *Teacher's notes*

Quick revision

- Write up on the board the words:
  *What ...?   Where ...?   How ...?
  Are ...?   Can ...?*

- Tell the students they have three minutes to write as many questions as possible starting with these words. If necessary, get them started by quickly making a few suggestions like *What's your first name?*, *Where's Brad Pitt from?*, *Can you spell that?* To make it competitive, look at your watch and then tell them to begin.

- Go round and check or help.

- After three minutes, tell them to stop. Ask a student to read out their list of questions. Encourage the others to correct if necessary. Ask if another person has the same question. If they have, then everybody crosses the question off their list. Then ask another student to do the same, etc. The winner is the person who has the most questions that are not crossed out.

Reading (SB page 22)

1 ● 1.47

- Focus the students' attention on the 'objective' headline and the plan of the shopping centre. Allow them time to have a good look at the plan, and to identify the situation and what the two lines are for (the two different routes taken by a man and a woman who each want to buy a pair of jeans). Then ask them to read the article. Answer any questions they may have about vocabulary.

- Ask the students to complete the article with *He* or *She*. Ask them to work on their own at first, and then to compare their answers in pairs or small groups.

- Play the recording for them to check their answers.

> 1 He   2 He   3 She   4 She   5 She
> 6 She   7 She   8 She   9 He   10 She
> 11 She   12 He

Cultural note

Gap

Gap is an American clothes shop specialising in casual clothes, jeans, T-shirts, etc. Gap is now found in many countries, including Canada, the UK, France and Japan.

2

- Ask the students to look back at the text and decide if they think the situations described in the text are true or false. Give them a few minutes to think about their own experience and to put a tick or a cross next to each statement.

- Tell the students to compare their results with a partner.

Reading & Listening (SB page 23)

1

Focus the students' attention on the three words in the box. Ask the students if they think men and women generally have the same opinions about these things, or if their opinions are generally different. Help them express their opinions by providing any necessary vocabulary.

2 ● 1.48

- Focus the students' attention on the headline and the photos. Explain that they have to complete what the people say with the words in the box in Exercise 1. Give them a few minutes to do this.

- Play the recording for the students to check their answers.

- Find out how many pairs of shoes male and female students in the class have. This information will be useful when you come to look at the next exercise.

> a) shoes; shoes
> b) cars
> c) football; football

3

- Go through the first sentence with the students, finding out who would underline the affirmative form, and who the negative form. Then ask them to work on their own to underline the appropriate forms in the other sentences. Go round monitoring and giving help where necessary.

- Ask the students to compare their results with a partner and find out how many sentences they completed in the same way.

Grammar (SB page 23)

1 🌐 1.49

- Focus the students' attention on the information in the margin. Remind them that they studied questions and short answers using the verb *be* in Units 1 and 2. Point out the third person singular forms *does* and *doesn't*.

- Go through the examples in the exercise with the class, and then ask the students to work on their own to complete the questions and answers. Go round, monitoring and giving help.

- Play the recording for the students to check their answers. Then play it again for them to repeat the questions and answers.

---

a) 'Do you like shopping?'
   'Yes, I do.' 'No, I don't.'
b) 'Does your father do the housework?'
   'Yes, he does.' 'No, he doesn't.'
c) 'Do you think about chocolate all the time?'
   'Yes, I do.' 'No, I don't.'
d) 'Does your mother work at the weekend?'
   'Yes, she does.' 'No, she doesn't.'
e) 'Do you and your friends chat online?'
   'Yes we do.' 'No, we don't.'
f) 'Do your friends go out a lot?'
   'Yes they do.' 'No, they don't.'

Language note

Vocabulary: *chat*

To chat means to talk to someone in a friendly and informal way. The expression is now also used to describe instant messaging on the internet, where you don't actually talk but write.

2

Put the students in pairs and ask them to take turns asking and answering the questions for themselves.

Language note

Grammar: *do* auxiliary

- Tell students that *do*, in its role as an auxiliary verb, helps to form questions and negatives in the present simple. Other languages form questions and negatives in different ways, often without an auxiliary verb.

- You may like to explain that *Yes, I do* and *No, I don't* sound softer and more natural than simply *Yes* or *No*, but both are correct.

- Point out that *do + not* is usually contracted to *don't* in spoken English.

3

- Read the example sentence with the class, and ask the students to raise their hands if this sentence is true for them. If anyone doesn't raise their hand, ask them to change the sentence so that it is true for them. If there is no one who doesn't raise their hand, ask a confident student to say what the opposite sentence would be (*I work in a restaurant*).

- Ask the students to work on their own to write sentences which are true for them. Go round, monitoring and giving help.

4

Pairwork. Put the students in pairs to take turns asking and answering questions using the prompts in Exercise 3. Tell them to write the answers down and point out that they should use the third person singular in the sentences they write, as in the example.

5 *Grammar Extra* 4

Ask students to turn to *Grammar Extra* 4 on page 126 of the Student's Book. Here they'll find an explanation of the grammar they've been studying and further exercises to practise it.

---

1 a) I   b) I   c) My teacher   d) I
   e) My teacher   f) My teacher   g) I
   h) My teacher

   a) I don't live in the city centre.
   b) I don't like doing housework.
   c) My teacher doesn't wear a watch.
   d) I don't work in a shop.
   e) My teacher doesn't speak French.
   f) My teacher doesn't have a mobile phone.
   g) I don't study computer science.
   h) My teacher doesn't do yoga.

2 a) Do you play the guitar?
   b) Do your friends study English?
   c) Does your teacher smoke?
   d) Does your father drive a sports car?
   e) Do you drink gin and tonic?
   f) Does your mother go to the gym?

Vocabulary & Listening (SB page 24)

Likes and dislikes

1 🌐 1.50

- Focus the students' attention on the key and explain that the strongest way of saying that you like something is on the left of the key, and the strongest way of saying that you dislike something is on the right. Ask them to look at the symbols and decide which of the phrases in the box should go with each symbol. To help them, you could read the items in the box aloud, showing with your intonation which are the stronger expressions.

- When the students have decided where the words go, play the recording for them to check their answers. Then play it again for them to repeat the words.

1 I love it.	4 I don't mind it.
2 I really like it.	5 I don't like it.
3 I like it.	6 I hate it.

Language notes

Vocabulary: *don't mind*

- *Mind* here means to dislike, be annoyed by or object to. You use it in the negative form rather than in the affirmative, e.g. *I don't mind cooking.* (I think cooking is OK: I don't really enjoy it, but I don't hate it.)

- It's usual to ask the question *Do you **like** cooking?* when asking about someone's feelings about cooking. When you ask the question *Do you **mind** cooking?*, you're politely asking the other person to do the cooking.

2

Focus the students' attention on the photos and the two texts. Explain that the texts tell us about the things Jack and Layla like and don't like. Ask them to read the texts and answer any questions they may have.

3 🌐 1.51

- Read the items in the box aloud. Ask the students to work in pairs, and to decide which of these things Jack likes and which Layla likes. Go round, monitoring and giving help. If anyone is having trouble, give them some hints by pointing out that Jack doesn't like loud music. Ask them if clubbing and going to rock concerts involve loud music. Then point out that Layla likes dancing, and ask them if clubbing and rock concerts involve dancing.

- Play the recording for the students to check their answers. Then ask them to decide in their pairs whether they are similar to Jack or Layla.

- Finally, point out the structures *like + ing* and *like + noun*.

clubbing: L	jogging: J
eating out in restaurants: L	playing football: J
going to rock concerts: L	shopping: L
going to the gym: J	swimming: J

> 🌐 1.51
>
> Jack loves water, really likes being outside and really likes sport and keeping fit. He hates towns and cities and he doesn't like loud music. He loves playing football, swimming, jogging and going to the gym. But he doesn't like shopping, clubbing, eating out in restaurants or going to rock concerts. ... Oh, and he really likes Layla.

> Layla loves spending money. She hates doing housework and she doesn't like cooking. She likes dancing and she doesn't mind loud music. She hates sport. She loves shopping, clubing, eating out in restaurants and going to rock concerts. But she doesn't like playing football, swimming, jogging or going to the gym. ... And Jack? She really likes him.

Speaking (SB page 24)

1

- Focus the students' attention on the table and explain that it will help them with the spelling of *ing* forms. Ask them to look at the three column headings and the examples to see how the different *ing* forms are spelled.

- Ask the students to work on their own to complete the table. Allow them to compare notes in pairs before checking answers with the class.

1	read – reading; study – studying; cook – cooking
2	dance – dancing; smoke – smoking; drive – driving
3	swim – swimming; shop – shopping; jog – jogging

2

Go through the speech bubbles with the class. Then put the students in pairs to take turns asking and answering questions about the things they like doing. Go round, monitoring and giving help. Take note of any errors which may need particular attention later, and also any examples of good language use which you can praise.

3 Pairwork

- The pairwork exercise for this unit is on pages 117 and 122 of the Student's Book. Put the students in pairs and tell them who will be Student A, and who will be Student B.

- While they are doing the pairwork exercise, go round monitoring and giving help. Take note of any errors which may need paying particular attention to later and also any examples of good language use which you can praise.

Pronunciation (SB page 24)

1

- Ask the students to say the three words *flying, talking* and *thinking* aloud.

- Then read out the first of the chants and ask the students to say which word will sounds best at the end. Explain that *talking* rhymes with *walking*, so it completes the chant nicely.

- Ask the students to discuss in pairs which words they think best complete the other two chants.

A: talking   B: thinking   C: flying

2 🌐 1.52

Play the recording for the students to listen and check their answers. Then play it again for them to repeat the chants.

Grammar (SB page 25)

Object pronouns

1 🌐 1.53

- Focus the students' attention on the example and read it aloud. Point out the subject pronoun *I* in front of the verb in the first sentence. There is another subject pronoun in the question (*you*), again in front of the verb. *Them*, after the verb in the question, is an object pronoun. It refers back to the Beatles.

- Do the next one together with the whole class. If they seem to have understood what to do, ask them to complete the rest of the exercise on their own, and then compare answers in pairs. Go round, monitoring and giving help with any problems.

- Play the recording for them to check their answers. Then play it a second time for them to listen and repeat.

a) them   b) him   c) her   d) him e) them   f) it

Language notes

Grammar: object pronouns

- Subject pronouns *I, you, he, she, it, we* and *they* replace the person or thing performing the action of the verb. In affirmative sentences they go before the verb.

- Object pronouns *me, you, him, her, it, us* and *them* replace the person or thing that the action of the verb is done to. In affirmative sentences they go after the verb. For example:
Maria (= subject) likes *Paul* (= object).
She (= subject pronoun) likes *him* (= object pronoun).

Cultural notes

The Beatles
Paul McCartney, John Lennon, George Harrison and Ringo Star formed the band the Beatles, which became the most famous pop group of the 1960s. Paul McCartney and John Lennon wrote some of the best-known songs in rock and pop music, including *Yesterday*, *Hey Jude* and *Let it Be*. The Beatles broke up in 1970.

Robbie Williams
British singer songwriter who originally came to fame as a member of the boyband, Take That. He's now famous as a solo artist all over the world for songs such as *Angels*, *Millenium* and *Radio*.

Mariah Carey (born 1969)
American singer songwriter who is said to be the most successful artist of the 1990's in the US. She's recorded the most US number one singles for a female solo artist (seventeen).

Eminem (born 1972)
American rapper, record producer and actor. He's famous for the violence of the words of his songs. He appeared in the semi-autobiographical film *8 Mile* (2002), which included to song *Lose Yourself*. It won an Academy Award for Best Song. He's sold over 65 million albums worldwide so far.

The Sugababes
The Sugababes are three friends from England who liked the same music – hip hop, dance and garage, and enjoyed singing along to the radio. They formed a girl band in 1998, and became famous with songs such as *Freak Like Me*.

Madonna (born 1958)
Madonna is one of the most successful recording artists of all time, with songs such as *Material Girl* and *Into the Groove*. She has also appeared in a number of films, including *Desperately Seeking Susan* and *Evita*. In 2000, she married British film director Guy Ritchie. She continues to produce best-selling albums.

Note that when you refer to a band like the Beatles or the Sugababes you use *they/them*.

2

- Remind the students that you can use *like* + verb + *ing*, or *like* + noun to talk about our likes and dislikes, e.g. *I like reading, I like walking, I like football, I like music.*

- Go through the two example sentences with the class and point out the two different structures.

- Ask the students to work on their own to write their sentences. Encourage them to use examples of both structures. Go round, monitoring and giving help.

- Pairwork. Put the students in pairs and ask them to take turns reading out their sentences, and asking for their partner's opinion. Demonstrate the activity first with a confident student by reading out the first speech bubble and encouraging the student to reply. Go round, monitoring and giving help.

Extra activity

- Grammar Exercise 2 can be taken a stage further if students find it relatively easy. Ask them to report back to the class where their partner has a different opinion. This involves manipulating the *don't / doesn't* forms. For example:
I don't like Madonna, but Juan likes her. I don't like dogs, but Juan loves them.

- Encourage other students to join in, saying *I like her* or *I don't mind them.*

Reading & Writing (SB page 25)

1 🔊 1.54

- Ask the students to look at Cathy's web profile. Point out that this is information on the internet about a young woman who would like to meet other people over the internet. Ask them to read the text and complete it with the object pronouns in the box.

- Go round while the students are working on the text and answer any questions about vocabulary. Make sure they are not having much difficulty completing the text. Allow them to work in pairs if they wish.

- Play the recording for the students to listen and check their answers. Then go through the text and ask the students to say what each of the object pronouns refers to (*me* – Cathy, *it* – her job, *him* – her brother, *her* – her brother's girlfriend, *us* – Cathy, her parents and her brother, *her* – Cathy's sister, *it* – the saxophone, *them* – Cathy's friends, *you* – the people reading the web profile).

1 me	2 me	3 it	4 him	5 her	6 us
7 them	8 it	9 them	10 you		

Cultural note

Astrological signs

Scorpio is one of the twelve astrological signs. The full list of astrological signs is:

Capricorn (22nd December – 19th January)
Aquarius (20th January – 18th February)
Pisces (19th February – 19th March)
Aries (20th March – 19th April)
Taurus (20th April –20th May)
Gemini (21st May – 20th June)
Cancer (21st June – 22nd July)
Leo (23rd July – 22nd August)
Virgo (23rd August – 22nd September)
Libra (23rd September – 22nd October)
Scorpio (23rd October – 21st November)
Sagittarius (22nd November – 21st December)

2

- Encourage the students to use Cathy's model text but to add details of their own lives. Go round, monitoring and giving help. Encourage them to use object pronouns where appropriate.

- You could display some of the web profiles on the walls of your classroom, or put them on a class website if you have one.

Extra activity

When your students have finished their web profiles, read one out, but don't give the name of the person who wrote it. Let the other students guess who it is.

Useful phrases (SB page 26)

1 🔊 1.55

- Ask the students to look at the photos and say if they recognise any of the people (singer Beyoncé Knowles, actor Jude Law, rock group the Rolling Stones, footballer Wayne Rooney). Play the recording and ask the students to underline the adjectives they hear. You may need to play it more than once.

- Check answers with the class and make sure that everyone understands that *great* indicates a very positive response, *OK* is rather neutral, and *terrible* indicates strong dislike.

a) great	c) great; terrible
b) terrible; OK	d) great

Cultural notes

Beyoncé Knowles (born 1981)
American R&B singer known as Beyoncé. She was first in the girl band Destiny's Child, and is now a solo artist, actor and fashion designer. Her first solo album *Dangerously in Love* (2001) became one of the biggest commercial successes of that year. She received five Grammy Awards in 2004 and had a worldwide number one hit with *Irreplaceable* in 2006.

Jude Law (born 1972)
English actor who starred with Matt Damon in the film *The Talented Mr Ripley* (1999). After leaving school when he was seventeen, he acted in theatres in London and then in the film *Wilde*. He then moved to Hollywood and has starred in many films since, such as *Cold Mountain* (2003), *Closer* (2004) and *The Holiday* (2006).

Leonardo DiCaprio (born 1974)
Leonardo DiCaprio started acting when he was fourteen, appearing in TV commercials and educational films. He's starred in a number of successful films, such as *Romeo and Juliet* (1995), *Titanic* (1996), *The Man in the Iron Mask* (1998), *Gangs of New York* and *Catch Me If You Can* (2002), and *The Aviator* (2005). He's also greatly involved in environmental work in the US.

The Rolling Stones
English rock band, often referred to as 'the greatest rock and roll band in the world'. The band was formed in 1962 by Brian Jones, Mick Jagger and Keith Richards. They originally played American Blues, R&B and Rock n' Roll. They later played country and disco music. They've released 29 albums, and had 37 top ten singles, including *Satisfaction*, *Honky Tonk Woman* and *Brown Sugar*.

Wayne Rooney (born 1985)
English football player. In 2004, he was named PFA Young Player of the Year. He currently plays for Manchester United. Despite suffering from a foot injury, he took part in the 2006 Fifa World Cup, but was sent off in a match against Portugal.

2 🌐 1.56

- Focus attention on the two columns of the table. Point out that there are two types of phrases here: those that are asking for an opinion and those that are giving an opinion. Read the example aloud to the class, then ask them to categorise the other phrases in the box.

- Play the recording for the students to listen and check their answers. Then play it again for them to repeat.

Asking for an opinion
What do you think of Beyoncé?
What about you?

Giving an opinion
I think she's great.
I think he's OK.
I prefer Leonardo DiCaprio.
I think they're terrible.
I don't know.

3

- Ask the students to look back at the conversations in Exercise 1, and to circle the adjectives that best give their own opinion of these people.

- Pairwork. Put the students into pairs and ask them to practise the conversations, taking turns to be the person who asks the initial question, and using their own opinions to give a response. Go round, monitoring and giving help.

4

Pairwork. Ask the students to work on their own to write their lists. Then put them in pairs and ask them to take turns asking for their partner's opinion on the people on their lists.

Vocabulary *Extra* (SB page 27)

Common verbs

1

- Focus students' attention on the list of verbs. Check that the students can pronounce the verbs correctly.

- Ask the students to look at the pictures and match each one with one of the verbs. Point out that the first one has been done for them.

- Now ask the students to complete the verbs with a phrase. Again, point out that the first one has been done for them. Go round, giving help and encouragement. They can then report back to the class.

---

  5 buy a pair of shoes
  7 drink beer
  3 drive a car
12 eat chips
10 live in a big city
  8 play football
  4 smoke a cigarette
  1 speak French

---

11 spend $50
  6 think about chocolate
  2 watch television
  9 work for a big company

2

Pairwork. Demonstrate the activity with a confident student. Cover the words, point to the first picture and ask *What is number 1?* Elicit the answer. Then put the students into pairs to continue the activity. Go round, checking that everyone is pronouncing the words correctly.

Focus on instructions (2)

Ask the students to look at the pictures and complete the instructions with the correct words from the box.

---

1 Tick   2 Circle   3 Underline   4 Match
5 Complete   6 Cross out

Further practice material

Need more writing practice?

→ Workbook page 19
- Punctuation review
- Writing an email to a new friend

Need more classroom practice activities?

→ Photocopiable resource materials pages 160 to 162
 Grammar: *Find out*
 Vocabulary: *I love playing charades!*
 Communication: *What do you really think?*
→ TOP 10 activities pages xv to xx

Need DVD material?

→ DVD – Programme 2: *Martine and Jamie go shopping*

Need progress tests?

→ Test CD – *Test Unit 4*

Need more on important teaching concepts?

→ Key concepts in *New Inside Out* pages xxii to xxxv

Need student self-study practice?

→ CD-ROM – Unit 4: *Different*

Need student CEF self-evaluation?

→ CEF Checklists pages xxxvii to xliv

Need more information and more ideas?

→ www.insideout.net

Review A *Teacher's notes*

These exercises act as a check of the grammar and vocabulary that the students have learnt in Units 1–4. Use them to find any problems that students are having or anything that they haven't understood and which will need further work.

Grammar (SB page 28)

Remind the students of the grammar explanations they read and the exercises they did in the *Grammar Extra* on pages 126 and 127.

1

This exercise reviews language from Units 1 and 2.

Subject	Verb (be)	Contraction	Question
I	am	I'm	Am I ...?
You	are	You're	Are you ...?
He/She/It	is	He's/She's/It's	Is he/she/it ...?
We	are	We're	Are we ...?
You	are	You're	Are you ...?
They	are	They're	Are they ...?

2 🌐 1.57

This exercise reviews *this* and *these* from Unit 1.

> 1 this   2 these   3 this   4 this   5 this
> 6 these

3

This exercise reviews subject pronouns and possessive determiners from Unit 2.

> 1 my   2 you   3 his   4 she   5 its   6 we
> 7 their

4

This exercise reviews the possessive *'s* and family words from Unit 3.

> a) sisters'   b) father's   c) son's   d) cousins'
> e) parents'   f) brother's

5

This exercise reviews present simple questions from Unit 3.

> a) Do you work?
>   (Yes, I do. / No, I don't.)
> b) Does your mother like shopping?
>   (Yes, she does. / No, she doesn't.)
> c) Do you and your family eat together every day?
>   (Yes, we do. / No, we don't.)
> d) Do you have a Japanese car?
>   (Yes, I do. / No, I don't.)
> e) Does your father speak another language?
>   (Yes, he does. / No, he doesn't.)
> f) Do you and your friends go out every night?
>   (Yes, we do. / No, we don't.)

6

This exercise reviews object pronouns from Unit 4. When you've checked answers with the class, ask the students to tick the ones that are true for them and to compare with a partner.

> a) her   b) it   c) him   d) them   e) her
> f) him

Cultural notes

Halle Berry (born 1966)
Halle Berry is won of the highest paid actresses in Hollywood. She starred in the James Bond film *Die Another Day* (2002) with Pierce Brosnan, and won an Academy Award for best actress in *Monster's Ball* (2001). In 2005, she won a 'Razzie award' as worst actress for her role in the film *Catwoman*.

X-Men
X-Men (2000) is a film adaptation of a comic book series about a superhero team, who were born with extra powers. They fight off another group of people who were also born with extra powers, but who use their powers for evil purposes.

Brad Pitt (born 1963)
(See notes about Brad Pitt in Unit 2, page 9.)

The Arctic Monkeys
The Arctic Monkeys are a band from Sheffield, England who became famous by promoting their own music on the internet. They gave people who saw them in concert demo CDs of their songs, and these were put on the web for other people to listen to. Their album *Whatever People Say I Am, That's What I'm Not* (2006) was the fastest selling album in history.

Beyoncé Knowles (born 1981)
(See notes about Beyoncé Knowles in Unit 4, page 28.)

7

This exercise reviews structures used in Units 1 to 4.

> 1 b) ~~She is Italian?~~
> 2 b) ~~What's these?~~
> 3 a) ~~Is you're family from Poland.~~
> 4 a) ~~They likes Japanese food.~~
> 5 a) ~~He work in a shop.~~
> 6 a) ~~Do you lives in London?~~

Vocabulary (SB page 29)

1

This exercise reviews country and language words from Unit 1. When checking answers, make sure that the students can pronounce both the country and language words, putting the stress on the correct syllables.

> a) Russian   b) Portuguese   c) Spanish
> d) German   e) Chinese   f) Polish
> g) Italian   h) Japanese   i) English

2

This exercise reviews numbers *0* to *10* and telephone numbers from Unit 1.

> a) oh one double seven nine, four oh six two, five double three
> b) oh five seven oh four, two nine four, double oh five six
> c) oh two oh, one double six three, four one five six
> d) double oh three one oh, two three double nine, eight one oh four

3

This exercise reviews the categories of favourite things from Unit 2. When you've checked answers with the class, ask the students to work on their own to answer the questions, and then take turns asking and answering the questions with a partner.

> a) actor   b) film   c) singer   d) drink
> e) food   f) writer   g) sport

Cultural notes

Tom Cruise (born 1962)
American actor Tom Cruise has been in some of the top selling films of the 1980s, such as *Top Gun* (1986), *Rain Man* (1988), and *Born on the Fourth of July* (1989). In 1996, he took the role of Ethan Hunt in the *Mission Impossible* films. He was married to Nicole Kidman (1990–2001). He got married to Katie Holmes in 2006.

The Matrix
The Matrix (1999) is the first of a series of science fiction/action films starring Keanu Reeves as 'Neo', who discovers that the world has been turned into a virtual reality world, created by a computer.

Madonna (born 1958)
(See notes about Madonna in Unit 4, page 27.)

Dan Brown
(See notes about Dan Brown in Unit 2, page 10.)

4

This exercises reviews the way numbers can be written as words.

> a) forty-five   e) seventy-four
> b) eleven   f) one hundred and eighty-seven
> c) twelve   g) seven hundred and eighty-six
> d) twenty

5

This exercise reviews job words from Unit 2.

> a) doctor   e) sales manager
> b) hairdresser   f) nurse
> c) IT technician   g) shop assistant
> d) lawyer   h) taxi driver

6

This exercise reviews the different ways of saying that you either like or dislike something from Unit 4.

> a) like   d) don't like
> b) don't mind   e) love
> c) really like   f) hate

7

This exercise reviews family words from Unit 3.

> a) husband   e) niece
> b) cousin   f) sister-in-law
> c) uncle   g) aunt
> d) nephew

Pronunciation (SB page 29)

These two exercises review work students did on word stress, using words they met in Units 1–4.

1

Focus the students' attention on the table and explain that the boxes show the syllables in a word and the large boxes indicate the stressed syllables. Read the example words in the table aloud so that the students can hear the stress clearly. Tell them that they should complete the table by classifying the words according to how many syllables each one has, and where the main stress falls. Encourage them to say each word aloud.

> (See Exercise 2 for answers)

2 🌐 **1.58**

Point out the main stresses in the example words which are underlined. Ask the students to do the same for the other words in the table. Play the recording for them to check their answers. Then play it again for them to listen and repeat the words.

> 1 and 2
> A: <u>cou</u>sin, <u>hus</u>band, <u>law</u>yer
> B: <u>hair</u>dresser, <u>man</u>ager, <u>Por</u>tugal
> C: a<u>ddress</u>, Bra<u>zil</u>, Chi<u>nese</u>
> D: as<u>sis</u>tant, com<u>pu</u>ter, um<u>bre</u>lla

Reading & Listening (SB page 30)

1

Suggest to the students that they read the questions first, so that they know what information they're looking for when they read and listen to the text.

> a) Rona Cameron.
> b) Kate Cameron.
> c) Rona likes: eating out (Chinese food), cooking, reading, listening to jazz, travelling, (watching) football, relaxing
> d) Rona doesn't like: shopping, loud music.

2

Go through the sentences with students before they read the text again, then ask them read the text and decide which sentences are true and which are false. When you've checked their answers, ask them to correct the false information.

> a) False.
> b) True.
> c) False. She's a nurse.
> d) False. She doesn't have time to meet new people.
> e) True.
> f) False. She thinks Rona works hard.

3 🌐 1.59

Tell the students that they're going to listen to a conversation between Rona and Kate. They'll talk about three men who have responded to the profile of Rona that Kate put on the website. The three men are pictured below. The students should listen to Kate and Rona, and decide which man Rona calls.

> James Clark.

> 🌐 **1.59** (K = Kate; R = Rona)
>
> K: Hi, Rona. It's me.
> R: Oh, hi, Kate.
> K: So, did you look at the website?
> R: Yes, I did. Amazing!
> K: And? Did you see anyone interesting?
> R: Well, Ben looks nice.
> K: The doctor?
> R: Yes. He's tall, with dark hair, and he's very good-looking.
> K: Yes, but he doesn't like football, and he doesn't like travelling.
> R: Oh.
> K: What about Raj?
> R: Mmm. Maybe.
> K: He likes eating out and travelling.
> R: Yes, but he lives in London. And he likes shopping. I don't like shopping, Kate!
> K: Well, there's James. He lives in Glasgow too!
> R: Oh ... yes.
> K: He's an IT technician.
> R: Yeah.
> K: He likes holidays, reading and football. His favourite football team is Glasgow Rangers! Go on, Rona. Call him!
> R: OK. OK. Where's his number? ... OK. Talk to you later. Bye. ... Right, here goes. 07785 7844 532.

4

Go through the three profiles with the class, then play the recording again and ask the students to complete them with the missing information. You may need to play the recording more than once, and pause it to give the students time to take down the information they need. When you've checked answers, ask the students which man they would choose, if any.

> Ben Harris
> Doesn't like: football, travelling
>
> Raj Singh
> City: London
> Likes: shopping
>
> James Clark
> City: Glasgow
> Job: IT technician
> Likes: holidays, reading, football
> Telephone: 07785 7844 532

Writing & Speaking (SB page 31)

1

Ask the students to look at the punctuation marks and the words in the box. See how many they can match up, then help them with the rest.

a) a full stop	d) an apostrophe
b) a comma	e) a capital letter
c) a question mark	

2

Go through the example and the sentences with the class. Then ask the students to match the punctuation features to their uses. Check answers with the class.

a) a question mark	d) a comma
b) a full stop	e) an apostrophe
c) a capital letter	

3

Go through the example with the class, then ask the students to write the other questions. Go round checking that they are using capital letters and question marks correctly. Check answers with the class.

a) What's your name?
b) Where do you live?
c) What's your job?
d) What languages do you speak?
e) What things do you like?
f) Who's your favourite singer?
g) What's your favourite food?

4

Pairwork. Put the students in pairs and tell them to take turns asking the questions in Exercise 3, and completing the form with their partner's answers. Go round monitoring and giving help. Ask some pairs to report back to the class on what they found out about their partners.

5

Give the students plenty of time to write their profiles. Remind them of the work they've just done on punctuation and go round, monitoring and giving help. When the students have finished, ask them to exchange texts with the same partner whose profile they've written. Ask them to check each other's work and to pay particular attention to the punctuation. You could display the profiles in the classroom for everyone to read.

Further practice material

Need more classroom practice activities?

→ Photocopiable resource materials page 163
  🔘 1.60 **Song:** *I Like The Way …*
→ TOP 10 activities pages xv to xx

Need progress tests?

→ Test CD – *Test Review A*

Need more on important teaching concepts?

→ Key concepts in *New Inside Out* pages xxii to xxxv

Need student self-study practice?

→ CD-ROM – *Review A*

Need more information and more ideas?

→ www.insideout.net

5 Days *Overview*

Section	Aims	What the students are doing
Reading **SB page 32**	*Reading skills*: reading for specific information	• Listening and repeating times. • Reading and completing a text with times. • Responding to a text about body clocks.
Grammar **SB page 33**	*Grammar*: telling the time; routine activities	• Studying ways of telling the time. • Talking about routine activities.
Pronunciation **SB page 33**	*Pronunciation*: long vowel sounds	• Practising saying words with long vowel sounds in isolation and in sentences.
Vocabulary **SB page 33**	*Vocabulary*: days of the week	• Completing the days of the week.
Listening **SB page 34**	*Listening skills*: listening for detail	• Predicting the days of the week when people do certain things. • Talking about weekend activities.
Vocabulary & Speaking **SB page 34**	*Vocabulary*: verb phrases with *have* and *go* *Conversation skills*: talking about routines	• Completing verb phrases with *have* and *go*. • Talking about weekend and weekday routines.
Reading **SB page 35**	*Reading skills*: reading for detail	• Completing a text with correct information. • Changing information to make it true for them.
Writing **SB page 35**	*Writing skills*: writing a paragraph	• Writing a paragraph about their perfect weekend. • Comparing paragraphs with a partner.
Useful phrases **SB page 36**	*Vocabulary*: asking prices, asking for tickets, asking for the bill in a restaurant	• Matching conversations to pictures. • Listening and repeating useful phrases. • Writing and practising new conversations.
Vocabulary *Extra* **SB page 37**	*Vocabulary*: revision of words from the unit: daily routine. Focus on *have*	• Matching pictures with words.
Writing **WB page 23**	Sequencing: *then, after (that)* Describing a perfect day	

Days *Teacher's notes*

Warm-up

Books closed. Whole class. Tell the students that you're going to mime some things that you do every day. Ask them to work in groups and to write down in English what they think you do. Mime a few daily activities such as getting up, brushing your teeth, driving to work, etc. At the end, see which group got most activities correct.

Reading (SB page 32)

1 🌐 **1.61**

- Look at your watch or point to the classroom clock, if you have one, and tell the students what time it is now. Then focus their attention on the times in the box. Explain *a.m.*, *p.m.*, midday and its opposite *midnight*.
- Then play the recording and ask the students to repeat the times.
- Ask individual students to say whether the times are before or after midday.

> a) Before midday: 6.30 a.m., 7.45 a.m.
> b) After midday: 6.00 p.m., 11.00 p.m., 12.30 p.m.

Language note

Vocabulary: *a.m.* and *p.m.*

a.m. stands for *ante meridian* (before midday) and *p.m.* for *post meridian* (after midday). They're used to differentiate between times in the morning and those in the afternoon / evening. Note that 12.00 a.m. is midnight, and 12.00 p.m. is midday. These two are often confused, and, as a result, *midnight* and *midday* or *noon* are the preferred terms. However *a.m.* or *p.m.* are not usually said unless it isn't clear from the context whether it's the morning or evening. For example, if you're going to the cinema with friends, you'd say *It starts at 7.00*, because it's obviously in the evening.

2 🌐 **1.62**

- Explain *body clock*: the idea that the human body has its own internal time-telling mechanism and that certain times of day are better than others for doing certain activities. Explain also *routine activities*: things people do regularly, and ask the students to look at the text and find some examples of routine activities (*get up, have breakfast, work*, etc.).
- Ask the students to read the text carefully. Go through any unknown vocabulary with the class.

Then ask them to work in pairs and to decide where the times in Exercise 1 should go to complete the text.
- Play the recording for the students to check their answers.

> 1 6.30 a.m.   2 7.45 a.m.   3 12.30 p.m.
> 4 6.00 p.m.   5 11.00 p.m.

3

- This exercise calls for a personal response from the students to the text they've just read. Ask them to work on their own to decide if they agree or disagree with the times and explanations in the article. Then ask them to compare their results with a partner.
- Finally, find out from the class if the students agree or disagree with the ideas in the text. Encourage them to say what is true for them.

Grammar (SB page 33)

1 🌐 **1.63**

- Focus the students' attention on the information in the margin. Tell them that *quarter* and *half* are fractions, but that when referring to the time, you write them out as words not $\frac{1}{4}$ or $\frac{1}{2}$. Explain that you use *past* for times between the hour, and half past and *to* for times between half past and the hour.
- Point out that there's always more than one way to talk about a particular time, and it largely depends on personal preference. Explain that the example shows two different ways of saying exactly the same thing. Ask the students to match the other times in the exercise with those in the article on page 32.
- Play the recording for the students to check their answers. Then play it again for them to listen and repeat. Ask for individual repetition of the times.

> a) 9.00 a.m.   b) 6.00 p.m.   c) 11.00 p.m.
> d) 6.30 a.m.   e) 7.45 a.m.   f) 8.15 a.m.

Language notes

Vocabulary: *in/at*

- You say *in the morning / afternoon / evening*, but *at night*.

Vocabulary: American use of *after*

- In American English, you usually say *ten after four* rather than *ten past four*.

2 🌐 1.64

Go through the example with the class, and perhaps do the next one as well. Then ask them to complete the exercise. Play the recording for them to check their answers, then play it again for them to listen and repeat.

a) It's half past two.	d) It's three forty-five.
b) It's seven fifteen.	e) It's five to five.
c) It's ten past one.	f) It's twenty to ten.

3 Pairwork

- The pairwork exercise for this unit is on pages 117 and 122 of the Student's Book. Put the students in pairs and tell them who will be Student A, and who will be Student B.

- While they are doing the exercise, go round monitoring and giving help. Take note of any errors which may need particular attention later, and also any examples of good language use which you can praise. Check answers with the class.

> Honolulu: It's one o'clock in the morning.
> Los Angeles: It's four o'clock in the morning.
> Mexico City: It's six o'clock in the morning.
> Sao Paulo: It's eight o'clock in the morning.
> London: It's twelve o'clock, midday.
> Berlin: It's one o'clock in the afternoon.
> Moscow: It's three o'clock in the afternoon.
> Hong Kong: It's seven o'clock in the evening.
> Sydney: It's nine o'clock in the evening.

4

- Ask the students to look back at the article on page 32, and to call out the verb phrases for routine activities. Write them on the board. Focus their attention on the first speech bubble and ask the students to form questions for the other routines on the board.

- Demonstrate the activity with a confident student. Ask the question in the speech bubble and encourage the student to give a true answer. Then tell the student to ask you the same question. Again, give a true answer.

- Put the students in pairs and ask them to continue the activity, taking turns to ask and answer questions about their daily routines. Go round monitoring and giving help. Take note of any difficulties they have with expressing times for remedial work later.

5 Grammar Extra 5

Ask students to turn to Grammar Extra 5 on page 128. Here they'll find an explanation of the grammar they've been studying and further exercises to practise it.

1 a) It's one oh five.
   b) It's quarter past three.
   c) It's eight twenty-five.
   d) It's seven thirty-five, OR It's twenty-five to eight.
   e) It's ten forty-five, OR It's quarter to eleven.
   f) It's eleven fifty-five, OR It's five to twelve.

2 a) What time do children start school?
   b) What time do children finish school?
   c) What time do banks open?
   d) What time do banks close?
   e) What time does your English lesson start?
   f) What time does your English lesson finish?

Pronunciation (SB page 33)

1 🌐 1.65

Focus the students' attention on the table. Remind them that phonemic script will help them find out how to pronounce unknown words. Point out that the symbols here represent three long vowel sounds. Read the vowels at top of the columns and the example words to the class. Then play the recording for them to listen and repeat.

2 🌐 1.66

- This exercise puts the words with long vowel sounds in the context of sentences. Play the recording for the students just to listen to the sentences. Then ask them to practise saying the sentences aloud to a partner.

- Play the recording again, pausing after each sentence for the students to repeat.

Vocabulary (SB page 33)

1

Focus the students' attention on the shortened forms in the box. Tell them that they'll sometimes see shortened forms of the days of the week on such things as timetables. Then ask them to complete the other days of the week.

Language notes

Vocabulary: days of the week

- You always write the days of the week with a capital letter in English.

- Some students may have difficulty differentiating between *Tuesday* and *Thursday*. Point out the pronunciation of /tʃ/ in *Tuesday* and /θ/ in *Thursday*. If necessary, give an exaggerated demonstration of how the tongue is behind the teeth in /tʃ/ and well in front of them with /θ/.

2 🌐 1.67

- Play the recording for the students to check their answers. Then play it a second time for them to repeat. Point out that that *Wednesday* is spelled with a *d* in the middle, but that this isn't pronounced. You pronounce *Wednesday* /ˈwenzdi/ or /ˈwenzdeɪ/. Ask for individual repetition of the word.

- Ask the students to say what day it is today. Then ask someone to say what the time is now.

1 Monday	2 Tuesday	3 Wednesday
4 Thursday	5 Friday	6 Saturday
7 Sunday		

Listening (SB page 34)

1 🌐 **1.68**

- Focus the students' attention on the photos of Tanya, Bill and Mary, and ask the them to think about what sort of people they might be.
- Go through the lists of activities with the class and explain any that they don't understand.
- Ask the students to decide when they think the three people do the various activities listed. Ask them to mark them *Sat* or *Sun*. Allow them to discuss it in pairs if they wish.
- Play the recording for the students to check their answers. Then find out from the class how accurate their predictions were.

> **Tanya**
> - go out with friends; go dancing; drink cocktails;
> - have a good time – *Sat*
> - read magazines – *Sun*
>
> **Bill**
> - go to work; listen to the radio – *Sat*
> - go home; have a shower; go to bed – *Sun*
>
> **Mary**
> - stay in; have dinner; watch television;
> - go on the internet – *Sat*
> - go shopping – *Sun*

> 🌐 1.68 (I = Interviewer; T = Tanya)
>
> I: *What do you do on Saturday night?*
> T: *I go out with my friends.*
> I: *Where do you go?*
> T: *We go to the cinema and then we go dancing. We drink cocktails and we have a good time.*
> I: *What do you do on Sunday morning?*
> T: *Sunday morning? Oh, I get up late. I don't have breakfast. I drink black coffee and read magazines.*
>
> (I = Interviewer; B = Bill)
>
> I: *What do you do on Saturday night?*
> B: *I go to work. I'm a taxi driver.*
> I: *Oh. Do you listen to music in your taxi?*
> B: *Yes, I listen to the radio.*
> I: *What do you do on Sunday morning?*
> B: *I go home and have a shower. Then I go to bed and I sleep.*
>
> (I = Interviewer; M = Mary)
>
> I: *What do you do on Saturday night?*
> M: *I don't go out – I stay in … with my parents.*

> I: *What do you do with your parents?*
> M: *We have dinner and we watch television. Then I go on the internet and chat with my friends. I go to bed late.*
> I: *What do you do on Sunday morning?*
> M: *We have breakfast. Then we go shopping.*

2

Pairwork. Ask the students to work on their own to tick the activities that they do at the weekend, and to note down the day on which they do them. Then ask them to compare notes with a partner. Encourage the pairs to report back to the class in a feedback session.

Vocabulary & Speaking (SB page 34)

1 🌐 **1.69**

- Students should be able to identify fairly quickly which verb goes in which gap. Encourage them to read all the phrases aloud as they do the exercise, so that they get used to hearing them.
- Play the recording for the students to check their answers. Then play it again for them to listen and repeat.

> a) go   b) have

Language notes

Vocabulary: *have*

- The verb *have* can be used in different ways: to express possession: *I have two cats* (see Unit 3), or as an auxiliary: *Have you done it yet?* (see Unit 15). Here it's used to talk about actions: *I have breakfast at 6.30.*
- When doing the freer speaking activity, students may want to use other expressions such as *have a bath / a drink / coffee / a rest / a nice day / a walk*.

Vocabulary: expressions with *go*

- *Go* is one of the most frequent verbs in English. You use it in a lot of expressions. Students have already seen the expressions *go to bed; go out; go to the shopping centre; go to the pub; go on holiday*.

2

- Go through the two lists with the students and make sure they understand that one list is activities at the weekend, and the other weekday activities.
- Ask the students to make their own lists, using full sentences as in the example. Go round, monitoring and giving help with any extra vocabulary they may need.
- Put the students in pairs and ask them to tell each other about their weekend and weekday routines. Ask a few confident pairs to report back to the class.

Reading (SB page 35)

1 🔊 1.70

- You may need to explain to the students that the information they need to complete the reading text is in the two lists headed *Saturday night* and *Saturday morning* underneath the gapped text.
- Give the students plenty of time to read the text and to decide how to complete the gaps. Allow them to discuss it in pairs or small groups if they wish.
- Play the recording for the students to check their answers. Then ask them if Ms Dynamite's perfect weekend is similar to a perfect weekend for them.

1 DVD	2 restaurant	3 club	4 vodka
5 breakfast	6 book	7 TV	8 jeans

Cultural notes

Ms Dynamite (born 1981)
Ms Dynamite is a British R&B / hip hop musician. Her debut album *A Little Deeper* (2002) received good reviews both in the UK and the US.

Thai food
The food in the south of Thailand is spicy with many curry dishes, some of them extremely hot. In the north, meat is more popular. Some of the best Thai food can be bought from stalls in the crowded streets of Bangkok. Thai food is very popular in Britain.

Red Bull
Red Bull is an energy drink. It comes in a can like a beer and is mixed with vodka as a cocktail.

Armani and D&G
Giorgio Armani is an Italian fashion designer who is particularly noted for his menswear. He was one of the first designers to ban models who are too thin (American size 0). There are now Emporio Armani shops selling ready-to-wear clothes and accessories for young people throughout the world.
(See notes about Domenico Dolce and Stefano Gabbana (D&G) in Unit 2, page 13.)

The Observer
One of the quality national British newspapers which comes out Sunday. It specializes in reporting UK and world news and politics.

Robert T Kiyosaki
Robert T Kiyosaki is an author who writes self-help books. He's sold over 26 million books including the *Rich Dad, Poor Dad* series.

Soaps
Soaps or soap operas are TV series about the daily lives of a fictional group of characters. The series is often broadcast several times a week for years.

Billie Holiday (1915–1959)
American jazz singer of the 1930s to 1950s. She's considered to have one the greatest jazz voices of all time, despite having no technical training in singing. She died at the age of 44.

2

- Explain the task and focus the students' attention on the example. Ask them to make similar changes to the items mentioned by Ms Dynamite, to change it into a perfect weekend for them. They only need to make rough notes at this stage in the style of the example, but they should put one new item for each of those listed under the gapped text. As they do this, go round, monitoring and giving help.
- Make sure the students keep their notes safe if this is the end of the lesson as they'll need them in the Writing section which follows.

Cultural note

George Clooney (born 1961)
American actor, director, producer and screenwriter. He became known in the television drama *ER* (1994–1999). His film roles included *The Perfect Storm* (2000), *Ocean's Eleven* (2001), *Syriana* and *Good Night, and Good Luck* (2005).

Writing (SB page 35)

1

Using the notes they made in Exercise 2 in the Reading section, the students write paragraphs about their perfect weekends. Allow them to use the text at the top of page 35 as a model. Go round, monitoring and giving help, and allow plenty of time for them to work on their texts. Remind them of the work on punctuation that they did in Review A.

2

- Put the students in pairs and ask them to read about each other's perfect weekend.
- Then find out from the class if any pairs had similar or vastly different ideas for a perfect weekend.

Useful phrases (SB page 36)

1 🔊 1.71

- Give the students a minute or so to have a good look at the pictures so they can see what is happening in each one. Then play the recording and ask them to listen to and read the four conversations.
- Ask the students to decide which conversation goes with each picture. Check answers with the class.

a) 2	b) 3	c) 1	d) 4

Language notes

Pronunciation

- You pronounce *receipt* as /rɪˈsiːt/.
- You pronounce *ID* as /aɪˈdiː/.

2 🔘 **1.72**

Go through the useful phrases with the class, asking individual students to supply the missing words. Then play the recording for them to check, and play it a second time for them to repeat after the speakers.

a) How much is it	d) Can I have
b) Can I have	e) Can I have
c) How much is	f) Can I have

3

- Pairwork. Go through the three situations with the class. Tell them that they should base a) on the conversation in the bar in Exercise 1; b) on the conversation outside the club; and c) on the conversation with the taxi driver.
- Put the students in pairs to write their conversations. Go round, monitoring and giving help. Then ask them to practise them in pairs. Go round helping with any pronunciation problems. Take note of a few good pairs who can be asked to perform their conversations for the class.

Language note

Vocabulary: *18 certificate*

A film has an 18 certificate when it isn't suitable for people under eighteen years old.

Vocabulary *Extra* (SB page 37)

Daily routine

1

- Focus the students' attention on the list of verb phrases and point out that they're all to do with daily routine. Remind students that the underlining indicates the syllable of the word that has the strongest stress. Check that the students can pronounce the phrases correctly.
- Ask students to look at the pictures and match each one with one of the verb phrases. Point out that the first one has been done for them.

11	do exercise	3	have a shower
8	finish work	4	have breakfast
2	get up	13	have dinner
10	go home	7	have lunch
14	go on the internet	12	listen to music
9	go shopping	5	read the newspaper
15	go to bed	1	wake up
6	go to work		

2

Ask students to work individually and to tick the things in Exercise 1 that they do as part of their daily routine. They should then add three more items that they do to the list. The students can then compare with a partner

3

Focus the students' attention on the words for the parts of the day in the table. Ask the students to complete the table with the verb phrases from Exercise 1 according to when they do these things. They can then compare with their partner to see if there are any differences.

Focus on *have*

1

Ask the students to look at the table and complete it with the correct phrases from the box.

1	have dinner	4	have a shower
2	have lunch	5	have a BMW
3	have a meal	6	have a good time

2

Ask the students to write a sentence of their own for each use of *have* from the table.

Further practice material

Need more writing practice?

→ Workbook page 23
- Sequencing: *then, after* (*that*)
- Describing a perfect day

Need more classroom practice activities?

→ Photocopiable resource materials pages 164 to 166
  Grammar: *Breakfast survey*
  Vocabulary: *Daily routines*
  Communication: *Time dominoes*
→ TOP 10 activities pages xv to xx

Need progress tests?

→ Test CD – *Test Unit 5*

Need more on important teaching concepts?

→ Key concepts in *New Inside Out* pages xxii to xxxv

Need student self-study practice?

→ CD-ROM – Unit 5: *Days*

Need student CEF self-evaluation?

→ CEF Checklists pages xxxvii to xliv

Need more information and more ideas?

→ www.insideout.net

6 Living *Overview*

Section	Aims	What the students are doing
Reading **SB page 38**	*Reading skills*: reading for detail	• Predicting which of two people are described in a set of sentences. • Reading an article to check their answers. • Asking and answering personal questions.
Vocabulary **SB page 39**	*Vocabulary*: verb phrases with *make* and *do*	• Completing verb phrases with *make* and *do*. • Talking about who does certain things at home.
Grammar **SB page 39**	*Grammar*: present simple with adverbs of frequency	• Completing a chart. • Making sentences true for them. • Asking and answering questions about the frequency of activities.
Pronunciation **SB page 39**	*Pronunciation*: ordinal numbers 1st to 10th	• Listening and repeating ordinal numbers. • Listening and ticking groups of numbers.
Vocabulary **SB page 40**	*Vocabulary*: months and dates	• Completing the names of the months. • Talking about seasons. • Completing a table with dates. • Discussing important dates.
Grammar **SB page 40**	*Vocabulary*: prepositions of time	• Completing sentences with prepositions of time. • Writing true sentences and comparing with a partner.
Reading & Listening **SB page 41**	*Reading skills*: reading for detail *Listening skills*: listening for gist	• Matching festival information with photos. • Matching descriptions with festivals. • Listening to two people talking about a festival and answering questions. • Talking about festivals they would like to go to.
Speaking: anecdote **SB page 41**	*Conversation skills*: fluency practice	• Talking about favourite festivals or parties.
Useful phrases **SB page 42**	*Vocabulary*: opening and closing times	• Listening and matching conversations to pictures. • Completing useful phrases. • Listening to and repeating useful phrases. • Asking and answering about opening and closing times of places in their city.
Vocabulary *Extra* **SB page 43**	*Vocabulary*: revision of words from the unit: times of the year and dates. Focus on *go*	• Matching pictures with seasons. • Completing months of the year and days of the week.
Writing **WB page 27**	Organising a text Describing a festival	

6 Living *Teacher's notes*

Warm-up

Write the words *city* and *country* on the board. Find out which students live in the country and which in the city. Ask them to say what they think are the good and bad points of each.

Reading (SB page 38)

1 🔘 1.73

- Focus the students' attention on the two photos. Tell the students that the woman is Jodie Kidd and the man is Asashoryu.

- Go through the sentences with the class and explain any difficult vocabulary. You may need to tell them that *reggae* is a type of music from Jamaica, and a *Maserati* is an expensive Italian sports car. If anyone asks about the adverbs of frequency which are highlighted in the text, tell them that their function is to say how often something happens, and that you will be studying these in detail later in the unit.

- Ask the students to work in pairs and to decide which sentences describe Jodie Kidd and which Asashoryu. Make sure they understand that they aren't expected to know this information, but they should make guesses based on the photos. Discourage them from trying to find the answers in the article at this stage. You could tell them to cover the text if necessary.

- Play the recording and ask the students to listen to the article and read it. Then find out how many sentences the students guessed correctly. Ask if they find any of the information surprising.

> a) She b) He c) He d) He e) He
> f) He g) He h) She i) She

Language notes

Pronunciation: *wrestler*

The pronunciation of *wrestler* is /ˈreslə/.

Vocabulary: *have a nap*

have a nap is an expression meaning to have a short sleep during the day.

Cultural note

Roast dinners

Roast dinners are the traditional meals that British people eat on Sundays. They consist of roast meat (beef, lamb, chicken or pork), roast potatoes, vegetables. Yorkshire pudding (which is made from flour, milk and eggs) is also traditionally served with roast beef. The meal is popular in Britain, Ireland, Canada and Australia.

2

- Focus the students' attention on the speech bubbles. Point out that the question in the first bubble is formed from sentence a) in Exercise 1. Ask one of the students this question, using their own name, and encourage them to give a truthful reply. Then ask the students to form a question with sentence b) of Exercise 1. Once you are sure they understand what to do, put them in pairs and ask them to form questions for the other items in Exercise 1.

- Then ask pairs to take turns asking and answering their questions. Tell them that they should make brief notes of their partner's replies. Go round, monitoring and giving help.

- Ask the students to use their notes to write sentences about their partners. Encourage several students to read their sentences to the class.

Vocabulary (SB page 39)

1 🔘 1.74

- Tell the students to say the phrases aloud as they decide whether they take *make* or *do*.

- Play the recording for the students to check their answers. Then play it again for them to listen and repeat. Ask them to turn back to the article on page 38 and find which of these verb phrases were used and who they were describing (*make my bed, do the housework* in the text about Asashoryu).

> a) do b) make

Extra activity

Tell the students that you're going to mime some of the verb phrases in Exercise 1. Ask them to call out the verb phrase as soon as they think they know what you're doing.

2

- Ask the students to work individually to make a list of the people in their home who do the various things in Exercise 1. Draw the students' attention to the speech bubbles and remind them of the use of *does* and *makes* with the third person singular, and that the possessive determiner changes for *homework*. Go round, monitoring and giving help.

- Put the students in pairs and ask them to tell each other about their lists.

Language notes

Vocabulary: *do* and *make*

- *Do* and *make* are combined with nouns to talk about actions you perform.

- *Do* is often used when the action is a noun ending in *ing*. For example, *do the shopping, do the cooking, do some sightseeing,* etc. It's also used to talk about daily activities or jobs. For example, *do (your) homework / the housework / the ironing / the dishes / a job.*

- *Make* is often used to talk about an activity that creates something. For example, *make food / a cup of tea / a mess.*

- However, there are a number of fixed expressions using *do* and *make* that don't fit into these categories. For example, *do business / make your bed.*

- Encourage the students to learn these as complete phrases.

Grammar (SB page 39)

Adverbs of frequency

1

- Focus the students' attention on the adverbs of frequency in the margin. Tell them they are used to say how often someone does something. Look at the first section with the students and explain the difference between a main verb and an auxiliary ('helping') verb. Point out that in the second and third example sentences the adverbs go before the main verbs (*drink* and *walk*), not before the auxiliaries (*doesn't* and *Do*).

- Look at the second section and point out that when the verb in a sentence is *be*, the adverb comes immediately after it.

- Tell the students to turn back to the article on page 38 and ask them to read out the highlighted adverbs of frequency in the text. Write them on the board as they call them out. Then focus their attention on the chart on page 39. Point out that the left-hand side is marked 100% and the right-hand side 0%. The adverbs of frequency can be put in order to show exactly how often something happens. Ask the students to work in pairs or groups to decide where in the chart they should put the adverbs of frequency you've written on the board. Check answers with the class.

---

a) always   b) usually   c) often
d) sometimes   e) hardly ever   f) never

2

- Go through the sentences with the class. As you read each one, ask the students to raise their hands if the sentence is true for them.

- Then ask the students to use adverbs of frequency to make the sentences true for them. Go round, monitoring and giving help. Then, for each sentence, ask a number of students to call out their new versions. Check that they're using the adverbs of frequency correctly.

3

- Go through the instructions with the class and explain that you use questions with *ever* to ask about how frequently someone does something. Tell them that you use *Are you ever ...?* for questions with *be* (*Are you ever late?*) and *Do you ever ...?* for other verbs (*Do you ever wake up before 7.00 a.m.?*). Read the question in the example speech bubble and encourage several students to give you their answers. If the students are having difficulty with these questions, go through the list of sentences in Exercise 2 with the class, and ask the students to say what question they should ask for each one. Make sure that they make any changes that are necessary. For example, they'll need to change *my* to *your* in question c) (*Do you visit **your** relatives at the weekend?*).

- Put the students in pairs to complete the activity, taking turns to ask and answer questions based on the sentences in Exercise 2.

---

a) Do you ever wake up before 7.00 a.m.?
b) Do you ever have a nap in the afternoon?
c) Do you ever visit your relatives at the weekend?
d) Are you ever home in the evening?
e) Do you ever drink alcohol when you go out?
f) Are you ever late for work?

Language notes

Vocabulary: *ever*

- Students sometimes have difficulty with the meaning of *ever*. It means *at any time*, and it's generally used in questions: *Do you ever go to bed after midnight?* The question can be answered with a simple *Yes, I do* or *No, I don't,* or with an adverb of frequency: *Yes, always* or *No, never / hardly ever.*

- *Hardly ever* means *almost never.*

4 Pairwork

- The pairwork exercise for this unit is on pages 117 and 122 of the Student's Book. Put the students in pairs and tell them who will be Student A, and who will be Student B.

- While they're doing the exercise, go round monitoring and giving help. Take note of any errors which may need particular attention later, and also any examples of good language use which you can praise in a feedback session.

5 *Grammar Extra* 6

Ask students to turn to *Grammar Extra* 6 on page 128 of the Student's Book. Here they'll find an explanation of the grammar they've been studying and a further exercise to practise it.

---

1 a) Tom is always happy.
  b) Janet sometimes has eggs for breakfast.
  c) Dick usually goes out on Saturday evenings.
  d) Sue is often tired on Friday evenings.
  e) Harry hardly ever does the housework.
  f) Maggie never answers her mobile phone.

Pronunciation (SB page 39)

Ordinal numbers

1   1.75

- Focus the students' attention on the list of ordinal numbers in the margin. Point out that the numerals in the first column have abbreviations (*st, nd, rd, th*) after them; these correspond to the ordinal number words in the second column. Ordinal numbers are used to show order rather than quantity. Students will need to know them so that they can talk about dates, which they'll study in the next section of this unit.

- Play the recording and ask the students to repeat the ordinal numbers after the speaker. When they've done this chorally, ask individual students to repeat numbers after you. Give extra practice of *sixth* /sɪksθ/ and *eighth* /eɪtθ/, which are quite difficult to say. Also point out the spelling of *fifth, eighth* and *ninth*.

2   1.76

- Ask individual students to read out the groups of ordinal numbers. Help them when they come to *12th* /twelfθ/ and *20th* /'twentiəθ/ which are not in the list in the margin. Tell them that for each item a) to d) they'll hear one of the groups, and they should tick the one they hear. The first one has been done for them as an example.

- Play the recording and check answers with the class.

---

a) 1st 2nd 3rd   c) 5th 1st 4th
b) 7th 6th 2nd   d) 10th 20th 12th

Extra activity

Ask the students to write down six ordinal numbers and to dictate them to a partner. They then change roles and write down their partner's dictated numbers.

Vocabulary (SB page 40)

Months and dates

1   1.77

- Focus the students' attention on the pictures and the names of the seasons. Ask them what season it is at the moment, and find out what is their favourite season.

- Now focus their attention on the months. Ask the students how many of the names of the months they know. Ask them to call them out and then find them in the list and complete them. Remind them that they should always write the names of months with a capital letter at the beginning. Point out that you don't use capital letters with the names of seasons when they occur in the middle of a sentence. (They have capital letters here because they are captions for the pictures.)

- Play the recording for the students to check their answers. Then play it again for them to listen and repeat. Ask them if the seasons are the same months in their country / countries.

- Ask them to underline the stressed syllables in the names of the months. Then play the recording again so they can check their answers.

Spring: March, <u>A</u>pril, May
Summer: June, Ju<u>ly</u>, <u>Au</u>gust
Autumn: Sep<u>tem</u>ber, Oc<u>to</u>ber, No<u>vem</u>ber
Winter: De<u>cem</u>ber, <u>Ja</u>nuary, <u>Feb</u>ruary

---

2   1.78

- Ask the students to look at the table. Point out the two columns headed *How to write dates* and *How to say dates*. Read out the two examples and ask the students what they notice about the way you say dates (we add the words *the* and *of* which do not appear in written dates).

- Ask the students to complete the table. Then play the recording for them to check their answers. Play it a second time for them to listen and repeat. When they've done this chorally, ask individual students to repeat the dates after you.

---

1 the first of January
2 the fourteenth of February
3 1st May
4 the thirty-first of October
5 25th December

Vocabulary: dates

- Point out that months are written, like days of the weeks, with a capital letter.

- Variants do exist, but in standard British English, you write *10ᵗʰ May*, but you say *the tenth of May*. However, in American English, you write *May 10*, and you say *May tenth*.

- In British English, when you write the date in figures, you write *10/5/2007*. However, because in American English you say the month first, you write *5/10/2007* when referring to May 10.

3

Pairwork. Ask the students to look at the dates in the table. Explain briefly the significance of these dates in the UK (see below), then put the students in pairs to discuss the questions. Go round, monitoring and giving help with any vocabulary that they need. Take note of any errors which may need focusing on later, and also any examples of good language use which you can praise. Encourage students to tell the class about any interesting information they found out from their partners.

Cultural notes

New Year's Day (1ˢᵗ January)
In Britain, 1ˢᵗ January is called New Year's Day and is a national holiday. People celebrate the evening before on New Year's Eve, when they go to parties or pubs, and stay up until midnight. There's also an annual firework display on the River Thames in London, a big celebration in Edinburgh in Scotland, and live concerts in cities throughout the UK.

(Saint) Valentine's Day (14ᵗʰ February)
(Saint) Valentine's Day is the traditional day on which lovers send each other cards. These are often anonymous. Approximately 85 percent of these cards are bought by women.

May Bank Holiday (1ˢᵗ May)
May Bank Holiday or May Day is a national holiday to celebrate workers. In the UK, it's celebrated on the first Monday in May.

Halloween (31ˢᵗ October)
Halloween was originally an Irish celebration. On the evening of 31ˢᵗ October, the day before the Christian feast of All Saints, people believed that evil spirits would try to come back from the dead. So, they'd dress up in costumes to frighten the spirits away. Halloween is now a popular celebration in the United States and in Britain. Children dress up as witches and ghosts and play 'trick or treat'. They knock on their neighbours' doors to ask for treats such as sweets, or play tricks on the neighbours if they receive nothing.

Christmas Day (25ᵗʰ December)
Christmas Day is a religious holiday celebrating the birth of Jesus Christ. It's a national holiday in the UK. People normally spend the day with their family and exchange presents. They also eat a big meal, usually turkey, roast potatoes and vegetables, followed by a special Christmas pudding. Lots of people also have a special Christmas tree in their house which they decorate.

Grammar (SB page 40)

Prepositions of time

1 🌐 1.79

- Ask the students to look at the information in the margin about prepositions of time. Begin with the expressions using *in* and ask several students to read them aloud. Point out the use of the definite article with *in the morning*, *in the afternoon* and *in the evening*. No article is used with the names of months. With seasons, use of the article is, to some extent, optional. It's given here, but you can also say *in spring, in summer*, etc. Then ask several students to read out the expressions which use *on*. When they come to the dates, make sure they say them as they were taught in the last section, using *the* and *of* correctly. Point out the lack of an article with *on Sunday, on Monday*, etc. Finally ask some students to read out the expressions with *at*. Again, point out the use of the article with *at the weekend*.

- Give the students a few minutes to complete the sentences. Allow them to compare results in pairs before you play the recording for them to check their answers. Play it a second time for them to listen and repeat.

a) on	b) in	c) at	d) on	e) on	f) in

2

- Point out the use of the adverbs of frequency, which the students learnt earlier, in the items in Exercise 1. Ask them to write true sentences about the ideas in Exercise 1. Go round, monitoring and giving help.

- Put the students in pairs and ask them to compare their sentences. Get some students to read their sentences out to the class.

Reading & Listening (SB page 41)

1 🌐 1.80

- Focus the students' attention on the photos. Play the recording and ask the students to read the three texts as they listen. Answer any questions about vocabulary and tell them to discuss in pairs which text goes with which photo.

- Check answers with the class.

a) 3	b) 2	c) 1

Cultural notes

Oktoberfest

The first Oktoberfest was held in 1810 in Munich to celebrate the marriage of the Crown Prince and it has continued since then. Although it's called *Oktoberfest*, it traditionally starts in September.

San Fermín festival

The origins of San Fermín festival date back to the 13th century. The festival evolved from three events which took place around the same time: a religious festival celebrating Saint Fermín, a commercial fair, and a bull fighting festival.

The Rio Carnival

The Rio Carnival is probably the most famous carnival in the world. The first records of the Carnival in Rio de Janeiro are in 1723. Gradually over the years elements have been added to the carnival to make it what it is today – four days of music, parades and dancing.

2

Go through the sentences with the class, then ask the students to look back at the texts and decide which festival each one describes. Allow them to compare notes in pairs before checking answers with the class.

a) Rio Carnival	b) San Fermín	c) San Fermín
d) Rio Carnival	e) Oktoberfest	f) Oktoberfest

Language note

Vocabulary: *goes on*

to go on is a phrasal verb which means to last. You could also say that the carnival lasts four days.

3 🌐 1.81

- Tell the students that they're going to listen to a man and a woman talking about one of the festivals in Exercise 1. Go through the questions with them before you play the recording so that they know what information they're listening out for.

- Play the recording and ask the students to answer the questions. Check answers with the class.

- Pairwork. Put the students in pairs and ask them to talk about which festival they would like to go to and why. Go round, monitoring and giving help. Take note of any errors which may need focusing on later, and also any examples of good language use which you can praise in a feedback session.

> a) Rio Carnival
> b) Yes she does. She likes the music and dancing all night on the beach.
> c) No, he doesn't. He doesn't like all the people, or the drumming. (He likes listening to music at home and watching the parades on television.)

🌐 1.81 (M = Man; W = Woman)

M: Are you going to carnival this year?
W: Of course. I go every year. What about you?
M: No. I hate carnival. I'm going to the mountains for a week.
W: Really? Why?
M: I don't like all the people.
W: But it's fun. And the music is fantastic. I love it.
M: I don't like all that drumming. I like listening to music at home.
W: But what about the parades and the costumes?
M: Yes, I like the parades and costumes. I think they're great. But I like watching them on television.
W: On television?! Oh no, that's terrible. Carnival on television! I love dancing all night on the beach.

Speaking: anecdote (SB page 41)

For more information about how to set up, monitor and repeat anecdotes, see Practical methodology, page xx in the Introduction.

1 🌐 1.82

- Focus the students' attention on the photo in the margin and tell them that this is a young man called Conor. Tell them that they're going to listen to him talking about his favourite festival.

- Before you play the recording, give the students time to read the questions and the choices.

- Play the recording for the students to listen and underline the correct information. You may need to play it more than once.

- Check answers with the class.

a) Saint Patrick's Day	e) Green clothes
b) In March	f) Beer
c) For four days	g) Traditional
d) A parade and dancing	

🌐 1.82

My favourite festival is Saint Patrick's Day. It takes place in Dublin, in the city centre.

It takes place in March and it goes on for four days.

On 17th March – the most important day – we have a big parade in the city centre.

At the end of the parade, thousands of people do traditional Irish dancing together. It's fantastic.

People wear green clothes and paint their faces green.

We drink a lot of beer – that's Guinness, of course. And we listen to traditional Irish music in the pubs.

Ah, Irish people love a good party!

Cultural notes

Saint Patrick's Day (17ᵗʰ March)
Saint Patrick's Day celebrates Saint Patrick (386–493), the patron saint of Ireland. It's a national holiday in the Republic of Ireland. It's also celebrated in many countries by people of Irish descent. Parades are a large part of the celebrations, the largest one in New York City.

Halloween (31ˢᵗ October)
(See notes about Halloween on page 44.)

Samba
Samba is one of the most popular forms of music in Brazil. Its roots come from Africa with *semba*, a type of ritual music from Angola. Samba developed at the beginning of the 20ᵗʰ century in Rio de Janeiro under the strong influence of African immigrants.

2

- Give the students a minute or two to decide what their favourite festival or party is.

- Then ask them to look back at the questions in Exercise 1 and write answers about their favourite festival or party. Go round, monitoring and giving help with any additional vocabulary they may need.

- Tell them that they're going to tell their partner about their favourite festival or party, but that they need to do more than simply read out their sentences. Ask them to think about the language that they'll need to describe the event and to make notes.

- Pairwork. Put the students in pairs and ask them to take turns to tell their partner about their favourite festival or party. Encourage them to ask each other questions to get further information. You could talk about the sort of questions they might ask first and put them on the board (*Does it take place every year? How often do you go to the festival? What do you eat?* etc.).

- Ask some pairs to report back to the class about what they found out.

Useful phrases (SB page 42)

1 ● 1.83

- Focus the students' attention on the pictures and give the students time to take in what is happening in them.

- Play the recording for the students to listen and read the conversations. Ask them to match the conversations with the pictures. You may need to play the recording more than once.

- Check answers with the class. Then ask the students what the three conversations have in common (they are people asking about the opening and closing times of shops).

> a) 2   b) 3   c) 1

Cultural note

7/11

7/11 or 'seven eleven' is a chain of convenience stores which can be found throughout the United States and Canada.

2 ● 1.84

- Focus the students' attention on the example and explain that the students have to rewrite the phrases correctly by inserting the words in brackets in the right place. Do the second one with the whole class to make sure that they understand what to do.

- Ask the students to work on their own to complete the exercise. Allow them to compare their results in pairs before playing the recording for them to check their answers.

- Play the recording again for the students to repeat the phrases after the speaker. Make sure that they match the speaker's intonation. When they've done this chorally, ask individual students to read out the phrases.

> a) What time do you open?
> b) We open at nine o'clock.
> c) What time does it open?
> d) What time does it close?
> e) What time do you close?
> f) We close at 5.30.
> g) We're closed at the weekend.

3

Pairwork. Students work in pairs and practise the conversations in Exercise 1, taking it in turns to play each role.

4

- Pairwork. Demonstrate the activity by asking a confident student the questions at the bottom of the page. Then put the students in pairs and ask them to take turns asking and answering about the opening and closing times of the places in the box. Remind them to use real information about places in their cities.

- While they're doing the exercise, go round monitoring and giving help. Take note of any errors which may need focusing on later, and also any examples of good language use which you can praise. When the students have finished, invite pairs to perform their conversations for the rest of the class. Encourage them to make eye contact with each other when they say their lines, rather than simply reading them out.

Vocabulary *Extra* (SB page 43)

Times of year and dates

1

- Focus the students' attention on the list of seasons. Check that they can pronounce the words correctly.
- Ask students to look at the pictures and match each one with one of the words. Point out that the first one has been done for them.

3	autumn	2	summer
1	spring	4	winter

2

Ask the students to work individually to write either the words for the ordinal numbers, or the ordinal numbers for the words. Ask for choral and individual repetition to check that they're pronouncing the words correctly.

1st = first	21st = twenty-first
2nd = second	22nd = twenty-second
3rd = third	23rd = twenty-third
4th = fourth	24th = twenty-fourth
5th = fifth	25th = twenty-fifth
6th = sixth	26th = twenty-sixth
7th = seventh	27th = twenty-seventh
8th = eighth	28th = twenty-eighth
9th = ninth	29th = twenty-ninth
10th = tenth	30th = thirtieth
11th = eleventh	31st = thirty-first
12th = twelfth	
13th = thirteenth	
14th = fourteenth	
15th = fifteenth	
16th = sixteenth	
17th = seventeenth	
18th = eighteenth	
19th = nineteenth	
20th = twentieth	

3

Ask the students to complete the months of the year. Then check that the students can pronounce all the months correctly.

January, February, March, April, August, September, October, November, December

4

Ask the students to complete the days of the week. Then check that the students can pronounce all the days of the week correctly.

Monday, Tuesday, Wednesday, Thursday, Friday, Saturday, Sunday

Focus on *go*

1

Ask the students to look at the table and complete it with the correct phrases from the box.

1	go to bed	4	go riding
2	go to work	5	go for a walk
3	go shopping	6	go on the internet

2

Ask the students to write their own example sentences for each use of *go* in the table in Exercise 1.

Further practice material

Need more writing practice?

→ Workbook page 27
- Organising a text
- Describing a festival

Need more classroom practice activities?

→ Photocopiable resource materials pages 167 to 169
   Grammar: *A question of time*
   Vocabulary: *Make or do?*
   Communication: *Snakes and ladders*
→ TOP 10 activities pages xv to xx

Need DVD material?

→ DVD – Programme 3: *A day in the life*

Need progress tests?

→ Test CD – *Test Unit 6*

Need more on important teaching concepts?

→ Key concepts in *New Inside Out* pages xxii to xxxv

Need student self-study practice?

→ CD-ROM – Unit 6: *Living*

Need student CEF self-evaluation?

→ CEF Checklists pages xxxvii to xliv

Need more information and more ideas?

→ www.insideout.net

7 Sea Overview

Section	Aims	What the students are doing
Vocabulary & Listening **SB page 44**	*Vocabulary*: water sports; time expressions; *ago* *Listening skills*: listening for specific information	• Listening to and repeating names of water sports. • Listening to two interviews about water sports and circling time expressions. • Completing a table with time expressions. • Discussing the water sports they like.
Grammar SB page 45	*Grammar*: past simple (*be, go*) – affirmative forms	• Rewriting questions using *be* and *go* in the past simple. • Asking questions about past activities.
Reading SB page 45	*Reading skills*: reading for gist; reading for specific information	• Explaining the meaning of an article title. • Completing sentences about an article on the inventor of the wetsuit.
Grammar SB page 46	*Grammar*: past simple, regular and irregular verbs	• Categorising verbs as regular or irregular. • Matching sentence halves to make rules about forming past forms. • Completing a table with irregular past forms. • Practising the pronunciation of past forms.
Pronunciation **SB page 46**	*Pronunciation*: present and past forms	• Practising past forms which do and don't have extra syllables.
Reading & Vocabulary **SB page 47**	*Reading skills*: reading for detail *Vocabulary*: time linkers	• Reading a story and identifying true and false statements. • Using time linkers to complete a story.
Useful phrases **SB page 48**	*Vocabulary*: useful phrases about the weather	• Listening to conversations about the weather and matching them to pictures. • Completing a table with useful phrases about the weather. • Practising conversations with a partner.
Vocabulary *Extra* **SB page 49**	*Vocabulary*: revision of words from the unit: sports. Focus on *make* and *do*	• Matching pictures with words.
Writing WB page 31	Using time expressions Telling a story	

Sea *Teacher's notes*

Warm-up

Find out how many of the students live near the sea, a lake or a river. How many go to the beach for their holidays?

Vocabulary & Listening (SB page 44)

1 🌐 2.01

- Focus the students' attention on the photos and the captions. Ask them what all these sports have in common (they all take place in or around water). Read out the sports one by one and ask the students which ones they have taken part in.

- Play the recording for the students to repeat the names of the sports. When they've done this chorally, ask individual students to repeat the sports after you.

2 🌐 2.02

- Tell the students that they're going to hear two people, Pam and Sergio, talking about water sports. Focus their attention on the table and point out the time expressions which all refer to the past. Ask the students to listen and circle the expressions they hear in each interview.

- Play the recording. You may need to pause it several times during each interview, and between the two interviews, to give the students time to circle the time expressions. Allow them to compare their results in pairs before checking answers with the class.

---

a) in August   d) a long time ago
b) last summer   e) last year
c) yesterday

🌐 2.02

Pam
(I = Interviewer; P = Pam)

I: *Excuse me. I'm from a new sports shop. Can I ask you some questions about water sports?*
P: *Sure.*
I: *Um, what's your name?*
P: *It's Pam.*
I: *OK, Pam. Do you ever go swimming?*
P: *Oh, yes, I love swimming.*
I: *And when was the last time you went swimming?*
P: *Er, the last time I went swimming was … in August. I was on holiday.*

I: *And do you ever go sailing?*
P: *No – I'd like to, but I don't know anybody with a boat.*
I: *OK, how about other water sports?*
P: *I sometimes go windsurfing.*
I: *When was the last time you went windsurfing?*
P: *I went windsurfing last summer with my friend. We were on holiday.*
I: *Great. Well, come along to our shop some time. Here's the address.*
P: *Yeah, thanks.*

Sergio
(I = Interviewer; S = Sergio)

I: *Excuse me. I'm from a new sports shop. Can I ask you some questions about water sports?*
S: *Water sports?*
I: *Yes, what's your name?*
S: *Sergio Fernandez Almira Olivera.*
I: *OK, er, Sergio. Do you ever go swimming?*
S: *Yes, yes, I go swimming a lot.*
I: *Oh great. When was the last time you went swimming?*
S: *Yesterday!*
I: *Right, and do you ever go sailing?*
S: *Yes, but not often.*
I: *When was the last time you went sailing?*
S: *I can't remember. A long time ago.*
I: *Do you ever do other water sports?*
S: *Yes, I love scuba diving.*
I: *Wow. When was the last time you went scuba diving?*
S: *Last year. I was on holiday in Egypt.*
I: *Lovely. Well, our new shop is in the centre of town …*

Extra activity

- Tell the students, working individually, to write three sentences, two of them true and one false using time expressions from Exercise 2, or their own ideas. For example, *I was at university in 2004.* (True); *I saw a good film yesterday. I went kite surfing last August.* (False). Tell them not to discuss their sentences with anyone else.

- In pairs, the students take turns to read their sentences to each other. Their partner has to guess which one is false.

Vocabulary: water sports

The water sports in this exercise collocate with
the verb *go*. Other possible water sports which
collocate with *go* include *water skiing, jet skiing*
and *kayaking*.

3

Focus attention on the table and explain that it shows
two ways of saying the same thing. Point out that all
these expressions refer to the past. Look at the example
with the class and read it aloud. Then ask the students
what they think the answer to b) is (this will depend
what day of the week it is today). Go through each of the
others and ask for the answers.

Extra activity

Put the students in pairs. Ask one student to say
an expression with *on, in* or *last*. The other says the
same thing using *ago*. They then swap round.

Language note

Vocabulary: *ago*

Ago counts back in time from now. It's always
used after a time expression, and you can use it
with all units of time:
two minutes ago
an hour ago
two days ago (Note you don't say *one day ago*. You
say *yesterday*.)
three weeks ago
five months ago
years ago
Ages ago is a common expression meaning *a long
time ago*.

4

Pairwork. Put the students in pairs and ask them to talk
about any water sports that they like. Go round,
monitoring and giving help. Take note of any errors
which may need particular attention later, and also any
examples of good language use which you can praise.
Encourage students to report back to the class on any
interesting information they learnt from their partners.

Grammar (SB page 45)

Past simple

1 🌐 2.03

- A table of the past simple of the verbs *be* and *go* is
  shown in the margin. Focus the students' attention
  on this and point out that while both *was* and *were*
  are used (according to the person) as the past simple
  of *be*, there's only one form for all persons with *go*
  (*went*). Ask the students to read the two lists of verbs
  aloud, prefacing each verb form with the pronoun
  each time (*I was, you were, he was, she was*, etc.).

- Tell the students to look at two jumbled questions.
  Explain that these questions appeared in the
  interviews in the previous section (both in the
  interview with Pam). Ask them to put the words in
  the correct order.

- Play the recording for the students to check their
  answers. Explain the difference between the two
  questions (the first asks about swimming in general;
  the second asks about a specific experience of
  swimming in the past). Then play the recording a
  second time for the students to repeat the questions.
  Encourage them to match the intonation of the
  speaker on the recording. In the first question, the
  emphasis is on *swimming*. In the second, it is on
  last time.

> a) Do you ever go swimming?
> b) When was the last time you went swimming?

2

- Pairwork. Students work in pairs and take turns to
  ask each other more questions about past activities.
  Read the speech bubbles aloud with the class first
  and explain any words in the box that they don't
  understand.

- While they're doing the pairwork exercise, go round
  monitoring and giving help.

Language note

Vocabulary: other expressions with *go*

All the expressions in this activity collocate with
the verb *go*, but they aren't limited to water sports.
Students are asked to use their own ideas, but they
must follow this pattern and collocate with the
verb *go*. They've already seen other collocations on
page 34 of the Student's Book, including *go on
holiday, go home, go on the internet, go out with
friends*, which they can use as well as the other
water sports.

Reading (SB page 45)

1 🌐 2.04

- Focus the students' attention on the photos that
  accompany the article. Then tell them to look at the
  title and the choices in the exercise. Ask them to read
  and listen to the article to find out which one is the
  best explanation of the title.

- Play the recording and ask the students to make their
  choices. Check answers and then go through any
  difficulties the students may have with the article.

> b

2

- Ask the students to work on their own to complete
  the sentences using information from the article.
  Allow them to compare results in pairs before
  checking answers with the class.

- You could then ask the students if they have any clothes by O'Neill, which other brands of sports clothes they know, and which brand they like best.

> a) in his free time
> b) in California
> c) because the Californian ocean was cold / he wanted to stay warm in the water
> d) in 1952
> e) in a bath of ice
> f) in a surfing accident

Grammar (SB page 46)

Past simple

1

- Explain that English verbs can be classified as regular or irregular according to their past forms. Focus the students' attention on the information in the margin and point out that the verb *work* is regular and it takes *ed* at the end to form the past simple. Tell them that *have* is irregular and point out that it doesn't take *ed* to form the past simple.

- Students should now be able recognise quite easily which of the two boxes of verbs in the exercise is regular and which irregular. Check answers with the class.

> Box A: Regular verbs
> Box B: Irregular verbs

- Remind the students of the two verbs they saw in the past simple in the last grammar section: *be* and *go*. Ask whether they think these two verbs are regular or irregular (irregular).

2

Tell the students that the two sentence halves need to be matched to make rules about forming regular past forms. Refer them back to the regular verb *work* in the margin, and ask them to work in pairs to match the sentence halves. Check answers with the class.

> a) add *ed* (*watched*)
> b) add *d* (*liked*)
> c) delete *y* and add *ied* (*studied*)
> d) add a consonant + *ed* (*stopped*)

Language note

Grammar: past forms

If you want to give your students further practice of recognising regular and irregular verbs, ask them to go back to the reading text on page 45 of the Student's Book and make a list of regular verbs and a list of irregular verbs.

Regular verbs: *loved, wanted, started, opened, demonstrated, asked, pointed, worked*

Irregular verbs: *sold, took, wore, lost, sat, went, was*

3 🌐 2.05

- Point out that all the past forms in the box are irregular. Go through the examples with the class and then ask them to work on their own to match the past forms with the verbs. (The reason why the verbs are grouped as they are will become apparent in the next exercise.) Allow them to compare answers in pairs.

- Play the recording for the students to check their answers. Then play it again for them to listen and repeat. Point out the difference in pronunciation between *read* (present simple) /riːd/ and *read* (past simple) /red/.

> a) go – went, do – did, send – sent
> b) hold – held, sell – sold, tell – told
> c) think – thought, catch – caught, hear – heard
> d) take – took, break – broke, speak – spoke
> e) see – saw, come – came, wear – wore
> f) read – read (/red/), say – said, give – gave

Language notes

Grammar: teaching irregular verbs

- There are approximately 180 irregular verbs. Some of these are very rare but the majority are extremely frequent. Indeed, as the following list shows, eleven out of the top twelve most common lexical verbs are irregular: *say, get, go, know, think, see, make, come, take, want, give, mean*.

- Students need to learn the irregular past forms of the most common verbs as soon as possible. Some will prefer trying to learn a list by heart. Others may prefer chanting them: *say – said, get – got, go – went*, etc. In the classroom you should spend as much time as you can on a wide range of extra activities with the express purpose of helping students to learn these forms.

4 🌐 2.06

- Explain that the verbs in Exercise 3 are grouped so that in each line two of the past forms have the same sound and one is different. Demonstrate by reading out the example and pointing out that *did* is circled because it has a different sound from *went* and *sent*.

- Ask the students to work in pairs and to decide which past form in each of the other groups has a different sound. Encourage them to say the words aloud as they do this so that they get a feel for how they sound.
- Play the recording for the students to check their answers. Then play it again for them to listen and repeat.

> a) did   b) held   c) heard   d) took
> e) came   f) gave

5 Pairwork

- The pairwork exercise for this unit is on pages 118 and 123 of the Student's Book. Put the students in pairs and tell them who will be Student A, and who will be Student B.
- While they are doing the exercise, go round monitoring and giving help. Take note of any errors which may need particular attention later, and also any examples of good language use which you can praise.

> **Student A**
> a) went   b) travelled   c) used   d) spoke
> e) drove   f) earned
>
> **Student B**
> a) had   b) telephoned   c) made
> d) held   e) gave   f) took

6 *Grammar Extra* 7

Ask students to turn to *Grammar Extra* 7 on page 128 of the Student's Book. Here they'll find an explanation of the grammar they've been studying and further exercises to practise it.

> 1 a) worked   b) called   c) stop   d) studied
>   e) liked   f) completed   g) try   h) listen
> 2 a) went   b) wore   c) saw   d) was
>   e) sat   f) woke up

Pronunciation (SB page 46)

1

Focus the students' attention on the table and explain that the boxes show the syllables in a word, with a large box to indicate stressed syllables. Point out the difference between the pronunciation of the past forms of *asked* /ɑːskt/, which has one syllable, and *pointed* /ˈpɔɪntɪd/, which has two. Encourage the students to read the words aloud as they decide which column each one should go in. Allow them to compare notes in pairs.

> A: No extra syllables   B: Extra syllable
> ask – asked   point – pointed
> love – loved   start – started
> stop – stopped   want – wanted
> use – used
> work – worked

Pronunciation: of past regular verbs

- The *ed* ending on regular past simple verbs ending in /t/ or /d/ is pronounced with an extra syllable (/ɪd/). For example, *started, waited, added, ended*.
- For all other regular past simple verbs there's no extra syllable. After unvoiced sounds: /k/, /p/, /f/, /s/, /ʃ/ and /tʃ/, *ed* is pronounced /t/. For example, *stopped, walked, watched*. After voiced sounds, *ed* is pronounced /d/. For example *arrived, changed, used*.
- Here the exercise concentrates on verbs ending with the pronunciation /ɪd/. If your students would benefit from extra practice, ask them to do the same with the other regular verbs they've seen in Grammar Exercise 1 at the top of page 46 of the Student's Book.

2 🌐 2.07

- Play the recording for the students to check their answers. Then play it again for them to repeat after the speaker. When they've done this chorally, ask individual students to repeat the past forms after you. Point out that some of the one-syllable forms end in a /t/ sound (*asked, stopped, worked*) and others with a /d/ sound (*loved, used*).

Reading & Vocabulary (SB page 47)

1 🌐 2.08

- Focus the students' attention on the photo of Richard E Grant and that of the shark. Teach the word *shark* and ask them what they think the connection between the two might be. Then go through the statements with the class and explain any difficulties.
- Play the recording as the students read the text. Then ask them to say if the statements are true or false.

> a) False.   b) True.   c) False.   d) False.
> e) True.   f) False.

Cultural notes

Richard E Grant (born 1957)
Richard E Grant is a British actor, director and author. He was born in Swaziland in Africa, and went to university in South Africa before coming to London. The films he's appeared in include *Withnail and I* (1987), *Jack and Sarah* (1995) and *Gosford Park* (2001).

Mozambique
Mozambique is a republic bordering on the Indian Ocean in south-eastern Africa. It lies north of South Africa and south of Tanzania, with Zambia and Zimbabwe to the west. Portuguese is the official language.

2 🔊 2.09

- Point out the words that are highlighted in the text in Exercise 1. Explain that these are called linkers and that they're used to make clear the order of events in a story, and to join it together so that it reads smoothly.
- Pairwork. Ask the students to work in pairs to put the linkers from the story in Exercise 1 into a new text. Tell them to read the new story first, ignoring the gaps. As they work, go round and give any help that they might need.
- Play the recording for the students to check their answers.

1 One day	4 eventually
2 After an hour	5 Suddenly
3 At first	6 Two or three weeks later

3

Groupwork. Ask the students to work in small groups and to discuss what they think happened to the couple in the story. Offer help with any vocabulary they may need to express their ideas. Rather than just settling for *A shark ate them*, encourage the students to come up with more elaborate explanations. Allow time for them to tell the rest of the class their opinions.

Useful phrases (SB page 48)

1 🔊 2.10

- These short conversations will enable students to talk about the weather.
- Play the recording and ask the students to read the conversations and match each one with one of the sports in the box. Check answers with the class and then ask the students what is good weather for windsurfing, skiing and fishing. Ask them also what the weather is like today where you are.

a) windsurfing   b) skiing   c) fishing

Language note

Vocabulary: talking about the weather

When the sun is shining, you can say *It's sunny*. When there are clouds, you say *It's cloudy*. When there's fog, you say *It's foggy* and when there's wind, you say *It's windy*.

2 🔊 2.11

- Remind the students that all three conversations in Exercise 1 were about the weather. Ask them to complete the table with words from the conversations. Go round, monitoring and giving help where necessary.
- Play the recording for them to listen and check their answers. Then play it again for them to repeat the weather phrases. Ask several students to repeat the phrases individually.

1 weather	2 sunny	3 windy	4 cloudy
5 raining	6 snowing	7 foggy	

Extra activity

Ask the students to look through the conversations in Exercise 1 and find two other words that are connected to the weather (*cold, warm*).

3

Pairwork. Ask the students to take turns taking the different roles in the conversations and to practise them.

Extra activity

Ask the students to think of other situations where the weather is important and to write their own conversations in pairs. Go round, monitoring and giving help with vocabulary. Ask some pairs to perform their new conversations for the class.

Vocabulary *Extra* (SB page 49)

Sports

1

- Focus the students' attention on the list of words and point out that they're all to do with sports. Remind students that the underlining indicates the syllable of the word that has the strongest stress. Check that the students can pronounce the words correctly.
- Ask students to look at the pictures and match each one with one of the words. Point out that the first one has been done for them.

8	cycling
10	fishing
5	football
7	jogging
6	kite surfing
2	riding
11	sailing
3	scuba diving
1	surfing
4	swimming
9	tennis
12	windsurfing

2

Pairwork. Demonstrate the activity with a confident student. Cover the words, point to one of the pictures and ask *What sport is number 1?* Elicit the answer. Then put the students into pairs to continue the activity. Go round, checking that everyone is pronouncing the sports correctly.

1

- Focus the students' attention on expressions with
  make and *do* in the table. Check that they can
  pronounce the expressions correctly. Then ask them
  to add the words in the box to the appropriate list
  a or *b* in the table. Point out that the first one has
  been done for them.

> 1 dinner
> 2 a decision
> 3 a noise
> 4 exercise
> 5 my homework
> 6 the washing up

2

Ask students to work individually and write six
expressions of their own with *make* or *do*. They can then
compare their expressions with a partner.

Further practice material

Need more writing practice?

→ Workbook page 31
- Using time expressions
- Telling a story

Need more classroom practice activities?

→ Photocopiable resource materials pages
  170 to 172
  Grammar: *I did the same!*
  Vocabulary: *Weather forecast*
  Communication: *What's the sport?*
→ TOP 10 activities pages xv to xx

Need progress tests?

→ Test CD – *Test Unit 7*

Need more on important teaching concepts?

→ Key concepts in *New Inside Out* pages
  xxii to xxxv

Need student self-study practice?

→ CD-ROM – Unit 7: *Sea*

Need student CEF self-evaluation?

→ CEF Checklists pages xxxvii to xliv

Need more information and more ideas?

→ www.insideout.net

8 Alone *Overview*

Section	Aims	What the students are doing
🌐 Vocabulary **SB page 50**	*Vocabulary*: feelings	• Listening to and repeating adjectives for feelings. • Matching adjectives to photos.
Speaking **SB page 50**	*Conversation skills*: talking about feelings	• Saying how they feel in different situations. • Talking about feelings with a partner.
🌐 Reading & Writing **SB page 51**	*Reading skills*: reading for specific information *Writing skills*: writing sentences	• Reading an article and answering questions. • Matching words from the article. • Writing sentences about the article.
🌐 Listening & Vocabulary **SB page 51**	*Listening skills*: listening for gist *Vocabulary*: prepositions with adjectives to do with feelings	• Listening to a radio programme and underlining the correct information. • Completing sentences with prepositions.
🌐 Reading **SB page 52**	*Reading skills*: reading for specific information	• Reading a text about Greta Garbo. • Putting the events of Garbo's life in order. • Talking about favourite Hollywood stars.
Writing **SB page 52**	*Writing skills*: a life summary	• Writing a summary of the life of a retired person.
🌐 Grammar **SB page 53**	*Grammar*: past simple affirmative, negative and question forms	• Completing questions and answers about their family's past. • Asking and answering questions.
🌐 Pronunciation **SB page 53**	*Pronunciation*: past forms of irregular verbs	• Completing lists with past forms of irregular verbs. • Matching past forms with similar sounds.
🌐 Speaking: anecdote **SB page 53**	*Conversation skills*: fluency practice	• Listening to a description of a summer holiday. • Talking about their last summer holiday.
🌐 Useful phrases **SB page 54**	*Vocabulary*: complaints and suggestions	• Listening to conversation and matching them with pictures. • Listening and repeating useful phrases. • Completing conversations with useful phrases. • Writing and practising new conversations about feelings.
Vocabulary *Extra* **SB page 55**	*Vocabulary*: revision of words from the unit: feelings. Focus on the weather	• Matching pictures with words.
Writing **WB page 35**	Describing a holiday	

8 Alone *Teacher's notes*

Warm-up

Tell the students how you are feeling at the moment, e.g. *I'm happy because it's sunny today. I'm nervous because it's my driving test tomorrow.* Ask the students to say how they are feeling. Help them with vocabulary.

Vocabulary (SB page 50)

1 🌐 2.12

- Play the recording for the students to listen and repeat the adjectives. Remind them that the underlining shows the stressed syllables. When they've done this chorally, ask individual students to repeat the adjectives after you.

- Ask the students to tick the words they know. Then read them out one by one. Ask students to raise their hands if they know the meaning, and to give examples of situations when they might feel this particular emotion.

2

Pairwork. Focus the students' attention on the photos and point out that the woman shown is experiencing the feelings in the box in Exercise 1. Put the students in pairs and ask them to match the feelings with the photos. Tell them that they can match more than one word with some of the photos. Check answers with the class.

a) excited, happy	d) bored
b) sad	e) frightened, nervous, worried
c) angry	f) embarrassed

Extra activity

Ask the students to work in pairs and to take turns making a facial expression to demonstrate one of the adjectives in Exercise 1. Their partner guesses how they feel. For example, *Are you nervous? No, I'm not. I'm angry.*

Speaking (SB page 50)

1

Go through the situations in the box and make sure that everyone understands them. Then read out each one in turn and ask the students to call out adjectives for how they feel in these situations.

Language note

Vocabulary: *feel*

More confident students may want to make negative sentences using the verb *feel*. Point out that the negative of *I feel happy* is *I don't feel happy*. If they wish to contradict, then, instead of saying *Me too*, they say *I don't*.

2

- Pairwork. Read the example speech bubbles with the class. Point out the use of *really* as an intensifier in the second bubble. Choose a confident student and ask another question, e.g. *How do you feel in a club or disco?* Encourage the student to reply and then agree with *Me too*, using positive intonation to show that you agree. To give them the option of disagreeing, ask another student another question. When the student replies, say *Oh, I feel (embarrassed)*, using a different adjective, emphasising the *I*, and using intonation to show that you are disagreeing.

- Put the students in pairs and ask them to continue the exercise, taking turns to ask the questions. Go round, monitoring and giving help, but don't insist that they sometimes disagree.

Reading & Writing (SB page 51)

1 🌐 2.13

- Focus the students' attention on the photos. Go through the questions with the class and ask them to read the article as they listen to the recording.

- When they've finished, ask them who the photos show (Debra and Andrew Veal). Check the answers to the questions with the class.

- Remind the students of the adjectives describing feelings that they've just studied and ask them to imagine that they are Debra, and to say how they feel at the various points of the story: setting out, when Andrew left, rowing alone, arriving in Barbados.

a) Debra and Andrew.
b) Andrew.
c) Debra.

Debra and Andrew Veal

This is a true story that happened in 2001. Debra and Andrew Veal entered a race in which a team of two rows a 23 foot wooden boat across the Atlantic. Normally the race takes about six weeks, but Debra took three and a half months. She was disqualified from the race because she did it alone, not in a team of two. However, she became the hero of the race and there was a lot of media interest in her. She's now a motivational speaker using her experience as inspiration.

2

Look at the example with the class and ask them to find it in the text (in the first two sentences). Then ask the students to match the other items. Allow them to compare in pairs before you check with the class.

> a) a 3,000-mile rowing race
> b) thirty-four other rowing teams
> c) two weeks
> d) 2,290 miles alone
> e) 113 days

3

Go through the instructions with the class. Give them a minute or two to remind themselves of what the items in Exercise 2 refer to. Then ask them to cover the article in Exercise 1 and write their sentences. Make sure that they cover the article, so that they don't just copy their sentences from it. Allow them to compare results in pairs before checking answers with the class. Sample answers taken from the text are given below, but accept any others that are factually and grammatically correct. Ask the students to compare their answers with those in the text.

> Sample answers
> a) Debra and Andrew Veal entered a 3,000-mile rowing race across the Atlantic.
> b) There were thirty-four other rowing teams.
> c) After two weeks, Andrew left the race because he was frightened of the ocean.
> d) Debra rowed the remaining 2,290 miles alone.
> e) The journey took 113 days.

Listening & Vocabulary (SB page 51)

1 🌐 2.14

- Tell the students that they're going to listen to a radio programme about Debra Veal. Ask them what questions they would like to ask about Debra if they were putting together a programme about her. Prompt them to make questions using *How did she feel when …?*

- Go through the sentences with the students and encourage them to predict what they think the correct information will be.

- Play the recording and ask them to underline the correct information. Then check answers with the class.

> a) wasn't b) was c) was d) wasn't
> e) wasn't f) was

> 🌐 2.14 (I = Interviewer; N = Nelly)
>
> I: *Welcome to this week's edition of 'Heroes'. Today we have the popular television presenter, Nelly B, in the studio. Nelly, hello and welcome.*
> N: *Thank you. It's lovely to be here.*
> I: *Nelly, who is your hero and why?*
> N: *My hero is Debra Veal because she rowed across the Atlantic alone.*
> I: *Alone?! That's amazing! Why did she do it?*
> N: *Well, she started a trans-Atlantic race with her husband, Andrew. But he left after two weeks. He was frightened of the ocean.*
> I: *Oh dear. Was she angry when Andrew left?*
> N: *No, she wasn't angry. She was relieved when he left. She just wanted him to be happy.*
> I: *Was it difficult for Debra to continue the journey alone?*
> N: *Yes, it was difficult for her to sleep. She was worried about big ships. Some ships are enormous and she was in a very small boat.*
> I: *Did she have any bad experiences?*
> N: *Yes. She was frightened of sharks. One night there was a very big shark under the boat – but it wasn't interested in her – it was only interested in eating the fish under the boat.*
> I: *I understand that Debra finished the race seventy days after the winners. How did she feel about that? Was she embarrassed?*
> N: *No, she wasn't embarrassed about it. She was just happy about finishing the race.*
> I: *Well, that's an incredible story. Nelly, thank you so much. Debra Veal is an inspiration. Next week we'll be talking to …*

2 🌐 2.15

- Explain to the students that you use certain prepositions with adjectives when you talk about feelings. Focus their attention on the sentences in Exercise 1 and read out a couple of them, emphasising the prepositions.

- Ask the students to complete the exercise by putting the correct prepositions from the box into the sentences. Check answers by getting individual students to read out their sentences.

- Then play the recording, once as a check and once for the students to listen and repeat.

- Ask the students to tick the sentences that are true for them and to compare their sentences with a partner.

> a) about b) with c) of d) in e) about

Ask the students to make five more sentences using *worried about, angry with, frightened of, interested in* and *embarrassed by*. One of the sentences should be false. They then show their sentences to a partner who has to guess which is the false one.

Reading (SB page 52)

1 🌐 2.16

- Focus the students' attention on the photo and tell them that it's a photo of Greta Garbo. Ask the students if they've heard of Greta Garbo and what, if anything, they know about her.

- Explain to the students that Greta Garbo changed her name more than once. Ask them to listen to the recording, read the text and find out how many times she changed her name.

> She changed her name twice.

2 🌐 2.17

- Give the students time to look back through the article and decide on the correct order of the events in Greta Garbo's life. Point out that the information is in the form of a continuous text, not separate sentences, so they'll have to make sure that the end of one part makes sense when joined to the beginning of the next. The first two have been done for them.

- Play the recording for them to check their answers.

> 1 a   2 f   3 b   4 e   5 g   6 c   7 h
> 8 d

3

- Give the students a few minutes to decide on their favourite Hollywood star and what they know about the person's life.

- Pairwork. Put the students in pairs and ask them to take turns to tell their partner about their chosen Hollywood star. Go round, monitoring and giving help. Take note of any errors which may need particular attention later, and also any examples of good language use which you can praise.

Extra activity

- Write a number of activities on the board, such as *study, drive, do exercise, have lunch, watch TV, go clothes shopping, go on holiday.* Ask the students (working on their own) to copy down the list, and put a tick next to activities they like doing alone, and three ticks next to activities they like doing with other people.

- Draw the following speech bubbles on the board.

  Do you like studying alone?
  Yes, I do.
  No, I don't. I like studying with other people.

  Ask a confident student the question and encourage them to reply with one of the answers.

- Put the students into small groups and ask them to compare and discuss their lists.

Writing (SB page 52)

1

- Explain *retired* and ask the students to think of someone they know who is retired. You might like to use an example of someone you know and tell the students a little about this person's life.

- Focus attention on the prompts in the box and tell the students to use these to write a summary of the life of the person they've chosen. Explain that they don't have to use all the prompts as some may not be relevant. Give them plenty of time to do this (it could also be done for homework and brought to the next class). Go round, monitoring and giving help, and remind them that they can use the summary of Greta Garbo's life in Exercise 2 as a model.

2

- Pairwork. Ask the students to exchange summaries and read each other's.

- Encourage them to ask questions to find out more about the person their partner has written about.

Grammar (SB page 53)

Past simple: affirmative, negative and question forms

1 🌐 2.18

- Focus the students' attention on the information in the margin, which shows the affirmative, negative and question forms of the past simple of *work* and *go*. Point out the note about not using *did* and *didn't* with *be*. Ask the students to make affirmative and negative sentences and questions with *was* and *were*.

- Ask the students to look at the questions and answers and complete them. Point out that they are all questions about their family's past.

- Play the recording for them to check their answers. Then play it again for them to listen and repeat.

> a) 'Did you go to primary school near here?'
>   'Yes, I did.' 'No, I didn't.'
> b) 'Did you walk to school?'
>   'Yes, I did.' 'No, I didn't.'
> c) 'Did you move house when you were a child?'
>   'Yes, I did.' 'No, I didn't.'   ➤

> d) 'Did your father leave school at sixteen?'
>   'Yes, he did.' 'No, he didn't.'
> e) 'Did your mother study English at school?'
>   'Yes, she did.' 'No, she didn't.'
> f) 'Did your parents go to university?'
>   'Yes, they did.' 'No, they didn't.'

2

Pairwork. Put the students in pairs and tell them to take turns asking and answering the questions in Exercise 1.

3 Pairwork

• The pairwork exercise for this unit is on pages 118 and 123 of the Student's Book. Put the students in pairs and tell them who will be Student A, and who will be Student B.

• While they are doing the exercise, go round monitoring and giving help. Take note of any errors which may need particular attention later, and also any examples of good language use which you can praise.

4 *Grammar Extra* 8

Ask students to turn to *Grammar Extra* 8 on page 128 of the Student's Book. Here they'll find an explanation of the grammar they've been studying and further exercises to practise it.

> **1**
> a) I didn't get up late.
> b) I didn't wear jeans.
> c) I didn't do the housework.
> d) I didn't play tennis.
> e) I didn't have lunch with my family.
> f) I didn't go shopping.
> g) I didn't buy a DVD.
> h) I didn't read the newspaper.
>
> **3**
> a) Did you get up late last Sunday?
> b) Did you wear jeans last Sunday?
> c) Did you do the housework last Sunday?
> d) Did you play tennis last Sunday?
> e) Did you have lunch with your family last Sunday?
> f) Did you go shopping last Sunday?
> g) Did you buy a DVD last Sunday?
> h) Did you read the newspaper last Sunday?

Pronunciation (SB page 53)

1 🔘 2.19

• Look at the example with the class. Tell them to ignore the link line for the moment and concentrate on the past simple forms of the verbs. Tell them that all the verbs in the lists are irregular and ask them to complete them with the past simple forms.

• Play the recording for the students to listen and check their answers. Then play it again for them to repeat the verbs. When they've done this chorally, ask individual students to repeat the verbs after you.

> | A | B |
> |---|---|
> | feel – felt | break – broke |
> | know – knew | fly – flew |
> | mean – meant | spell – spelt |
> | see – saw | spend – spent |
> | speak – spoke | teach – taught |
> | think – thought | wear – wore |

2 🔘 2.20

• Focus attention on the line joining *felt* and *spelt*. Say the words aloud and point out that they have the same sound. Ask the students to repeat them after you.

• Tell the students to look at the other past forms which they wrote down in Exercise 1. Tell them that for each of the past forms in column A, there's one in column B which has a similar sound. Ask them to match them. Encourage them to say the words aloud as they do this so that they hear how they sound.

• Play the recording for the students to listen and check their answers. Then play it again for them to repeat the verbs. When they've done this chorally, ask individual students to repeat the verbs after you.

> | felt – spelt | saw – wore |
> |---|---|
> | knew – flew | spoke – broke |
> | meant – spent | thought – taught |

Speaking: anecdote (SB page 53)

For more information about how to set up, monitor and repeat anecdotes, see Practical methodology, page xx in the Introduction.

1 🔘 2.21

• Tell the students that they're going to listen to a woman called Lottie talking about her last summer holiday. Go through the information with the class. Play the recording and ask them to listen and underline the correct information.

• Allow the students to compare notes in pairs before checking answers with the class.

> | a) to the beach | e) in a hotel |
> |---|---|
> | b) in July | f) two weeks |
> | c) alone | g) went to the beach |
> | d) by plane and by car | h) went to the bars and clubs |

🔵 10 (F = Frank; L = Lottie)

F: I don't know where to go on holiday this year. Where did you go for your last summer holiday?

L: I went to the beach – to Tarifa in the south of Spain.

F: Oh, lovely. When did you go there?

L: Um, in July.

F: Nice. Who did you go with?

L: I went alone. I always go on holiday alone.

F: Oh, right. … How did you get there?

L: I went by plane and by car. I flew from London to Malaga, and then I drove from Malaga to Tarifa. There's a really good motorway.

F: Great. Where did you stay?

L: In a hotel – the Hurricane Hotel. Do you know it?

F: No – what's it like?

L: Fantastic. The rooms are wonderful. And it's near the beach.

F: Mm, you are lucky. How long did you stay?

L: Just two weeks, unfortunately.

F: Oh, well. So what did you do all day?

L: I went to the beach, of course – you can do everything there. I tried kite surfing – it's amazing.

F: Wow – and what did you do in the evening?

L: I went out to the bars and clubs. There's a lot to do in Tarifa.

F: Mm, and did you meet anybody nice?

L: Well, yes, I did actually. He's a windsurfing instructor, and the first time we went out …

Language note

Grammar: questions with *Who*

- Students have already seen the questions *Who started the race?*, etc. on page 51 of the Student's Book. Now they see the question *Who did you go with?* and may ask why this question uses *did* and not the first.

- If a question word (i.e. *who*) is the subject of the question, you don't use *do*, *does* or *did*. Compare:
  Who went to the party? (*Who* is the subject)
  Who did you go with? (*Who* is the object – *you* is the subject)
  Who saw him? (*Who* is the subject)
  Who did he see? (*Who* is the object – *he* is the subject)

2

- Pairwork. Tell the students that they're going to tell a partner about their last summer holiday. Give them a moment or two to think back and visualise this holiday. Then ask the students to go through the questions in Exercise 1, making the answers true for their last summer holiday. Ask them to work individually to do this.

- Tell the students to think about the language they want to use when they talk about their holidays and to make notes. Remind them of the work they've done on expressing feelings, and encourage them to include some of this language in their notes. Remind them too that they'll be talking about something that happened in the past, and to note down the past simple forms of any verbs that they want to use. Discourage them from writing whole sentences so that when it comes to the pairwork, they don't simply read out their notes.

- Put the students in pairs and ask them to take turns telling their partner about their holidays. Tell them that they can use their notes to help them, but they shouldn't just read from the paper. Encourage them to maintain eye contact with their partner as they speak.

Useful phrases (SB page 54)

1 🔵 2.22

- Focus the students' attention on the pictures and give them time to take in what is happening in them. Ask the students to say how they think each person feels.

- Play the recording and ask the students to read the conversations and match them with the pictures.

- Check answers with the class.

a) 3	b) 1	c) 4	d) 2

Extra activity

You could then ask several pairs of confident students to read and act out the conversations for the class. Encourage them to copy the intonation on the recording and play the parts in character.

Language notes

Grammar: *I like* versus *I'd like*

In conversation a), the man says *I'd like a beer* (= *I would like a beer*). So far, students have only learnt *I like* for talking about likes and dislikes, and may find this confusing. Explain that *I'd like …* is one way of asking for something. In this sentence, the man doesn't mean that he likes beer, but that he wants one.

Vocabulary: *Let's*

- In conversation a), the woman says *Let's have a nice cup of tea.* and in conversation d), the wife says *Let's stay at home tonight.*

- *Let us* (formal) or *Let's* (informal) is used to make a suggestion which includes the speaker.

- *Why don't you …?* is used to make a suggestion which is only for the other person.

2 🔊 2.23

• Play the recording and ask the students to repeat the phrases. Point out that *Why don't you ...?* is used to suggest that other people should do things, and that *Let's ...* is an invitation to do things together.

• Then play the recording again and ask several students to repeat the phrases individually.

3 🔊 2.24

Ask the students to work on their own to complete the conversations. Allow them to compare results in pairs before playing the recording for them to check their answers. Play it a second time for them to repeat the sentences.

a) I'm bored.	d) I'm hungry.
b) I'm hungry.	e) I'm thirsty.
c) I'm tired.	f) I'm bored.

4

• Pairwork. Go through the ideas in the box and ask the students to think of situations in which people might say these things. Then put them in pairs to write new conversations similar to those in Exercise 1. Explain that they can use the ideas in the box, or they can make up their own if they prefer. Go round, monitoring and giving help with vocabulary.

• When the students have written their conversations, ask them to practise them, taking turns to play the different roles. Ask several pairs to perform their conversations for the class.

Vocabulary *Extra* (SB page 55)
Feelings

1

• Focus the students' attention on the list of phrases and point out that they're all to do with feelings. Check that the students can pronounce the adjectives.

• Ask the students to look at the pictures and match each one with one of the phrases. Point out that the first one has been done for them.

(See Exercise 2 for answers.)

2

Ask the students to match the sentence beginnings from Exercise 1 with their sentence endings. Point out that the first sentence has been done for them.

4–f)	She's angry with her son.
6–h)	She's bored with her job.
3–a)	He's embarrassed about his body.
7–c)	They're excited about their holiday.
1–g)	He's frightened of dogs.
5–e)	She's very interested in horses.
2–d)	She's sad about going.
8–b)	He's worried about the future.

1

• Focus the students' attention on the list of phrases and point out that they're all to do with the weather. Check that the students can pronounce the weather words correctly.

• Ask the students to look at the pictures and match each one with one of the phrases. Point out that the first one has been done for them.

6 It's cloudy.	5 It's cold.	3 It's foggy.
1 It's hot.	7 It's raining.	4 It's snowing.
8 It's sunny.	2 It's windy.	

2

Ask the students to describe the weather today, using the phrases from Exercise 1.

Further practice material

Need more writing practice?

→ Workbook page 35
• Describing a holiday

Need more classroom practice activities?

→ Photocopiable resource materials pages 173 to 175
  Grammar: *I think ...*
  Vocabulary: *How do you feel?*
  Communication: *Last summer, I ...*
→ TOP 10 activities pages xv to xx

Need DVD material?

→ DVD – Programme 4: *Bob Marley*

Need progress tests?

→ Test CD – *Test Unit 8*

Need more on important teaching concepts?

→ Key concepts in *New Inside Out* pages xxii to xxxv

Need student self-study practice?

→ CD-ROM – Unit 8: *Alone*

Need student CEF self-evaluation?

→ CEF Checklists pages xxxvii to xliv

Need more information and more ideas?

→ www.insideout.net

Before the next lesson ...

Find some pictures that show the contents of rooms from magazine, newspapers or holiday brochures and bring to class for Grammar Exercise 3 on page 61.

Review B *Teacher's notes*

These exercises act as a check of the grammar and vocabulary that the students have learnt in Units 5–8. Use them to find any problems that students are having or anything that they haven't understood and which will need further work.

Grammar (SB page 56)

Remind the students of the grammar explanations they read and the exercises they did in the *Grammar Extra* on pages 128 and 129.

1

This exercise reviews the language of daily routines from Unit 5.

> a) work   b) goes   c) live   d) does
> e) get up   f) has
>
> a) I don't work from 9.00 a.m. to 5.00 p.m.
> b) My mother doesn't go to the supermarket on Fridays.
> c) We don't live near the station.
> d) Sue doesn't do exercise after work.
> e) John and Ella don't get up early in the morning.
> f) Pete doesn't have breakfast at work.

2

This exercise reviews different ways of telling the time from Unit 5.

> a) 4   b) 6   c) 2   d) 5   e) 1   f) 3

3

This exercise reviews adverbs of frequency from Unit 6.

> 1 always   2 usually   3 often   4 sometimes
> 5 hardly ever   6 never

4

This exercise reviews adverbs of frequency and their position in a sentence from Unit 6. Check answers before moving on to the second part of the exercise.

> a) I sometimes have a nap at work.
> b) I never make long phone calls.
> c) I always make my bed.
> d) I hardly ever listen to reggae.
> e) I often go to the gym.
> f) I usually have dinner with my family.

5

This exercise reviews prepositions of time from Unit 6.

> at: 8.15, night, eleven o'clock, the weekend
> in: the evening, 1997, the summer, July, the morning
> on: Wednesday, 10th March, Thursday morning
> last: Wednesday, night, July, Thursday morning

6

This exercise reviews the past simple from Unit 7. Check answers with the class before moving on to the next exercise.

> 1 asked   2 had   3 sat   4 wasn't   5 went
> 6 saw   7 thought   8 jumped   9 lost
> 10 saved

7

This exercise reviews the formation of past simple questions from Unit 8. Check that the students have formed all the questions correctly before putting them in pairs to take turns asking and answering the questions.

> a) When did Ron and Lulu go to the beach?
> b) Who sat on Lulu's sunglasses?
> c) What did Lulu do in the afternoon?
> d) Who saw something in the water?
> e) What did Ron lose?
> f) Who saved Ron?

> **Answers to questions**
> a) Last Saturday.   d) Ron.
> b) Ron.   e) He lost his glasses.
> c) She went swimming.   f) A lifeguard.

8

This exercise reviews structures used in Units 5 to 8.

> 1 a) ~~It twelve o'clock.~~
> 2 a) ~~He work with me.~~
> 3 b) ~~What time you go to bed?~~
> 4 b) ~~I saw that film the last week.~~
> 5 a) ~~We go to town yesterday.~~
> 6 b) ~~Did you were there on Monday?~~

Vocabulary (SB page 57)

1

This exercise reviews the days of the week from Unit 5. When checking answers, make sure that the students can pronounce the words correctly, paying particular attention to *Wednesday* /ˈwenzdɪ/.

> a) Monday   b) Sunday   c) Wednesday
> d) Friday   e) Tuesday   f) Saturday
> g) Thursday

2

This exercise reviews daily routines used with the verbs *have* and *go* from Unit 5.

> a) have breakfast   f) go home
> b) go to work   g) have dinner
> c) go shopping   h) have a shower
> d) have lunch   i) have a good time
> e) go on the internet   j) go to bed

3

This exercise reviews dates from Unit 6. When you've checked answers, make sure all the students can pronounce the months and the dates correctly.

> a) the sixth of January
> b) the twenty-second of February
> c) the fifteenth of March
> d) the fifth of April
> e) the twelfth of May
> f) the twenty-third of June
> g) the first of July
> h) the twenty-fourth of August
> i) the twentieth of September
> j) the seventeenth of October
> k) the eighth of November
> l) the thirty-first of December

4

This exercise reviews activities with *make* and *do*. Check answers before putting the students into pairs to take turns asking questions about these activities. Remind the students to use *last, on, in* and *at*.

> a) do   b) make   c) do   d) do   e) make
> f) do   g) make   h) do

5

This exercise reviews words used to talk about feelings from Unit 8.

> a) happy   b) bored   c) angry   d) excited
> e) frightened   f) embarrassed   g) sad
> h) worried   i) nervous

6

This exercise reviews water sports vocabulary from Unit 7.

> a) fishing   b) kite surfing   c) sailing
> d) scuba diving   e) surfing   f) swimming
> g) windsurfing

Pronunciation (SB page 57)

These two exercises review work students did on word stress, using words they met in Units 5–8.

1

Remind the students that the boxes show the syllables of a word and the large boxes indicate the stressed syllables. Read the example words in the table aloud so that the students can hear the stress clearly. Tell them that they should complete the table by classifying the words according to how many syllables each one has and where the main stress falls. Encourage them to say each word aloud to get a feeling for what sounds right.

> (See Exercise 2 for answers.)

2 🌐 2.25

Point out the main stresses in the example words which are underlined. Ask the students to do the same for the other words in the table. Play the recording for them to check their answers. Then play it again for them to listen and repeat the words.

> 1 and 2
> A: <u>Au</u>gust, <u>break</u>fast, <u>frigh</u>tened, <u>ner</u>vous, <u>Thurs</u>day
> B: <u>ex</u>ercise, <u>in</u>ternet, <u>Sa</u>turday, <u>ter</u>rible, <u>u</u>sually
> C: em<u>ba</u>rrassed, ex<u>ci</u>ted, No<u>vem</u>ber, Oc<u>to</u>ber, Sep<u>tem</u>ber

Reading & Listening (SB page 58)

1

Pairwork. Put the students in pairs to discuss the question. Give them plenty of time to do this and then ask them to report back to the class on the results of their discussion.

2 🌐 2.26

Give the students a few minutes to look at the photos and take in what they see in them. Then ask them to read the article as you play the recording and to decide how to match the two sets of photos. Ask them if they find any of the information in the article surprising.

> a) 3   b) 1   c) 2

Angelina Jolie (born 1975)
(See notes about Angelina Jolie in Unit 2, page 11.)

Bono (born 1960)
Bono is the lead singer of the Irish rock band U2. He performed in the original Band Aid in 1984, in 1985 at Live Aid, and at Live 8 in 2005. He also campaigns for third-world debt relief, and in raising awareness about the problems of Africa.

Sean Penn (born 1960)
Sean Penn is one of Hollywood's most talented and controversial actors. He's admired for films such as *Dead Man Walking* (1995), *Sweet and Lowdown* (1999) and *Mystic River* (2003). He's also drawn much media attention for his stormy relationships, most notably his marriage to Madonna, and for his political views.

Hurricane Katrina, New Orleans (2005)
Hurricane Katrina was a category 5 hurricane, and was the deadliest and most costly hurricane in the history of the US. At least 1,836 people lost their lives, and the storm is estimated to have cost $81.2 billion in damage. It was the sixth-strongest Atlantic hurricane ever recorded and the third strongest one to reach land in the US. It devastated the Gulf coast as far as 100 miles from the centre of the storm.

UNICEF /'juːnisef/
UNICEF or the United Nations Children's Fund works for the rights of children throughout the world.

Live 8
Live 8 was a series of ten simultaneous music concerts around the world. The concerts took place in July 2005. More than 1,000 musicians performed at the concerts.

3

Tell the students to read the article again and complete the sentences with the information in the box.

a) UNICEF   b) time   c) 1979   d) Live 8
e) New Orleans   f) boat

4 🌐 2.27

Ask students to look at the photo and describe what they see. Tell them a little about David Walliams and explain that he did a swim to raise money for charity. Then play the recording and ask the students to complete the sentence with the name of the country.

France

🌐 **2.27**

This is the news for Tuesday, 4th July 2006.

This morning, actor and writer, David Walliams, walked into the sea at Dover in the south of England. At 5.30 a.m. David started his swim across the English Channel. Greg Whyte, his trainer, followed him in a boat and gave him bananas and chocolate. David Walliams swam 34 kilometres from Dover to Calais in France. The swim took 10 hours and 30 minutes. The sea was cold – 15 degrees centigrade, but David didn't have any problems and arrived in Calais at 4.00 p.m. He was very happy to finish so quickly.

David made more than £1 million for the charity, Sport Relief. The money goes to help poor children all over the world.

David Walliams (born 1971)

David Walliams is an English comedy actor. He appears with fellow comedian Matt Lucas in the British TV comedy show *Little Britain*, which became a huge success in the UK in 2003.

5

Ask the students to read the choices before they listen again so they know what kind of things they should be looking out for.

a) trainer   b) 34   c) 10 hours 30 minutes
d) 4.00 p.m.   e) happy   f) £1,000,000

Writing & Speaking (SB page 59)

1

Ask the students to read the text and the notes and then match the notes with the questions.

a) 3   b) 1   c) 6   d) 5   e) 2   f) 4

2

Put the students in pairs to read the notes and complete the story. Remind them that the notes are prompts to help them find the missing words; they may not always be the missing words themselves.

1 two years ago   2 Rome   3 Italy   4 sunny
5 my boyfriend   6 dancing competition
7 won   8 tired

3

Remind the students of the two sets of notes they've looked at in the previous exercises and to model their notes on these. Tell the students that they can use the photos at the bottom of the page for inspiration if they wish.

4

Give the students plenty of time to write their stories. Remind them of the texts they've just read on memorable days and go round, monitoring and helping. When the students have finished, ask them to exchange texts with a partner. Ask them to check each other's work. You could display the texts in the classroom for everyone to read.

Further practice material

Need more classroom practice activities?

→ Photocopiable resource materials page 176

   🔊 2.28

   Song: *Don't Worry, Be Happy*

→ TOP 10 activities pages xv to xx

Need progress tests?

→ Test CD – *Test Review B*

Need more on important teaching concepts?

→ Key concepts in *New Inside Out* pages xxii to xxxv

Need student self-study practice?

→ CD-ROM – *Review B*

Need more information and more ideas?

→ www.insideout.net

9 Hotel *Overview*

Section	Aims	What the students are doing
🌐 Reading & Listening SB page 60	*Reading skills*: reading for specific information *Listening skills*: listening for specific information	• Reading and listening to an article about two hotels. • Matching sentences with the correct hotel. • Talking about favourite hotels.
🌐 Vocabulary SB page 61	*Vocabulary*: rooms and furniture	• Matching words with pictures. • Talking about what furniture you find in various rooms.
🌐 Grammar SB page 61	*Grammar*: *there is/there are; some/any*	• Completing sentences about things in a hotel room. • Writing sentences about a hotel room.
🌐 Vocabulary SB page 62	*Vocabulary*: prepositions of place	• Matching beginnings and endings of sentences to describe the location of things. • Completing sentences about their homes. • Discussing the location of things in their homes.
🌐 Grammar SB page 62	*Grammar*: *Is/Are there …*	• Completing questions and answers with *there is* and *there are*. • Asking and answering questions.
🌐 Pronunciation SB page 62	*Pronunciation*: silent letters	• Practising saying words with silent letters.
🌐 Vocabulary SB page 63	*Vocabulary*: prepositions of place	• Circling the prepositions they hear. • Writing sentences about where they live.
🌐 Reading SB page 63	*Reading skills*: reading for detail	• Completing horoscopes with prepositions. • Discussing horoscopes.
🌐 Useful phrases SB page 64	*Vocabulary*: phrases which are useful when complaining in a hotel	• Listening to three conversations and identifying problems. • Listening and repeating useful phrases. • Writing and practising new hotel conversations.
Vocabulary *Extra* SB page 65	*Vocabulary*: revision of words from the unit: houses. Focus on prepositions of place (2)	• Matching pictures with words.
Writing WB page 39	Describing your home and the area near it	

9 Hotel *Teacher's notes*

Warm-up

- Write the word *hotel* on the board. Ask the students what a hotel is like and put any ideas they come up with on the board.
- Find out when the students last stayed in a hotel and if they can describe it.

Reading & Listening (SB page 60)

1 🌐 2.29

- Focus the students' attention on the pictures. Give them a moment or two to think about what they show. Then ask them to read the two hotel descriptions.
- Tell the students to match the names of the hotels to the descriptions, and ask them what information they used to help them decide which hotel was which. Go through any difficult vocabulary with the class.
- Play the recording for them to listen and check. Point out the pronunciation of *Palm*: /pɑːm/. Ask them to repeat it and make sure that they aren't pronouncing the letter *l*. They'll be doing more work on words with silent letters later in this unit.

> 1 Little Palm Island
> 2 The Emirates Palace Hotel

Cultural notes

The Little Palm Island Resort

- The Little Palm Island Resort is on one on the many islands that makes up the Florida Keys in the United States.

The Emirates Palace Hotel

- Opened in 2005, the Emirates Palace Hotel is in Abu Dhabi in the United Arab Emirates.

2 🌐 2.30

- Go through the instructions with the class, then ask them to go through the sentences one by one and decide which hotel it refers to. Allow them to compare in pairs or small groups before playing the recording for them to check their answers.
- Check once more with the class before asking for a show of hands to find out which hotel the students prefer.

> a) L   b) E   c) E   d) L   e) E   f) L

🌐 2.30

The Little Palm Island is exclusive. There isn't a road to the hotel: guests arrive by boat or seaplane. Come here for total peace and quiet. There aren't any phones or televisions, and there aren't any children – sixteen is the minimum age.

The Emirates Palace Hotel offers you excellent service. There are 2,600 employees – that's four for every guest in the hotel. The rooms are beautiful and well-equipped. There are 1,000 crystal chandeliers, and there's a 125-centimetre plasma TV in every room.

3

Pairwork. Ask the students to think of their favourite hotel and to tell a partner about it. Go round, monitoring and giving help. Encourage the students to report back to the class on what they learnt.

Vocabulary (SB page 61)

Rooms and furniture

1 🌐 2.31

- Ask the students to look at the pictures and match them with the words in the box.
- Go round, monitoring and giving help. Allow the students to compare in pairs before playing the recording for them to check their answers. Play it a second time for them to repeat and ask for individual repetition of difficult words such as *cushion* /ˈkʊʃən/, *cupboard* /ˈkʌbəd/ and *mirror* /ˈmɪrə/. Again, you might like to point out the silent letters in *cupboard* and tell the students that they'll be doing more work on words with silent letters later. You could also take this opportunity to explain to the students the difference between a *cook* (someone who cooks) and a *cooker* (the apparatus on which they cook).

> a) a lamp   b) a bath   c) plants
> d) a mirror   e) curtains   f) a cooker
> g) an armchair   h) a bookcase   i) a shower
> j) a rug   k) a fridge   l) a sofa
> m) cushions   n) a carpet   o) a cupboard
> p) a washbasin   q) a coffee table   r) a desk

2

- Focus the students' attention on the names of four rooms and make sure everyone understands what they are. Demonstrate the activity by asking the class to call out things that you can usually find in a bathroom. Allow them to add things which are not in Exercise 1 if they wish. Put any new vocabulary items on the board. Emphasise that there are no fixed answers. For example, in some cultures you would never see a carpet in a bathroom; in others, this is quite common.

- Then ask them to complete the exercise by saying which things they would find in the other three rooms.

> *Possible answers:*
> a) a bathroom: a bath, a carpet, a cupboard, curtains, a mirror, plants, a shower, a washbasin
> b) a living room: an armchair, a bookcase, a carpet, a coffee table, a cupboard, curtains, cushions, a desk, a lamp, a mirror, plants, a rug, a sofa
> c) a kitchen: a cooker, a cupboard, a fridge, plants
> d) a bedroom: an armchair, a bookcase, a carpet, a cupboard, curtains, cushions, a desk, a lamp, a mirror, plants, a rug

Extra activity

Put the students in teams and give them five minutes to list other things that they would find in the rooms of a house. At the end of the time limit, the team with the most items wins.

Language note

Vocabulary: *living room*

A living room is the room in the house where people sit together and relax, but in general, don't eat. It's also called the sitting room or lounge.

Grammar (SB page 61)

there is / there are; some / any

1

- Focus the students' attention on the four sentences in the margin and point out that two are singular and two are plural. Explain that you use *there is a/an* to talk about single things that are present in a room, and *there isn't a/an* to talk about things that aren't present in a room. You use *there are + some* to talk about plural things in affirmative statements, and *there aren't + any* to talk about plural things in negative statements. Give a few examples of things in your classroom to demonstrate, e.g. *There is a board. There isn't a carpet. There are some students. There are some chairs. There aren't any cushions.*

- Focus the students' attention on the photo. Ask them to look at it closely and decide which hotel it is. Remind them of the descriptions of the two hotels they looked at on page 60.

> In the Emirates Palace Hotel.

2 🌐 **2.32**

- Now ask the students to look closely at the photo again and complete the sentences with the words in the box.

- Allow students to compare answers in pairs before playing the recording for them to check. Play it a second time for them to repeat the sentences.

> a) There's a bed.
> b) There isn't a bookcase.
> c) There are some curtains.
> d) There aren't any clocks.

3

- Now ask the students to write more sentences about the hotel room in the photo using the sentence beginnings in Exercise 2. Go round, monitoring and giving help. Make sure everyone is using *there is / there are* and *some/any* correctly.

- Ask several students to read their sentences aloud to the class. Ask the others if they agree with them.

Extra activities

- Give extra practice in describing the contents of rooms by bringing in pictures of rooms from magazines, newspapers or holiday brochures, and asking the students to say what there is and what there isn't in these rooms.

- Ask the students to write sentences about what there is/isn't and are/aren't in their ideal hotel room.

Language notes

Grammar: *some/any*

- In this unit, students practise *there is* and *there are* to talk about things that exist. They use *there are* followed by *some* + a plural noun in affirmative sentences, and *Are there* and *There aren't* followed by *any* + a plural noun in questions and negative sentences. At this level, it's probably not appropriate to go into any more detail on the uses of *some* and *any*.

- Students may come across the phrase *Would you like some tea?* It would appear to contradict the rule that the students have studied here, i.e. that *some* is used in affirmative sentences, *any* in negatives and questions. In fact, *some* is used in situations where the question isn't a real question, but a request or an invitation and the answer *yes* is expected. Encourage students to learn these as complete phrases.

Vocabulary (SB page 62)

1 ⊕ 2.33

- Point out the sentence beginnings (a–f) and the sentence endings in the box. The sentence beginnings are similar to sentences they worked with in the previous section. The sentence endings contain prepositions of place which are used to say the exact location of things. Focus the students' attention on the example and ask them to find the lamp in the photo. Explain that it's *in the corner* of the room.
- Demonstrate the prepositions of place, if necessary, using objects in your own classroom, moving things onto desks, under desks, etc. to show the various locations. Then ask the students to study the photo and match the beginnings and endings of the sentences.
- Play the recording and ask the students to check their answers. Then play it a second time for them to listen and repeat.

a) There's a rug on the floor.
b) There's a lamp in the corner.
c) There's a magazine under the coffee table.
d) There's a plant next to the sofa.
e) There are some cushions on the sofa.
f) There are some pictures on the wall, above the sofa.

Extra activity

Ask the students to work on their own to complete the following sentences. *There are ____ clocks. There are ____ mirrors. There are ____ phones. There are ____ plants. There are ____ televisions. There are ____ lamps.* Make it clear that they are to base their answers on the number of things in their own homes, and to think carefully about this as they'll need to expand on the information in Exercise 2.

2

- Pairwork. Focus the students' attention on the example. Read it out to the class. Tell them to take turns describing the location of things in their homes.
- Go round, monitoring and giving help. Ask several students to report back to the class on what they learnt about their partner's house.

Extra activity

Make various false statements about where things are in your classroom, such as *The board is next to the door*, *The computer is under the table*, etc. and invite students to correct you.

Grammar (SB page 62)

Is / Are there …?

1 ⊕ 2.34

- Focus the students' attention on the information in the margin and remind them that they've just studied affirmative and negative statements with *there is* and *there are*. Tell them that in this section the two question forms have been added and point out the use of *any* with plural questions.
- Ask the students to work on their own to complete the questions and answers.
- Allow them to compare results in pairs or small groups before playing the recording for them to check. Play it a second time for them to repeat the sentences. Point out that in the questions, it's most often the noun that is stressed.

a) 'Is there a computer in your living room?'
  'Yes, there is.' 'No, there isn't.'
b) 'Are there any plants in your kitchen?'
  'Yes, there are.' 'No, there aren't.'
c) 'Are there any pictures in your bedroom?'
  'Yes, there are.' 'No, there aren't.'
d) 'Is there a carpet in your bathroom?'
  'Yes, there is.' 'No, there isn't.'
e) 'Is there a television in your bathroom?'
  'Yes, there is.' 'No, there isn't.'
f) 'Are there any cushions in your bedroom?'
  'Yes, there are.' 'No, there aren't.'

Language note

Grammar: questions with *Are there some …?*

Note that in some circumstances it's possible to ask questions using *some* (generally when the speaker is confident of an affirmative response), but these aren't presented at this level.

2

- Pairwork. Demonstrate the activity with a confident student. Ask the first question and encourage the student to reply truthfully. Then put the students in pairs to take turns asking and answering the questions.

3 *Grammar Extra* 9

Ask students to turn to *Grammar Extra* 9 on page 130 of the Student's Book. Here they'll find an explanation of the grammar they've been studying and further exercises to practise it.

1	2
a) some	a) There aren't any shops.
b) a	b) There isn't a hotel.
c) some	c) There aren't any bars.
d) an	d) There isn't an Italian restaurant.
e) a	e) There isn't a park.
f) some	f) There aren't any trees.

4 Pairwork

- The pairwork exercise for this unit is on pages 118 and 123 of the Student's Book. Put the students in pairs and tell them who will be Student A, and who will be Student B.

- While they are doing the exercise, go round monitoring and giving help. Take note of any errors which may need particular attention later, and also any examples of good language use which you can praise.

Pronunciation (SB page 62)

1 🌐 2.35

Focus the students' attention on the words in the box and point out that some of the consonants are printed in red. Ask the students to listen to the recording and decide whether these letters are pronounced or not. Play the recording for them to listen and repeat. When they've done this chorally, ask individual students to repeat the words after you, and make sure that no one is trying to pronounce the silent letters. Also check that they know all the words – they may not know *receipt* (a document you receive to show that you have paid a bill).

No.

Extra activity

Ask the students if they can remember any other words they've learnt in earlier units that have silent letters. They may remember *daughter, Wednesday, half, know, lawyer, night,* etc.

2

- Ask the students to practise saying the words in pairs.

Vocabulary (SB page 63)

Prepositions of place

1 🌐 2.36

- Ask the students to look at the pictures in the margin. Remind them that they looked at some prepositions of place earlier in the unit, when they were talking about the location of furniture within rooms. Ask them to circle the correct prepositions.

- Go round, monitoring and giving help. Allow the students to compare in pairs before playing the recording for them to check their answers. Play it a second time for them to repeat and ask for individual repetition.

- You may need to explain why you say *I live on a hill* but *I live in the mountains.* In the first sentence, the meaning is literally *on* – the house is on a hill. In the second, because *mountains* is plural, the meaning is *among* – the house is in a mountainous area, surrounded by mountains.

---

a) in   b) on   c) near   d) in   e) in
f) on   g) near   h) in   i) on   j) on
k) near   l) near

2

- Ask the students to work on their own to write their three sentences. Go round, monitoring and giving help. Then ask them to compare their sentences with a partner.

Reading (SB page 63)

1 🌐 2.37

- Ask the students if they know what star sign they were born under. Go through the horoscope and do some practice of dates. Ask a confident student when their birthday is and then say *Oh, you're (Taurus),* etc. Students can then do the same in pairs.

- Ask the students to complete the horoscope text with prepositions. Do the first couple with them as an example, and then ask them to complete the exercise. Go round, monitoring and giving help. Allow the students to compare in pairs before playing the recording for them to check their answers.

---

1 in   2 on   3 near   4 near   5 in   6 on
7 near   8 in   9 on   10 in   11 on
12 near

2

Groupwork. Put the students in small groups and ask them to discuss the descriptions of their star signs, answering the questions in the book. Encourage them to report back to the rest of the class in a feedback session.

Useful phrases (SB page 64)

1 🌐 2.38

- The phone conversations here all take place in a hotel between a hotel receptionist and a hotel guest. First, focus the students' attention on the pictures and give them time to take in what they see.

- Play the recording and ask the students to read the conversations as they listen. Then ask them to say what the problems are.

- Play the recording again for a final check.

---

a) The television doesn't work.
b) There aren't any towels in the bathroom.
c) The shower doesn't work. There isn't any hot water for the bath.

Language note

Vocabulary: *work*

The students have seen the verb *work,* meaning what people do to earn a living. Here it's used to mean to function or operate.

2 🔘 **2.39**

- Point out where the useful phrases appear in the conversations in Exercise 1. Ask the students who says each one.
- Play the recording and ask the students to listen and repeat the phrases. Then ask several students to repeat the phrases individually.
- Put the students in pairs to practise the conversations.

3

- Pairwork. Put the students into pairs and ask them to write similar conversations, using the problems from the box, or ones they've thought of themselves. Go round, giving help and encouragement.
- When the students have finished, ask them to practise their conversations. As you monitor this, take note of any particularly good ones that can be performed for the class. When groups perform for the class, encourage them to act out the situation sitting back to back, pretending to hold telephones.

Vocabulary *Extra* (SB page 65)

Houses

1

- Focus the students' attention on the list of words and point out that they're all to do with things in a house. Remind students that the underlining indicates the syllable of the word that has the strongest stress. Check that the students can pronounce the words correctly.
- Ask students to look at the pictures and match each one with one of the words. Point out that the first one has been done for them.
- Then ask the students to name the four rooms in the house.

23	an armchair	14	a floor
3	a bath	13	a fridge
6	a bed	5	a lamp
21	a bookcase	15	a mirror
8	a carpet	4	a picture
10	a clock	9	a plant
20	a coffee table	19	a rug
12	a cooker	1	a shower
11	a cupboard	17	a sofa
7	a curtains	16	a wall
18	a cushion	2	a washbasin
22	a desk		

a) bathroom   b) bedroom   c) kitchen
d) living room

2

Pairwork. Demonstrate the activity with a confident student. Cover the words, point to one of the pictures and ask *What this?* Elicit the answer. Then put the students into pairs to continue the activity. Go round, checking that everyone is pronouncing the items correctly.

Focus on prepositions of place (1)

1

- Focus the students' attention on the prepositions in the table. Point out the words that go with them.
- Ask the students to work individually and complete the table with the words from the box. Ask for choral and individual repetition to check that they're pronouncing the words correctly.

1	a village	4	the top floor
2	the country	5	a park
3	an island	6	the shops

2

Ask students to look back at the phases in Exercise 1 and tell their partner which phrases are true for them.

Further practice material

Need more writing practice?

→ Workbook page 39
- Describing your home and the area near it

Need more classroom practice activities?

→ Photocopiable resource materials pages 177 to 179
   Grammar: *Spot the different*
   Vocabulary: *Where are they?*
   Communication: *In my room …*
→ TOP 10 activities pages xv to xx

Need DVD material?

→ DVD – Programme 5: *Unusual hotels*

Need progress tests?

→ Test CD – *Test Unit 9*

Need more on important teaching concepts?

→ Key concepts in *New Inside Out* pages xxii to xxxv

Need student self-study practice?

→ CD-ROM – Unit 9: *Hotel*

Need student CEF self-evaluation?

→ CEF Checklists pages xxxvii to xliv

Need more information and more ideas?

→ www.insideout.net

10 Food *Overview*

Section	Aims	What the students are doing
Vocabulary **SB page 66**	*Vocabulary*: food	• Matching names of food groups to photos. • Completing lists of food. • Categorising food according to personal preferences.
Pronunciation **SB page 67**	*Pronunciation*: sound discrimination	• Circling words with different sounds.
Grammar **SB page 67**	*Grammar*: countable and uncountable nouns	• Completing tables with countable and uncountable food nouns. • Completing questions and answers about food. • Asking and answering about food items in photos.
Speaking **SB page 67**	*Conversation skills*: talking about food	• Making shopping lists and playing a guessing game about a partner's list.
Reading & Listening **SB page 68**	*Reading skills*: reading for specific information *Listening skills*: listening for specific information	• Reading an article about an unusual diet and completing sentences. • Identifying the correct food category to lose weight according to the article. • Listening to a conversation to check answers.
Writing & Speaking **SB page 68**	*Writing skills*: writing menus *Conversation skills*: fluency work	• Discussing and writing menus using rules learnt in the previous section.
Grammar **SB page 69**	*Grammar*: *How much ...?* and *How many ...?*	• Completing questions and answers with *How much ...?* and *How many ...?* and countable and uncountable nouns. • Talking about the contents of their fridge.
Speaking: anecdote **SB page 69**	*Conversation skills*: fluency work	• Listening to a description of a meal and underlining the correct information. • Talking about a delicious meal.
Useful phrases **SB page 70**	*Vocabulary*: phrases which are useful when buying food in a shop	• Listening to a conversation and answering questions. • Completing the conversation. • Listening and repeating useful phrases. • Writing and practising a new food shop conversation.
Vocabulary *Extra* **SB page 71**	*Vocabulary*: revision of words from the unit: food. Focus on prepositions of place (2)	• Matching pictures with words.
Writing **WB page 43**	Writing an invitation	

Warm-up

- Revise food vocabulary by playing a game. Tell the students, for example, *Every day for lunch I have pasta*. Ask a student to repeat your sentence and to add a food item of their own, e.g. *Every day for lunch I have pasta and salad*. The next student adds a third food item, and so on. If students don't have enough vocabulary to do this, you could brainstorm some food items to begin with.

- When the students have finished the unit, play the game again to see how many of the food items they can remember from the unit.

Vocabulary (SB page 66)

1

Read out the four words in the box and make sure that the students can pronounce them. Be especially careful with *vegetables* /ˈvedʒtəbəlz/. They should have no difficulty matching the words *fruit* and *vegetables* to the photos. *Proteins* and *carbohydrates* may present more problems so make sure students have understood these terms when checking answers. Perhaps ask them to suggest further items for these lists.

> a) Proteins   b) Vegetables   c) Fruit
> d) Carbohydrates

2 🌐 2.40

- Ask the students to use the words in the box to complete the lists in Exercise 1.

- Play the recording for them to check their answers. Then check the answers with the class and ask the students to suggest one more item of their own for each list.

- Play the recording again for them to listen and repeat. When they've done this chorally, ask individual students to repeat some of the food words after you. Be careful with *cauliflower* /ˈkɒlɪflaʊə/.

> a) fish   c) bananas, apples
> b) carrots, onions, olive oil   d) rice, pasta

Extra activity

Put the students in pairs and ask them to take turns calling out the name of a food. Their partner responds with the name of the list it is in.

Language notes

Vocabulary: fruit and vegetables

- Technically, tomatoes and olives are fruit, but most people regard them as vegetables because of the way they're used (cooked or in salads rather than used as desserts). Olive oil, because it's considered to come from a vegetable, is in the vegetable category.

- Although potatoes are vegetables, when talking about food groups they tend to be put in the carbohydrate or starch category.

3

- Go through the categories with the whole class and make sure that everyone understands. Remind the students that they studied adverbs of frequency in Unit 6. Ask them to work on their own to create their lists.

- Put the students in pairs to compare and discuss their answers.

Pronunciation (SB page 67)

🌐 2.41 and 2.42

- Go through the instructions with the class and read out the example. Point out that the vowel sound in all three words is represented by the letters *ea* but that they are pronounced differently in *bread* /bred/. (You might like to point out that the sound /iː/ can also be represented by other letter combinations, such as *eo* as in *people*, *ee* as in *sleep* and *i* as in *police*.)

- Play the first recording and ask the students to circle the words with the different vowel sounds.

- Play the second recording for them to check their answers and repeat the words.

> a) bread   b) garlic   c) potato   d) cereal

Language note

Pronunciation: *tomato*

The British English pronunciation of *tomato* is /təˈmɑːtəʊ/, whereas the American English pronunciation of *tomato* is /təˈmeɪtəʊ/. Interestingly, *potato* /pəˈteɪtəʊ/ has the same pronunciation in both American and British English.

Grammar (SB page 67)
Countable and uncountable nouns

1

- Focus the students' attention on the information about countable and uncountable nouns in the margin. Demonstrate with board drawings that you can count items such as grapes, melons, etc. but that you can't count liquids, such as milk, or foods such as pasta, rice, cereal, etc. which are regarded as a whole rather than as individual grains or pieces. Point out the use of *some* rather than *a* or *an* with uncountable nouns.

- Ask the students to turn back to the photos on page 66 and decide whether the food items shown are singular and countable, plural and countable or uncountable. They should complete the table with some of these items. As they work, go round, monitoring and checking that all the students have understood the concept of countable and uncountable nouns, and are choosing appropriate items to complete the table.

- Go through answers with the class, making sure that all the items chosen by the students are checked.

> *Possible answers:*
> Singular countable: cauliflower, lemon, melon
>
> Plural countable: apples, bananas, beans, cakes, carrots, eggs, grapes, mushrooms, onions, oranges, pears, peppers, potatoes, strawberries, tomatoes
>
> Uncountable: bread, cereal, cheese, chicken, fish, garlic, meat, pasta, rice, seafood

Language notes
Vocabulary: countable/uncountable

- Countable nouns are the names of individual objects, people or ideas which can be counted, e.g. *a man, two women, five chairs*. With countable nouns you can use numbers and the indefinite article *a/an* (*two oranges and an apple*). Countable nouns have plurals (*lemon, lemons*). You can use *some* with plural countable nouns: *some strawberries*.

- Uncountable or mass nouns are the names of materials, liquids, collections without clear boundaries, which aren't seen as separate objects, e.g. *water, weather, air*. Uncountable nouns don't have plurals (*weathers*). You can use *some* with uncountable nouns: *some water*.

- It's sometimes possible to 'package' an uncountable noun and make it countable, e.g. *three bottles of water, two pieces of steak*.

- The distinction between countable and uncountable objects can seem a little difficult to determine in some cases. For example, you say *two chairs* and *three tables* (as both *chair* and *table* are countable), but you say *some furniture* (because *furniture* is uncountable in English). However, *furniture* is countable in some languages, and this may confuse some students.

- Certain food items can be both countable and uncountable with a difference of meaning, e.g. *cheese, meat, chicken, lamb, fish, cake, cereal*.

  Cheese: in the photo (SB page 66), there's a plate with three different cheeses, i.e. different types of cheese. However, you say *Would you like some cheese?* because you're offering a quantity rather than a whole cheese.

  Chicken: when you talk about the bird itself, it's countable, e.g. *My parents have some chickens on their farm.* When you talk about the meat of the bird, it's uncountable, e.g. *We had some chicken for dinner. Would you like some chicken?*

  Fish: in the photo (SB page 66), there are two fish on the plate. Each fish is an individual item and can be counted. (Note that the plural of *fish* is *fish*, which can add extra confusion.) However, when you talk about what you eat, *fish* is uncountable and you say, *We had some fish for lunch. Would you like some fish?*

2 🌐 2.43

- Remind the students that they used *any* in questions in Unit 9, when they asked questions about plural things in rooms (*Are there any chairs?*). Focus the students' attention on the examples in the table and point out that you use *Are there any …?* with plural countable nouns and *Is there any …?* with uncountable nouns. With singular countable nouns, you use *Is there a/an …?*

- Tell the students to refer back to the food photos on page 66 to help them complete the table.

- Play the recording for them to check their answers. Then play it a second time for them to listen and repeat.

> a) 'Are there any mushrooms in photo *b*?'
>   'Yes, there are.' 'No, there aren't.'
> b) 'Is there any cheese in photo *c*?'
>   'Yes, there is.' 'No, there isn't.'
> c) 'Is there a cauliflower in photo *b*?'
>   'Yes, there is.' 'No, there isn't.'
> d) 'Is there any pasta in photo *d*?'
>   'Yes, there is.' 'No, there isn't.'
> e) 'Are there any bananas in photo *d*?'
>   'Yes, there are.' 'No, there aren't.'
> f) 'Is there any bread in photo *a*?'
>   'Yes, there is.' 'No, there isn't.'

3

- Pairwork. Put the students into pairs to take turns asking and answering the questions in Exercise 2.

- When they've finished, ask them to work individually to prepare more questions about the food photos on page 66. They can take turns to ask and answer these new questions. Alternatively, allow them to work in pairs to make new questions, and then join another pair to ask and answer the questions.

- Go round, monitoring and giving help. Make sure everyone has understood the concept and is using uncountable and countable nouns correctly.

a) Yes, there are.	d) Yes, there is.
b) No, there isn't.	e) No, there aren't.
c) Yes, there is.	f) No, there isn't.

Speaking (SB page 67)

1

Ask the students to work on their own to prepare their lists and not to show them to anyone else. Make one for yourself to use in the next exercise for demonstration purposes.

2

- Pairwork. Focus the students' attention on the example speech bubbles. Tell them that you've made your own list of favourite food items, and ask them to ask you questions to find out what is on the list. When a few students have asked correct questions, put them in pairs to complete the activity using their own lists. Tell them to take turns asking and answering questions.

- Go round, checking that they're forming questions and answers correctly.

Reading & Listening (SB page 68)

Warm-up

Tell the class that they're going to read a text about a diet in which you have to eat certain foods in combination and avoid other combinations. For a bit of fun, ask the students to work in small groups and to think up a menu with the most disgusting combinations of food they can think of, e.g. chocolate-covered fish with a strawberry curry sauce. They should think up a starter, main course and dessert. The class can then vote on the most revolting menu.

1 🌐 2.44

- Tell the students that they're going to read about a special diet. Explain that *diet* /ˈdaɪət/ can mean simply 'the things you eat', but is often used to refer to an eating plan undertaken in order to lose weight. Teach *I'm on a diet*.

- Play the recording and ask the students to read the article as they listen.

- Read out the three sentences and ask the students to complete them.

a) carbohydrates   b) fruit   c) vegetables

2

- Remind the students of the food categories they studied at the beginning of the unit. Ask them to work in pairs and to decide which of the meals will help you lose weight. If they have difficulty, go through the food items individually and ask them to tell you which food category each should go in (remind them that chips are made of potatoes but go in the carbohydrate rather than vegetable category). They should then be able to make their decision about which meal is best according to the rules in the article.

- They can check their answers in the next exercise.

c) Fish and vegetables

Language and cultural notes

Steak and chips
Note also that you always say *steak and chips*, never *chips and steak*. There are several combination like this which are fixed expressions, for example, *salt and pepper*, *bread and butter*, etc.

Spaghetti bolognese
Spaghetti bolognese is a name used in Britain to describe a pasta dish which originally came from Bologna in northern Italy. The traditional dish is served with tagliatelle rather than spaghetti, and is served with a meat sauce (*ragù alla bolognese*). This sauce is made with beef, pancetta, onions, carrots, celery, tomatoes, and white wine. It's cooked very slowly.

3 🌐 2.45

Play the recording for the students to check their answers to Exercise 2. Then ask them for suggestions as to what the 'seafood diet' is. If necessary, explain the pun to the students. You may need to put the words *seafood* and *see food* on the board so that they can see the difference. *Seafood* is the collective term for such things as prawns, shrimps, crab, mussels, etc. Alan jokes that the seafood diet is 'when you see food, you eat it', in other words, you eat everything you can see – not a good way to lose weight.

When he sees food, he eats it.

A: I want to lose weight but I love my food. How do you stay so slim?

K: I follow the food-combining rules.

A: Food-combining? What's that?

K: Well, for example, I never eat protein and carbohydrates together.

A: What? Do you mean you never eat steak and chips?

K: No, because steak is protein and chips are carbohydrates.

A: Oh. What about fish and rice. That's healthy.

K: No, fish is protein and rice is carbohydrate. Fish and vegetables is OK.

A: Well, how about my favourite meal – spaghetti bolognese with fruit salad for dessert.

K: No, sorry. There's meat in bolognese and spaghetti is carbohydrate. And you can't eat fruit as a dessert.

A: Oh dear. I don't like this. My favourite diet is the seafood diet.

K: Oh, what's that?

A: When you see food, you eat it.

K&A: Ha ha ha.

Writing & Speaking (SB page 68)

- Pairwork. Students use the rules in the article on food combining to write two menus. Tell them they can use the food items on page 66 of the Student's Book. They then discuss their menus and decide which one they like best. Go round, monitoring and giving help if necessary.

- When the students have finished, ask them to join other pairs and discuss their menus together. With a strong class, ask the students what they think of the food-combining diet. Would they like to try it?

Grammar (SB page 69)

How much/many ...?

1 2.46

- Focus the students' attention on the information in the margin and go through it with the class. Tell them that you use *many* in questions about countable nouns and *much* in questions about uncountable nouns, and point out the different uses of *a lot, many, much* and *none* when talking about quantity.

- Ask the students to work in pairs to complete the questions and answers. Allow them to compare their results with other pairs before you play the recording. Then check answers with the class.

- Play the recording again for the students to listen and repeat.

a) 'How much bread is there?'
   'There isn't much.'
b) 'How many eggs are there?'
   'There are a lot.'
c) 'How many lemons are there?'
   'There aren't any.'
d) 'How much meat is there?
   'There's a lot.'
e) 'How much milk is there?'
   'There isn't any.'
f) 'How many peppers are there?'
   'There aren't many.'

2

- Pairwork. Go through the speech bubbles with the class and ask them to ask you questions about your fridge or kitchen. Then ask some of them questions about theirs. Once you're sure that everyone is handling the question and answer forms correctly, put them in pairs to continue the activity. Go round, monitoring and giving help.

3 Pairwork

- The pairwork exercise for this unit is on pages 119 and 124 of the Student's Book. Put the students in pairs and tell them who will be Student A, and who will be Student B.

- While they're doing the exercise, go round monitoring and giving help. Take note of any errors which may need particular attention later, and also any examples of good language use which you can praise in a feedback session.

Student A
a) many   b) much   c) many   d) many
e) much   f) much

Student B
a) much   b) many   c) much   d) much
e) many   f) many

4 *Grammar Extra* 10

Ask students to turn to *Grammar Extra* 10 on page 130 of the Student's Book. Here they'll find an explanation of the grammar they've been studying and further exercises to practise it.

1
a) I eat a lot of bread. / I don't eat much bread.
b) I drink a lot of tea. / I don't drink much tea.
c) I do a lot of exercise. / I don't do much exercise.
d) I read a lot of books. / I don't read many books.
e) I buy a lot of magazines. / I don't buy many magazines.
f) I get a lot of emails. / I don't get many emails.
g) I meet a lot of people. / I don't meet many people.
h) I have a lot of free time. / I don't have much free time.

2
a) How much bread do you eat?
b) How much tea do you drink?
c) How much exercise do you do?
d) How many books do you read?
e) How many magazines do you buy?
f) How many emails do you get?
g) How many people do you meet?
h) How much free time do you have?

Speaking: anecdote (SB page 69)

For more information about how to set up, monitor and repeat anecdotes, see Practical methodology, page xx in the Introduction.

1 2.47

- Tell the students that they're going to listen to a woman talking about the last time she had a delicious meal. Before you play the recording, ask them to think back to the last time they had a delicious meal.

- Give them a minute or two to read the questions and the answer choices. Then play the recording and ask them to underline the correct information in the answers. You may need to play the recording more than once. Check answers with the class.

a) last weekend
b) my brother's 18th birthday
c) in an Italian restaurant
d) fifteen of us
e) my grandmother
f) pizza
g) for nearly three hours
h) a really good evening

🌐 2.47

We had a delicious meal last weekend. It was my brother's 18th birthday, and the whole family went out. We had a meal in an Italian restaurant. It's called Mario's, and they do fantastic pizzas there. There were fifteen of us – me, my brother, our parents, our grandmother, our cousins and my brother's best friends. I sat next to my grandmother, but she fell asleep after two glasses of wine. Everybody had pizza. The restaurant made my brother a special birthday cake, and we all sang 'Happy birthday' – I think he was a bit embarrassed. The cake was delicious, and we had some champagne too. I think we stayed in the restaurant for nearly three hours. I didn't get home till 1.00 a.m. It was a really good evening.

2

- Pairwork. Give the students time to think of their own answers to the questions in Exercise 1, and to note them down. Go round, monitoring and giving help with any additional vocabulary they may need

- Tell them that they're going to tell their partner about the last time they had a delicious meal, but that they need to do more than simply read out their sentences. Ask them to think about the language that they will need to describe the meal and to make notes.

- Pairwork. Put the students in pairs and ask them to take turns to tell their partner about their meal. Encourage them to ask each other questions to get further information. You could talk about the sort of questions they might ask first and put them on the board (*Was it expensive? Who cooked the meal? Who did the washing up?*)

- Ask some pairs to report back to the class about what they found out.

Useful phrases (SB page 70)

1 🌐 2.48

Focus the students' attention on the picture and ask them what type of shop it is (a food shop or a shop that sells sandwiches). Go through the questions with the class so that the students know what information they're listening for. Then play the recording and ask them to answer the questions.

a) A chicken sandwich.
b) Five dollars.

2

- Remind the students of the use of *I'd like …* (*I would like …*) when asking for things in shops, and the difference between this and sentences such as *I like football*. Ask them to complete the conversation with the words in the box. Go round, monitoring and giving help.

- Play the recording again for the students to listen and check their answers. Then focus students' attention to the shop assistant's questions *Would you like …?* and *Would you like anything to drink?* Remind them of the use of *any* in questions such as *Are there any chairs?*, and explain that you use *anything* when you ask people general questions about what they would like. *Would you like anything to eat?* would also be possible.

1 I'd   2 Would   3 like   4 you'd   5 like
6 you   7 Would   8 like   9 you
10 Would

3 🌐 2.49

Play the recording for the students to listen and repeat the useful phrases. Check that they are copying the intonation of the speakers, and ask several students to repeat the phrases individually.

4

- Pairwork. In pairs, the students write similar conversations about a customer who wants a different sort of sandwich, and who would also like a drink. Go round monitoring and giving help with any extra vocabulary that they may need, and check that they're using *I'd like …* and *Would you like …?* correctly. Encourage them to use the useful phrases from Exercise 3 in their conversations.

- When they've finished, ask them to practise their conversations. Choose a few pairs to perform their conversations for the class.

Vocabulary *Extra* (SB page 71)

Food

1

- Focus student's attention on the groups of words and point out that they're all to do with food. Remind students that the underlining indicates the syllable of the word that has the strongest stress. Check that the students can pronounce the words correctly.

- Ask students to look at the pictures in each group and match each one with one of the words. Point out that the first one has been done for them.

A		**B**	
3	an apple	4	beans
7	banana	8	a carrot
1	grapes	2	a cauliflower
6	a lemon	5	garlic
2	a melon	3	mushrooms
5	an orange	7	an onion
8	a pear	1	a pepper
4	strawberries	6	a tomato
C		**D**	
2	bread	5	cheese
6	a cake	3	chicken
1	cereal	6	eggs
4	pasta	1	fish
3	potatoes	2	seafood
5	rice	4	meat

2

Pairwork. Demonstrate the activity with a confident student. Cover the words, point to one of the pictures and ask *What's this?* Elicit the answer. Then put the students into pairs to continue the activity. Go round, checking that everyone is pronouncing the words correctly.

1

- Focus the student's attention on the sentences and point out that the words in bold are prepositions of place.

- Ask students to look at the pictures and match each one with one of the sentences. Point out that the first one has been done for them.

3	It's on the wall.
1	It's in the cupboard.
6	It's on the coffee table.
5	It's under the rug.
2	It's above the door.
4	It's next to the plant.

2

- Pairwork. Demonstrate the activity with a confident student. Cover the words, ask the students a question with *Where's the …?* about an object in the classroom. Elicit the answer. Then put the students into pairs to continue the activity about other items in the classroom. Go round monitoring and giving help.

Further practice material

Need more writing practice?

→ Workbook page 43
- Writing an invitation

Need more classroom practice activities?

→ Photocopiable resource materials pages 180 to 182
  Grammar: *How much milk is there?*
  Vocabulary: *Describe it!*
  Communication: *Healthy or hopeless?*
→ TOP 10 activities pages xv to xx

Need progress tests?

→ Test CD – *Test Unit 10*

Need more on important teaching concepts?

→ Key concepts in *New Inside Out* pages xxii to xxxv

Need student CEF self-evaluation?

→ CD-ROM – Unit 10: *Food*

Need student CEF self-evaluation?

→ CEF Checklists pages xxxvii to xliv

Need more information and more ideas?

→ www.insideout.net

Before the next lesson …

Collect some magazine and newspaper photos of famous people to use in the warm-up activity for the next unit.

11 Looks *Overview*

Section	Aims	What the students are doing
Vocabulary SB page 72	*Vocabulary*: physical description	• Guessing family relationships based on photos. • Completing descriptions of people. • Completing a table with words to describe people.
Speaking SB page 73	*Conversation skills*: describing people	• Describing people and guessing their identities. • Writing short descriptions of people and telling a partner about them.
Vocabulary SB page 73	*Vocabulary*: clothes	• Identifying items of clothing in a photo. • Completing a table with clothes and accessories.
Listening SB page 73	*Listening skills*: listening for specific information	• Listening to an interview and underlining correct information. • Asking and answering questions about clothes.
Reading SB page 74	*Reading skills*: reading for specific information	• Reading and completing a magazine quiz about the clothes and spending habits of the average British man. • Discussing the quiz with a partner.
Pronunciation SB page 74	*Pronunciation*: sound discrimination	• Listening to and repeating chants with clothing words. • Matching sounds to coloured letters.
Listening SB page 75	*Listening skills*: listening for specific information	• Listening to a radio commentary and putting photos in order. • Matching verb phrases and noun phrases. • Identifying who is doing certain actions.
Grammar SB page 75	*Grammar*: present continuous	• Completing a table of questions and answers. • Asking and answering questions. • Guessing what three members of their family are doing at the moment.
Useful phrases SB page 76	*Vocabulary*: phrases which are useful when buying clothes	• Circling the clothes they see in a picture. • Listening to a conversation in a clothes shop and answering questions. • Deciding who says which useful phrases. • Writing and practising a new conversation.
Vocabulary *Extra* SB page 77	*Vocabulary*: revision of words from the unit: clothes. Focus on *get*	• Matching pictures with words.
Writing WB page 47	Linking sentences: *and, with* Describing a person	

Warm-up

- If students already have some knowledge of words used to describe people, play *Who am I?* using famous people. Describe the appearance of someone famous and ask the students to guess who it is. A student who guesses correctly can then think of another famous person to describe.

- Pre-teach some of the vocabulary that the students will encounter in this unit. Bring to class some magazine or newspaper photos of famous people, and use them to illustrate items such as *curly hair, shaved head, medium-length hair, highlights, sweet,* etc.

Vocabulary (SB page 72)

Physical description

1 🌐 2.50

- Focus the students' attention on the photos. Tell them that each person in the top row is related to one of the people in the bottom row and they have to guess the relationships. Look at the example with the class. Teach *look like* and explain that it has nothing to do with *like* in the sense of liking somebody. (Remind them that when you use *I'd like …* to ask for something in a shop, this is also different from talking about likes and dislikes.) Ask them if they think Will looks like Sue.

- Play the recording and ask the students to listen and check their answers. Find out if anyone guessed all the relationships correctly. Ask them which of the children look like their parents. Then find out if any of the students think they look like their parents or look like their brothers and sisters.

> a) son   b) daughter   c) brother   d) father

2 🌐 2.51

- Look at the list of descriptions with the class. Explain any words they don't know, using members of the class to demonstrate where possible.

- Ask the students to complete the descriptions with the names of the people in the photos in Exercise 1.

- Play the recording for them to listen and check. Then play it a second time for them to repeat.

> a) Will   b) Jem   c) Sue   d) Albert
> e) Gus   f) Nancy   g) Zainab   h) Simon

3

- Go through the headings in the table with the class and make sure they understand them. Make sure they are aware that the *Opinion* column is for things that depend on the point of view of the speaker.

- Put the students in pairs and ask them to complete the table with words and phrases from Exercise 2. Go round, monitoring and helping.

- Check answers with the class.

Exercises 3 and 4

Hair length	Hair colour	Hair style	Eyes	Opinion	Other
a shaved head short medium-length	dark grey	straight blond highlights curly	green dark brown	very good-looking very sweet lovely smile	
long	fair	wavy	blue	beautiful handsome	a beard a moustache a tattoo

4 🌐 2.52

- Play the recording for the students to listen and repeat the words in the box. Make sure that they can say *moustache* /məˈstɑːʃ/ correctly. Then give them a few minutes to add the words to the table. Allow them to work in pairs if they wish.

- Check answers with the class. Then ask the students to say which words they think are usually used to describe men, which to describe women and which can be used for both. (The words describing hair length, hair colour, hair style and eyes can be used for both men and women; *very sweet* and *beautiful* would generally only be used of a woman, whereas *handsome* and *good-looking* tend to be used more of men. *Lovely smile* could be used for either, but is perhaps more likely to be used of a woman. Either sex could have a tattoo, but a *beard* and *moustache* would only be used on men.)

5 Pairwork

- The pairwork exercise for this unit is on pages 119 and 124. Put the students in pairs and tell them who will be Student A, and who will be Student B.
- While they are doing the exercise, go round monitoring and helping. Take note of any errors which may need particular attention later, and also any examples of good language use which you can praise in a feedback session.

> **Student A**
> 1 Jane   2 Emma   3 Mickey   4 Jason
> 5 Max
>
> **Student B**
> 1 Marco   2 Karen   3 Lily   4 Paul
> 5 Susanna

Speaking (SB page 73)

1

Pairwork. Focus the students' attention on the speech bubbles. Read them out to the class. Then give a short description of one of the students. Ask them to try to identify who it is. Respond to their guesses with *Yes, that's right* or *No, that's wrong*. Then put them in pairs to continue the activity. Make sure they take turns to be the one who gives the description.

Language notes

Grammar: word order

- In this exercise, the students are asked to combine adjectives and nouns to describe people. When two or more adjectives come before a noun, they usually have to be put in a particular order. You say *short grey hair*, not *grey short hair*. Although the rules are complex, generally, when there are two adjectives, the order is:

  judgement (*beautiful, pretty, lovely*)
  size (*long, short*)
  other (*straight, curly, wavy*)
  colour (*black, red, dark, blond*)

- So, for example, you could say:

  She has beautiful, long, straight, red hair.
  He has lovely, blue eyes.

- At this stage in the course don't worry too much about the correct word order of the adjectives. This issue will be dealt with in detail in a later level.

2

- Give the students plenty of time to write their descriptions or ask them to do it for homework.
- In pairs, the students take turns to talk about the people they've described. Encourage them to ask follow-up questions to extract more information where possible.

Vocabulary (SB page 73)

Clothes

1 🌐 **2.53**

- Focus the students' attention on the photograph of Stuart. Ask them what they think of his clothes collection. They then identify the items shown in the photo and tick the correct ones. Check answers with the class. Point out the use of *accessories* to describe things such as belts, hats, jewellery, etc. and the difference between *formal* and *casual*.
- Check comprehension by asking the students for other items that could go in the five categories.
- Play the recording for the students to listen and repeat the words.

> Footwear: shoes
> Underwear: —
> Formal clothes: jackets, shirts, suits, ties, trousers
> Casual clothes: —
> Accessories: belts, rings

Language notes

Vocabulary: clothes

- *Trainers* are light comfortable shoes for playing sport, although they're often worn for everything but sport! In American English, they're called *sneakers*.
- In British English, you generally refer to the underwear worn by men as *underpants* or *pants*, and to the underwear worn by women as *pants* or *knickers*. *Underwear* is the general term for all items of clothing worn next to the skin.
- *Tops* are light items of clothing worn on the upper part of the body above the waist.
- *Tracksuits* are a loose top and trousers worn for sport or exercise, but now also worn as casual clothing.

2 🌐 **2.54**

- Focus the students' attention on the table and point out the two headings. Go through the examples with them and then ask them to complete it.
- Students should have no trouble with the concept of shoes and boots being described as *a pair of*, as they consist of two separate items. They may have more difficulty identifying that you also use *a pair of* with trousers, underpants, etc. where there appears to be only one item. It's worth pointing out that items of clothing with two legs (and, in the case of glasses and sunglasses, with two lenses) are always plural and don't have a singular form. Whilst you can talk of *one shoe*, you can't talk of *one trouser*.
- Play the recording for the students to check their answers. Then play it a second time for them to listen and repeat the words.

A: Singular nouns (*a* …)
a coat, a jacket, a shirt, a suit, a tie, a sweater,
a top, a tracksuit, a T-shirt, a belt, a hat, a ring
B: Plural nouns (*a pair of* …)
a pair of boots, a pair of shoes, a pair of trainers,
a pair of socks, a pair of underpants, a pair of
trousers, a pair of jeans, a pair of sunglasses

Listening (SB page 73)

1 🌐 **2.55**

- Remind the students that the clothes in the photo in
  the previous section belong to a man called Stuart.
  Tell them that they're going to listen to Stuart talking
  about his clothes.

- Play the recording for the students to listen and
  underline the correct information.

- Check answers with the class and ask them for their
  reactions to what they've heard. Do they know
  anyone like Stuart who owns a lot of clothes?

---

a) 350   b) 200   c) 150   d) 125

🌐 **2.55** (I = Interviewer; S = Stuart)

I: *Stuart, you really like buying clothes,*
     don't you?
S: *Oh yes, I love it.*
I: *How many items of clothing do you have?*
S: *Well … I have 350 shirts. I wear three or four*
     different shirts every day.
I: *Goodness. 350 shirts! Er … who does the*
     washing?
S: *My wife does the washing, and I do the ironing.*
     Then I have 200 suits. I like bright colours –
     red, blue and green.
I: *Mm, I see.*
S: *Then I have 150 pairs of trousers.*
I: *150 pairs of trousers!*
S: *Yes, and 125 pairs of shoes.*
I: *Stuart, why do you have so many clothes?*
S: *Well, it's my hobby. Some people spend lots of*
     money on cars, or holidays. I don't have a car,
     and I never go on holiday. I buy clothes.

2

- Pairwork. Ask one of the students the question in the
  speech bubble, and encourage them to give a truthful
  answer, and to then ask you the question back. Give
  your answer. Then ask a similar question with one of
  the plural nouns.

- Put the students in pairs to continue the activity. Go
  round, monitoring and helping. Make sure they take
  turns to ask questions, and that the person answering
  the question then asks the questioner the question
  each time. Find out who in the class has the most
  clothes.

Reading (SB page 74)

1

- Ask the students to look at the photo and get their
  reactions to it. Remind the students of Stuart from
  the previous section. Explain the meaning of *average*
  and tell them that Stuart was not average. Ask them
  if they think they have a lot of clothes, not many
  clothes or if they think they are about average.

- Give the students plenty of time to look at the quiz
  and decide what they think Mr Average's answers
  would be. They should do this individually.

2

When the students have compared their answers with a
partner, they should look at the answers in the book.
Ask them if any of the answers surprise them.

Extra activity

Ask the students to discuss how many items of
clothing they think Ms Average has and how
much she spends.

3

Pairwork. Ask the students to discuss the questions in
pairs. When they've finished, ask them to join another
pair and tell them about their discussion.

Pronunciation (SB page 74)

1 🌐 **2.56**

Play the recording and ask the students to listen and
repeat the chants.

2

Ask the students to look back at the first line in chant A
and draw their attention to the final *s* in the words
highlighted in red. Tell them that the *s* in plural words
can be pronounced with a /z/ sound or a /s/ sound.
Focus the students' attention on where these two words
go in the table, and ask them to put the other words
from the chants in the correct column. Encourage them
to say the words aloud as they do this so that they get a
feel for how they sound. Check answers with the class,
then get them to practise the chants in chorus.

Listening (SB page 75)

Warm-up

- Find out how many students watch the Oscars ceremony on television. Ask them what they think of the clothes that the celebrities wear to the event.
- Ask which actors won the most recent Oscars awards for best actor and best actress, and if they can remember what they wore to the ceremony.

1 🌐 **2.57**

- Focus attention on the photos and ask the students if they know these actors and have seen any of their films. Ask them if they like the clothes they are wearing. Tell them to listen to the radio commentary and to number the photos in the correct order.
- Check answers with the class.

> 1 a   2 c   3 b

> 🌐 **2.57**
>
> *Good evening. I'm Ross White and I'm standing outside the Kodak Theatre in Hollywood. I'm waiting for the big stars to arrive for this year's Oscars ceremony.*
>
> *And here comes Keira Knightley. She's wearing a beautiful red dress.*
>
> *Oh, wow – there's Charlize Theron. She's talking to the photographers. Oh, and what's she doing now – she's turning around. Hi, Charlize! Good luck! Oh, what a gorgeous woman!*
>
> *Right, Jake Gyllenhaal's arriving now. He's wearing a black bow tie. Oh, he's so good-looking! And he's smiling at everybody.*

2

- Focus attention on the verb phrases and explain that the students heard these in the radio commentary of the Oscars ceremony. Tell them that they'll be looking at the verb form (the present continuous) in the next section and that it's used for describing things that are happening right now.
- Ask the students to discuss in pairs which noun phrase they think should go with each of the verb phrases.
- Check answers with the class. Then play the recording again for them to listen and check.
- Finally, ask them to identify who is doing each action.

> a) I'm waiting for the big stars. (Ross White)
> b) She's wearing a beautiful red dress. (Keira Knightly)
> c) She's turning around. (Charlize Theron)
> d) He's wearing a black bow tie. (Jake Gyllenhaal)
> e) He's smiling at everybody. (Jake Gyllenhaal)

Extra activity

In groups of four, students could act out the radio commentary of the arrival of three film stars at the Oscars ceremony, with one student playing the part of the commentator and the others the actors. Give them time to prepare their commentaries, using descriptions of the clothes the students are actually wearing. Make sure that they include some actions that the arriving film stars can be doing. Go round, checking that they use correct present continuous forms. Ask them to perform their Oscars ceremonies for the class.

Cultural notes

Keira Knightley (born 1985)
Keira Knightly was born in London. She plays the role of Elizabeth Swan in the *Pirates of the Caribbean* films. She also starred in *Bend it Like Beckham* (2002), and *Love Actually* (2003).

Jake Gyllenhaal (born 1980)
American actor Jake Gyllenhaal starred in the title role in the cult film *Donnie Darko* (2001), and was nominated for an Academy Award as Best Supporting Actor in *Brokeback Mountain*. He takes an active role in politics and social causes.

Charlize Theron (born 1975)
Charlize Theron grew up in South Africa and studied to be a ballet dancer. However, a leg injury put a stop to her dancing career. At the age of eighteen, she went to Los Angeles to become an actress. She's starred in films such as *The Devil's Advocate* and *The Cider House Rules*. She received an Academy Award for Best Actress as the serial killer Aileen Wuornos in the film *Monster* (2003).

Grammar (SB page 75)

Present continuous

1 🌐 **2.58**

- Focus the students' attention on the information in the margin. Go through the present continuous of *work* with the class and point out that it's formed with the present simple of *be* (*I am, you are, he is,* etc.) and a verb ending in *ing*. Remind them that they saw examples in the last section and that the present continuous is used for things which are happening at the moment of speaking.

- Ask the students to complete the table of questions and answers. Go round, monitoring and helping.
- Play the recording for the students to check their answers. Then play it a second time for them to listen and repeat.

---

a) 'Are you wearing jeans?'
   'Yes, I am.' 'No, I'm not.'
b) 'Are you sitting next to a window?'
   'Yes, I am.' 'No, I'm not.'
c) 'Is your teacher standing up?'
   'Yes, he/she is.' 'No, he/she isn't.'
d) 'Is the traffic making a noise?'
   'Yes, it is.' 'No, it isn't.'
e) 'Are you all wearing watches?'
   'Yes, we are.' 'No, we aren't.'
f) 'Are the birds singing outside?'
   'Yes, they are.' 'No, they aren't.'

Language notes

Grammar: present continuous

- The difference between the present simple and the present continuous can be confusing for students, even at an advanced level. This will be particularly true for students whose own language has a single present tense. However, at this level the difference is relatively simple. You use the present simple to talk about permanent situations (*We live in Paris.*) or about things that happen regularly/every day (*I usually get up at 7.00 a.m.*). Note that the action may not be happening at the time of speaking (*Tom goes to work by bus – but today he's ill.*) In contrast, you use the present continuous to talk about what is happening at or around the time of speaking ('*Where's Anna?*' '*She's doing her homework.*') You can also use the present continuous for temporary situations (*I live in Rome, but I'm doing an English course in Oxford for the summer.*)

- Note that some verbs (e.g. *like, love, hate, prefer, see, hear, know, mean, understand, want*) are not normally used in the continuous form. For example, you can say *Do you like London?* and *Does he know you?*, but not ~~*Are you liking London?*~~ and ~~*Is he knowing you?*~~

- The present continuous is a composite tense formed with an auxiliary (*be*) and the present participle. Students may on occasions forget to include the auxiliary (~~*She writing a letter*~~ rather than *She's writing a letter*).

- The use of the present continuous to talk about the future will be covered at a later stage in the course.

2

Pairwork. The students take turns to ask and answer the questions in Exercise 1. Make sure they answer truthfully.

3

- Go through the example speech bubble with the class. Ask the students to work individually to write down the names of three family members and make guesses about what they are doing at the moment.

- Pairwork. The students take turns to tell a partner what they think their relatives are doing.

4 *Grammar Extra* 11

Ask students to turn to *Grammar Extra* 11 on page 130 of the Student's Book. Here they'll find an explanation of the grammar they've been studying and further exercises to practise it.

1
Verbs ending in *e*: come – coming, have – having, make – making, phone – phoning, use – using, write – writing
Verbs ending in one + vowel + one consonant: get – getting, run – running, sit – sitting
All other verbs: eat – eating, listen to – listening to, read – reading, sleep – sleeping, study – studying, talk – talking, wear – wearing

2
1 're having	6 's swimming
2 'm sitting	7 's sleeping
3 'm drinking	8 're eating
4 's reading	9 'm getting
5 's listening	10 're thinking

Useful phrases (SB page 76)

1

Focus the students' attention on the picture. Ask them to concentrate on the type of clothes they can see and to circle the right word.

---

c) evening dresses

Language note

Vocabulary: *Here you are*

You use *Here you are* when giving something to someone. For example:

Can you pass the sugar, please?
Here you are.

2 🌐 2.59

- Tell the students they are going to listen to a conversation in the dress shop in the photo. Point out that they only have to answer a single question.

- Play the recording ask the students for the answer to the question.

Erica chooses a black dress.

3 🔘 2.60

- Ask the students to cover the conversation in Exercise 2.
- Go through the useful phrases one by one and ask the students to write E if they think Erica (the customer) says it and SA if they think the shop assistant says it.
- Play the recording for the students to check their answers. Play it again for them to repeat the useful phrases. Then ask several students to repeat the phrases individually.
- Go back over the conversation and answer any questions the students have about difficult vocabulary. Make sure they understand *a medium* (short for *a medium size*) and teach *a small* and *a large* as well. Point out the use of *one* in *this yellow one* and explain that here it's used to avoid repeating the word *dress*.

a) SA   b) E   c) E   d) SA   e) SA   f) E
g) E   h) SA

4

Pairwork. As the students write their conversations, go round, offering help and encouragement. When they've finished, get them to practise them aloud. Take note of any particularly good conversations and ask the students involved to perform them for the class.

Vocabulary *Extra* (SB page 77)

Clothes

1

- Focus the students' attention on the list of words and point out that they're all to do with clothes. Remind students that the underlining indicates the syllable of the word that has the strongest stress. Check that the students can pronounce the words correctly.
- Ask the students to look at the pictures and match each one with one of the words. Point out that the first one has been done for them.

6	a belt	12	socks
15	boots	5	a suit
2	a coat	7	a top
1	a hat	4	a tracksuit
3	a jacket	13	trainers
8	a shirt	10	trousers
11	a skirt	9	a T-shirt
14	shoes		

2

Pairwork. Demonstrate the activity with a confident student. Cover the words, point to one of the pictures and ask *What's this?* Elicit the answer. Then put the students into pairs to continue the activity. Go round, checking that everyone is pronouncing the words correctly and using *It's* and *They're* appropriately.

Focus on *get*

1

Ask the students to look at the table. Focus their attention the uses of *get* and their examples. Then ask the students to complete the table with the correct phrases from the box.

1	get an new car	4	get home
2	get an email	5	get married
3	get a job	6	get up at 7.00 a.m.

2

Ask the students to write a sentence of their own for each use of *get* from the table.

Further practice material

Need more writing practice?
→ Workbook page 47
- Linking sentences: *and, with*
- Describing a person

Need more classroom practice activities?
→ Photocopiable resource materials pages 183 to 185
  Grammar: *What are they doing?*
  Vocabulary: *Fashion and style*
  Communication: *Fashion show*
→ TOP 10 activities pages xv to xx

Need DVD material?
→ DVD – Programme 6: *The new look*

Need progress tests?
→ Test CD – *Test Unit 11*

Need more on important teaching concepts?
→ Key concepts in *New Inside Out* pages xxii to xxxv

Need student self-study practice?
→ CD-ROM – Unit 11: *Looks*

Need student CEF self-evaluation?
→ CEF Checklists pages xxxvii to xliv

Need more information and more ideas?
→ www.insideout.net

12 Money *Overview*

Section	Aims	What the students are doing
Reading **SB page 78**	*Reading skills*: reading for specific information	• Reading an article and identifying a problem. • Marking sentences true or false. • Putting sentences in order.
Vocabulary **SB page 79**	*Vocabulary*: money	• Completing sentences with words from the reading text. • Identifying sentences about money that are true for them.
Grammar **SB page 79**	*Grammar*: comparative adjectives	• Underlining comparative adjectives. • Completing a table with comparative adjectives. • Writing sentences using comparative adjectives. • Completing sentences with comparative adjectives.
Pronunciation **SB page 80**	*Pronunciation*: schwa /ə/	• Repeating chants and practising the schwa sound.
Vocabulary & Listening **SB page 80**	*Vocabulary*: big numbers *Listening skills*: listening for detail	• Writing out prices in words. • Matching prices and objects. • Talking about their most valued possession.
Speaking **SB page 80**	*Conversation skills*: talking about prices	• Discussing how much they usually pay for things.
Grammar **SB page 81**	*Grammar*: superlative adjectives	• Completing questions with superlative adjectives. • Asking and answering questions.
Reading **SB page 81**	*Reading skills*: reading for detail	• Talking about the most common objects to lose • Reading a text about losing things. • Discussing questions about losing things.
Useful phrases **SB page 82**	*Vocabulary*: phrases which are useful when describing objects	• Reading and listening to a conversation. • Matching questions and answers. • Listening to and repeating useful phrases. • Writing and practising a new conversation.
Vocabulary *Extra* **SB page 83**	*Vocabulary*: revision of words from the unit: common adjectives. Focus on *like*	• Matching pictures with words.
Writing **WB page 51**	Writing a summary of graphic data	

Warm-up

Ask the students to brainstorm ways of getting money without actually working. Start them off with a few ideas, such as *ask your parents*, *rob a bank* and write their suggestions on the board.

Reading (SB page 78)

1 🌐 2.61

Focus attention on the photo and tell the students that this is a woman called Karyn. Ask them to read the article and find out what Karyn's problem was. When they've given the answer, ask them how Karyn got such a big debt – what did she spend her money on?

> She had a huge credit card debt.

Language note

Pronunciation: silent letters

The 'b' in *debt* is silent. You say /det/.

2

- Ask the students to read the sentences and decide whether they are true or false. Sentence c) contains a comparative adjective (*better*). The next grammar section will focus on comparative adjectives, so you might like to draw the students' attention to it.
- Check answers with the class.

> a) False. b) True. c) False. d) True.
> e) True. f) False.

3 🌐 2.62

- Point out that when the students put the items in order, they form a continuous text summarising the article. When they've decided on the order, tell them to check that the end of each item fits onto the beginning of the next.
- Play the recording for the students to check their answers.
- Ask the students if they think that Karyn's website was a good idea? Do they feel sorry for her? Would they have sent her any money?

> 1 f)   2 b)   3 e)   4 c)   5 h)   6 d)
> 7 g)   8 a)

Vocabulary (SB page 79)

1 🌐 2.63

Make sure that the students realise that the words they need to complete the sentences are all in the article about Karyn on page 78. Give them a few minutes to find the words and complete the sentences. Then play the recording for them to check their answers. Play it a second time for them to listen and repeat.

> a) save   b) spent   c) salary   d) bills
> e) credit

2

- Ask the students to work individually to tick the sentences that are true for them.
- Put the students into pairs and ask them to compare their sentences with their partner. Encourage them to ask follow-up questions where appropriate. For example, *What do you spend your money on? What did you buy last weekend? What things do you buy on the internet?*

Grammar (SB page 79)

Comparative adjectives

1

- Focus the students' attention on the information in the margin. Explain that comparative adjectives are used to describe the difference between two things. Demonstrate by drawing two objects on the board, one with a price tag of £10, the other with a price tag of £100. Point to the cheaper one and tell the students that it's cheaper than the other one. Go through the other short adjectives and point out that they form the comparative by adding *er*. Explain that adjectives ending in *e*, such as *nice*, add only an *r*, those that end in a short vowel and a consonant, such as *big*, double the consonant before adding *er*, and those that end in *y*, such as *lucky*, drop the *y* and add *ier*.
- Now point to the more expensive object you drew on the board and tell the students that this is more expensive than the other one. Explain that long adjectives take *more* in the comparative form because it's easier to say than adding *er* on the end. Finally, explain that some two-syllable adjectives, such as *careful*, also take *more* in the comparative.
- Focus their attention on the irregular forms and remind them of the sentence *Her new job was better than her old job* which they saw in Exercise 2 on page 78.

- Ask them to underline the comparative adjectives in the sentence. Check answers with the class.

> smaller, cheaper, more careful

2 🌐 2.64

Focus attention on the headings of the table. Ask the students to decide which of the adjectives in the box goes in each column and to write their comparative forms. Allow them to compare notes in pairs or small groups, then play the recording for them to check their answers. Play it a second time for them to listen and repeat.

> Shorter adjectives: bigger, cleaner, faster, happier, older, richer
> Long adjectives: more beautiful, more important, more interesting
> Irregular forms: better

3

- Remind the students that they've met *I'd like …* in several of the *Useful phrases* sections where it was used to ask for things in shops and restaurants.
- Go through the example sentences with the class and then ask them to work individually to write new sentences for themselves. Go round, monitoring and helping. Make sure everyone is using comparative adjectives correctly and encourage them to use a variety of different types: short, long and irregular.
- Pairwork. Put the students in pairs to compare and discuss their sentences.

4 🌐 2.65

- Focus the students' attention on the cartoon in the margin and the example sentences. Ask them to work individually to complete the remaining sentences with the comparative forms of the adjectives in brackets. Go round, monitoring and helping. Remind them of the information in the margin if they need help, especially for c) and e).
- Play the recording for the students to check their answers, then play it again for them to listen and repeat.

> a) taller   b) older   c) worse   d) smaller
> e) further from   f) more expensive

5

- Do the first one as an example for the class, choosing a student who is shorter than you. Ask him or her to stand up and say *I'm taller than (Ana).* Ask the students to complete the exercise by replacing the other names in Exercise 4 with those of people in the class. They'll need to ask each other questions to find out some of the information. With weaker classes, put these questions on the board: *How old are you? Where is your house? How much was your pen?*

- Ask several students to read out their sentences and ask the others to listen and challenge if they think any of them are untrue.
- Ask the students to make further true sentences using the comparative forms of the adjectives in the box. Go round, monitoring and helping. Ask several students to read out their sentences. Again, allow challenges if anyone thinks a sentence is untrue.

Pronunciation (SB page 80)

1 🌐 2.66

- Play the recording and ask the students to listen and repeat the chants.
- Ask the students to look at the letters in red and ask them how you pronounce these vowel sounds. Ask individual students to say the words aloud.
- Point out that this is one of the most common sounds in English and ask the students for examples of other words that contain this sound. Point out that the schwa sound can be represented by a variety of letters and letter combinations. Here there are examples of the schwa being represented by the letters *er, or, our,* and *a (than).*

> The schwa sound (/ə/).

2

Tell the students to decide which lines in the chant are true for them. Ask for a show of hands.

Vocabulary & Listening (SB page 80)

1 🌐 2.67

- Go through the example with the class. Point out the use of the word *and.* Tell them that this is pronounced weakly, and the vowel sound is an example of the schwa which they practised in the previous section.
- Ask the students to work in pairs and to read the other numbers aloud, deciding when to use *and.* (See *Language notes* on page 89.) Give them a few minutes to do this and then ask several pairs to read out the numbers to the class. Ask the other students to say whether or not they agree with each reading.
- Play the recording for the students to check. Then play it again for them to listen and repeat. When they've done this chorally, ask individual students to repeat the numbers after you.

> a) One million, two hundred and fifty thousand, six hundred and twenty dollars
> b) Eighty-five thousand, five hundred and ninety dollars
> c) Eleven million, three hundred and two thousand, six hundred and fifty dollars
> d) Sixty-five thousand, two hundred and eight dollars

Language notes
Vocabulary: big numbers

- In British English, you always put *and* before the tens in a number, e.g. *six hundred and twenty*. You don't put *and* before the hundreds. You say *one thousand, six hundred and twenty*.

- Note that with thousands, you write a comma after the thousands. However, if the number has just four figures, you can write the number without a comma, e.g. *1,500* or *1500*. You don't use the comma to indicate decimals. Here you use the full stop as the decimal point, e.g. *5.7* is *five point seven*.

- When saying big numbers, if students have difficulty getting the rhythm and intonation right, build the number backwards. For example, with the number *$1,250,620*, say *twenty dollars* and ask them to repeat. Then say *six hundred and twenty dollars*, and ask them to repeat. Then say *fifty thousand, six hundred and twenty dollars*. Gradually build the number until it's complete.

2 ⊕ 2.68

- Pairwork. Focus the students attention on the objects in the photos. Tell them that they're all valuable, i.e. they're very expensive. Ask the students to try to predict which thing goes with which price. When they've made their decisions, allow them to compare results with another pair.

- Play the recording for the students to check their answers.

> 1 c) $11,302,650   2 d) $65,208
> 3 a) $1,250,620   4 b) $85,590

> ⊕ 2.68
>
> 1 *The most valuable watch is by Patek Phillippe. It's made of 18-carat gold and is worth $11,302,650.*
> 2 *The most valuable pair of jeans are an original pair of 115-year-old Levis. A Japanese collector bought them on the internet in 2005. The jeans cost $65,208.*
> 3 *The most valuable dress is the dress worn by Marilyn Monroe when she sang 'Happy Birthday, Mr President' to JF Kennedy in 1962. In 1999 a collector bought the dress for $1,250,620.*
> 4 *The most valuable pair of shoes are a pair of shoes worn by Emperor Bokassa of the Central African Republic in 1977. The shoes cost $85,590.*

Extra activity

Ask the students to make as many sentences as they can about the objects in Exercise 2 using comparative adjectives. Award a point for each correct sentence and see who can win the most points. For example, *The watch is more expensive than the jeans. The jeans are cheaper than the dress.*

3

- Pairwork. Read the example speech bubble with the class. Tell them if this is true for you or not. If not, repeat the sentence, substituting your most valuable possession. Then give the students a moment or two to decide what their most valuable possession is.

- Put them into pairs to tell their partner about their most valuable possession.

Speaking (SB page 80)

1

Go through the items with the class and ask the students to work individually to decide how much they usually pay for these things. Make sure that they all give the prices in the same currency, if possible.

2

- Choose a confident student and ask *How much do you usually pay for a pair of shoes?* Encourage the student to answer and then to ask you a question using *How much do you usually pay for …?*

- Put the students into pairs and ask them to take turns asking and answering about how much they pay for things.

Grammar (SB page 81)
Superlative adjectives

1 ⊕ 2.69

- Remind the students that so far they have looked at comparative adjectives, which are used to compare two things. Tell them that they're now going to look at superlative adjectives, which are used to compare three or more things.

- Focus the students' attention on the information in the margin. Go through the different sections, pointing out that once again long adjectives behave differently from short adjectives and that some adjectives are irregular.

- Focus the students' attention on the questions and point out that they're all asking about family members.

- Ask them to complete the questions with the superlative forms of the adjectives in brackets. Play the recording for them to check their answers, then play it a second time for them to listen and repeat.

> a) the youngest   f) the luckiest
> c) the oldest   g) the worst driver
> d) the most interesting h) the best cook

2

- Pairwork. Go through the speech bubbles with the class, then ask a confident student the question. Encourage them to give a true answer and then to ask you the same question. Give your answer.

- Put the students in pairs to take turns asking and answering the questions in Exercise 1 about each other's family. Go round, monitoring and helping. Make sure all the students are handling the superlative forms correctly.

3 Pairwork

- The pairwork exercise for this unit is on pages 119 and 124. Put the students in pairs and tell them who will be Student A, and who will be Student B.

- While they're doing the exercise, go round monitoring and helping. Take note of any errors which may need particular attention later, and also any examples of good language use which you can praise in a feedback session. Check answers with the class.

Student A
a) the ugliest   b) the most famous
c) the oldest   d) the most expensive
e) the biggest   f) the most popular

Student B
a) the most interesting   b) the most beautiful
c) the most modern   d) the busiest
e) the cheapest   f) the quietest

---

4 *Grammar Extra* 12

Ask students to turn to *Grammar Extra* 12 on page 130 of the Student's Book. Here they'll find an explanation of the grammar they've been studying and further exercises to practise it.

---

1 a) Driving is more dangerous than flying.
  b) French food is better than English food.
  c) Meat is healthier than fish.
  d) English is more difficult than my language.
  e) Men are more romantic than women.
  f) Cats are nicer than dogs.

3 a) The most beautiful beach I know is Ipanema beach in Rio de Janeiro.
  b) The ugliest city I know is …
  c) The most expensive restaurant I know is …
  d) The funniest person I know is …
  e) The worst driver I know is …
  f) The luckiest person I know is …

Reading (SB page 81)

1

- Focus attention on the pictures and give the students a moment or two to take in what they see. Then ask the students to raise their hands if they have one or more of these things.

- Explain *lose* and ask the students to discuss in pairs which of these things they think are easy to lose. Get them to report back to the class on their discussion. Explain *common* and have a class vote on which three are the most common things to lose.

2 🌐 2.70

Play the recording and ask the students to listen and read the article. Ask them to say what the answer to the question in Exercise 1 is. Then ask them for their reactions to the text. Does anything surprise them?

Money, keys, a TV remote control.

3

Groupwork. Ask the students to discuss the questions in small groups. When they've finished, ask them to report back to the class. Encourage them to tell any funny stories that emerged about losing things.

Extra activity

Ask the students to say what is the most unusual thing they have ever lost.

Useful phrases (SB page 82)

1 🌐 2.71

- Explain *lost property office(r)* and ask the students if they've ever been to a lost property office to ask about something they've lost, and if they have, to provide details (What did they lose? Where did they lose it? What happened? Did they get the object back?).

- Go through the questions with the class and ask three confident students to describe the three bags in the picture.

- Play the recording and ask them to listen and read the conversation. Allow them to discuss their answers to the questions in pairs.

---

a) Bag 2
b) a mobile phone, some glasses and
   a plastic snake

---

2 🌐 2.72

- Focus the students' attention on the example, then ask them to match the other questions and answers. Check answer with the class.

- Tell the students to find the questions in the conversation in Exercise 1 and underline the answers that Judy gives.

- Play the recording for them to listen and check. Then play it again for them to repeat the useful phrases.

---

a) 2: It's black.   b) 4: It's made of leather.
c) 1: It's a handbag.
d) 3: There's a plastic snake.

Extra activities

- Collect various possessions from your students to create your own lost property office. Ask the students to come up one by one and describe the objects they've 'lost'. After a while, choose a confident student to play the part of the lost property officer.

- Use the question *What's it made of?* to teach some more vocabulary for materials. Remind them of *leather, plastic* and *nylon* from the conversation in the Student's Book and teach *wood, paper, glass, metal, wool, china* and *cloth*. Put the students into groups and give them one minute to write down as many objects as they can which are made of plastic, then leather, then wood, etc. Award one point for each object.

3

- Pairwork. Put the students in pairs to write a new conversation similar to that in Exercise 1. Go round, monitoring and helping with vocabulary.

- When the students have written their conversations, ask them to practise them, taking turns to play the different roles. Ask several pairs to perform their conversations for the class.

Vocabulary *Extra* (SB page 83)
Common adjectives

1

- Focus the students' attention on the list of words and point out that they're all adjectives. Remind students that the underlining indicates the syllable of the word that has the strongest stress. Check that the students can pronounce the adjectives correctly.

- Ask students to look at the pictures and match each one with one of the adjectives. Point out that the first one has been done for them.

> See Exercise 2 for answers.

2

Focus the students' attention on the words in the box. Check that the students can pronounce the adjectives correctly. Then ask them to match each adjective in the box with their opposite adjective in Exercise 1.

10 big – small	5 good – bad
4 boring – interesting	11 happy – sad
9 cheap – expensive	8 long – short
13 difficult – easy	14 loud – quiet
1 dirty – clean	2 lucky – unlucky
3 early – late	7 rich – poor
6 fast – slow	12 ugly – beautiful
	15 young – old

3

Pairwork. Demonstrate the activity with a confident student. Cover the words and ask what the opposite of one of the adjectives is. Elicit the answer. Then put the students into pairs to continue the activity. Go round, checking that everyone is pronouncing the adjectives correctly.

Focus on *like*

1

Ask the students to look at the table. Focus their attention the uses of *like* and their examples. Then ask the students to complete the table with the correct phrases from the box.

> 1 Do you like Sushi?
> 2 She doesn't like him.
> 3 I don't like washing up.
> 4 They like cooking.
> 5 They'd like a holiday.

2

Ask the students to write a sentence of their own for each use of *like* from the table.

Further practice material

Need more writing practice?
→ Workbook page 51
- Writing a summary of graphic data

Need more classroom practice activities?
→ Photocopiable resource materials pages 186 to 188
  Grammar: *Quiz time*
  Vocabulary: *Ready, steady, search*
  Communication: *What is it?*
→ TOP 10 activities pages xv to xx

Need progress tests?
→ Test CD – *Test Unit 12*

Need more on important teaching concepts?
→ Key concepts in *New Inside Out* pages xxii to xxxv

Need student self-study practice?
→ CD-ROM – Unit 12: *Money*

Need student CEF self-evaluation?
→ CEF Checklists pages xxxvii to xliv

Need more information and more ideas?
→ www.insideout.net

Review C *Teacher's notes*

These exercises act as a check of the grammar and vocabulary that the students have learnt in Units 9–12. Use them to find any problems that students are having or anything that they haven't understood and which will need further work.

Grammar (SB page 84)

Remind the students of the grammar explanations they read and the exercises they did in the *Grammar Extra* on pages 130 and 131.

1

This exercise reviews countable and uncountable nouns from Unit 10.

> Countable: apples, strawberries, bananas, eggs
> Uncountable: meat, milk, water, bread

2

This exercise reviews countable and uncountable nouns from Unit 10. Give the students time to study the picture before they start to complete the conversation. Make sure they understand that some of the words in the box can be used more than once.

Check answers with the class before putting the students into pairs to have similar conversations about other items in the picture. As they do this, go round, offering help and encouragement where necessary.

> 1 Are   2 are   3 many   4 lot   5 is
> 6 is   7 much   8 isn't

3

This exercise reviews the present continuous from Unit 11. Check answers to the first part of the exercise before moving on to the second part.

> a) 'm wearing   d) 'm sitting
> b) are working   e) 'm reading
> c) is talking   f) 'm holding
>
> a) I'm/am not wearing a T-shirt.
> b) My parents aren't / are not working today.
> c) Our teacher isn't / is not talking to us.
> d) I'm/am not sitting near the door.
> e) I'm/am not reading a newspaper.
> f) I'm/am not holding a pencil.

4

This exercise reviews comparative adjectives from Unit 12. Check answers with the class before moving on to the second part of the exercise. Then ask the students agree or disagree with the statements.

> a) more beautiful   b) cheaper   c) better
> d) nicer   e) more interesting   f) bigger

Cultural notes

Angelina Jolie (born 1975)
(See notes about Angelina Jolie in Unit 2, page 11.)

Julia Roberts (born 1967)
American actress, Julia Roberts is one of the most popular actresses in Hollywood and one of the best paid. She's appeared in a number of romantic comedies, such as *Pretty Woman* (1990), *My Best Friend's Wedding* (1997) and *Notting Hill* (1999). She won the Best Actress Academy Award as the title role in *Erin Brockovich* (2000).

Brad Pitt (born 1963)
(See notes about Brad Pitt in Unit 2, page 9.)

Jake Gyllenhaal (born 1980)
(See notes about Jake Gyllenhaal in Unit 11, page 83.)

Keira Knightley (born 1985)
(See notes about Keira Knightley in Unit 11, page 83.)

Charlize Theron (born 1975)
(See notes about Charlize Theron in Unit 11, page 83.)

5

This exercise reviews superlative adjectives from Unit 12. Check answers before the students go on to discuss possible answers to the questions.

> a) tallest   b) youngest   c) best
> d) most interesting   e) furthest   f) loveliest

6

This exercise reviews a variety of structures used in Units 9 to 12.

1 a) I working with my father today.
2 a) You are studying Spanish?
3 b) He is better as me at sport.
4 b) I'm the most happiest person in the world!
5 a) There aren't some curtains.
6 b) Are there any cheese?

Vocabulary (SB page 85)

1

This exercise reviews household objects and furniture from Unit 9. When checking answers, make sure that the students can pronounce the words correctly, paying particular attention to *cupboard* /ˈkʌbəd/ and *picture* /ˈpɪktʃə/.

armchair, coffee table, cushions, lamp, mirror, picture, plant, rug, sofa

2

This exercise reviews rooms and household objects from Unit 9. Allow the students to compare answers in pairs before checking with the class. Encourage them to say in which rooms the 'odd things out' belong.

a) bath   b) shower   c) cooker

3

This exercise reviews prepositions of place from Unit 9.

1 in   2 in   3 on   4 near   5 near   6 in
7 near   8 in

4

This exercise reviews types of food from Unit 10.

a) pasta   b) apple   c) banana   d) bread
e) potato   f) rice   g) carrot   h) egg   i) fish
j) cheese   k) orange

5

This exercise reviews words used for describing people from Unit 11. Encourage the students to look carefully at the two pictures before completing the gaps.

1 beautiful   2 straight   3 green   4 T-shirt
5 jeans   6 belt   7 trainers   8 rings   9 grey
10 blue   11 handsome   12 smile   13 suit
14 shirt   15 tie   16 shoes

6

This exercise reviews talking about amounts of money from Unit 12 and practises large numbers.

a) 3   b) 5   c) 1   d) 2   e) 4

Pronunciation (SB page 85)

These two exercises review work students did on word stress, using words they met in Units 9–12.

1

Remind the students that the boxes show the syllables of a word and the large boxes indicate the stressed syllables. Read the example words in the table aloud so that the students can hear the stress clearly. Tell them that they should complete the table by classifying the words according to how many syllables each one has and where the main stress falls. Encourage them to say each word aloud to get a feeling for what sounds right.

(See Exercise 2 for answers)

2 🌐 3.01

Point out the main stresses in the example words which are underlined. Ask the students to do the same for the other words in the table. Play the recording for them to check their answers. Then play it again for them to listen and repeat the words.

A: <u>arm</u>chair, <u>cur</u>ly, <u>gar</u>lic, <u>lem</u>on
B: <u>beau</u>tiful, <u>in</u>teresting, <u>sal</u>ary, <u>veg</u>etable
C: mou<u>stache</u>, tat<u>too</u>
D: ba<u>na</u>na, ex<u>pen</u>sive, im<u>por</u>tant, po<u>ta</u>to

Reading & Listening (SB page 86)

1 🌐 3.02

Give the students a few minutes to read the texts. Then ask them to decide if the statements are true or false. Encourage them to correct the false statements or say why they are wrong. Allow them to work in pairs, if they wish.

a) False. (It's 450 years old.)
b) False. (There's steak, chicken and fish on the menu.)
c) False. (He's especially famous for his strange dishes.)
d) True.
e) True.
f) False. (Aragawa is famous for its beef.)

2

Give the students a few minutes to read the texts again and decide which restaurants to recommend for these people. Remind them to give reasons for their choices.

a) El Bulli   b) Aragawa   c) The Fat Duck

3

Give the students plenty of time to discuss the question. Go round monitoring and helping, and take note of anything interesting that can be reported back to the whole class.

4 🌐 3.03

Focus the student's attention on the notepad and the photo. Tell them that they're going to hear a conversation between a waiter in a restaurant and a customer, Lara, who is phoning to reserve a table. Play the recording and ask the students to complete the notes.

1 Dinner	2 Saturday 16th August	3 Six
4 Nine o'clock	5 Lara Gluck	

🌐 3.03 (R = (male) Receptionist; L = Lara)

R: *The Fat Cat. Can I help you?*
L: *Yes, I'd like to make a reservation, please.*
R: *Of course. What day?*
L: *Friday 15th August.*
R: *Is that for lunch or dinner?*
L: *Dinner.*
R: *I'm sorry. We have tables for lunch, but there aren't any tables for dinner on the 15th. There's a big party that night. The chef's getting married.*
L: *Oh. It's my birthday.*
R: *Would you like a different day?*
L: *What about Saturday – Saturday 16th August?*
R: *For dinner?*
L: *Yes.*
R: *Yes. We have some tables for dinner on Saturday.*
L: *Great.*
R: *How many people?*
L: *Six. Do you have a window table?*
R: *Sorry?*
L: *Do you have a table near the window, with a view of the river?*
R: *Certainly. What time would you like, 7.30 or nine o'clock?*
L: *Er, nine, I think.*
R: *And what's your name?*
L: *Lara Gluck.*
R: *Can you spell that, please?*
L: *L–A–R–A G–L–U–C–K.*
R: *OK. That's a window table for six people at 9.00 p.m. on Saturday 16th August.*
L: *Thank you. Er, is there a dress code?*
R: *Yes. No jeans, and we ask men to wear a jacket and tie.*
L: *OK. Oh, and can I pay by credit card?*
R: *Yes, that's no problem. See you on Saturday.*

5

Ask the students to read the choices before they listen again so they know what kind of things they should be looking out for.

a) dinner	b) Friday	c) are some	d) can
e) formal	f) takes		

Writing & Speaking (SB page 87)

1

Ask the students to read the email and answer the question.

The email starts *Dear* + the name of the people she's writing to.
It ends *See you soon* and *Love* + her name.

2

Ask the students to read Patricia's email again and to find the relevant paragraphs.

a) 2   b) 1   c) 4   d) 3

3

Remind the students that adjectives are words that describe nouns. When you check answers, ask the students to say what each adjective describes.

(very) relaxed, beautiful, blue, amazing, white, big, (really) quiet, fantastic, great

4

Give the students time to imagine where they are and what they're doing. Then put them into pairs to take turns asking and answering questions about their holidays. Go round offering help and encouragement. When they've finished, ask them to tell the class whether their holidays were similar to their partner's or not.

5

Remind the students that they read an email from Patricia in Exercise 1 and that this was also divided into four paragraphs. Ask what the topics of these paragraphs were (see Exercise 2). As the students write their emails, go round offering help and encouragement. You might like to display the finished emails in the classroom.

Further practice material

Need more classroom practice activities?

→ Photocopiable resource materials page 189
   🌐 3.04 **Song:** *Sailing*
→ TOP 10 activities pages xv to xx

Need progress tests?

→ Test CD – *Test Review C*

Need more on important teaching concepts?

→ Key concepts in *New Inside Out* pages xxii to xxxv

Need student self-study practice?

→ CD-ROM – *Review C*

Need more information and more ideas?

→ www.insideout.net

13 Talent *Overview*

Section	Aims	What the students are doing
Listening **SB page 88**	*Listening skills*: listening for specific information	• Matching photos of famous people to names. • Listening to a radio show and identifying who can do different things.
Grammar **SB page 88**	*Grammar*: *can* (for ability)	• Completing questions and answers with *can* and *can't*. • Asking and answering questions.
Pronunciation **SB page 89**	*Pronunciation*: stress with *can* and *can't*	• Practising chants and identifying when *can* and *can't* are stressed and unstressed.
Grammar **SB page 89**	*Grammar*: adverbs of manner	• Completing sentences. • Matching adjectives and adverbs. • Studying adverb formation. • Putting words in order to make sentences.
Reading **SB page 90**	*Reading skills*: reading for detail	• Matching headings to sections of an article on a dancer. • Matching beginnings and endings of sentences.
Grammar **SB page 90**	*Pronunciation*: frequency expressions	• Putting expressions in order of frequency. • Putting words in the correct place in questions. • Asking and answering the questions.
Vocabulary **SB page 91**	*Vocabulary*: adjectives	• Matching character adjectives with their meanings. • Using adjectives to describe themselves.
Reading **SB page 91**	*Reading skills*: reading for detail	• Reading and completing a questionnaire on how people see you. • Discussing the results of the questionnaire.
Useful phrases **SB page 92**	*Vocabulary*: phrases which are useful when making excuses.	• Matching excuses with pictures. • Listening to a conversation and ticking the excuses one person makes. • Listening to and repeating useful phrases. • Writing and practising a new conversation.
Vocabulary *Extra* **SB page 93**	*Vocabulary*: revision of words from the unit: common adverbs. Focus on *be*	• Matching pictures with words.
Writing **WB page 55**	Correcting mistakes with capital letters and spelling Writing about a talented person	

13 Talent *Teacher's notes*

Warm-up

Teach the words *talent* and *talented* and tell the students that you know a very talented woman. Write a couple of examples of things this person can do on the board. For example *She can play the piano. She can speak Spanish*. Ask all the students to stand up and tell them to ask you questions using *Can she …?* If the verb and the noun in a question begin with the same letter, say *Yes, she can*, write the equivalent sentence on the board and tell the student who asked the question that they can sit down. If not, say *No, she can't* and leave the student standing. If students ask questions without nouns such as *Can she swim?*, only say *yes* if the verb begins with the same letter as the pronoun, i.e. *s*. Continue until all the students have worked out what questions they have to ask in order to be allowed to sit down.

Listening (SB page 88)

1

- Pairwork. Focus attention on the photos. Ask the students to work in pairs and to match the photos with the names. Ask them to make notes of anything they know about the people in the photos.

- Check answers with the class and ask the students to share the information they noted down about the famous people.

> 4 Bono   3 Shakira   2 Bruce Willis
> 1 Madonna

Cultural notes

Madonna (born 1958)
(See notes about Madonna in Unit 4, page 27.)

Bruce Willis (born 1955)
American actor who found fame in the TV series *Moonlighting* (1985–1989), but is best known for his roles in the *Die Hard* films (1988 and 1989). His other films include *Pulp Fiction* (1994), *The Jackal* (1997), and *The Sixth Sense* (1999). He was married to Demi Moore.

Shakira Isabel Mebarak Ripoll (born in 1977)
Colombian singer-songwriter known as Shakira. She achieved great success in Latin America before breaking into the English speaking market in 2001 with her album *Laundry Service*. She's best known for mixing different sound styles in her songs and her dancing.

Bono (born 1960)
(See notes about Bono in Review B, page 64.)

2 🌐 3.05

- Explain that the students are going to hear a radio show called *Hidden talents*, which focuses on things that famous people can do in addition to those for which they are famous. Go through the list of possible talents with the class and make sure everyone understands them. Give them a minute or two to discuss in pairs or small groups which of the famous people in Exercise 1 they think can do these things.

- Play the recording for the student to check their answers. Find out if anyone guessed them all correctly. Then ask for a show of hands to find out how many of the students can do each of the things listed.

> a) Bruce Willis   b) Bono   c) Shakira
> d) Madonna

> 🌐 3.05
>
> *It's time for 'Hidden talents'!*
>
> *Hi everybody. In 'Hidden talents' today we look at some of the things you didn't know about your favourite stars.*
>
> *First up we have Bruce Willis, our favourite Hollywood actor. Did you know that Bruce can play the harmonica? It's true!*
>
> *Next is Bono from our favourite band in the world, U2. Even rock stars relax, and Mr Bono can play chess really well.*
>
> *Shakira has everything – she's beautiful and talented __and__ she can speak Spanish, English, Italian, Arabic and Portuguese. Wow. Five languages!*
>
> *And finally what about the queen of pop, Madonna? Well, she loves horses and she can ride really well. She has some beautiful horses at her big country house in England.*
>
> *And now …*

Extra activity

If you can juggle, or you have any other talent that is easy to demonstrate in the classroom, do so (saying *I can juggle*), and then ask the students to reveal any hidden talents that they might have.

Grammar (SB page 88)

can/can't

1 🌐 3.06

- Focus attention on the information in the margin and read the question, affirmative answer and negative answer with the class. Ask various students if they can read music and encourage them to reply with *Yes, I can* or *No, I can't.*

- Give the students a few minutes to complete the questions and answers. Then play the recording for them to check their answers. Play it a second time for them to listen and repeat.

---

a) 'Can you play the harmonica?'
  'Yes, I can.' 'No, I can't.'
b) 'Can your father play chess?'
  'Yes, he can.' 'No, he can't.'
c) 'Can you speak five languages?'
  'Yes, I can.' 'No, I can't.'
d) 'Can your mother ride a horse?'
  'Yes, she can.' 'No, she can't.'
e) 'Can you dance flamenco?'
  'Yes, I can.' 'No, I can't.'
f) 'Can your parents ski?'
  'Yes, they can.' 'No, they can't.'

Language notes

Grammar: *can* for ability

- Earlier in the course, students looked at *can* for requesting and giving permission, e.g. *Can you repeat that?* Another major use of *can* is to do with ability, i.e. to say that you know how to do something.

  I can swim.
  I can't dance.
  Can you play golf?

- Note the pronunciation of *can*: when stressed *can* is pronounced /kæn/, when unstressed it's pronounced /kən/, and *can't* is pronounced /kɑːnt/.

- When you're talking about the ability to speak languages, do sports, or play musical instruments, you often leave out *can*, and just use the present simple, with the same meaning.

  I can play the guitar.
  I play the guitar.

2

Pairwork. Put the students into pairs and ask them to take turns asking and answering the questions in Exercise 1

3 *Grammar Extra* 13

Ask the students to turn to *Grammar Extra* 13 on page 132 of the Student's Book. Here they'll find an explanation of the grammar they've been studying and further exercises to practise it.

1
a) I can speak English but I can't speak Spanish.
b) I can ride a bicycle but I can't ride a motorbike.
c) I can drive a car but I can't drive a bus.
d) I can play the guitar but I can't play the drums.
e) I can read music but I can't read Japanese.
f) I can play chess but I can't play poker.

Pronunciation (SB page 89)

1 🌐 3.07

- Play the first chant and ask the students just to listen and to notice which words are stressed (remind them that the underlining indicates words with the most stress). Then play it again and ask them to repeat the chant. Make sure that they're stressing the correct words and that their pronunciation of *can* is quite weak. Remind them of the work that they did on the schwa sound in Unit 12 and point out that *can* has the schwa sound in affirmative statements and questions where it isn't the first word.

- Focus attention on the second chant and play the recording. Then ask the students to repeat it. Again pay attention to the words they're stressing and make sure that the correct words are stressed. Point out that in short answers *can* is always pronounced strongly with the /æ/ rather than the /ə/ sound, and that when *can* is the first word of a question, either the strong or weak form is used.

- Focus attention on the third chant and play the recording. Point out that *can't* is never pronounced with a schwa sound and that it's stressed in negative statements and short answers. Play the recording again and ask the students to repeat it.

2

- Ask the students to identify the chants where *can* and *can't* are stressed and those in which they aren't stressed.

- Then divide the class in three groups and ask each group to practise one of the chants.

---

can is stressed in chant B. *can't* is stressed in chant C. *can* isn't stressed in chant A.

Grammar (SB page 89)

Adverbs of manner

1

- Focus the students' attention on the photo and say *He's a bad cook. He can't cook very well.* Explain that you use *very well* to say how good or bad you are at doing something. Give a few examples of your own abilities, sounding cheerful when you say, for example, *I can speak French very well* and sad when you say, for example, *I can't play the piano very well.*

- Tell the students to look at the three gapped sentences and to complete them so that they are true. Point out that they can use the activities in the box or their own ideas. When they've finished, go round the class asking students to read out their sentences.

2

- Focus the students' attention on the lists of adjectives and adverbs. Remind them that adjectives are used to describe nouns. Ask the students for a sentence or two using a couple of the adjectives in the list. Then explain that adverbs describe verbs; they tell you how someone does something. Explain that many adverbs are formed from adjectives. Tell them to look at the list of adverbs and to decide which adjective they think each one is formed from. This should present little difficulty as most adverbs resemble or are the same as the adjectives from which they come.

- Ask the students to look at the adverbs and their corresponding adjectives and say how most are formed. Then ask which ones are irregular.

- Check answers and then focus their attention on the information in the margin. Point out the spelling changes in *carefully* and *happily*. Remind them that in Exercise 1 they used *well*, the adverb from *good*.

---

bad – badly	happy – happily
careful – carefully	loud – loudly
fast – fast	quiet – quietly
good – well	slow – slowly

a) You add *ly*.
b) *well* and *fast*

---

3 🌐 3.08

- Go through the example with the class, pointing out the order in which the parts of the sentence occur when the verb takes an object. Compare this with the simpler sentences they formed in Exercise 1 where there's no object and the adverb comes immediately after the verb. Putting the adverb in the wrong place in the sentence is a common student error, so spend some time making sure that they get this right.

- Ask the students to work in pairs to put the words in the right order to make sentences. Go round, monitoring and helping. Make sure that the students are putting the adverbs in the correct place.

- Play the recording for the students to check their answers. Then play it a second time for them to listen and repeat.

- Ask the students to put a tick by the sentences that are true for them. Then put them in pairs to compare results with a partner. Ask several students if they can change the sentences that are not true for them into true sentences by changing the adverbs.

---

a) I eat my food very slowly.
b) I drive my car quite fast.
c) I play the guitar very badly.
d) I spend my money very carefully.
e) I play the drums very loudly.
f) I don't eat my soup very quietly.
g) I do my homework very happily.
h) I don't speak English very well.

Extra activity

Ask the students to change all the adverbs in the sentences in Exercise 3 so that they have the opposite meaning. You may need to teach *carelessly* as the opposite of *carefully*.

I eat my food very fast.
I drive my car quite slowly.
I spend my money very carelessly.
I play the drums very quietly.
I play my CDs very loudly.
I do my work very unhappily.
I speak English very well.

Reading (SB page 90)

Warm-up

Ask the students to discuss with a partner what dances are typical in their country. If possible, get them to explain or show their partners how to do them. If any students attend a dance class, ask them to talk about it and to demonstrate a dance they've learnt.

1

- Ask the students to call out all the different types of dance that they know. Write their ideas on the board. This could be done as a team game with points awarded for suggestions.

- Find out if any of the students can do any of the dances listed on the board.

Example answers: flamenco, ballet, tap, salsa, samba, jive, disco, ballroom dancing (e.g. waltz, tango, foxtrot).

---

2 3.09

- Focus attention on the photo and ask the students if they've heard of the Spanish flamenco dancer Joaquín Cortés.

- Go through the words in the box and then ask the students to read the article as they listen to the recording and match the headings to the different sections of the text.

- Check answers with the class and go through any problems of understanding that they have with the text.

> a) Early life   b) Travel   c) Sleep
> d) Practice   e) Meals   f) Family
> g) Hidden talents

3 3.10

- Focus the students' attention on the second column and explain that these expressions tell you how often Joaquín Cortés does certain things. Ask them to match the beginnings and endings of the sentences according to the information in the article.

- Play the recording for them to check their answers. Ask them if they find any of the information surprising. Don't ask them how often they do all the things in the list as they will be doing that in the next section.

> a) He travels all the time.
> b) He sleeps for five or six hours a night.
> c) He practises for more than five hours a day.
> d) He buys new shoes every month.
> e) He eats three times a day.
> f) He calls his family every day.

Grammar (SB page 90)
Frequency expressions

1 3.11

- Focus the students' attention on the frequency expressions in the margin and point out that they are arranged with the most frequent at the top and the least frequent at the bottom. Ask several students to read them aloud.

- Ask the students to look at the frequency expressions in the box. Explain that they should number these in order of frequency with *1* being the most frequent and *6* the least frequent. Allow them to work in pairs and to compare answers with another pair before you play the recording for them to check their answers. Play it again for the students to listen and repeat the expressions.

> 1 three times a day   4 every two weeks
> 2 every day   5 once a month
> 3 twice a week   6 four times a year

2 3.12

- Look at the example with the whole class and point out the correct position of the auxiliary verb *do*. Ask the students to complete the remaining questions with the words in brackets.

- Play the recording for them to check their answers. Play it a second time for them to listen and repeat.

- Put the students into pairs. Remind them of the information they learnt in the previous section about Joaquín Cortés and how often he travels, buys new shoes and calls his family. Tell them to take turns asking each other. Encourage them to report back on their partner's answers and compare them with those of Joaquín Cortés.

> a) How often do you travel?
> b) How often do you buy new shoes?
> c) How often do you call your family?

3 Pairwork

- The pairwork exercise for this unit is on pages 120 and 125. Put the students in pairs and tell them who will be Student A, and who will be Student B.

- While they are doing the exercise, go round monitoring and helping. Take note of any errors which may need particular attention later, and also any examples of good language use which you can praise in a feedback session.

Extra activity

Put the students in pairs and ask them to write three more questions using *How often do you …?* Then put pairs together to take turns asking and answering each others questions.

Vocabulary (SB page 91)
Character adjectives

1 3.13

- Read out the list of adjectives and ask the students what they think they describe (people's characters). Point out the example which shows that *confident* means you are very sure of yourself. Ask the students to match the other adjectives to their meanings. Allow them to compare results in pairs or small groups.

- Play the recording for the students to check their answers, then answer any questions they may have about vocabulary. Explain *positive* and *negative* and ask which one they think always has a negative meaning.

> a) 3   b) 1   c) 5   d) 6   e) 4   f) 2
> *Selfish* always has a negative meaning.

2

- Ask the students to work individually to choose their three adjectives. Point out that they can use adjectives of their own if they find the ones in Exercise 1 too limiting. Go round, monitoring and helping with any vocabulary they need.

- Put the students in pairs to compare their adjectives. Encourage them to explain their choices.

Extra activity

Ask each student to think of an adjective to describe themselves which begins with the same letter as their first name. Do the same yourself. Start them off by saying, for example, *Hello, I'm energetic Eric*. Go round the class with students introducing themselves together with their adjectives.

Reading (SB page 91)

1

- Look at the title of the questionnaire with the class and ask if you can ever really know what other people think of us. Tell them that they're going to answer a questionnaire that claims to be able to reveal this. Ask them to read the questionnaire and work individually to choose their own answers. Suggest that they circle the answers that are best for them. Go round, monitoring and helping with any queries.

- Explain how to add up their scores and then tell them to read the *What your score means* section. They should compare with a partner.

2

- Tell the students to work individually and write short descriptions of three people they know well. Point out the example and encourage students to begin their descriptions with *People think …* as in the *What your score means* section of the questionnaire. Go round, monitoring and offering help and encouragement.

- Put the students in pairs and tell them to take turns to read out their descriptions to each other.

Useful phrases (SB page 92)

1 🌐 3.14

- Ask the students if they like doing exercise. If anyone says they don't, explain *excuse* and ask what excuse they give when someone asks them to do some exercise.

- Focus the students' attention on the pictures and explain that these show the top six excuses that people give for not doing exercise. Ask the students to match the excuses in the list to the pictures.

- Allow students to compare results in pairs before playing the recording again for them to check. Explain any unknown vocabulary. Then play the recording again for the students to repeat the excuses.

> a) 2   b) 4   c) 1   d) 5   e) 6   f) 3

2 🌐 3.15

Focus attention on the illustration and ask the students for adjectives to describe Dan and Lisa. Then play the recording and ask the students to listen and read their conversation. Tell them to tick the excuses from Exercise 1 that they hear Lisa make. Check answers with the class.

> a) 'I have a bad back.'
> c) 'I'm really tired.'
> d) 'I have a cold.'
> f) 'I don't have any money.'

Language notes

Grammar: *can't*

- Here *can't* isn't used to talk about not having the ability to do something, but about not having the possibility.

- When you say *I can't swim*, you mean that you don't know how to.

- When you say *I can't go swimming at the moment*, you mean that it isn't possible.

3 🌐 3.16

- Play the recording for the students to listen and repeat the useful phrases.

- Point out Dan's use of *you should* (*You should go swimming*) for giving advice. Ask them to find another place in the conversation where he gives advice (*… you should have a massage*).

4

- Pairwork. Put the students into pairs and ask them to write a similar conversation using their own excuses. You could have a brainstorming session with the whole class first and put their suggestions for good excuses on the board.

- As the students write their conversations, go round offering encouragement and assistance. When they've finished, get them to practise them aloud. Take note of any particularly good conversations and ask the students involved to perform them for the class.

Vocabulary *Extra* (SB page 93)

Common adverbs

1

- Focus the students' attention on the sentences and point out that they all include common adverbs. Check that the students can pronounce the adverbs correctly.

- Ask the students to look at the pictures and match each one with one of the sentences. Point out that the first one has been done for them.

> 3 She's driving carefully.
> 5 He's winning easily.
> 9 She's typing fast.
> 4 They're playing happily.
> 7 He's working hard.
> 8 He's laughing loudly.
> 1 She's reading quietly.
> 2 He's speaking slowly.
> 6 He's singing well.

2

Pairwork. Demonstrate the activity with a confident student. Cover the words, point to one of the pictures and ask *What's he/she doing?* Elicit the answer. Then put the students into pairs to continue the activity. Go round, checking that everyone is pronouncing the adverbs correctly.

Focus on *be*

1

Ask the students to focus their attention on the table and the uses of *be* and their examples. Then ask the students to complete the table with the correct phrases from the box.

> 1 She's an architect.
> 2 He's twenty-one.
> 3 I'm cold.
> 4 They're bored.
> 5 Be careful!
> 6 There are some new students.
> 7 We're waiting for a bus.

2

Ask the students to write a sentence of their own for each use of *be* from the table.

Further practice material

Need more writing practice?

- → Workbook page 55
- Correcting mistakes with capital letters and spelling
- Writing about a talented person

Need more classroom practice activities?

- → Photocopiable resource materials pages 190 to 192
  Grammar: *How do you do it?*
  Vocabulary: *Character jumble*
  Communication: *How many people can do it?*
- → TOP 10 activities pages xv to xx

Need progress tests?

- → Test CD – *Test Unit 13*

Need more on important teaching concepts?

- → Key concepts in *New Inside Out* pages xxii to xxxv

Need student self-study practice?

- → CD-ROM – Unit 13: *Talent*

Need student CEF self-evaluation?

- → CEF Checklists pages xxxvii to xliv

Need more information and more ideas?

- → www.insideout.net

14 TV *Overview*

Section	Aims	What the students are doing
Vocabulary & Listening **SB page 94**	*Vocabulary*: TV programmes *Listening skills*: listening for gist	• Completing questions with TV words. • Asking and answering questions about TV viewing. • Listening and identifying TV programmes by genre.
Speaking SB page 94	*Conversation skills*: fluency work	• Discussing TV viewing.
Reading SB page 95	*Reading skills*: reading for specific information.	• Reading a web page about *Big Brother* and answering questions. • Matching people with reasons why they want to be on *Big Brother* and discussing the reasons people give.
Grammar SB page 95	*Grammar*: future forms – *want to*, *would like to*, *hope to*, *(be) going to*	• Underlining the target verb structures in sentences. • Studying the structure of future forms. • Putting words in order to make sentences.
Listening & Reading **SB page 96**	*Reading and listening skills*: listening for specific information	• Reading and listening to an interview with a *Big Brother* winner. • Completing the interview with future forms.
Grammar SB page 96	*Grammar*: *(be) going to* + base form	• Completing questions and answers. • Asking and answering questions. • Writing and discussing sentences expressing good intentions.
Speaking SB page 97	*Conversation skills*: asking about future plans and intentions	• Asking and answering questions about future plans and intentions.
Pronunciation **SB page 97**	*Pronunciation*: stress in sentences with *going to*	• Listening to and repeating chants. • Practising weak pronunciation of *to*.
Speaking: anecdote **SB page 97**	*Conversation skills*: fluency practice	• Talking about favourite TV programmes.
Useful phrases **SB page 98**	*Vocabulary*: phrases which are useful for making and responding to suggestions and offers	• Listening to a conversation and completing it. • Completing a table with useful phrases. • Listening to and repeating useful phrases. • Practising a conversation.
Vocabulary *Extra* **SB page 99**	*Vocabulary*: revision of words from the unit: television. *What ...?* and *How ...?*	• Matching pictures with words.
Writing WB page 59	Linking sentences: *and, but, because* Completing a form, giving reasons	

14 TV Teacher's notes

Warm-up

Write *TV* in the centre of the board and create a mind map. Ask the students to call out any words that they know of that are connected to TV. Arrange them in groups on the mind map, so that all types of TV programmes are grouped together, any technical words are grouped together, words for people who appear on TV are grouped together, etc.

Vocabulary & Listening (SB page 94)

1 🌐 3.17

- Go through the words in the box and make sure the students understand them. Then ask them to work individually to complete the questions.

- Allow them time to discuss their results in pairs before playing the recording for them to check their answers. Play it a second time for them to repeat the questions.

a) televisions	b) watch	c) switch on
d) channels	e) programme	f) on

Language note

Pronunciation: *TV*

- *TV* is pronounced /ˈtiːˈviː/.

2

Pairwork. Ask the students to take turns asking and answering the questions in Exercise 1. They can then tell the class what they learnt about their partners. Then find out who in the class has the most / least televisions, who watches the most hours of TV per *day*, etc.

3 🌐 3.18

- Focus the students' attention on the pictures. Give them a few moments to take in what they can see. Explain *reality TV show* (making TV programmes with ordinary people) and make sure that they understand all the other captions.

- Tell the students that they're going to hear short extracts from each of the programmes illustrated. Play the recording and tell them to number the programmes in the order they hear them. Check answers with the class. Then ask the students to work individually to write down the names of TV programmes and what kind of programmes they are. Have a class feedback session on the various programmes.

1 a game show	4 a chat show
2 the news	5 a documentary
3 a soap opera	6 a reality TV show

🌐 3.18

1 (A = game show host; B = contestant)
A: Next question. On the border of which two South American countries can you find the Iguaçu Falls?
B: Oh. Um. Mm, I know this one. Is it Argentina and Chile? No – Argentina and Brazil.
A: Is that your final answer?
B: Yes.
A: Are you sure?
B: Um, yes.
A: It's the correct answer – YOU'VE JUST WON £125,000!!!

2
Police arrested two men after they attempted to rob a bank in the centre of London this morning. The men were armed, but nobody was hurt.

3 (W = woman; M = man)
W: Oh, hello, Mr Jones. How are you today?
M: Oh, can't complain. Here, have you heard about that Andy Clifford?
W: No, what?
M: Well, I've heard he's going to get married to Rachel Smedley.
W: Rachel Smedley – no!

4 (A = chat show host; B = film star)
A: Well, Michael, you've had a very successful career in the film business. Did you always want to be a movie star?
B: Not exactly. I grew up on a farm in the Mid-West and when I was a young boy all I wanted to be was a farmer like my dad.
A: So what made you change your mind?
B: Well, it was …

5
The shark is the king of the sea. It fills people with fear. But that's not the whole story. Yes, some kinds of shark are dangerous, but most of them are harmless and shy. Take the Spotted Wobbegong – not a beautiful specimen – quite ugly in fact …

6 (BB = Big Brother; V = Vicky)
BB: This is Big Brother. The nominations for eviction are … Vicky!
V: Oh … I knew it
BB: And … Clyde!

Language notes

Vocabulary: TV programmes

- A *soap opera*, or a *soap*, is a series of TV programmes about the daily life of a group of characters. It's often broadcast several times a week over many years.
- A *chat show*, or talk show, is an informal discussion with a host asking celebrities about themselves or work.

Speaking (SB page 94)

- Groupwork. Go through the questions with the class, then put the students into small groups to discuss them. Go round, monitoring and helping.
- Ask the groups to report back to the class on their discussions.

Reading (SB page 95)

1 3.19

- If the students aren't aware of the reality TV show *Big Brother*, wait until they've finished this exercise and then give them some more details about the programme. (See *Cultural note* below.)
- Ask the students to listen and read the web page and answer the questions. Then check answers with the class.

> a) A sociable, interesting and competitive person.
> b) The contestants live in the *Big Brother* house with eleven strangers, twenty-four hours a day, seven days a week.
> c) £100,000.

Extra activity

Ask the students what reality TV programmes are popular in their country or countries, what they think of them and whether they watch them. Find out if any of them would ever consider applying to be a contestant on one of these shows.

Cultural note

Big Brother

Big Brother is a reality TV show that lasts for about fifteen weeks. In it a number of contestants, usually about twelve, live together in a house and are filmed twenty-four hours a day. They have to try to avoid being voted out of the house by the public until only one is left. This person wins a cash prize.

2 3.20

- Focus attention on the photographs and tell the students that these are all people who would like to be on *Big Brother*. Ask them who they think look the most interesting.
- Ask the students to read the reasons why the people want to be on *Big Brother*. Ask them to guess from the photos who made which statement.
- Play the recording and ask the students to match the people to the statements.
- Check answers with the class before putting them into pairs to discuss which is the best and which is the worst reason to be on *Big Brother*.

> a) 1   b) 5   c) 2   d) 6   e) 4   f) 3

Extra activity

Ask the students to think of their own reasons for wanting (or not wanting) to be on *Big Brother*. Have a class vote on the best and worst.

Grammar (SB page 95)

Future forms

1

- Focus the students' attention on the reasons the contestants gave in the last section. Ask them to underline the verb structures listed.
- Ask them to discuss the two questions in pairs.
- Check answers with the class.

> a) The future.
> b) The infinitive with *to*.

2 3.21

- Look at the example with the class and then ask the students to work individually to put the words in the other sentences in the correct order.
- Allow them to compare results in pairs before playing the recording for them to check their answers. Play it a second time for them to listen and repeat the sentences.
- Tell the students to tick the sentences that are true for them and then to compare with a partner. Encourage them to ask follow-up questions. For example, if their partner says they want to live in a foreign country, they could ask *Which foreign country do you want to live in?* If they say they'd like to have lots of children, they could ask *How many children do you want to have?*

Extra activity

Ask the students to write more sentences with *hope to*, *want to* and *I'd like to* which are true for them.

Listening & Reading (SB page 96)

1 🌐 3.22

- Remind the students that Lynne was one of the candidates for *Big Brother* that they met on page 95. Ask them what her reason for wanting to go on the show was (she wanted to meet people, have a good time and buy her mother a house). Tell them that Lynne has now won *Big Brother* and her prize is £100,000. Tell them that they're going to listen to an interview with Lynne in which she says what she's going to do with the money. Before you play the recording, ask the students for a few suggestions about what they think she's going to do.

- Play the recording and ask the students to listen and read (tell them to ignore the gaps for the moment). Ask them what job Lynne would like to do. You may need to play the recording more than once.

A singer and an interviewer on TV.

Language notes

Vocabulary: *miss*

- The verb *miss* has several meanings. It can mean to be late for something, e.g. *I missed the train this morning and had to take a taxi*, or to notice that someone isn't there, e.g. *Nobody missed the boy until the evening when he didn't come home.*

- In this unit, *miss* means that you're sorry not to be with someone. For example:

  My children have gone away with their grandparents. I really miss them.
  My best friend has moved to London. I miss her.

2

- Go through the phrases in the box with the class. Then ask the students to work individually and use them to complete the conversation in Exercise 1. Point out that they'll need to use some of them more than once. Allow them to compare results with a partner.

- Play the recording again for the students to check their answers. Then ask a couple of confident students to take the roles of Lynne and the interviewer and to perform the conversation for the class.

1 you're going to	6 I'm not going to
2 I'm going to	7 Are you going to
3 are you going to	8 we're going to
4 I'm going to	9 I'm going to
5 are you going to	10 I'm going to

Language notes

Grammar: *(be) going to*

- There's no future tense in English, but there are various ways of talking about the future including *(be) going to*, the present continuous and *will*.

- *(be) going to* is the most common way to talk about future plans and intentions, and is the future form presented in this unit. It's usually used when you've already decided about a future action – you know what you're going to do.

- When *(be) going to* is used with *go*, it's often shortened. For example: *I'm going to go shopping* becomes *I'm going shopping.*

- *going to* is often written in an abbreviated form as '*gonna*' in pop songs. Encourage students to use the full form when doing their own writing. (Unless they're writing pop songs!)

Grammar (SB page 96)

(be) going to + base form

1 🌐 3.23

- Focus attention on the information in the margin and read out the sentences to the class. Then give the students time to look at the table of questions and answers about Lynne's plans and intentions and to complete it. Allow them to compare results in pairs or small groups.

- Play the recording for the students to listen and check their answers. Then play it again for them to listen and repeat.

a) 'Is she going to have a big party?'
   'Yes, she is.' 'No, she isn't.'
b) 'Is she going to buy a house for her mum?'
   'Yes, she is.' 'No, she isn't.'
c) 'Is she going to see Sheryl and Josh?'
   'Yes, she is.' 'No, she isn't.'
d) 'Is she going to see Eddie?'
   'Yes, she is.' 'No, she isn't.'
e) 'Is she going to go out and spend some money?'
   'Yes, she is.' 'No, she isn't.'
f) 'Is she going to record a CD?'
   'Yes, she is.' 'No, she isn't.'

2

Pairwork. Put the students in pairs to ask and answer the questions in Exercise 1. Remind them to take turns and that they'll find the answers in the interview in the previous section if they've forgotten Lynne's plans.

a) Yes, she is.	d) Yes, she is.
b) Yes, she is.	e) Yes, she is.
c) No, she isn't.	f) Yes, she is.

3 🌐 **3.24**

- Remind the students of the word *intentions* from Exercise 1. Tell them that, like *plans*, it means things that you decide that you're going to do. Ask the students what they think *good intentions* are (usually things that you decide to do in order to improve your health, to help other people, etc.). Go through the example with the class, pointing out the correct position of *to*, and find out if any of the students has this particular good intention.

- Ask the students to complete the other sentences. Play the recording for them to check their answers. Then play it again for them to listen and repeat. When they've done this chorally, ask individual students to repeat the sentences after you.

> a) I'm going to do more exercise.
> b) I'm going to eat healthier food.
> c) I'm going to save more money.
> d) I'm going to spend more time with my family.
> e) I'm not going to watch so much TV.
> f) I'm not going to arrive late for appointments.

4

Pairwork. Put the students in pairs to discuss the good intentions in Exercise 3. Go round, monitoring and helping. Ask if any of the students has other good intentions.

5 *Grammar Extra* **14**

Ask students to turn to *Grammar Extra* 14 on page 132 of the Student's Book. Here they'll find an explanation of the grammar they've been studying and further exercises to practise it.

> 1
> a) I'm/I'm not going to buy a new car tomorrow.
> b) I'm/I'm not going to get up early tomorrow.
> c) I'm/I'm not going to see my parents tomorrow.
> d) I'm/I'm not going to play golf tomorrow.
> e) I'm/I'm not going to watch my favourite TV programme tomorrow.
> f) I'm/I'm not going to wear jeans tomorrow.
>
> 2
> a) Are you going to buy a new car tomorrow?
> b) Are you going to get up early tomorrow?
> c) Are you going to see your parents tomorrow?
> d) Are you going to play golf tomorrow?
> e) Are you going to watch your favourite TV programme tomorrow?
> f) Are you going to wear jeans tomorrow?
>
> 3
> a) She's going to have a pizza.
> b) She's going to do the washing.
> c) She's going to wash her hair.
> d) She's going to read a magazine.
> e) She's going to drink some wine.
> f) She's going to watch a DVD.

Speaking (SB page 97)

1

- Pairwork. Focus the students' attention on the example speech bubbles. Read them to the class, then choose a confident student and ask them the question. Encourage the student to answer truthfully and then to ask you the same question.

- Put the students in pairs to continue asking and answering the questions. Make sure they take turns to ask and answer. Go round, monitoring and helping with any vocabulary that they need. Discourage them from answering too many questions with *I don't know*.

2 Pairwork

- The pairwork exercise for this unit is on pages 120 and 125. Put the students in pairs and tell them who will be Student A, and who will be Student B.

- While they are doing the exercise, go round monitoring and helping. Take note of any errors which may need particular attention later, and also any examples of good language use which you can praise in a feedback session.

Pronunciation (SB page 97)

1 🌐 **3.25**

- Play the recording and ask the students what the missing word is in the chants (*to*). Remind them of the use of the *to* infinitive after *want* and *going*. Play the recording again and ask the students to notice how *to* is pronounced (weakly, with a schwa sound).

- Play the chants again for the students to repeat. Make sure they are pronouncing *to* correctly.

> The missing word is *to*.
> You pronounce *to* with the schwa sound (/ə/).

2

- Ask the students to underline the stressed words in the chants in Exercise 1. Play the recording for them to listen and check.

- Divide the class in half and ask each half to practise one of the chants. They then perform it for the others.

Speaking: anecdote (SB page 97)

For more information about how to set up, monitor and repeat anecdotes, see Practical methodology, page xx in the Introduction.

1 🌐 **3.26**

- Start by asking a few students around the class *What are you going to watch on TV tonight?* When they answer, ask *Is that your favourite programme?*

- Then tell them that they're going to listen to a woman called Juliet talking about her favourite programme. Give them a minute or two to go through the questions and answers so that they know what they are listening out for. Then ask them to listen and underline the correct information for each question.
- Check answers with the class and find out if students are familiar with the two programmes mentioned in the exercise. If anyone is familiar with them, ask them to say a little about them to the class.

a) *Desperate Housewives*	e) Bree
b) a comedy drama	f) Wednesdays
c) five women	g) Bree met a new man
d) the five women's lives	h) the humour

🌐 **3.26** (M = Max; J = Juliet)

M: *OK, Juliet. So what's your favourite TV programme?*

J: *My favourite TV programme? 'Desperate Housewives'.*

M: *What sort of programme is it?*

J: *It's a drama, but it's funny too. So I suppose it's a comedy drama.*

M: *Who are the main characters?*

J: *There are five women – Susan, Bree, um Lynette, Gabrielle and Edie. They all live in the same street and they're all friends. Well, sometimes they're friends.*

M: *What's it about?*

J: *It's about their lives.*

M: *Who's your favourite character?*

J: *Hm, I like Bree. She's crazy.*

M: *What day is it on?*

J: *Wednesdays.*

M: *Did you see it last Wednesday?*

J: *Yes, of course.*

M: *What happened?*

J: *Oh, um, Bree met a new man.*

M: *Oh. Why do you like it?*

J: *I like the humour – it's very dark. Anyway, what's your favourite programme.*

M: *Um, 'Who wants to be a Millionaire?'*

Cultural note

Desperate Housewives
Desperate Housewives is an American TV comedy drama that follows the lives of five fictional women who live on a street called Wisteria Lane in the suburbs of Fairview. Bree is one of the five women.

Who wants to be a millionaire?
Who wants to be a millionaire? is a TV game show which offers contestants cash prizes of up to £1,000,000 for answering a series of multiple-choice questions correctly. The questions start off by being extremely easy and get increasingly difficult. The emphasis of the show is on suspense rather than speed. The show originated in the UK in 1998.

2
- Pairwork. Give the students a moment or two to decide which TV programme they're going to talk about. Then ask them to go through the questions in Exercise 1, making the answers true for them. Ask them to work individually to do this.
- Tell the students to think about the language they want to use when they talk about their favourite TV programme and to make notes. Give help with any vocabulary that they think they'll need, but discourage them from writing whole sentences so that when it comes to the pairwork, they don't simply read out their notes.
- Put the students in pairs and ask them to take turns to talk about their favourite TV programme. Tell them that they can use their notes to help them, but they shouldn't just read from the paper. Encourage them to maintain eye contact with their partner as they speak.

Useful phrases (SB page 98)

1 🌐 3.27
Focus attention on the illustration. Tell the students that these people are talking about what they're going to do tonight. Read out the question, then play the recording and ask them to read the conversation and find the answer as they listen to it.

Ruby

Cultural notes

Pirates of the Caribbean
Pirates of the Caribbean (2003–2007) is a series of three films about pirate adventures, and is set in the early to mid-18th century. It was inspired by one of the attractions in the Disney theme parks. The films have become a huge success worldwide. It stars Johnny Depp, Orlando Bloom and Keira Knightley.

Johnny Depp (born 1963)
(See notes about Johnny Depp in Unit 2, page 10.)

2
Ask the students to complete the conversation with the words in the box. Play the recording again for them to check their answers.

1 Let's	2 OK	3 No	4 Shall I

3
- Go through the table with the class. Explain the difference between a suggestion and an offer. Ask them to look back at the conversation in Exercise 1 and complete the example suggestion in the table. Then ask them to complete the offer.

- Ask the students to work in pairs to complete the table with other phrases from the conversation. Go round, offering encouragement and checking that they're putting the phrases in the correct columns. Then check answers with the class.

> Make a suggestion: *Shall we ...?*; *Let's ...*
> Agree: *Good idea*; *OK*
> Offer to do something: *I'll*; *Shall I ...?*
> Disagree: *It's OK*; *No*

Language note

Grammar: *will/shall*

- In modern English, *shall* is only really used in questions with *Shall I...?*, or *Shall we ...?* You use it to make suggestions:

  Shall I help you with that?
  Shall we go out for a walk?

- However, you use *will* to offer to do something:

  I'll look on the internet.
  I'll choose a film.

4 🌐 3.28

Play the recording for the students to listen and repeat the useful phrases. When they've done this chorally, ask individual students to repeat the phrases after you.

5

Pairwork. Put the students in pairs to practise the conversation. Tell them to take turns being Ruby and Joe and to change the name of the film and the actor each time. Ask some pairs to perform their conversations to the class.

Vocabulary *Extra* (SB page 99)

Television

1

- Focus the students' attention on the list of words and point out that they're all types of TV programmes. Remind students that the underlining indicates the syllable of the word that has the strongest stress. Check that the students can pronounce the programmes correctly.

- Ask students to look at the pictures and match each one with one of the words. Point out that the first one has been done for them.

9	a cartoon	4	a reality TV show
3	a chat show	6	a soap opera
5	a documentary	7	a sports programme
1	a game show	8	the weather
2	the news		

2

Pairwork. Demonstrate the activity with a confident student. Cover the words, point to one of the pictures and ask *What's number ...?* Elicit the answer. Then put the students into pairs to continue the activity. Go round, checking that everyone is pronouncing the programmes correctly.

Focus on *What ...?* and *How ...?*

1

Ask the students to look at the table. Focus their attention the uses of *What* and *How* and their examples. Then ask the students to complete the table with the correct questions from the box.

> 1 What's it made of?
> 2 What do you do?
> 3 What time does it open?
> 4 How do you do?
> 5 How much was it?
> 6 How far is it?

2

Ask the students to write an example question and answer for each use of *What* and *How* from the table.

Further practice material

Need more writing practice?

→ Workbook page 59
- Linking sentences: *and, but, because*
- Completing a form, giving reasons

Need more classroom practice activities?

→ Photocopiable resource materials pages 193 to 195
  Grammar: *Make a sentence with ...*
  Vocabulary: *Television*
  Communication: *What's your future?*
→ TOP 10 activities pages xv to xx

Need DVD material?

→ DVD – Programme 7: *Video diary*

Need progress tests?

→ Test CD – *Test Unit 14*

Need more on important teaching concepts?

→ Key concepts in *New Inside Out* pages xxii to xxxv

Need student self-study practice?

→ CD-ROM – Unit 14: *TV*

Need student CEF self-evaluation?

→ CEF Checklists pages xxxvii to xliv

Need more information and more ideas?

→ www.insideout.net

15 Experiences *Overview*

Section	Aims	What the students are doing
● **Reading & Listening** SB page 100	*Reading skills*: reading for specific information *Listening skills*: listening for specific information	• Reading a magazine letter and answering questions. • Listening to three people and identifying places they have visited. • Deciding on the top five places to visit.
● **Grammar** SB page 101	*Grammar*: present perfect	• Studying the use of the present perfect. • Completing a table with present perfect forms. • Completing questions and answers about experiences. • Asking and answering questions.
● **Vocabulary** SB page 101	*Vocabulary*: past participles	• Matching pictures with past participles. • Writing sentences about what they have and haven't done. • Asking and answering questions.
● **Pronunciation** SB page 102	*Pronunciation*: past participles	• Completing chants using past participles. • Practising chants.
● **Reading & Listening** SB page 102	*Reading skills*: reading for gist *Listening skills*: listening for specific information	• Reading a web page to find out about a travel company. • Identifying the meaning of numbers from the web page. • Listening to someone talking about travel experiences. • Discussing questions about travel.
● **Grammar** SB page 103	*Grammar*: present perfect or past simple?	• Differentiating between the use of the present perfect and the past simple. • Completing a table with past simple questions. • Asking and answering questions.
● **Speaking: anecdote** SB page 103	*Conversation skills*: fluency practice	• Talking about their oldest friend.
● **Useful phrases** SB page 104	*Vocabulary*: phrases which are useful when ordering food in a restaurant	• Putting a conversation in the correct order. • Listening to and repeating useful phrases. • Identifying items from a menu. • Practising the conversations.
Vocabulary *Extra* SB page 105	*Vocabulary*: revision of words from the unit: in a restaurant. Focus on verb + prepositional phrase	• Matching pictures with words.
Writing WB page 63	Forming and answering *Wh* questions Building a text from notes	

Warm-up

- Have a 'Spelling bee' to revise any vocabulary you feel needs reviewing.

- Say a word and ask one of the stronger students to spell it. Write what they say on the board and ask the class to check if the spelling is correct. Continue with other words and other students.

Reading & Listening (SB page 100)

1 🌐 3.29

- Focus the students' attention on the letter and explain that it's a letter that appeared in a magazine on international travel. Go through the questions with the class and then ask them to listen to the recording as they read the letter and find the answers.

- Check answers with the class, making sure they pronounce *fifteen* clearly and don't confuse it with *fifty*.

> a) Fifteen years old.
> b) Colleagues at *International Travel Magazine*.
> c) Janet Dean, the Editor.

2 🌐 3.30

- Remind the class that the people who chose the top fifteen places to visit were employees of the magazine. Tell them that they're going to listen to three of them talking about places they've visited. Focus attention on the photo of the people and ask the students to speculate about the kind of places they think these people would like to visit. Explain *urban* (in towns and cities) and *rural* (in the countryside).

- Play the recording for the students to listen and match the people to the places they've been to. You may need to pause the recording after each speaker to allow the students time to put their initials in the boxes. Check answers with the class.

> Steve: Hong Kong, Istanbul, the Seychelles, the Greek islands
> Ben: the Amazon
> Rose: Tuscany, the Loire Valley, the North Island in New Zealand, Petra in Jordon, the Great Wall of China

🌐 3.30

1 *Steve*
I love shopping. I've been to Hong Kong, and there are fantastic shops there. But my favourite place to shop is the Grand Bazaar in Istanbul. It's amazing.
I also love beaches. So I've been to the Seychelles and I've been to some Greek islands. But I haven't been to Hawaii. I'm getting married next year and I want to go there for my honeymoon.

2 *Ben*
I don't like cities – there are too many cars and people everywhere. I love going to wild places. I've been to the Amazon – that was amazing. I love deserts, but I haven't been to the Sahara yet. That's my next trip.

3 *Rose*
I enjoy walking. So I've been to Tuscany, the Loire Valley and the North Island in New Zealand. I also love historical places. I've been to Petra in Jordan and the Great Wall of China. One day, I'd like to visit Angkor Wat in Cambodia.

3 🌐 3.31

- Play the recording and ask the students to repeat the names of the places.

- Ask the students to work individually to decide on their five top places. Allow them to choose places that aren't on the list if they wish. Then put them in pairs to compare with a partner. You could have a class vote on the top five.

- Prepare for the next section by introducing the question *Have you ever been to?* and the answers *Yes, I have. / No, I haven't.* and ask individual students around the class if they've ever been to the places on the list.

Cultural notes

Wonders of the world
Traditionally there are seven wonders of the ancient world built by man, but today there are lists of different wonders, usually top tourist sites.

Petra, Jordan
Petra is an archaeological site in Jordan. It's a city carved out of rock. It has over 800 individual monuments, including buildings, tombs, baths, temples, and gateways. It was rediscovered in 1812 after being lost for almost 300 years.

Angkor Wat, Cambodia

Angkor is in northwestern Cambodia. It's the capital of the ancient Khmer Empire and was possibly founded around the ninth century AD. Angkor Wat is the most beautiful and most famous monument in the city. It's since been turned into a Buddhist temple and is now a World Heritage Site.

The Great Wall of China

The construction of the Great Wall of China began over 2,000 years ago, and wasn't completed until the beginning of the 17th century. It's the longest man-made structure, and is over 6,500 kilometres long. It was built in order to protect the various dynasties from invasion.

Grammar (SB page 101)

Present perfect

1

- Remind the students that the speakers in the last section used *I have been to …* to describe their past experiences of travel. Focus their attention on the information in the margin and go through it with the class. Point out the use of *ever* in questions about past experience (meaning 'at any time up to now'). Students commonly make the mistake of trying to include the word *ever* in their answers ~~Yes, I have ever been~~, etc. Explain that you don't use *ever* in the answers to *Have you ever …?* questions or in statements about our past experiences.

- Ask the students to look at the questions and discuss them in pairs. Check answers with the class.

> a) No.   b) Yes.   c) No.

Language notes

Grammar: present perfect

- Many students have difficulty with the present perfect tense. To some students (e.g. French, Spanish, Italian, German) the tense may look similar to a composite tense (auxiliary *have/be* + past participle) they use in their own language. However, these students will find that the present perfect in English is used rather differently from the tense they know.

- The present perfect has many different usages. At this stage in the course the focus is on questions about past experience (completed events in the past) using the adverb *ever* (*Have you ever visited New York?*). In this context *ever* means *at any time (in your life up to now)*. Note that no precise time is given for the event in the past.

- In contrast with the present perfect, the past simple is used to describe completed events in the past where a precise time (e.g. *at 10.00 a.m., yesterday, two days ago*) is specified (*I visited New York in 2005*).

- In this unit questions with *Have you ever* + present perfect are answered with either simple *Yes, I have* or *No, I haven't*, or with past simple statements which provide precise time details of the experience. (*'Have you ever visited New York?' 'Yes, I have. I visited New York in 2005.'*) The present perfect is never used with precise past time references.

- *been* is the past participle of *be*, but it's often used as a past participle of *go* (or *come*). Note that this use of *been* is only for completed visits, i.e. gone and returned. (*She's been to New York many times … but now she is in London.*) If the visit does not involve a return trip, then *gone* should be used. (*She's gone to New York … and she's still there.*)

2 🌐 3.32

- Ask the students to work individually to complete the table. Then allow them to compare their results in pairs before playing the recording for them to check their answers.

- Play the recording a second time for the students to repeat the sentences. Then ask them to say the full forms of *I've* and *He's*.

> a) 've   b) haven't   c) 's   d) hasn't
> I have   He has

3 🌐 3.33

- As the students complete the questions and answers, go round checking that everyone has understood the form of the present perfect.

- Play the recording for the students to check their answers. Then play it a second time for them to listen and repeat.

> a) 'Have you ever been to Angkor Wat?'
>   'Yes, I have.' 'No, I haven't.'
> b) 'Has your father ever been to London?'
>   'Yes, he has.' 'No, he hasn't.'
> c) 'Have you ever been to a big pop concert?'
>   'Yes, I have.' 'No, I haven't.'
> d) 'Has your mother ever been to a football match?'
>   'Yes, she has.' 'No, she hasn't.'
> e) 'Have you and your family ever been to Paris?'
>   'Yes, we have.' 'No, we haven't.'
> f) 'Have students in the class ever been to your house?'
>   'Yes, they have.' 'No, they haven't.'

4

Pairwork. Ask the students to take turns asking and answering the questions, making the answers true for them.

Extra activity

- Get the students to work in small groups to prepare a questionnaire containing questions starting *Have you ever been to …* Go round and check the questions, helping with vocabulary.
- Form new groups with one person from each of the old groups. Tell the students to ask and answer each other's questionnaire.

Vocabulary (SB page 101)

1 🌐 3.34

- Focus the students' attention on the pictures and give them time to look at them and take in what they see. Then point out the past participles in the box. Remind them that they've already met one past participle (*been*) and explain that past participles are used to form the present perfect.
- When they've matched the pictures with the past participles and you've checked their answers, ask the students to say the infinitive form of each verb (*buy, do, drive, meet, swim, work*). Point out that regular verbs like *work*, form the past participle with *ed* and it's the same as the past simple form. Irregular verbs have their own past participle forms. Point out the list of irregular verbs on page 143 in the Student's Book.
- Play the recording for the students to check again and to repeat the past participles. Pay particular attention to the pronunciation of *bought* /bɔːt/.

> 2 bought   3 done   6 driven   4 met
> 5 swum   1 worked

2

Go through the example statements with the class and ask several students if they are true for them. Then ask them to write down what they have and haven't done. While they are writing, go round monitoring and helping with vocabulary. Make sure everyone is forming the present perfect correctly.

3

- Go through the example question with the class, pointing out that it's formed from the example statement in the previous exercise. Ask several students to answer the question, making sure you get at least one negative answer.
- Give the students a minute or two to form questions with their own statements from the previous exercise. Then put them in pairs to ask and answer their questions. Go round checking that everyone is forming the questions and answers correctly.

4 Pairwork

- The pairwork exercise for this unit is on pages 120 and 125. Put the students in pairs and tell them who will be Student A, and who will be Student B.

- While they are doing the exercise, go round monitoring and helping. Take note of any errors which may need particular attention later, and also any examples of good language use which you can praise in a feedback session.

Pronunciation (SB page 102)

1

Go through the first line of the first chant with the class. Explain that the three forms are the infinitive, past simple and past participle. Ask the students to look at the next line and say which of the past participles in the box they think should complete it. If they seem to have the right idea, ask them to complete the rest of the exercise, matching the past participles in the box with the correct lines of the chants. If not, do a few more examples with the whole class. Check their answers.

> A: broken, spoken, done, swum
> B: shaken, taken, flown, known
> C: given, driven, said, read

Language note

Grammar: past participle

The past participles of regular verbs are formed with *ed* (the same as the past simple). The verbs presented here are irregular verbs. Note that as with the past simple, irregular verbs are not totally irregular, there are some patterns. These chants illustrate this.

2 🌐 3.35

Play the recording the first time just for the students to listen. Then play it again and ask them to repeat the chants.

Reading & Listening (SB page 102)

1 🌐 3.36

- Focus attention on the web page. Give the students a minute or two to look at the photos and see the kinds of holidays the company offers.
- Play the recording and ask them to read the text as they listen.
- Ask them to say what *Adventure World Travel* does. You may need to explain that 'overland adventure trips' are journeys in which people travel by truck rather than by plane. They usually take food and camping equipment with them so that they can stay in places where there are no facilities for tourists.

> It organises overland adventure trips

2

Go through the numbers in the box and ask the students to find them in the text and make a note of what they refer to. Check answers with the class.

> four = the four continents (Africa, Asia and North and South America) that the company travels to
> eighteen to fifty = the age of most of their travellers
> twenty-five = the number of trucks they have
> thirty = the number of years of experience the company has

3 🌐 3.37

Focus attention on the photo of the two men. Explain that one of them (Rick) works for *Adventure World Travel* and that they're going to listen to him talking on the phone to his friend Will. Ask them to listen and say where Rick is phoning from. You may need to play the recording more than once. Ask them what happens at the end. (Rick is cut off.)

> Rick is phoning from Ecuador.

> 🌐 3.37 (W = Will; R = Rick)
>
> W: Hello.
> R: Hi, Will!
> W: Rick! ...
> R: How are you, Will?
> W: I'm fine. Hey, where are you?
> R: In Ecuador.
> W: Ecuador? Amazing. How's it going?
> R: Really well. I'm enjoying the job. I've seen a lot of South America.
> W: Where have you been?
> R: Argentina, Chile, Peru, Ecuador ... I've driven 12,000 kilometres in the last six months.
> W: 12,000 kilometres! What's the best place you've been to?
> R: I've seen so many beautiful places – but I think Patagonia was the best.
> W: Have you been to Brazil?
> R: Yeah, I have,
> W: When did you go?
> R: In February. I went to the Carnival in Rio.
> W: Amazing!
> R: Yeah, I met some great people in Rio. We had parties on the beach. It was really good fun.
> W: What about the people on the trips?
> R: Well, I've had a few problems.
> W: Oh dear. What happened?
> R: Well, one girl lost her passport. And a man got ill – I took him to hospital.
> W: Ah. Have you had any accidents?
> R: No, no, I haven't had any accidents.
> W: Oh, good.
> R: But ... I have had a few problems with the police.
> W: Really? What happened?
> R: Oh, it's a long story – I'll write to you.
> W: OK. Have you met any nice people?
> R: Yes – lots of nice people. I met a very nice woman last month in Peru. Her name's Ana and ...
> W: Rick? RICK? Oh no, he's gone.

4

Ask the students to work individually to match the sentence halves. Then ask them to compare results in pairs before checking with the class. Play the recording again as a further check.

> a) 5   b) 2   c) 3   d) 6   e) 1   f) 4

5

Go through the questions with the class and then put them into pairs or small groups to discuss them. Encourage them to report back to the class on their discussion. Be prepared to share your own answers to the questions, either as an example at the beginning of the activity or during feedback at the end.

Grammar (SB page 103)

Present perfect or past simple?

1 🌐 3.38

- Go through the information in the margin and explain the different uses of the present perfect and past simple. Then play the recording and ask the students to read the extract from the conversation between Rick and Will. Ask the students as a class to answer the questions below.

- Ask several students *Have you been to ...?* questions and if they answer that they have, follow up with *When did you go?*

> a) Present perfect.
> b) Past simple.
> c) Past simple.

2 🌐 3.39

Give the students plenty of time to complete the past simple questions. Go round, monitoring and helping. Allow them to compare answers in pairs before playing the recording for them to check. Then play the recording a second time for them to repeat the questions.

> a) When did you go? Who did you go with?
> b) When did you move? Where did you move to?
> c) When did you lose it? What did you do?
> d) What did you win? When did you win it?
> e) When did you see it? Which one did you see?

3

Invite the students to ask you some of the questions in Exercise 2. Then put them in pairs to ask and answer the questions. If a present perfect question produces a *No* answer (*No, I haven't*), then the questioner should move on to the next question. If a present perfect question produces a *Yes* answer (*Yes, I have*), then the questioner should find out further details by asking the past simple follow-up questions. Go round, monitoring and helping.

4 *Grammar Extra* **15**

Ask students to turn to *Grammar Extra* 15 on page 132 of the Student's Book. Here they'll find an explanation of the grammar they've been studying and further exercises to practise it.

1
a) I haven't been to New York.
b) I haven't seen the Pyramids in Egypt.
c) I haven't driven in a foreign country.
d) I haven't stayed in a five-star hotel.
e) I haven't eaten sushi.
f) I haven't slept on a beach.

3
a) Have you ever been to New York?
b) Have you ever seen the Pyramids in Egypt?
c) Have you ever driven in a foreign country?
d) Have you ever stayed in a five-star hotel?
e) Have you ever eaten sushi?
f) Have you ever slept on a beach?

Speaking: anecdote (SB page 103)

For more information about how to set up, monitor and repeat anecdotes, see Practical methodology, page xx in the Introduction.

1 🌐 3.40

- Start by telling the students that they're going to listen to someone talking about his oldest friend. Explain that your *oldest friend* is the person who has been your friend the longest, not necessarily the friend who is oldest in terms of age.

- Ask them to listen and underline the correct information for each question. Before you play the recording, give them a minute or two to go through the questions and answers so that they know what they're listening out for. With weaker classes, go through the questions and answers together.

- Check answers with the class.

---

a) Simon
b) secondary school
c) thirteen or fourteen
d) We laugh at the same things
e) a doctor
f) a few times a year
g) On his birthday
h) A holiday we had together

🌐 3.40

My oldest friend is Simon.

We first met at school – secondary school.

We were thirteen or fourteen – I can't remember exactly.

We became friends because we laugh at the same things. Simon is very funny.

Now he's a doctor. He's married and he lives in London. I see him a few times a year.

The last time I saw him was on his birthday. We went out for a lovely meal. His wife and my girlfriend get on really well.

My best memory of Simon is a holiday we had together in the USA. We were twenty-three, and it was the year we finished university. We drove from Chicago to Los Angeles. It was fantastic.

2

- Pairwork. Give the students a moment or two to decide which friend they're going to talk about. Then ask them to go through the questions in Exercise 1 on their own, making the answers true for them.

- Tell the students to think about the language they want to use and to make notes. Give help with any vocabulary that they think they'll need, but discourage them from writing whole sentences so that when it comes to the pairwork, they don't simply read out their notes.

- Put the students in pairs and ask them to take turns telling their partner about their oldest friend. Tell them that they can use their notes to help them, but they shouldn't just read from the paper. Encourage them to maintain eye contact with their partner as they speak. If necessary, demonstrate with a short account of your own oldest friend how much more interesting you sound if you look at your listeners as you speak rather than looking down and reading.

Useful phrases (SB page 104)

1 🌐 3.41

- Focus the students' attention on the picture and point out that the conversation takes place in a restaurant between a waiter and a man and woman who are customers. Explain that it's in the wrong order.

- Before you play the recording, ask the students to read the sections of the conversation and decide on the correct order. Play the recording for them to check their answers.

- Check answers with the class and ask the students what clues helped them decide (e.g. the initial greetings, ordering the bill, asking about dessert). Go through any difficult vocabulary with the class. You might like to teach *well-done* as an alternative to *rare* and *medium* when ordering steak.

---

1 d   2 b   3 c   4 e   5 a

Language note

Vocabulary: *sir* and *madam*

It's polite to address strangers as *sir* and *madam*. However, these are simply terms of address and can't normally be used as nouns. People who work in hotels (receptionists, waiters, etc.) often address their guests as *sir* or *madam*.

2

Ask the students to work individually to tick the items the people ordered. Allow them to compare with a partner before checking answers with the class.

> Main courses: steak
> Drinks: red wine, mineral water
> Hot drinks: espresso, tea

3 🌐 **3.42**

Go through the useful phrases and ask the students to find them in the conversations in Exercise 1. Then play the recording for them to listen and repeat. Ask for individual repetition of the items, checking that the students are pronouncing them correctly and using appropriate intonation.

Language notes

Grammar: *I'll have*

You say *I'll have* in the restaurant when you're ordering food and drinks. This is a contraction of *I will have*. You use *will* because you're making the decision as you speak.

Grammar: *could*

Here *could* is used when you're asking for something politely. It's possible to say *Can we have the bill?*, but *Could we have the bill?* is more polite.

4

Groupwork. The students practise the conversation in Exercise 1. Encourage them to act it out, using any suitable props and with the customers entering the restaurant and sitting down at a table. This will help them in getting the right intonation. Make sure they practise ordering different items from the menu and that they take turns to play the different roles.

Vocabulary *Extra* (SB page 105)

In a restaurant

1

* Focus the students' attention on the list of dishes. Check that the students can pronounce the dishes correctly.
* Ask the students to look at the pictures and match each one with one of the dishes. Point out that the first one has been done for them.

> 9 apple pie   2 prawns
> 5 chicken salad 6 salmon
> 8 fruit salad   4 steak and chips
> 7 ice cream   1 tomato soup
> 3 melon

2

Pairwork. Demonstrate the activity with a confident student. Cover the words, point to one of the pictures and ask *What's number …?* Elicit the answer. Then put the students into pairs to continue the activity. Go round, checking that everyone is pronouncing the dishes correctly.

3

Ask the students to tell their partner about their favourite meal.

Focus on verb + prepositional phrases

1

Ask the students to look at the table. Focus their attention on the common verb + prepositional phrases and their examples. Then ask the students to complete the table with the correct verbs from the box.

> 1 know   2 talk   3 arrive   4 look   5 wait
> 6 listen

2

Ask the students to write a sentence of their own for each verb in the table in Exercise 1.

Further practice material

Need more writing practice?

→ Workbook page 63
* Forming and answering *Wh* questions
* Building a text from notes

Need more classroom practice activities?

→ Photocopiable resource materials pages 196 to 198
  Grammar: *Where have they been?*
  Vocabulary: *Bingo!*
  Communication: *Life experience*
→ TOP 10 activities pages xv to xx

Need DVD material?

→ DVD – Programme 8: *Old friends*

Need progress tests?

→ Test CD – *Test Unit 15*

Need more on important teaching concepts?

→ Key concepts in *New Inside Out* pages xxii to xxxv

Need student self-study practice?

→ CD-ROM – Unit 15: *Experiences*

Need student CEF self-evaluation?

→ CEF Checklists pages xxxvii to xliv

Need more information and more ideas?

→ www.insideout.net

Section	Aims	What the students are doing
Reading **SB page 106**	*Reading skills*: reading for specific information	• Completing an article with headings. • Matching information with people. • Answering questions about journeys to work or school.
Vocabulary **SB page 107**	*Vocabulary*: prepositions	• Underlining correct prepositions in sentences. • Writing a detailed description of their journey to work or school.
Grammar **SB page 107**	*Grammar*: questions with prepositions	• Putting words in the correct order to make questions. • Asking questions about journeys.
Pronunciation **SB page 107**	*Pronunciation*: vowel sounds	• Matching words with similar vowel sounds.
Listening **SB page 108**	*Listening skills*: listening for specific information	• Listening to an interview with a cyclist and answering questions • Matching numbers to statements about the cyclist's experiences.
Grammar **SB page 108**	*Grammar*: tense review	• Completing a summary with a variety of tenses.
Vocabulary **SB page 109**	*Vocabulary*: places in a city / the country	• Matching vocabulary to postcards. • Talking about the things near their houses. • Talking about places to visit.
Speaking: anecdote **SB page 109**	*Conversation skills*: fluency practice	• Talking about an interesting drive.
Useful phrases **SB page 110**	*Vocabulary*: directions	• Matching pictures with directions. • Listening to three conversations and identifying destinations. • Completing a conversation with directions. • Writing and practising a new conversation involving giving directions.
Vocabulary *Extra* **SB page 111**	*Vocabulary*: revision of words from the unit: nature. Focus on prepositions of movement (*across, along, down, into, out of, past, through, up*)	• Matching pictures with words.
Writing **WB page 67**	Using adjectives to make a text more interesting Describing a journey	

16 Drive *Teacher's notes*

Warm-up

Ask students if they can remember any long car journeys from their childhood. Where were they driving to and why? How long did it take? Did they enjoy the journey? Did they play any games in the car on the journey? Can they play them in English? Common car games played by British children include 'I spy', in which one player says *I spy with my little eye something beginning with (A) ...* and the others have to guess words beginning with *A* until they identify the object.

Reading (SB page 106)

1 🔘 **3.43**

- Focus the students' attention on the photos. Tell them that these show the journey to work of two people, Jack and Siriwan. Ask them which journey they think they would prefer.

- Play the recording and ask the students to read the text. Go through any difficult vocabulary and ask the students to say which is the best drive and which the worst drive. Ask if anyone has a similar journey to Jack or Siriwan when they drive to work or school.

> a) The best drive   b) The worst drive

Cultural notes

The Great Ocean Road
The Great Ocean Road runs along some of the most scenic coastline in the world; the south-east coast of Australia. Construction began in 1919 and it was officially opened in 1932.

The Cape Otway lighthouse
The Cape Otway lighthouse is on the Great Ocean Road next to the Otway National Park where animals native to Australia, like koalas and kangaroos, are often seen.

2 🔘 **3.44**

- Look at the sentences with the class and go through the example. Ask the students to complete the other sentences with the correct pronouns.

- Play the recording for them to listen and check. Then play it a second time for them to repeat the sentences.

> a) He, his   b) She, her   c) her   d) him
> e) He   f) She

3

- Go through the questions with the class and make sure they understand them. Ask them to work individually to write their own answers to the questions. Go round, monitoring and helping.

- Put the students in pairs and ask them to compare their answers. Then have a feedback session with the class.

Vocabulary (SB page 107)

1 🔘 **3.45**

Focus the students' attention on the diagrams and prepositions in the margin. Give a demonstration with classroom objects if necessary. Then ask the students to look at the sentences describing someone's journey to work and to underline the correct prepositions. Encourage them to work individually at first but then to compare with a partner. Check answers with the class.

> a) down   b) out of   c) across   d) along
> e) past   f) up   g) through   h) over   i) into

Extra activity

Give further practice of prepositions by asking students to move various classroom objects / themselves around, e.g. *Put a pen under the table. Put your bag into the bin. Walk past my desk. Climb over this chair*, etc.

2

- Ask the students to work individually to tick the sentences that are true for them.

- Encourage them to modify any statements that are not true so that they are true for them Go round, offering help and encouragement.

3

- Ask the students to work individually to write their descriptions. Go round, offering help and encouragement. Emphasise that they should include as many of the prepositions in Exercise 1 as they can.

- Pairwork. Students compare their descriptions. Encourage them to report back to the class on any particularly interesting journeys.

Grammar (SB page 107)

Questions with prepositions

1 🔘 3.46

- Focus the students' attention on the questions in the margin and point out the position of the prepositions.
- Go through the example with the class. Then ask the students to put the remaining words in order to make questions. Check that students understand *scenery* (things, e.g. trees, hills, lakes, etc. that you can see in a particular place). Go round, monitoring and helping.
- Play the recording for the students to check their answers. Then play it again for them to listen and repeat the questions.

> a) Where do you start from?
> b) Who do you travel with?
> c) What do you talk about?
> d) What kind of music do you listen to?
> e) What kind of scenery do you go through?
> f) What kind of buildings do you go past?

Language note

Grammar: word order

When a question word is the object of a preposition, the preposition often comes at the end of the clause, especially in informal spoken language.

What are you interested in?
Where did you get it from?

2

- Give the students a few minutes to think of a journey they make regularly and to decide what their answers to the questions would be.
- Pairwork. Students take turns asking and answering the questions in Exercise 1 about their own journeys.

Pronunciation (SB page 107)

1 🔘 3.47

Play the recording and ask the students to listen and repeat the words. When they've done this chorally, ask for individual repetition and make sure everyone is producing the vowel sounds correctly.

2 🔘 3.48

- Ask the students to add the words from Exercise 1 to the lists of words with the same vowel sound. Encourage them to say all the words aloud as they do this so that they get a feel for what sounds right.
- Put the students in pairs to compare answers before you play the recording for them to check. Play it a second time for them to repeat all the words.

> a) past   b) turn   c) walk   d) through

Listening (SB page 108)

1 🔘 3.49

- Ask the students to look at the photo. Tell them that this is a German man called Heinz Stücke who is a very keen cyclist.
- Tell the students to listen to the recording and say when Heinz is going to finish his journey.

> Maybe never.

> 🔘 3.49 (P = Presenter; K = Kelly)
>
> P: *Welcome to 'Amazing Journeys'. Today's programme is about a man who has travelled round the world by bicycle. Kelly, what can you tell us about Heinz Stücke?*
> K: *Well, Heinz Stücke has actually been round the world ten times by bicycle.*
> P: *Ten times?! When did he start his journey?*
> K: *He started his journey in 1962. He left Germany when he was twenty-two years old. At first, he planned to travel only for a few years.*
> P: *What happened?*
> K: *Well, he forgot to stop!*
> P: *How many countries has he visited?*
> K: *Two hundred and eleven countries. He's filled fifteen passports.*
> P: *Fifteen passports! And what sort of bicycle does he have??*
> K: *It's a big, heavy bicycle – it weighs twenty-five kilos. He has very strong legs!*
> P: *I can imagine. Where does he sleep?*
> K: *He usually sleeps in a tent.*
> P: *And how does he make money?*
> K: *He sells postcards of his trip.*
> P: *I see. Where is he now?*
> K: *At the moment, he's cycling along the south coast of England.*
> P: *So, when is he going to finish his journey?*
> K: *I don't know. Maybe never.*

2

Focus attention on the numbers in the box, then play the recording again and ask the students to match the numbers to the questions. You may need to play the recording several times. Check answers with the class.

> a) 10   b) 1962   c) 22   d) 211   e) 15   f) 25

Extra activity

Ask the students for their reaction to the story of Heinz Stücke. Would they like to spend their lives on one long journey?

3

Pairwork. Ask the students to discuss the longest journey (by bicycle or some other means of transport) that they've ever made. When they've finished, ask them to join another pair and tell them about their journey.

Grammar (SB page 108)

Tense review

1 🔊 3.50

- Focus attention on the information in the margin and point out that the students have studied all these tenses in this coursebook. Ask them to produce further sentences for each tense, using different verbs.

- Ask the students to look at the summary of Heinz Stücke's journey and to underline the correct tense in each case. Encourage them to work individually at first and then to compare with a partner.

- Play the recording for them to check their answers, then check again with the class.

> 1 has been   2 started   3 left   4 was
> 5 has visited   6 has filled   7 weighs
> 8 sleeps   9 makes   10 is cycling
> 11 is he going to finish   12 doesn't know

Language notes

Grammar: tense review

- The present simple is used to talk about facts, habits or routines.

  I live in a small house in Oxford.

- The present continuous is used to talk about activities in progress now or around now.

  He's wearing an old pair of jeans.

- The past simple is used to talk about completed past actions, where a past time marker is mentioned or implied.

  She met him a long time ago.

- The present perfect is used to talk about completed past actions in 'time up to now'. There is no past time marker.

  They've visited fourteen different countries.

- The future *(be) going to* is used to talk about future plans and intentions: things you've decided to do.

  I'm going to see him on Thursday.

2 Pairwork

- The pairwork exercise for this unit is on pages 120 and 125. Put the students in pairs and tell them who will be Student A, and who will be Student B.

- While they are doing the exercise, go round monitoring and helping. Take note of any errors which may need particular attention later, and also any examples of good language use which you can praise in a feedback session. Check answers with the class.

> **Student A**
> a) do you go   b) did you get up
> c) are you reading   d) are you going to do
> e) have you been   f) do you like

> **Student B**
> a) do you play   b) did you go
> c) are you wearing   d) are you going to have
> e) have you been   f) do you like

3 *Grammar Extra* 16

Ask students to turn to *Grammar Extra* 16 on page 132 of the Student's Book. Here they'll find an explanation of the grammar they've been studying and further exercises to practise it.

> 1
> a) Present simple   d) Present continuous
> b) Past simple   e) Future: *(be) going to*
> c) Present perfect   f) Present simple
>
> 2
> a) I don't listen to British and American pop songs.
> b) I didn't see a film in English last month.
> c) I haven't written emails in English at work.
> d) I'm not studying for an English exam at the moment.
> e) I'm not going to do an English language course next summer.
> f) I don't like speaking English.

Vocabulary (SB page 109)

Warm-up

Find out how many students take photographs when they go on holiday. Ask what sort of things they take photos of (beautiful countryside, people they are travelling with, cities, sunsets, etc.).

1 🔊 3.51

- Focus attention on the photos and ask the students which ones they like best. Ask them to match each photo with one of the wordlists.

- Play the recording for them to check their answers, then play it again for them to repeat the lists of words. Explain any unknown vocabulary.

> a) 3   b) 4   c) 2   d) 1

2

Ask each student to draw a long horizontal line with *my house* at one end and *furthest away* at the other. They should then place the words from Exercise 1 along the line according to how near they are to their house. They should work individually to do this and then compare with a partner.

3

Pairwork. The students discuss whether or not they have been to any places like those in the photos in Exercise 1 and whether they would like to. Encourage them to report back to the class on their discussion.

Speaking: anecdote (SB page 109)

For more information about how to set up, monitor and repeat anecdotes, see Practical methodology, page xx in the Introduction.

1 🌐 3.52

- If your students are adults, ask them how many can drive and how many go out driving for pleasure. If they are younger teenagers, ask them if they like going out for a drive with their parents.
- Then tell them that they're going to listen to a woman called Carla talking about the last time she went on an interesting drive. Ask them to listen and underline the correct information for each question. Before you play the recording, give them a minute or two to go through the questions and answers so that they know what they are listening out for.
- Check answers with the class.

a) last spring	f) sunny
b) Tuscany	g) Green fields and hills
c) my friend	h) in a village
d) a Mazda	i) in the afternoon
e) in the morning	

> 🌐 3.52
>
> *Last spring, I went to Tuscany, one of my favourite places in Italy. I went with my friend, Julia. We had a little white Mazda. I drove and Julia read the map. I can't read maps.*
>
> *One day we decided to drive from Siena to Saturnia. We left Siena in the morning, and it was already sunny and hot. We drove through green fields and hills. Tuscany is so beautiful. We stopped in a small village on top of a hill. We visited an old church and bought some wine. Then we continued our drive through the Tuscan hills and arrived in Saturnia in the afternoon. There are hot springs in Saturnia, so we parked near a waterfall and went swimming in the river. It was amazing.*

2

- Pairwork. Give the students a moment or two to decide what they're going to talk about. Then ask them to go through the questions in Exercise 1, making the answers true for them. Ask them to work individually to do this.
- Tell the students to think about the language they want to use when they talk about their interesting drive and to make notes. Give help with any vocabulary that they think they'll need, but discourage them from writing whole sentences so that when it comes to the pairwork, they don't simply read out their notes.
- Put the students in pairs and ask them to take turns telling their partner about the last time they went on an interesting drive. Tell them that they can use their

notes to help them, but they shouldn't just read from the paper. Encourage them to maintain eye contact with their partner as they speak.

Useful phrases (SB page 110)

1 🌐 3.53

- Remind the students that Carla, the speaker in the last section, said that she couldn't read maps. Ask how many people in the class are good map readers. Ask also if they are good at giving people directions.
- Focus the students' attention on the pictures. Ask them to match them with the useful phrases for giving directions.
- Play the recording for them to check their answers. Then play it a second time for them to listen and repeat the useful phrases.

3	Go down College Road.
7	Opposite the church.
5	Take the second turning on the left.
6	Go straight on.
8	There's a pub on the left.
4	Go to the end of New Street.
2	Turn right.
1	Turn left.

2 🌐 3.54

- Tell the students that they're going to listen to three phone conversations in which people give directions. They have to listen and decide the number of the destination on the map.
- Play the recording, pausing after each conversation for the students to decide on the destination.

a) 2	b) 3	c) 1

> 🌐 3.54
>
> a)
> A: *Hi. Where are you?*
> B: *I'm at the roundabout.*
> A: *OK. Go down College Road and take the third turning on the right. That's Church Street.*
> B: *OK.*
> A: *Our house is opposite the church.*
> B: *OK, see you in ten minutes.*
> b)
> C: *Hello.*
> D: *Hi. I'm at the roundabout.*
> C: *OK. Go down London Road and take the second turning on the left. That's Henley Street.*
> D: *OK.*
> C: *Then go straight on and take the first turning on the right.*
> D: *OK.*
> C: *There's a pub on the left. We're there.*
> D: *Great. Get me a beer!*

c)

E: *Hello.*
F: *Hello. I'm lost.*
E: *Oh dear. Where are you?*
F: *At the roundabout.*
E: *OK. Go down Abingdon Road and take the second turning on the left.*
F: *OK.*
E: *Then go to the end of New Street and turn right. There's a bank on the right, and our house is opposite. It's number 21.*
F: *OK, thanks. See you soon.*

3 🔊 **3.55**

- Ask the students to find destination 4 and the roundabout on the map. Go through the conversation and ask the students to complete it with directions from the roundabout to destination 4. Go round, monitoring and helping.

- Play the recording for the students to check their answers. Then play it again for them to repeat the conversation.

- Go back over the conversation and answer any questions the students have about directions.

4

- Pairwork. As the students write their conversation, go round, offering help and encouragement. When they've finished, get them to practise it aloud. Take note of any particularly good conversations and ask the students involved to perform them for the class.

1 down	2 take	3 turning	4 end
5 turn	6 on	7 opposite	

Vocabulary *Extra* (SB page 111)

Nature

1

- Focus the students' attention on the list of words and point out that they're all words to do with nature. Check that the students can pronounce the words correctly.

- Ask the students to look at the pictures and match each one with one of the words. Point out that the first one has been done for them.

5	a beach	11	hills
9	a cliff	8	a mountain
12	a desert	6	a rock
2	a field	3	sand
1	a forest	10	a tree
4	grass	7	a waterfall

2

Pairwork. Demonstrate the activity with a confident student. Cover the words, point to one of the pictures and ask *What's number …?* Elicit the answer. Then put the students into pairs to continue the activity. Go round, checking that everyone is pronouncing the words correctly.

Focus on prepositions of movement

1

- Focus the students' attention on the list of phrases and point out that they're all include prepositions of movement. Check that the students can pronounce the prepositions correctly.

- Ask the students to look at the pictures and match each one with one of the phrases. Point out that the first one has been done for them.

3	across the street	1	out of the house
5	along the river	4	past the shops
2	down the stairs	6	through the park
8	into the building	7	up the hill

2

Pairwork. Ask the students to work in pairs and write another phrase for each of the prepositions in Exercise 1.

Further practice material

Need more writing practice?

➜ Workbook page 67
- Using adjectives to make a text more interesting
- Describing a journey

Need more classroom practice activities?

➜ Photocopiable resource materials pages 199 to 201
  Grammar: *Circuit training*
  Vocabulary: *Challenge*
  Communication: *It takes ages!*
➜ TOP 10 activities pages xv to xx

Need progress tests?

➜ Test CD – *Test Unit 16*

Need more on important teaching concepts?

➜ Key concepts in *New Inside Out* pages xxii to xxxv

Need student self-study practice?

➜ CD-ROM – Unit 16: *Drive*

Need student CEF self-evaluation?

➜ CEF Checklists pages xxxvii to xliv

Need more information and more ideas?

➜ www.insideout.net

Review D *Teacher's notes*

These exercises act as a check of the grammar and vocabulary that the students have learnt in Units 13–16. Use them to find any problems that students are having or anything that they haven't understood and which will need further work.

Grammar (SB page 112)

Remind the students of the grammar explanations they read and the exercises they did in the *Grammar Extra* on pages 132 and 133.

1

This exercise reviews questions with *can* from Unit 13. Check answers with the class before putting the students into pairs to ask and answer the questions.

> a) Can you swim?
> b) Can you ski?
> c) Can you play the guitar?
> d) Can you ride a motorbike?
> e) Can you drive a bus?
> f) Can you speak three languages?

2

This exercise reviews adverbs of manner from Unit 13. Here students have to form adverbs from adjectives.

> a) badly   b) carefully   c) fast   d) well
> e) happily   f) loudly   g) quietly   h) slowly

3

This exercise also reviews adverbs of manner from Unit 13. When they're working in pairs, go round, making sure they're forming the questions correctly. Answers will vary.

4

This exercise reviews the frequency adverbs from Unit 13. Go through the example with the whole class first. Allow students to compare their results in pairs before checking with the class. Answers will vary.

5

This exercise reviews ways of talking about the future from Unit 14. Remind the students that all the words in the box are used to talk about the future. Check answers with the class before moving on to the second part of the exercise. Go round while the students are talking, checking that they're using future forms correctly.

> 1 going to   2 hope   3 want to   4 like to
> 5 wouldn't like to

6

This exercise reviews the present perfect and the past simple from Unit 15. Check answers with the class before moving on to the second part of the exercise. When the students are asking each other about the places listed, go round, making sure they're using the present perfect and the past simple appropriately.

> 1 Have   2 have   3 did   4 went   5 Have
> 6 haven't

7

This exercise reviews a variety of tense forms from Units 13–16.

> 1 'm sitting   2 'm eating   3 is   4 are
> 5 arrived   6 was   7 'm going to see   8 lives
> 9 works   10 have visited   11 've been   12 love

8

This exercise reviews a variety of structures used in Units 13 to 16.

> 1 b) He can to speak three languages.
> 2 a) I play very well football.
> 3 b) Where do you from?
> 4 a) Have he ever been to Dubai?
> 5 b) She's going meet us later.
> 6 a) What are you listening?

Vocabulary (SB page 113)

1

This exercise reviews character adjectives from Unit 13. Check answers with the class before moving on to the second part of the exercise.

> a) confident   b) sensible   c) shy
> d) generous   e) selfish   f) serious

2

This exercise reviews types of TV programme from Unit 14. Check answers before the students go on to discuss their favourite types of programme.

a) game show   b) news   c) chat show
d) documentary   e) soap opera
f) reality TV show

3

This exercise reviews past participles from Unit 15.

buy – bought   go – been/gone   read – read
eat – eaten   meet – met   swim – swum

4

This exercise puts the past participles from Exercise 3 into contexts. Check answers with the class before putting the students into pairs to ask and answer the questions.

a) bought   b) eaten   c) read   d) been
e) met   f) swum

5

This exercise reviews prepositions from Unit 16.

1 down   2 out of   3 across   4 along
5 past   6 over   7 through   8 into   9 up

6

This exercise reviews the vocabulary of natural features from Unit 16. Check answers with the class before asking them which features they can find in the photo.

a) beach   b) cliff   c) desert   d) field
e) forest   f) grass   g) hill   h) mountain
i) rock   j) sand   k) snow   l) waterfall

In the photo: forest, grass, hill, mountain, rock, snow.

Pronunciation (SB page 113)

These two exercises review work students did on word stress, using words they met in Units 13–16.

1

Remind the students that the boxes show the syllables of a word and the large boxes indicate the stressed syllables. Read the example words in the table aloud so that the students can hear the stress clearly. Tell them that they should complete the table by classifying the words according to how many syllables each one has and where the main stress falls. Encourage them to say each word aloud to get a feeling for what sounds right.

(See Exercise 2 for answers.)

2 🌐 3.56

Point out the main stresses in the example words which are underlined. Ask the students to underline the stressed syllables for the other words in the table. Play the recording for them to check their answers. Then play it again for them to listen and repeat the words. Draw students attention to the spelling of *desert*, as in the Sahara desert, and *dessert*, a dish that follows the main course of a meal.

1 and 2
A: <u>cha</u>nnel, <u>de</u>sert, <u>sel</u>fish
B: <u>care</u>fully, <u>gen</u>erous, <u>sen</u>sible
C: des<u>sert</u>, re<u>spect</u>, week<u>end</u>
D: ad<u>ven</u>ture, app<u>oint</u>ment, ko<u>a</u>la
E: com<u>pet</u>itive, ex<u>per</u>ience, spec<u>tac</u>ular

Reading & Listening (SB page 114)

1 🌐 3.57

Give the students a few minutes to read and listen to the text. Then ask them for the name of Jasmine Smith's organisation.

Blind Hope

2

Give the students a few minutes to read the text again and decide which statements are true and which are false. Check answers before asking the students to correct the false statements.

a) True.
b) False. (She's travelled to forty-five countries.)
c) False. (She went to the local secondary school.)
d) True.
e) True.
f) False. (She thinks of them at night.)

3 🌐 3.58

Go through the statements with the class before you play the recording so that the students know what information they are listening for.

c)

🌐 3.58 (I = Interviewer; J = Jasmine)
I: *Good morning. I'm Bill Smiley, and today I'm talking to Jasmine Smith from the organisation, 'Blind Hope'. Welcome, Jasmine.*
J: *Thank you.*
I: *Jasmine, you and your husband John started 'Blind Hope' last year to help blind children in other countries. Two weeks ago, something fantastic happened. Tell us about it.*   ➤

J: Yes. Someone gave $1 million to 'Blind Hope'.
I can't say who gave us the money, but it was a
very rich film star. We were so excited!

I: And now you're organising a very special trip
to Kenya.

J: Yes, that's right. We'd like to help blind children
all around the world, and we're starting in
Kenya. 'Blind Hope' is going to use some of the
money to open a school there.

I: And now, Jasmine, I believe you are looking for
people from this area who want to go to Kenya
next year.

J: Yes, I'd like to find twelve people to help build
the school with me.

I: What sort of people?

J: Well, we're looking for people who are friendly,
confident, and who can work well with other
people. We don't want people who only want to
have a good time and travel. We want sensible
people, because this is a serious job. And it's
hard work. You need to be full of energy. It isn't
a holiday!

I: I see. And what are 'Blind Hope's' plans for the
future, Jasmine?

J: 'Blind Hope' has big plans, Bill. Every journey
starts with a single step. We hope to build one
school in a different country every year.

I: Wow! Good luck, Jasmine. It's a great plan!

J: Thank you.

I: If you would like to go to Kenya, or if you want
to give money to 'Blind Hope', you can find the
details on our website at www ...

4

Go through the choices with the class before you
play the recording so that the students know what
information they are listening for.

---

a) husband   b) fantastic   c) school
d) twelve   e) a serious job   f) year

Writing & Speaking (SB page 115)

1

Ask the students to read the email carefully, looking for
the mistakes. Make sure that they understand that
there's one mistake in each line of the email (except the
opening and closing greetings, which are correct).

Dear Jasmine

1 Do you <u>remember</u> me? I was in your class at
Willsby Secondary School. I <u>heard</u> the radio
programme about you and *Blind Hope*. I'd really
like to help <u>your</u> organisation.

2 What <u>did</u> I do after school? Well, I became
a firefighter. Then I got married <u>to</u> Linda Booker.
Do you remember her? She was in Mr Davis's
class. We moved to Grimsby and had two
<u>children</u>, a boy and a girl. Anyway, we got

---

divorced four year<u>s</u> ago and I <u>moved</u> back to
Purley.

3 Now, I'm doing something <u>different</u>. I'm not
a firefighter, I'm a baker! I <u>started</u> my own
business making bread and cakes. Yes, I know
I was a terrible cook at school, but I can [to]
cook really <u>well</u> now!

4 I've also travelled a lot. I love it! I<u>'ve</u> been to
fifteen countries and I've done a lot <u>of</u> work
with children.

5 I would really like <u>to</u> go to Kenya with *Blind
Hope*. <u>Do you think</u> I could help? I've done some
building work before. <u>I</u>'m very strong, I love
children, and I make great cakes!

Best wishes
Luigi Salvoni

2

Ask the students to read Luigi's email again and to
match the headings to the paragraphs.

---

a) Paragraph 3   b) Paragraph 2   c) Paragraph 5
d) Paragraph 1   e) Paragraph 4

3

Allow plenty of time for this as it will generate ideas
that the students can use in the writing exercise that
follows. If your students haven't yet left school or
college, encourage them to use their imaginations and
invent a life for themselves.

4

Give the students time to write their emails. Go round
offering help and encouragement. When they've finished,
ask them to read their partner's email and to correct each
other's work, looking for grammar and spelling mistakes.
Encourage them to be sensitive in doing this. When
they've finished, they could produce a corrected version
of their emails for display in the classroom.

Further practice material

Need more classroom practice activities?

→ Photocopiable resource materials page 202
🔘 **3.59 Song:** *Get Here*
→ TOP 10 activities pages xv to xx

Need progress tests?

→ Test CD – *Test Review D*

Need more on important teaching concepts?

→ Key concepts in *New Inside Out* pages
xxii to xxxv

Need student self-study practice?

→ CD-ROM – *Review D*

Need more information and more ideas?

→ www.insideout.net

Resource materials

Worksheet	Activity and focus	What students are doing
Unit 1		
1 Grammar *Landing card*	Pairwork *be*: present simple Personal information	Writing questions. Interviewing each other to complete a landing card.
1 Vocabulary *Common objects*	Pairwork: information gap crossword Alphabet and spelling	Completing a crossword using picture clues.
1 Communication *Where in the world?*	Groupwork: board game Countries, nationalities, languages	Identifying countries, cities and nationalities.
Unit 2		
2 Grammar *True or false?*	Pairwork: writing and asking questions Possessive determiners *be*: present simple	Finding out about a partner's favourite things and people.
2 Vocabulary *What's the job?*	Teamwork: guessing game Jobs	Guessing jobs from mime.
2 Communication *Match the numbers*	Pairwork and groupwork Pronunciation of numbers 13/30	Matching number cards. Pronouncing *teen* and *ty* correctly.
Unit 3		
3 Grammar *Who's who?*	Pairwork: family trees Possessive *'s*	Reading descriptions and writing names to complete family trees.
3 Vocabulary *Family photos*	Groupwork: inventing an identity Present simple Family	Inventing personal information from a picture and talking about a family member.
3 Communication *Am I right?*	Whole class: mingle activity Present simple	Guessing about lifestyles and habits of other students.
Unit 4		
4 Grammar *Find out*	Whole class: mingle activity Present simple questions	Asking about lifestyles and habits of other students.
4 Vocabulary *I love playing charades!*	Groupwork: miming game Word order Likes and dislikes Daily activities	Miming an activity for teams to guess the sentence.
4 Communication *What do you really think?*	Groupwork: game Opinions Object pronouns	Giving true or false opinions about famous things or people.
Review A *I Like The Way …*	Listening and reading Revision of vocabulary from Units 1–4	Listening to and reading a song. Giving opinions.

Worksheet	Activity and focus	What students are doing

Unit 5

5 Grammar
Breakfast survey

Groupwork: survey
Present simple
Daily routines
Food / drink

Asking questions to complete a group survey and interpreting results.

5 Vocabulary
Daily routines

Whole class: mingle activity
Verb phrases for daily routines
Present simple questions

Finding out about daily routines of other students.

5 Communication
Time dominoes

Groupwork: *Dominoes* game
Time

Matching clock face times to written times.

Unit 6

6 Grammar
A question of time

Pairwork
Present simple routines
Time phrases and prepositions

Grouping prepositions of time and asking questions about students' routines.

6 Vocabulary
Make or do?

Pairwork or groupwork: Pelmanism
make and *do*

Matching pairs of cards showing actions with *make* and *do*.

6 Communication
Snakes and ladders

Groupwork: board game
Adverbs of frequency
Dates

Asking about frequency and ordering sentences and questions.

Unit 7

7 Grammar
I did the same!

Whole class: mingle activity
Past simple

Talking about past events and finding someone with matching information.

7 Vocabulary
Weather forecast

Pairwork
Adjectives describing weather
will for prediction

Reading a weather forecast.
Identifying a picture slide.
Writing a weather forecast.

7 Communication
What's the sport?

Pairwork: information gap crossword
Sports

Miming clues to complete a crossword.

Unit 8

8 Grammar
I think …

Whole class: mingle activity
Past simple questions

Guessing which student experienced a particular past event or activity.

8 Vocabulary
How do you feel?

Groupwork
Adjectives and feelings

Guessing items associated with certain feelings.

8 Communication
Last summer, I …

Pairwork: dictation
Past simple
Punctuation

Memorising parts of a text and dictating to a partner.
Asking questions about holidays.

Review B
Don't Worry, Be Happy

Pairwork: listening and reading
Revision of vocabulary from Units 5–8

Listening to and reading a song.
Finding rhyming words.

Unit 9

9 Grammar
Spot the difference

Pairwork: describing a room
there is/are
some/any

Describing part of a room to a partner and finding seven differences.

9 Vocabulary
Where are they?

Pairwork: drawing dictation
Rooms and furniture
Prepositions of place

Listening to a description of where a simple item is in a room, and drawing it in the correct place.

9 Communication
In my room …

Groupwork
there is/are
Furniture vocabulary
Prepositions of place

Identifying a room from similar pictures by listening to a description and asking questions.

Unit 10

10 Grammar
How much milk is there?

Pairwork: information gap
How much/many …?
Countable and uncountable nouns
Food and drink

Asking questions about quantity and completing a picture.

10 Vocabulary
Describe it!

Groupwork: card game
Food

Guessing what's on a picture card from clues given by other students.

10 Communication
Healthy or hopeless?

Pairwork: questionnaire
How much/many …?
a lot / not much
Food and drink

Interviewing a partner with a questionnaire about food and drink.

Unit 11

11 Grammar
What are they doing?

Pairwork: identifying people
Present continuous
Clothes and actions

Describing a person in a party scene for a partner to identify.

11 Vocabulary
Fashion and style

Individual work: writing
Present continuous
Adjectives
Clothes and accessories

Labelling pictures and writing descriptions of other students' clothes.

11 Communication
Fashion show

Groupwork: board game
Present continuous
Clothes

Answering questions about people and clothes to play a board game.

Unit 12

12 Grammar
Quiz time

Groupwork: writing quiz
Comparative and superlative adjectives

Comparing and ordering three alternatives using given adjectives.

12 Vocabulary
Ready, steady, search

Pairwork: wordsearch
Adjectives and opposites

Finding adjectives in a wordsearch puzzle and matching with their opposite meaning.

12 Communication
What is it?

Pairwork: guessing game
Describing objects

Asking *yes/no* questions to identify an object in a picture.

Review C
Sailing

Pairwork: song
Revision of vocabulary from Units 9–12

Listening to and reading a song. Completing a text with missing adjectives.

Worksheet	Activity and focus	What students are doing
Unit 13		
13 Grammar *How do you do it?*	Team game Adverbs of manner Everyday activities	Miming actions for a team to guess the activity and adverb of manner.
13 Vocabulary *Character jumble*	Pairwork: crossword Character adjectives	Completing a crossword by rearranging the letters of jumbled character adjectives.
13 Communication *How many people can do it?*	Whole class: mingle activity *can* for ability	Asking questions to find someone who can do a certain thing.
Unit 14		
14 Grammar *Make a sentence with …*	Groupwork: Pelmanism Verb patterns with *want to, would like to, hope to, going to*	Making correct sentences using verb patterns.
14 Vocabulary *Television*	Groupwork: opinions Television	Discussing issues and opinions related to television viewing.
14 Communication *What's your future?*	Groupwork Questions with *want to, would like to, hope to, going to*	Making questions and interviewing other students about future hopes and plans.
Unit 15		
15 Grammar *Where have they been?*	Pairwork: information gap Present perfect Experiences	Completing information and guessing identities from asking about experiences.
15 Vocabulary *Bingo!*	Whole class: mingle activity Present perfect questions	Asking about experiences and completing Bingo cards with names of other students.
15 Communication *Life experience*	Whole class: mingle activity Present perfect / past simple	Completing questions and finding out details about past experiences.
Unit 16		
16 Grammar *Circuit training*	Whole class: revision game	Completing four team tasks: Grammar, Vocabulary, Pronunciation and English in use.
16 Vocabulary *Challenge*	Teamwork: revision game	Playing a team game revising: Grammar, Vocabulary, Pronunciation and Speaking.
16 Communication *It takes ages!*	Whole class: mingle activity Transport	Asking questions about methods of transport and completing a table about the class.
Review D *Get Here*	Pairwork: listening and reading Revision of vocabulary from Units 13–16	Listening to and reading a song. Identifying ways of travelling. Talking about travelling experiences.

Teacher's notes

1 Grammar Landing card

Page 151

Activity

Pairwork: completing personal details.

Focus

Asking questions.
Personal information.
The verb *be*.

Preparation

Make one copy of the worksheet for each student in the class.

Procedure

- Write *First name* on the board. Encourage your students to make the question *What's your first name?* and answer them.

- Give one copy of the worksheet to each student in the class. Ask your students to write the questions for each line of the landing card in Exercise 1. They mustn't complete the landing card with their own information. Check all questions together and write any questions they need on the board. (Note: *Where are you from?* is a more common question than *What's your nationality?*).

- Divide the class into pairs. Ask your students to interview each other and write down the answers their partner gives them in the correct space in Exercise 2. Remind students that they can ask for spellings: *How do you spell it?* or *Can you repeat that, please?* or *Sorry?* if they need to check information. You may like to write these on the board.

- After both students have finished, ask them to exchange pieces of paper. Each student checks that the information written down is correct, and then keeps the worksheet.

1 Vocabulary Common objects

Page 152

Activity

Pairwork: information gap crossword.

Focus

Common objects.

Preparation

Make one copy of the worksheet for each pair of students in the class, and cut up the copies as indicated.

Procedure

- Draw a simple crossword on the board and check or introduce students to: *crossword, clue, across, down*.

- Put the students into pairs and explain that you're going to give everybody the same crossword, but that Student A has the *Down* words already written in, and Student B has the *Across* words written in.

- Give a copy of Crossword A and Clues A to each Student A and a copy of Crossword B and Clues B to each Student B.

- Point out that their words have pictures they can show their partner. Ask them to check that they know the word for each picture. Explain that they must not show their crossword to their partner during the activity. They can fold it back to show the pictures.

- Ask them to sit facing one another and to take it in turns to ask their partner for clues to the missing words. Demonstrate with one Student A's worksheet, for example:

Teacher: *What is 6 across?*
Student B: (points to the picture of the sweets) *These.*

(Show students that you are writing *sweets* in the space.)

¹B												
O												
O				²T								
K	³P		I			⁴C					⁵M
⁶S	W	E	E	T	S		⁷D	I	A	R	Y	O
	N		S			M					B
	S		⁸U	M	⁹B	R	E	L	L	¹⁰A		I
		E	A	R			S		L
¹¹K	E	Y	S		G	A	¹²A	P	P	L	E
						I		P
		¹³T	O	O	T	H	B	R	U	S	H
					I		O
		¹⁴M	A	G	A	Z	I	N	E	N
					S		E

1 Communication Where in the world?

Page 153

Activity

Groupwork: board game.

Focus

Countries, nationalities and languages.

Preparation

Make one copy of the worksheet (this could be enlarged to A3 size if possible) and the answer key from this page for every group of two to four students. You may also want to give each student a copy of the worksheet at the end of the activity.

You will need one dice for each group and one counter for each student.

Procedure

- Put your students into groups of two to four and give each group a worksheet, a dice and one counter per student.

- Tell the students they are going to play a board game and explain the rules:

  1 Start on the DEPARTURES square. Roll the dice and move around the board. If you land on a:

  map, give the *country and the nationality.*
  flag, give the *country and the language.*
  famous building, give the *country and the capital city.*
  'Miss a turn' square, *miss your next turn.*

  There is a reminder of this on the board game.

  2 If the answer is correct, you can play the next turn. If it is incorrect, go back to the last 'Miss a turn' square and miss the next turn. One student in the group can be the 'checker' and have a copy of the answers.

  3 The winner is the first person to reach the ARRIVALS square.

1	
2	The United Kingdom, British
3	France, Paris
4	Italy, Italian
5	
6	Egypt, Cairo
7	Saudi Arabia, Arabic
8	Russia, Moscow
9	
10	India, Indian
11	China, Chinese (mainly Mandarin or Cantonese)
12	Japan, Japanese
13	
14	Thailand, Thai
15	Australia, Canberra
16	
17	Canada, English and French
18	Argentina, Spanish
19	Brazil, Portuguese
20	The United States of America, American

Extension

You could say the name of each country and check the country, nationality and language for each with the whole class. Pay attention to the correct word stress.

2 Grammar True or false?

Page 154

Activity

Pairwork: speaking.

Focus

Possessive determiners.
be: present simple affirmative and negative.

Preparation

Make one copy of the worksheet for each student.

Procedure

- Write three sentences about your own favourite things on the board. For example:

  My favourite food is potatoes.
  My favourite drink is apple juice.
  My favourite sport is baseball.

  Two sentences should be true and the other one false.

- Remind the students of the meaning of *true* and *false* and ask them to guess which of your sentences is the false one.

- Encourage the students to ask the question:
  Is your favourite drink apple juice? and answer:
  Yes, it is. or *No, it isn't.*

- Now ask the students to work in pairs and give one copy of the worksheet to each student.

- Tell the students that they are going to write true and false sentences about their own favourite things and then guess whether their partner's sentences are true or false.

- Ask them to complete the sentences on the worksheet with a mixture of true and false information.

- When they have done that, ask them to exchange worksheets with their partner. They should read their partner's sentences and put a *T* next to sentences they think are true and an *F* next to those they think are false. Pairs of students should not speak to one another during this part of the activity.

- When they have finished, students take it in turns to ask their partners questions to find out whether they have guessed correctly or not. Encourage them to use *Is your favourite ...?* They should keep a record of how many sentences they guessed correctly and write the score at the bottom of their partner's worksheet. The student with the most correct guesses is the winner.

Extension

For more practice of possessive determiners, choose a category and ask each of your students to choose a favourite (it can be one from the worksheet or one that's not on the worksheet). Tell them they are going to play a game where they have to listen carefully to each other to remember all the information. Select one student (Student A) to start by saying their favourite. The next student (Student B) has to first remember what Student A said and then add their own favourite. This continues until all the students have spoken. If a student can't remember, then the game starts again.

For example:
Student A (man): *My favourite food is chicken.*
Student B (woman): *His favourite food is chicken. My favourite food is fruit.*
Student C (woman): *His favourite food is chicken, her favourite food is fruit. My favourite food is pasta.* (etc.)

2 Vocabulary What's the job?

Page 155

Activity

Teamwork: miming card game

Focus

Jobs vocabulary.

Preparation

Make one copy of the worksheet and cut it up as indicated.

Procedure

- Write the word *Jobs* on the board and ask students to give you a few examples.
- Show the class the pack of cards and explain that each card has one job on it.
- Take one card, look at it and then place it face down. Mime the job and ask the class to guess what it is.
- Divide the class into two teams, A and B.
- Place the pack face down at the front of the class.
- One student from each team comes up to the front at a time and looks at the first card. They mime the job to the class and when someone guesses correctly their team gets a point. Then a student from the other team comes up to the front and mimes the next one.
- When the pack is finished, the team with the most points wins.

Variation 1

- Place the pack of cards face down at the front of the class.
- Divide the class into two teams, A and B.
- Ask one student from each team to come to the front of the class and sit with their backs facing the board.
- Pick up a card and write the job on the board.
- All the students in each team have to mime the job to their student at the same time.
- The student who is the first to call out the word correctly gets the point.

- Another student from each team comes to the front, and so on.
- When the pack is finished the team with the most points wins.

Variation 2

- Copy the worksheet several times so that there are enough cards for one pack per group of four or five students. Each group will need one large sheet of paper and a board pen or thick felt pen.
- One student from each group takes a card from the pack without showing the others and starts to draw someone doing the job. They must not speak, or answer any questions by nodding or shaking their heads.
- When someone in the group has guessed the job, the next student gets another card from the pack and draw the next job. Each student in the group should have a turn.
- The first group to finish the pack is the winning group.

2 Communication Match the numbers

Page 156

Activity

Pairwork and groupwork: Pelmanism.

Focus

Pronunciation of numbers (*13/30, 14/40* etc.).

Preparation

Make one copy of the worksheet for each pair of students (or group of four) and cut the copies up as indicated.

Procedure

- Put students into pairs or small groups (four students divided into two pairs).
- Give each pair / group a set of cards and tell them to place the cards face down on the table.
- Explain that the aim of the game is to turn over two cards which have the same number on them. If a student turns over a matching pair, they keep it. If they turn over two different cards, they should return them face down to the same place that they took them from. The idea is to remember the position of the cards.
- The students begin the game with the first player / pair turning over two cards and reading them aloud. Remind students to stress the first syllable on the *ty* numbers, and the second on the *teen* numbers. They either keep them or replace them. The next player (or pair of players) then takes a turn, and so on.
- This continues until all the matching numbers have been found. The winner is the player or pair with the most cards.
- The game can be repeated as often as necessary.

Extension

For further practice on the difference between *13* and *30*, *14* and *40* etc., write the numbers up on the board and divide the class into two teams. Call out a number and one student from each team has to run to the board and identify the number you call out. The student who first identifies the number correctly earns their team a point. The team with the most points at the end of the game is the winner.

3 Grammar Who's who?

Page 157

Activity

Pairwork: completing a family tree.

Focus

Possessive *'s*.

Preparation

Make one copy of the worksheet for each pair of students in the class and cut up as indicated.

Procedure

- Divide the class into two groups, Group A and Group B. Give each student in Group A a copy of the worksheet for Student A. Give each student in Group B a copy of the worksheet for Student B.

- Ask the students to work together in pairs to complete the sentences. Explain that more than one name is possible in some sentences, and they can choose either possibility. For example, for sentence 4, Student A could write either *Emily's* or *Grace's* to complete the sentence.

- When students have finished writing the sentences, ask each student from Group A to find a new partner from Group B. Ask students not to show their pieces of paper to each other.

- Ask Student A to read their sentences to Student B while Student B writes the names of the family in Family Tree A. Then Student B reads their sentences to Student A and Student A writes the names of the family in Family Tree B. Remind students that they can ask *Can you repeat that please?* or *How do you spell that?* for the names. Go round helping the students with the pronunciation of names.

- When both family trees have been completed, students compare worksheets.

Student A's sentences
1 Grace's grandfather is Stan.
2 Stan's wife is Liz.
3 Grace's sister is Emily.
4 Emily's/Grace's mother is Julie.
5 Julie's husband is Steve.
6 Steve's brother is Paul.
7 Emily's/Grace's aunt is Sandra.

8 Steve's/Julie's nephew is Daniel.
9 Steve's/Julie's niece is Olivia.

Student B's sentences
1 Kate's husband is Mike.
2 Mike's sister-in-law is Vicky.
3 Kate's/Vicky's brother is Alan.
4 Alan's/Vicky's nephew is Ben.
5 Ben's sister is Rose.
6 Rose's/Ben's/Annie's grandfather is Richard.
7 Richard's wife is Mary.
8 Richard's/Mary's granddaughter is Annie.
9 Annie's father is Dave.

3 Vocabulary Family photos

Page 158

Activity

Groupwork: inventing an identity.

Focus

Family vocabulary.
Present simple.

Preparation

Make one copy of the worksheet for each student. Cut out pictures from magazines of different people – at least one picture per group of three or four students.

Procedure

- You may like to demonstrate the activity before asking the students to do it. Choose a picture from a magazine and hold it up in front of the class. Go round the class asking students to invent personal information for the person in the picture. Each student has to repeat the information already invented by other students and then add another piece of information themselves.

- Ask the students to work in small groups of three or four and give each group a picture (see *Preparation*).

- Tell the students to imagine that this is a photograph of a member of their own family, and that they're going to talk to their partners about them.

- Give one copy of the worksheet to each student and ask them to invent an identity for the person in the photograph by writing information on the worksheet. Give them the time they need to do this.

- When the students have done this, ask them to take it in turns to show the picture to the other students in their group, and explain who the person in the photograph is.

Extension

Ask the students to bring photographs of real members of their family to class and do the same activity.

3 Communication Am I right?

Page 159

Activity

Class mingle: finding out about habits and lifestyles.

Focus

Present simple affirmative.

Preparation

Make one copy of the worksheet for each student in the class.

Procedure

- Give one copy of the worksheet to each student in the class. Ask your students to fold the worksheet where indicated and write the names of ten people in the class. If there are fewer than ten people in the class, ask them to repeat some names.
- After writing the names, ask students to unfold the worksheet and look at the sentences, for example: *Megumi does the housework.* If students think it's true, they put a tick (✓) in the next column or a cross (✗) if they think it's not true.
- Then ask students to find out if they were right by saying the sentence to the student they chose, and check their guess. For example:

Paolo: *Megumi, you do the housework.*
Megumi: *That's wrong. My mother does the housework.*

In this case, if Paolo had guessed that *Megumi does the housework* was incorrect (by putting a ✗) he could then put a ✓ in the final column, as his guess would have been right.

- The student with the most correct guesses is the winner.

4 Grammar Find out

Page 160

Activity

Class mingle: find someone who …

Focus

Present simple interrogative.

Preparation

Make one copy of the worksheet for every ten students in the class and cut up the copies as indicated.

Procedure

- If there are more than ten students in the class, divide them into groups. Give one card to each student in the class.
- Tell the students they are responsible for finding the answer to the questions on their card by speaking to

everybody in their group. Make sure the students know how to formulate the questions correctly and write an example on the board (each question starts with *Do you …?*).

- Ask the students to go round the class (or their group) asking and answering questions. Tell them that they may need to make notes on a separate piece of paper.
- When they have spoken to everyone in the class (or their group), they should take it in turns to report back to the class (or group) on what they have found out. For example:
Ana watches TV every day.
Rafael plays the piano.

4 Vocabulary I love playing charades!

Page 161

Activity

Groupwork: miming game.

Focus

Word order.
Vocabulary of likes and dislikes, and daily activities.

Preparation

Make one copy of the worksheet and cut it up as indicated.

Procedure

- Tell your students that they are going to guess the sentences being mimed to them. Explain that all the sentences are about likes and dislikes and daily activities.
- Demonstrate the activity yourself by miming the example sentences (below) to the whole class and asking the students to call out words to describe what you are doing. Use any gestures or point to any object in the classroom (a calendar, your watch, colours …) to make yourself understood. Indicate *yes* or *no* with your head, to direct the students, but do not say a word or draw anything on the board. As the students guess the right words, write them on the board. Example sentences:

I like getting up late.
I hate playing computer games.

- Divide the class into two teams (A and B). Place the cut-out sentences, face down, on your desk. Tell each team to send one player to the front of the class. The players pick up the same sentence and read it. They must then mime the sentence for their own team. They will have one minute per sentence. Explain that they can use any gestures or point to any object in the classroom to help their team guess the words.
- Students in each team then take it in turns to mime a sentence until all the sentences have been mimed. The team that guesses the sentence correctly gets two points.

Extension

Ask students to write six 'mimable' sentences about a member of their family, explaining his/her daily routines and likes and dislikes.

Variation

This game can also be played in pairs. Each player has half the sentences. Students take it in turns to mime to each other; if their partner guesses correctly, they get the sentences. The winner is the player with the most sentences at the end.

4 Communication What do you really think?

Page 162

Activity

Groupwork: opinions game.

Focus

Asking for and giving opinions.
Object pronouns (*him/her/it/them*).

Preparation

Make one copy of the worksheet for each group of four or five students and cut up as indicated.

Procedure

- Ask students to work in groups of four or five.
- Before students start, explain how to play.

1 Students take it in turns to ask each other for an opinion by picking up one of the smaller cards, which are in a pile face down on the table.

2 The student giving an opinion should follow the example below, giving their opinion and then adding a comment about liking/not liking the person or thing.

Copy this onto the board:

Ask for an opinion: *What do you think of …?*

Give an opinion:

| I think | he's
she's
it's
they're | great.
terrible. | – I really | like
don't like | him.
her.
it.
them. |

or: *I don't know him / her / it / them.*

3 Before giving the opinion, the student has to pick up one of the two larger cards (which are also lying face down on the table). The card says *Tell the truth* or *Tell a lie*. If they get *Tell the truth*, the student gives an honest opinion. If they get *Tell a lie*, the student gives a different opinion to what they really think. For example:

Student A picks up a card and asks Student B for an opinion.

*Student A: What do you think of the actor
              George Clooney?*

Student B doesn't like George Clooney but has picked up the *Tell a lie* card:

Student B: I think he's great – I really like him.

4 The other students in the group have to decide together whether the student has told the truth, or a lie. If the student manages to trick the other players, he or she gets two points.

5 Each member of the group takes it in turns to give an opinion until all the cards are used up. The student with the most points is the winner.

Review A Song: *I Like The Way …*

Page 163

Activity

Pairwork: song.

Focus

Revising vocabulary from *New Inside Out* Elementary Student's Book, Units 1–4.

Preparation

Make one copy of the worksheet for each student in the class. Get the recording ready.

Procedure

- Explain that you're going to listen to a song called *I Like the Way …* by The BodyRockers. Give one copy of the worksheet to each student in the class. Direct your students to the information box under the picture and ask some questions about the band (*How many people are there in the band? What are their names? Where are they from? When did they record this song? How long did it take to record?*)

- Ask your students to listen and draw a line joining the first half of each line and the second half. Play as many times as necessary.

- Ask your students what the singer likes most about the girl in the song.

- Encourage your students to write sentences starting with *I (don't) like the way …* about people they know and then ask them to compare their sentences in pairs.

> 1 a 4, b 6, c 1, d 5, e 3, f 2, g 8, h 9, i 10, j 7
> 2 He likes the way she moves.

5 Grammar Breakfast survey

Page 164

Activity

Groupwork: survey.

Focus

Present simple for daily routines.
Food and drink.

Preparation

Make one copy of the worksheet for each student in the class.

Procedure

- Ask your students to work in groups of five.
- Give one copy of the worksheet to each student in the class. Encourage them to make the questions for each column in the survey: *What time do you have breakfast? Who do you have breakfast with? What do you (usually) eat for breakfast? What do you (usually) drink at breakfast?* You may like to write them on the board as a reminder.
- Ask your students to complete the first row of the table with their own information. They then interview each student in the group with the questions above.
- When students have finished interviewing each other, ask them to sit down and complete the survey results together. In 1), if two of the five people in the group don't have anything for breakfast, the students need to write in 40% (as each person in a group of five has a value of 20%).
- After students have finished writing their results, compare results from different groups.

5 Vocabulary Daily routines

Page 165

Activity

Class mingle: daily routines.

Focus

Verb phrases for daily routines (*get up, have breakfast*).

Preparation

Make one copy of the worksheet for each student in the class.

Procedure

- Give one copy of the worksheet to each student in the class. Explain that they are going to complete the sentences with the verbs provided and then go round the class asking one another questions. Make sure your students are able to change the sentence into a question. For example … *gets up after ten on Sunday mornings. Do you get up after ten on Sunday mornings?*
- When they find someone who answers *yes* to a question, they can put that person's name in the space next to the sentence. Tell the students that they can only put the same name twice.
- When one student has found a name for each of the sentences on the worksheet, stop the activity.
- Ask different students to say one sentence each to the whole class.

> gets, goes, has, goes, reads, listens, has, has, goes, goes

5 Communication Time dominoes

Page 166

Activity

Groupwork: playing *Dominoes.*

Focus

Telling the time.

Preparation

Make one copy of the worksheet for every four students in the class and cut up as indicated.

Procedure

- Explain to the students that they are going to play a game of dominoes matching a clock time to a written time, and that the aim is to use all of their dominoes.
- Ask the students to work in groups of four and give each group a set of dominoes. Ask them to hand out three dominoes each and leave the rest in a pile, face down.
- Explain how to play.
- Player A puts down one of their dominoes, face up. The player on their left must put down one of their dominoes, making sure that the time on the half of their domino matches the time on Player A's domino, for example:

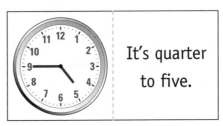

- If a player cannot put down one of their dominoes, they can take a domino from the top of the pile and put it down if they can. The first player to use all of their dominoes is the winner.

6 Grammar A question of time

Page 167

Activity

Pairwork: asking about times.

Focus

Prepositions of time.

Preparation

Make one copy of the worksheet for each student in the class.

Procedure

- Ask students to work in pairs.

- Give one copy of the worksheet to each student in the class. Ask them to work together to write the time phrases that go with the correct preposition, *in, on* or *at*.
- When they have finished, check their answers together as a class.
- Ask your students to think about their answers to the eight questions and then ask them to take it in turns, with the same partner, to ask and answer the questions. Write an example on the board:

Jon: *What time do you get up?*
Marc: *I get up at 7.30 .*
Jon: (writes) *Marc gets up at 7.30.*

- Encourage them to get as much practice as possible using the time prepositions.

on	in	at
Saturday night	the autumn	the weekend
Monday morning	February	quarter to six
Friday	the evening	four thirty
18th November	October	two o'clock
Sunday	the spring	6:15
24th April	the afternoon	night

6 **Vocabulary** *Make* or *do*?

Page 168

Activity

Pairwork or groupwork: *Pelmanism* game.

Focus

make and *do*.

Preparation

Make one copy of the worksheet for every pair of students in the class. Take enough pairs of scissors into the class for your students to cut up the worksheet after they have worked on it.

Procedure

- Ask students to work in pairs (or groups of four divided into two pairs).
- Give one copy of the worksheet to each pair and ask them to work together to complete the verb phrases by writing either *make* or *do* in the space provided.
- When they have finished, check the answers together as a class.
- When you have checked the answers, ask your students to cut the worksheet up as indicated. Ask them to place the cards face down on the table.
- Demonstrate that the aim of the game is to turn over two cards which show the same activity, for example 'do homework' and a picture of someone doing homework. If a student turns over a matching pair,

they keep it. If they turn over two different cards, they should return them face down to the place that they took them from. The idea is to remember the position of the cards.

- The students begin the game with the first player / pair turning over two cards and reading them aloud. Students should remember what the cards with a picture on them represent, and should read them out as if they were written. They either keep the cards or replace them. The next player (or pair of players) then takes a turn, and so on.
- This continues until all the matching cards have been found. The winner is the player (or pair) with the most cards.

6 **Communication** Snakes and ladders

Page 169

Activity

Groupwork: board game.

Focus

Dates, months, adverbs of frequency.

Preparation

Make one copy of the worksheet for each group of four or five students in the class. You will need a dice for each group and a counter for each player.

Procedure

- Divide the class into groups of four. Give each group a copy of the worksheet, a counter for each player and one dice.
- Tell the students they are going to play a game. The aim of the game is to reach the finish first by answering questions. Explain that the ladders are helpful – when you land at the bottom of a ladder, you can travel to the top of the ladder. But the snakes have the opposite effect. If you land on a snake's head, you have to move back to the end of its tail. After you have been up a ladder or down a snake, you don't answer the question at the top of the ladder or bottom of the snake.
- There are four types of question and there is a key on the page to help students understand what they have to do. One student in the group can be the referee and check the answers, or the other students in the group can check the player's answer.
  1 To start the game, each student puts their counter on the START square. Player 1 rolls the dice and moves forward the number of squares indicated on the dice.
  2 They must answer the question so that the other players or the referee are happy with their answer. If they answer the question correctly, they remain on the square. If they don't answer the question correctly, they have to move back to where they started.

3 The student to the left of Player 1 goes next. They roll the dice and move in the same way. The game continues until the first player reaches the FINISH square and wins the game.

7 Grammar I did the same!

Page 170

Activity

Class mingle.

Focus

Past simple affirmative.

Preparation

Make one copy of the worksheet for each student in the class.

Procedure

- Give one copy of the worksheet to each student in the class. Ask your students to complete true sentences.
- When everyone has finished, ask students to get up and move around the class and try to find someone with the same information as their own. For example:

Student A: *The last time I travelled in a car was two days ago. What about you?*
Student B: *I travelled in a car last week.*

- In this situation, neither student writes anything. However, if the answers are the same, the students can both write each other's name after the sentence. Ask students not to write the same name more than twice.
- As soon as one student completes their worksheet, stop the activity. Ask different students to tell the class who had the same information for one of the sentences.

7 Vocabulary Weather forecast

Page 171

Activity

Pairwork: weather forecast.

Focus

will and *might*.

Preparation

Make one copy of the worksheet for each pair of students in the class. Cut out the picture slides if you do the extension activity.

Procedure

- Tell students that they're going to practise talking about the weather in this lesson.

- Hand out one copy of the worksheet to each pair of students in the class. Ask students to do Exercises 1 and 2 in pairs. Check answers with the whole class.
- Give students five minutes to read the weather forecast in Exercise 3 and to identify which of the picture slides it refers to. Go round and listen, helping with vocabulary if necessary, e.g. *stormy*. Encourage those students who finish quickly to practise reading the forecast out aloud. As an alternative, you could read the forecast to the students yourself, and ask them to identify which of the picture slides it refers to.
- Ask students in each pair to choose one of the remaining picture slides (A or C) and to prepare a weather forecast to describe it. Tell students to use the forecast in Exercise 3 as a model. Less confident students could work together to produce their forecast. More confident students could write their own individual forecast.
- Students practise and then present their forecasts to their partner / other pairs / other students in the class.

Extension

1 Students cut up the weather slides and use the individual pictures to put on a map of their country and prepare their own TV weather forecast, which you could record and play back.

2 Students can look on the internet for weather forecasts in English from different parts of the world. Students compile a list of words and expressions that are used to talk about or describe the weather. www.met-office.gov.uk is one site to look at.

---

1 warm, wet, bad, cold, dry, good, hot, lovely
2 cloudy, foggy, sunny, windy, rainy, snowy, stormy
3 Slide B

---

7 Communication What's the sport?

Page 172

Activity

Pairwork: information gap crossword.

Focus

Sports vocabulary.

Preparation

Make one copy of the worksheet for each pair and cut up the copies as indicated.

Procedure

- Draw a simple crossword on the board and check that students know: *crossword, clue, across, down*.
- Put the students into pairs and explain that you're going to give everybody the same crossword, but that Student A has the *Across* words already written in, and Student B has the *Down* words written in.

- Give a copy of Crossword A to each Student A and a copy of Crossword B to each Student B. Point out that their words have pictures. Ask them to check that they know the word for each picture.

- Explain that they must not show their crossword to their partner.

- Ask them to sit facing one another and to take it in turns to ask their partner for clues to the missing words, for example:

  Student B: *What is 1 across?*
  Student A: *(says nothing but mimes someone playing football)*
  Student B: *Is it football?*
  Student A: *Yes, it is.*
  (Student B writes 'football' in the space)

- When they have finished, ask students to decide, in their pairs, which sports take the verb *play* and which sports take the verb *go*.

> You *play* football and tennis, but all the other sports here take the verb *go*.

8 Grammar I think ...

Page 173

Activity

Class mingle.

Focus

Past simple question forms.

Preparation

Make one copy of the worksheet for each student.

Procedure

- Give one copy of the worksheet to each student. Ask them to guess which of their classmates (or the teacher!) did each of the activities on the worksheet and then to complete the sentences by writing the names of their classmates in the appropriate spaces, for example, *Junko went to a party last weekend.* Encourage the students to write as many different names as possible.

- When they have completed all the sentences, the students walk around the class asking and answering questions. For example:

  Junko, did you go to a party last weekend?
  Yes, I did. / No, I didn't.

  Remind students that all the questions begin with *Did you ...?* even when the answer is negative (for *homework* and *breakfast*).

- The students tick their correct guesses and put a cross next to their incorrect guesses.

- The student with the most correct guesses is the winner.

8 Vocabulary How do you feel?

Page 174

Activity

Groupwork.

Focus

Adjectives related to feelings.

Preparation

Make one copy of the worksheet for the class and cut in half as indicated.

Procedure

- Divide the class into two teams, Team A and Team B.

- Give Team A the top half of the worksheet and Team B the bottom half.

- Explain that the students need to work together to agree on five things they associate with the five feelings shown on their worksheet. For example, for *five things that make you feel happy*, students may write: *the weekend, love, wine, friends, the sun.* They must make sure that the other team can't see what they're writing.

- The teams sit facing one another. Team A read out their category: *Things that make you feel happy* and Team B have one minute to say as many words as they can from Team A's list. If they say a word that Team A has on their list, they get a point. Team A are responsible for marking down the points and timing Team B.

- After Team B have had their go, it's Team A's turn. Team B read out their first category and Team A have one minute to guess Team B's words. The teams take it turns to guess each other's words until all the categories have been used up. The team with the most points is the winner.

8 Communication Last summer, I ...

Page 175

Activity

Pairwork: running dictation.

Focus

Past simple questions.

Preparation

Make a copy of the worksheet for each student, and one extra. Cut out the text at the top of the extra worksheet. Note: This activity is longer than usual and could be done in two or three stages.

Procedure

- Write two short sentences on the board and stand with your back to the board. Ask a student to dictate the two sentences on the board to you. As the student dictates, ask for repetition, clarification, spelling, etc. For example: *Wait a moment. What did you say? How do you spell that? What comes after … ?*

- Write these expressions on the board. Check that students know how to describe various punctuation marks – *full stop, comma, apostrophe,* etc.

- Stick the text from the top of the extra worksheet onto the wall outside the classroom. If it is a big class, you may like to stick two texts up.

- Put the students into pairs, with Student A as the 'writer' and Student B as the 'reader'. Explain to the students that the readers will dictate a text to their partner (the writer). Tell them that they must use only English.

- Ask the readers to stand up, go to the text, read it and then return and dictate it to their partner. Instruct readers to stand about one metre away from their partners as they dictate the text. Explain that they will probably have to return to the text several times, remembering a short piece of text each time. Check that the students are using only English.

- When the students have finished, the readers can sit with their writing partner to check the writing. After they have checked for a few minutes, give them two copies of the worksheet for the final check.

Extension 1

Ask the students to complete the questions using the prompts.

Tell the students to ask you their questions about your last holiday. After each answer, they should write notes in the first column of the table.

Students then write notes about their own holiday to complete the second column of the table and finally they can ask two other students about their holidays to complete the last two columns.

Extension 2

A logical next step is for students to write about their last holiday. You may wish to provide some input for the connecting words *and, but, so* and *because* (examples in dictation text) and encourage students to use them in their own writing.

```
1  When did you last go on holiday?
2  Where did you go?
3  Who did you go with?
4  How did you go?
5  Where did you stay?
6  What did you do?
7  Did you enjoy it?
```

Review B Song: *Don't Worry, Be Happy*

Page 176

Activity

Pairwork: song.

Focus

Revising vocabulary from *New Inside Out* Elementary Student's Book, Units 5–8.

Preparation

Make one copy of the worksheet for each student in the class. Get the recording ready.

Procedure

- Elicit an example of two words that rhyme (e.g. *cat* and *mat*). Then give students a minute or two to match the rhyming words in the two columns. Make sure that they all understand the meanings. *Litigate* will be a new word for many students. It means 'to take someone to court'. Check answers with the class.

- Draw students' attention to the information in the box. Find out if anyone has heard the song before. Ask them to read the song and complete the lyrics with the rhyming words from Exercise 1. You might like to point out that the first and second lines of each verse rhyme. Play the song for the students to check their answers. Then play it again for them to listen for enjoyment and sing along if they wish.

- Give students plenty of time to discuss and list, in pairs, the worries they think each of these people might have. Allow them to compare with other pairs and then have a class feedback session to determine how many ideas have been suggested and how much agreement there is.

- Ask students to work in pairs and discuss the effect this song has on them. Does it make them feel happy? Would it have that effect if they were worried about something? Ask them to discuss and report back to the class on what music makes them feel happy.

```
1  wrote – note   style – smile   trouble – double
   head – bed   frown – down   late – litigate
2  1 wrote  2 note  3 trouble  4 double  5 head
   6 bed  7 late  8 litigate  9 style  10 smile
   11 frown  12 down
```

9 **Grammar** Spot the difference

Page 177

Activity

Pairwork: describing a room.

Focus

there is/there are …
some and *any*.

Preparation

Make one copy of the worksheet for every pair of students in the class and cut in half as indicated.

Procedure

- Divide the class into two groups, Group A and Group B. Give a copy of worksheet A to each student in Group A and a copy of worksheet B to each student in Group B. Ask students to work in pairs, one student from Group A with one from Group B. Tell them not to look at each other's worksheets.

- Explain that each student has the same picture, but there are seven differences. They should take it in turns to describe something in the room while their partner listens and checks if their own picture can be described in the same way. If not, they should circle the difference.

- When the first pair has finished, stop the activity. Tell them not to look at each other's pictures yet. Ask the whole class about the differences. Then students can compare their pictures.

> The seven differences are:
> A: There are some plants next to the armchair.
> B: There's a lamp next to the armchair.
> A: There's a phone on the desk.
> B: There are some books on the desk.
> A: There's a mirror on the wall above the sofa.
> B: There's a picture on the wall above the sofa.
> A: There's a rug on the floor.
> B: There isn't a rug on the floor.
> A: There aren't any cushions on the sofa.
> B: There are some cushions on the sofa.
> A: There are some magazines under the coffee table.
> B: There's a cat under the coffee table.
> A: There's a picture on the television.
> B: There's a plant on the television.

9 Vocabulary Where are they?

Page 178

Activity

Pairwork: drawing dictation.

Focus

Vocabulary of rooms and furniture.
Prepositions of place.

Preparation

Make one copy of the worksheet for each student in the class.

Procedure

- Explain to your students that you are going to do a dictation, but instead of writing they are going to draw some simple items in the correct place on a picture.

- Give each student in the class a copy of the worksheet and make sure they know the names of each of the items at the bottom of the page. When they are ready, read out the sentences below one by one, allowing enough time for the students to draw them in on their pictures.
  1 The cushions are on the bed.
  2 The rug is next to the bed.
  3 The plants are on the table next to the armchair.
  4 The lamp is on the floor, next to the sofa.
  5 The clock is on the bookcase.
  6 The phone is on the bed.
  7 The books are on the sofa.
  8 The pen is on the coffee table next to the sofa.
  9 The mirror is on the wall, above the bookcase.
  10 The pictures are under the big coffee table.

- When you have read out all of the sentences, give students time to check their pictures in pairs.

- Go through the answers as a class. You may want to put a copy of the picture on an OHT and ask students to dictate back to you while you draw the items on your picture.

Extension

Ask your students to draw three more items in the picture (without showing the person next to them). Then, in pairs, each student should describe the location of their items to a partner, who draws them in their own picture. After they have finished describing and drawing, students compare worksheets to see if they have explained, or understood, clearly.

9 Communication In my room ...

Page 179

Activity

Groupwork: listen and describe.

Focus

there is/are.
Furniture vocabulary.
Prepositions of place.

Preparation

Make one OHT copy of the worksheet, or make one copy of the worksheet for each student.

Make one copy of the worksheet for each group of three or four students, and cut the copies up as indicated.

(Variation: only the OHT or one copy of the worksheet for each student is needed.)

Procedure

- Show the OHT of the worksheet or give one copy of the worksheet to each student, and encourage students to make sentences about picture 1.

- Ask the students: *Which room is mine?* and describe one of the pictures until a student guesses correctly, for example: *There are three pictures on the wall. There's a plant next to the armchair.* Repeat this one or two times.

- Now ask a student in the class to do the same. Repeat a few times.
- Demonstrate the activity with two or three strong students. Place a set of the picture cards face down on the table. One student picks up the top card and describes the room on that card. The other students listen and guess the room number (each student has only one guess per card). The first student to say the correct room wins the card for one point. Then the next student picks up a card, describes it, and so on.
- Divide the students into groups of three to four and give out one set of cards per group.
- Students play the game in their groups. Go round and listen carefully and suggest ideas where necessary.

Variation

- Show the OHT of the worksheet or give one copy of the worksheet to each student.
- Ask a student to choose a room and then you ask various *yes/no* questions to try to find out which room it is. Use *Is there a … ?* and *Are there any … ?* questions. Write notes on the board as the student answers your questions, for example, *one coffee table, no lamp*, etc. Encourage other students to ask questions as well.
- Demonstrate the game again, this time with students asking questions, in turn, around the classroom. Note that in this version, a student can only guess which room it is *after* they ask their question.
- Students then play the game in pairs or small groups.

10 Grammar How much milk is there?

Page 180

Activity
Pairwork: information gap.

Focus
How much …? / How many …?
Countable and uncountable nouns.
Food and drink.

Preparation
Make one copy of the worksheet for each pair of students in the class.

Procedure

- Divide the class into two groups, Group A and Group B. Give a copy of worksheet A to each student in Group A and a copy of worksheet B to each student in Group B. Ask students to work in pairs, one student from Group A with one from Group B. Tell students not to look at each other's worksheets.
- Explain that each student has the same picture, but there are some differences in quantities of food and drink, and they need to ask their partner. Then they can draw the correct amount of food or drink on their picture.
- Student A should decide if the food item is a countable or uncountable noun and then ask Student B the

question *How much (tea) is there?* or *How many (bananas) are there?* Student B then replies either *Not much, Not many* or *A lot*. Student A then draws the item in on the picture in the quantity that Student B says.
- Students take it in turns to ask and answer questions and draw in the answers. When they have finished, they can compare worksheets.

How much bread is there?	There's a lot of bread.
How much rice is there?	There isn't much rice.
How much tea is there?	There's a lot of tea.
How any bananas are there?	There aren't any bananas.
How many tomatoes are there?	There aren't many tomatoes.
How many apples are there?	There are a lot of apples.
How much pasta is there?	There isn't much pasta.
How much milk is there?	There isn't any milk.
How many oranges are there?	There are a lot of oranges.
How many onions are there?	There are a lot of onions.
How many steaks are there?	There are a lot of steaks.
How much coffee is there?	There isn't much coffee.

Extension

You may want to play a game using the completed picture. Divide the class into two teams. Take it in turns to ask one team: *Question: oranges*. The team should quickly respond with the question *How many oranges are there?* to get a point. If they make a correct question, say to the other team: *Answer* and they reply: *There are a lot* to get a point themselves.

Continue until all the items have been mentioned. Speed is essential in this game and any delays from either team means that the other team gets the points. The team with the most points at the end of the game is the winner.

10 Vocabulary Describe it!

Page 181

Activity
Groupwork: card game.

Focus
Food vocabulary.

Preparation
Make one copy of the worksheet for every group of four or five students in the class. Cut into cards as indicated.

Procedure

- Divide the class into groups of four or five and give one set of cards to each group. Ask them to place the cards in a pile on the table, face down.

- Explain that the students have to take it in turns to pick up a card and look at the word on it, but not show it to the other members of the team. They then have thirty seconds in which to describe the food item without saying the word. For example:

  It's a fruit. It's usually yellow. Monkeys like this. It's soft.

- If another student guesses the word, both players get one point. If nobody guesses after 30 seconds, the card is placed on the bottom of the pack and the next player takes a new card.

- Each group should choose one student to keep score. After all of the words have been used the game is over. The player with the most points is the winner.

Variation

This could also be played as a board drawing game. Divide the class into two teams. One player comes to the front from each team. They look at the word and then both start drawing it on the board for their teams. The first team to call out the correct word gets the points. After all students have had at least one go, the game ends. The team with the most points wins.

10 Communication Healthy or hopeless?

Page 182

Activity

Pairwork: questionnaire.

Focus

Food vocabulary.
how much ...?/how many ...?
a lot / not much.

Preparation

Make one copy of the worksheet for each student and cut the copies up as indicated.

Procedure

- Ask the students to work in pairs. Give one copy of the questionnaire to each student in the class but do not give out the *What it means* section yet.

- Give them a few minutes to read the questionnaire and to ask any questions about words they do not know.

- Now ask them to take it in turns to ask their partner the questions on the questionnaire and to note down their answers.

- When they have interviewed one another, they should add up their partner's score.

- Give the *What it means* section to each pair of students and ask them to read out their partner's results.

Variation

Ask the students to read the questionnaire and answer the questions silently, and then compare results with a partner.

11 Grammar What are they doing?

Page 183

Activity

Pairwork: identifying people.

Focus

Present continuous.
Clothes and actions.

Preparation

Make one copy of the worksheet for each student in the class and cut in half as indicated.

Procedure

- Ask your students to work in pairs and give Student A a copy of the worksheet for Student A, and B a copy of the worksheet for Student B. Ask your students not to show each other their worksheet.

- Explain that they are going to ask and answer questions about the picture and that they have to label the picture with the names of the people which are missing.

  For example:

  Student A: *What is Anna doing?*
  Student B: *She's standing up. She's smiling.*
  Student A: *What is she wearing?*
  Student B: *She's wearing a black skirt and a white top.*
  Student A: *Is she holding a glass of wine?*
  Student B: *Yes, she is.*

- When they think that they have identified the person, students write the name of the person in their picture. Encourage students to describe not only what the people are doing, but also what they're wearing. Draw attention to the useful verbs on their worksheets.

- When the students have finished their descriptions, ask them to compare worksheets to check that the names are all in the correct place.

Student A:	12 Anna	5 Ben
	11 Emily	6 Will
	9 Cathy	2 Rob
Student B:	1 Ed	3 Nick
	10 Olivia	7 Tom
	4 Louisa	8 Carla

11 **Vocabulary** Fashion and style

Page 184

Activity

Individual work: writing.

Focus

Clothes and accessories vocabulary.
Present continuous.

Preparation

Make one copy of the worksheet for each student.

Procedure

- Give out a copy of the worksheet to each student. Allow 1–2 minutes for them to read the instructions.
- Ask the students to look carefully at the two pictures and then to complete the 18 labels using the words from the boxes below.
- Go through the answers with the whole class.
- Ask the students to read the instructions for the second task. Explain to the students that they are going to write sentences describing what other students in the class are wearing, using the vocabulary from the first task and the present continuous.
- Allow students 5–7 minutes to do this task and then check the answers with the whole class. The students can also compare their answers in pairs.

Picture 1	Picture 2
1 hat	10 cap
2 ring	11 glasses
3 bracelet	12 shirt
4 top	13 T-shirt
5 bag	14 jacket
6 scarf	15 belt
7 skirt	16 trousers
8 coat	17 socks
9 boots	18 trainers

11 **Communication** Fashion show

Page 185

Activity

Groupwork: board game.

Focus

Present continuous.
Clothes vocabulary.

Preparation

Make one copy of the worksheet for each group of four or five students in the class. You will need a dice for each group and a counter for each player.

Procedure

- Divide the class into groups of four or five. Give each group a copy of the worksheet, a counter for each player and one dice.

- Tell the students they are going to play a game. The aim of the game is to reach the finish first, and to get there by answering questions. Explain that if you land on some squares, you can move forwards without even answering a question, but on others you have to move backwards.
- There are four types of question and there is a key on the page to remind students what they have to do.
- To start the game, each student puts their counter on the START square. Player 1 rolls the dice and moves forward the number of squares indicated on the dice. The other players must be happy with their answer. If they answer the question correctly, they stay on the square. If they don't answer the question correctly, they have to move back to where they started.
- The student to the left of Player 1 goes next. They roll the dice and move in the same way. The game continues until the first player reaches the FINISH square and wins the game.

12 **Grammar** Quiz time

Page 186

Activity

Groupwork: writing quiz.

Focus

Comparatives and superlatives.

Preparation

Make one copy of the worksheet for each team of two or three students and one copy of the worksheet for each student.

Procedure

- Put the students into teams of two or three and give each team a copy of the worksheet.
- Allow the students plenty of time to discuss the questions and write their answers. The students only have to write the letters as their answers at this stage.
- When the teams have completed the quiz, ask them to exchange worksheets with another team for marking and then check the answers with the whole class. Award three points if all three are in the correct order and one point if one is in the correct position. The team with the highest score is the winner.
- Give out one clean worksheet to each student for their records. Ask them to write out their answers as full sentences, with the comparative and superlative forms, using the example in question 1 as a model, for further practice or for homework.

1 b, a, c	4 c, a, b	7 b, c, a
2 c, a, b	5 b, a, c	8 c, a, b
3 a, c, b	6 a, c, b	9 a, b, c

12 Vocabulary Ready, steady, search

Page 187

Activity

Pairwork: wordsearch.

Focus

Adjectives and their opposites.

Preparation

Make one copy of the worksheet for each pair of students and cut up as indicated.

Procedure

- Put the students into pairs and give one the Student A worksheet and the other the Student B worksheet.

- Ask the students to find eight more adjectives in their wordsearch puzzle, circling the words and writing them in the 'My words' column of the table as they find them.

- When they have done this, Students A and B work together, exchanging their adjectives to complete the table. For example:

  A: What's the opposite of dirty?
  B: Clean. What's the opposite of …?

Extension

Ask the students, working in pairs, to produce some true sentences, either written or spoken, using the pairs of opposite adjectives. For example:

Some people think English is difficult, but we think it's easy.

fast / slow   ugly / beautiful   difficult / easy
dirty / clean   cheap / expensive   long / short
good / bad   big / small   young / old
rich / poor

A

F	A	S	T	Q	U	G	L	Y	X
D	D	Y	S	W	Z	X	Y	O	Z
G	I	I	W	R	L	R	T	U	L
J	F	D	R	Y	K	I	R	N	K
P	F	H	K	T	J	C	W	G	J
L	I	K	M	P	Y	H	Q	P	H
W	C	H	E	A	P	C	M	S	G
Q	U	L	G	S	G	V	B	I	G
Y	L	O	N	G	R	B	N	D	F
N	T	Z	R	D	F	G	O	O	D

B

S	M	A	L	L	Z	O	K	L	M
W	B	K	F	V	S	L	O	W	Q
C	L	E	A	N	D	D	J	R	S
R	J	W	A	C	V	S	H	T	H
B	A	D	F	U	T	W	G	Y	O
T	H	X	L	X	T	Q	D	P	R
E	X	P	E	N	S	I	V	E	T
Y	G	O	R	B	Y	Z	F	Q	R
P	F	O	H	G	P	V	X	U	D
S	D	R	M	E	A	S	Y	Z	L

12 Communication What is it?

Page 188

Activity

Pairwork: guessing game.

Focus

Describing objects.

Preparation

Make one copy of the worksheet for each student in the class.

Procedure

Put the students into pairs and give each student a copy of the worksheet. Explain the rules of the game:

1 Student A chooses an object from the worksheet without telling Student B what it is.

2 Student B asks the *yes/no* questions on the worksheet (in any order) and other questions to try to identify the object. Student A can only answer *Yes, it is. / No, it isn't.*, or *Yes, you do. / No, you don't.*, to Student B's questions.

3 If at any time Student B thinks he or she knows what the object is, he or she can make a guess. If correct, he or she gets a point and the round finishes. If not correct, this counts as one question and he or she continues asking more questions.

4 The student who is guessing can ask a maximum of ten questions. If after ten questions Student B doesn't know the object, he or she has one final guess at the object. If correct, he or she gets a point. If not correct, then Student A gets a point.

- At the end of the round, the students exchange roles and play again. You could set a time limit or play until the first student gets to, for example, five points.

Review C Song: *Sailing*

Page 189

Activity

Pairwork: song.

Focus

Reviewing vocabulary from *New Inside Out* Elementary Student's Book, Units 9–12.

Preparation

Make one copy of the worksheet for each student in the class. Get the recording ready.

Procedure

- Explain that you're going to listen to a song called *Sailing* by Rod Stewart. Give one copy of the worksheet to each student in the class. Ask students to match adjectives in column A with their opposites in column B. Check answers.

- Ask your students to complete the song with the words in Exercise 1. Play the song for students to check their answers. Then play it again for them to listen for enjoyment and sing along if they wish.

- Give students plenty of time to discuss with their partner which sentence best summarises the song.

---

1 a) 4, b) 5, c) 1, d) 3, e) 2
2 1 stormy   2 near   3 free   4 high   5 free
  6 dark   7 dark   8 stormy   9 near   10 free

---

13 Grammar How do you do it?

Page 190

Activity

Team game.

Focus

Adverbs of manner.

Preparation

Make one copy of the worksheet and cut it up as indicated.

Procedure

- Divide the class into two groups. Tell them they are going to play a game against each other.

- Explain that you are going to mime an action and they should call out what it is. Explain that the answer ends in an adverb of manner. Demonstrate by miming an action of your own choice (*Make a cup of tea quickly, brush your teeth slowly* etc.), making sure your students understand that they have to guess both the action and the adverb of manner.

- Tell each team to take it in turns to send one player to the front of the class. The player picks up one of the mime cards and silently reads the sentence. The player then has 30 seconds to mime the action on the card while their team calls out guesses. If the mime has not been guessed after 30 seconds, the other team can steal a point by giving the correct answer. Each team then takes it in turns to guess the answer until one team gets it right. Teams can score one point for a correct action and one point for a correct adverb of manner. Any team guessing both a correct action and adverb immediately, scores four points.

- The game continues until all the cards are used up. The team that has the most points at the end is the winner.

Extension

Students can make their own cards for the teacher to store and use at a later date as a short activity at the beginning or end of a class.

13 Vocabulary Character jumble

Page 191

Activity

Individual/pairwork: crossword.

Focus

Character adjectives.

Preparation

Make one copy of the worksheet for each student in the class.

Procedure

- Give one copy of the worksheet to each student and ask them to complete the crossword by rearranging the letters of jumbled character adjectives. You could help the students by telling them that the first letter of each adjective is in the correct position.

- Note: The word 'stubborn' may be new for your students so you may want to explain this one to them.

- The students can either do the crossword individually or work together in pairs. You could add a competitive element by making the first student or pair to finish the winner.

- When the students have finished the crossword, check the answers as a class.

- The students then work in pairs or small groups to discuss the questions in Exercise 2.

- Go through students' answers to Exercise 2.

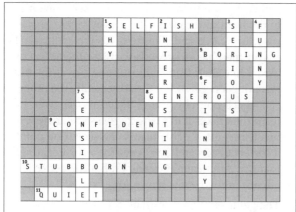

The stressed syllables are in bold: 1 across **sel**fish
1 down **shy**   2 **in**teresting   3 **se**rious   4 **fun**ny
5 **bor**ing   6 **friend**ly   7 **sen**sible   8 **gen**erous
9 **con**fident   10 **stub**born   11 **qui**et

13 **Communication** How many people can do it?

Page 192

Activity

Class mingle.

Focus

can for ability.

Preparation

Make one copy of the worksheet for every ten students in the class and cut up the copies as indicated.

Procedure

- If there are more than ten students in the class, divide them into groups. Give one card to each student in the class.
- Tell the students they are responsible for finding the answer to the questions on their card by speaking to everybody in their group. Make sure the students know how to form the questions correctly (each question starts with *Can you …?*).
- Ask the students to go round the class (or their group) asking and answering questions. Tell them that they may need to make notes on a separate piece of paper.
- When they have spoken to everyone in the class (or their group), they should take it in turns to report back to the class (or group) on the information they have found out.

14 **Grammar** Make a sentence with …

Page 193

Activity

Groupwork: Pelmanism sentence game.

Focus

Verb patterns with *want to, would like to, hope to,* and *going to.*

Preparation

Make one copy of the worksheet for each group of three to five students. Cut the copies up as indicated and sort into two piles: A and B.

Procedure

Version 1

- Divide the class into groups of three to five students.
- Demonstrate the activity to the class.
- Spread out the two sets of cards (A and B) face down on the table of your demonstration group.
- One student turns over two cards. If they are both A cards, or both B cards, he or she turns them back over, and the next student has a turn.
- If the two cards are an A card and a B card, the student uses the two verbs to make a sentence.
- If all the students in the group agree that the grammar and meaning of the sentence is correct, that student keeps the pair.
- The next student turns over two cards as above, and so on.

Version 2

- Divide the class into groups of three to five students.
- Put the cards face down in two piles – one for A cards, one for B cards.
- One student turns over the top card on each pile. The other students take turns to say a sentence using the two verbs shown.
- The student who turned over the cards judges which of the other students has said the best sentence. He or she gives the pair of cards to that student.
- The next student turns over the top card on each pile and the game continues.

Notes

Version 1 is easier as students are more likely to help their classmates as they try to produce correct sentences. Therefore, it is probably best to play the two games in the order given.

You may want to provide extra verbs to increase the number of possible verb combinations.

14 Vocabulary Television

Activity

Groupwork: opinions.

Focus

Television vocabulary.

Preparation

Make one copy of the worksheet for each student in the class.

Procedure

- Give one copy of the worksheet to each student in the class. Ask your students to tick the answer which best matches their opinion or situation for each one.
- When they have finished thinking about the statements and have selected an answer for each, ask them to work in small groups and discuss their answers.
- After students have finished discussing the statements, talk about them together as a class.

14 Communication What's your future?

Activity

Groupwork: asking questions.

Focus

want to, would like to, hope to, going to.

Preparation

Make one copy of the worksheet for each student in the class.

Procedure

- Write the first question from the worksheet on the board. Ask the class if anyone can complete the gap and write it on the board:

  What do you hope to study in the future?
- Give each student a copy of the worksheet and point out that the students must use *would, do* or *are* to make the questions.
- Now ask students to work individually to write their own short answers to the questions in the first column under 'You'.
- Go round helping with vocabulary if necessary.
- Now ask students to interview a partner, making sure they use the correct question form, and write their partner's answers in the second column.
- You may like to discuss any interesting answers as a class at the end of the activity.

15 Grammar Where have they been?

Activity

Pairwork: information gap.

Focus

Present perfect to talk about experience.

Preparation

Make one copy of the worksheet for each pair of students in the class.

Procedure

- Tell your students that they are going to play a game, but first they have to make sure their worksheets contain the same information.
- Divide the class into pairs, Student A and Student B. Give the top half of the worksheet to Student A and the bottom half to Student B. Explain that they need to ask and answer questions about the people on their card. Use the first person's name (Amy) as an example and encourage the students to help you write this conversation on the board:

  Student B: *Has Amy been to The Olympics?*
  Student A: *Yes, she has.* (Student B writes ✓)
  Student B: *Has she been to Buenos Aires?*
  Student A: *No, she hasn't.* (Student B writes ✗)
- Tell your students to ask and answer questions about everyone on their card. When they have done that, ask them to compare worksheets to check that the information is the same. Now tell them they are ready to play the game.

  1 Student A chooses a person on their card but doesn't tell Student B. Student B has to ask questions (as before) to eliminate the others on their card.

  2 The aim of the game is to find the selected person as quickly as possible (i.e. in as few questions as possible).

  3 The students can keep playing for as long as they enjoy it. The winner is the player who has guessed the most people in the fewest guesses.

  For example:

  Student A: *Is it a man or a woman?*
  Student B: *A woman.*
  Student A: *Has she been to Italy?*
  Student B: *Yes, she has.*
  Student A: *Has she been to Egypt?*
  Student B: *No, she hasn't.*
  Student A: *Has she been to The Olympics?*
  Student B: *No, she hasn't.*
  Student A: *It's Eva.*
  Student B: *Yes.*

  (Student A guessed in four questions. Student B can only win the round if he or she guesses in fewer than four questions.)

Note

In order to guess more quickly your students will probably stop using *Has (s)he been to…* and just use the name of the place. You may want to explain that the point of the exercise is to practise saying the stem as often as possible to make it sound more natural.

Point out to your students that the *have* is not stressed in the question and the *been to* is either pronounced /'bɪntə/ when it's followed by a consonant or /'bɪntuː/ (followed by a 'w' sound) when followed by a vowel.

15 Vocabulary *Bingo!*

Page 197

Activity

Class mingle.

Focus

Present perfect + *ever*.

Preparation

Make one copy of the worksheet for every six students in the class and cut it up as indicated.

Procedure

- Check students know the following vocabulary from the bingo cards: *bungee jump, credit card, drums, octopus, wallet, accident, celebrity, ID card, x-ray, tattoo, operation, break your leg, fall in love.*

- Give out one bingo card to each student. Explain that the aim of the game is to complete the bingo card with the names of students who have done the activities on their card.

- Remind students how to form the present perfect with *ever* and if necessary revise the irregular past participles: *done, been, gone, broken, had, lost, won, eaten, found, met, fallen, seen, ridden.*

- Tell students to walk around the class asking their classmates in turn *Have you ever …?* questions about the activities on their card, for example, *Have you ever visited New York? Have you ever done a bungee jump?* When a student answers *yes* to a question, his or her name is written in pencil next to the activity. Once the card is complete, with a name written in for each of the activities, the student should shout *Bingo!* If no-one in the class can answer *yes* to a question, the student can complete his or her card by writing *no-one* in the space. The first student to call out *Bingo!* is the winner.

- Ask the students to rub out the names, exchange their bingo cards and play the game again. Alternatively you may want to give out fresh bingo cards. Repeat this as many times as you feel is appropriate.

15 Communication Life experience

Page 198

Activity

Class mingle.

Focus

Present perfect and past simple.

Preparation

Make one copy of the worksheet for each student in the class.

Procedure

- Give one copy of the worksheet to each student in the class. Explain that they are going to complete some questions and then ask each other about their experiences.

- Direct your students' attention to the first verb on the worksheet (*lost*) and ask them to look at the example, where Student A has completed the question with … *any money* to make the question: *Have you ever lost any money?*. The example goes on to show that when Student A asked Carlo the question, he gave the answer *Yes*, and so his name was written down in the second column. Then Student A asked for details. This time the tense changes from present perfect to past simple. Ask your students to guess the two questions necessary to complete the third column with the note-form answer: *lost it last week in the city centre*. (The questions are *When did you lose it?* and *Where did you lose it?*) Both questions can be seen in the sample dialogue between Student A and Carlo.

- Encourage your students to be creative when completing their questions and try to think of questions that they would really like to hear answers to. When they have written them, ask your students to get up and mingle, asking and answering their questions.

- When the first student has finished, stop the activity and ask the class if they found out anything interesting about each other.

16 Grammar Circuit training

Page 199

Activity

Revision game.

Focus

To revise and practise structures, vocabulary and pronunciation from *New Inside Out* Elementary Student's Book.

Preparation

Make four copies of the worksheet and cut the copies up as indicated.

Make one copy of the key for each student for the final part of the activity.

Provide four English dictionaries if you have some.

Procedure

- Stick one of the photocopied activities: *Grammar, English in use, Pronunciation* and *Vocabulary* on the wall in each corner of the classroom.

- Divide the class into four teams and ask them to choose a name for their team. Tell students that they should try to complete the task in each corner of the classroom in their teams. They must remember to write their team name at the top of the task sheet.

- Tell students they will have eight minutes per task. At the end of the eight minutes, collect in the completed tasks and stick up a new blank task sheet. Each team then moves on to a different corner of the classroom.

- Once all the teams have completed all four tasks, tell students to sit down in their teams. Give each team a copy of the key, an English dictionary and another team's task sheets to mark.

- Go round, while students are marking the sheets, checking that they are marking fairly and helping with any language queries.

- Return the marked task sheets to the original teams and find out which group has the highest score.

Grammar

Give one point for each correct sentence.

1 She is a <u>very intelligent</u> woman.
2 Mary <u>always</u> has ~~the~~ dinner at 8.00 p.m.
3 After dinner he <u>saw</u> a film <u>on</u> TV.
4 David always <u>cooks</u> and Phillipa does the <u>washing up</u>.
5 My mother gets to <u>work</u> at ~~the~~ 9.30 a.m.
6 He has ~~the~~ toast and coffee <u>for breakfast</u> every day.
7 Where <u>are you going / are you going to go</u> on holiday next summer?
8 I <u>would like/'d like</u> to buy <u>some / a pair of</u> jeans tomorrow.

Vocabulary

Use your dictionaries and Student's Books to check the answers. One point for every correct word.

Pronunciation

/ʌ/	much	but	cut	son
/ɜː/	word	girl	first	work
/ɔː/	more	four	walk	door
/iː/	easy	meet	three	seat
/ɪ/	big	ship	rich	bit

English in use

1 h 2 e 3 f 4 b 5 i
6 j 7 a 8 c 9 d 10 g

---

16 **Vocabulary** Challenge

Page 200

Activity

Team game.

Focus

Revision of some of the grammar, vocabulary and pronunciation in *New Inside Out* Elementary Student's Book.

Preparation

Make two copies of the worksheet and cut one of the copies up as indicated. If possible, make an OHT so that you can reveal each question when you are playing the game.

Procedure

- Place the worksheet which has not been cut up, face up on your desk. Arrange the cards face down on top of the worksheet, so that you are using the worksheet as a grid.

- Divide the class into two teams. Explain the rules of the game:

  1 Students have to answer questions and win points for their team.

  2 There are four categories of questions, and four difficulty levels for each category. The more difficult the question, the more points the team can win.

  3 Teams take it in turns, one student at a time, to choose a category and a difficulty level for their question.

     If the question they have chosen has already been answered, they must choose a different category or difficulty level.

  4 If they answer the question correctly, the team is awarded the card and the number of points written on the card.

  5 The winning team is the one with the most points at the end of the game.

- Play the game. For each question, copy the text onto the board or show it on the OHT so that the whole class can read it.

Extension

If students enjoyed the game and if time allows, the teams could prepare revision questions for one another using the same categories.

Vocabulary
75 points: strong – weak; nephew – niece;
like – hate / dislike; near – far; go to sleep – wake up

Grammar

25 points: child – children; family – families; wife – wives; church – churches; bus – buses

50 points: Countable – lemon, carrot, grape, potato, egg; **Uncountable** – bread, pasta, meat, rice, oil

75 points: go – went; hear – heard; say – said; buy – bought; sleep – slept; can – could; fly – flew; see – saw

100 points: unhappy – unhappily; fast – fast; careful – carefully; good – well; early – early; loud – loudly

Pronunciation

25 points: after<u>noon</u>; thir<u>teen</u>; ex<u>pe</u>rience; <u>in</u>teresting; ho<u>tel</u>

50 points: cor<u>rect</u>; Chin<u>ese</u>; <u>chil</u>dren; <u>vis</u>it; <u>in</u>teresting

75 points:
/s/ envelopes, stamps
/z/ roads
/ɪz/ pages, horses

100 points:
/d/ enjoyed
/t/ washed
/ɪd/ divided, needed, created

16 Communication It takes ages!

Page 201

Activity

Class mingle.

Focus

Questions about transport.

Preparation

Make one copy of the worksheet for each student.

Procedure

- Ask the students to match the expressions at the top of the page – one has been done as an example.
- Ask the students to fill in the table – you may want to do the first line as an example. Then ask the students to complete the bottom line about themselves.
- Ask students to look at the table in Exercise 3. Ask them to tell you the questions and write on the board:

  How do you go to | *school?*
  | *work?*
  How long does it take?

- Ask the students to walk around the class, asking and answering the questions, and then complete the table.

Extension

You can use the students' completed tables to lead into a writing activity in which students write about how they and their classmates go to school/go to work (using the connectors *and* and *but*).

Note

This activity may be best used as a warmer/lead-in to the unit.

	Type of transport	Leave home	Arrive	How long does it take?
Ann	bus	8.10	8.55	*45 minutes*
Ben	car/ferry	7.30	9.00	90 minutes
Chris	foot/train	7.45	8.45	one hour

Review D Song: *Get Here*

Page 202

Activity

Pairwork: song.

Focus

Revising vocabulary from *New Inside Out* Elementary Student's Book, Units 13–16.

Preparation

Make one copy of the worksheet for each student in the class. Get the recording ready.

Procedure

- Explain that you're going to listen to a song called *Get Here*. Direct your students to the information box and ask some questions about the two women who have recorded it. (*How many people have had a hit with the song? What are their names? When did they each record this song?*)
- Ask your students to listen to the song and number the pictures that show the different ways of travelling. Play as many times as necessary.
- Ask your students to read the song and find two more ways of travelling.
- Students complete the table with the travel phrases in Exercise 1 and then compare travelling experiences in pairs.

> 1 a3 b7 c5 d2 e8 f6 g1 h4
> 2 by trail way, find and climb a tree and swing rope to rope, windsurfing

1 Grammar

Landing card

1 Look at the landing card. Write one question for each line.

- *What's your first name?*
- _____
- _____
- _____
- _____
- _____
- _____

2 Interview your partner and write your partner's answers on the card.

LANDING CARD

First name: ☐

Surname: ☐

Nationality: ☐

Home address: ☐

Email address: ☐

Phone (home): ☐

Phone (mobile): ☐

3 Give your partner the completed landing card to check, and keep.

1 Vocabulary

Common objects

A

fold

Grid A (crossword):

- 1 Down: B O O K S
- 2 Down (T): T I S S U E S
- 3 Down (P): P E N S
- 4 Down (C): C A M E R A
- 5 Down (M): M O B I L E P H O N E
- 6 Across: S E...
- 7 Across
- 8 Across: U S
- 9 Down: B A G
- 10 Down: A S P I R I N S
- 11
- 12 Down: P I R I N S
- 13
- 14

Clues A

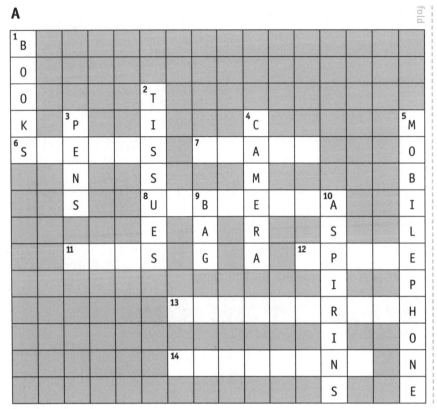

10 Aspirin
2
5
1
4
3
9

B

fold

Grid B (crossword):

- 6 Across: S W E E T S
- 7 Across: D I A R Y
- 8 Across: U M B R E L L A
- 9 Down: B R E L L A
- 10 A
- 11 Across: K E Y S
- 12 Across: A P P L E
- 13 Across: T O O T H B R U S H
- 14 Across: M A G A Z I N E

Clues B

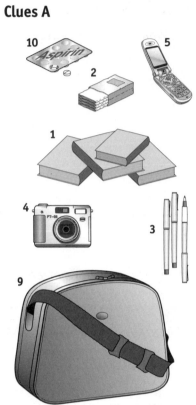

8
11
13
7
6
12
14 TIME
Has time run out for our planet
GLOBAL WARMING
Are we to blame

 New Inside Out Elementary Teacher's Book © Macmillan Publishers Limited 2007

1 Communication

Where in the world?

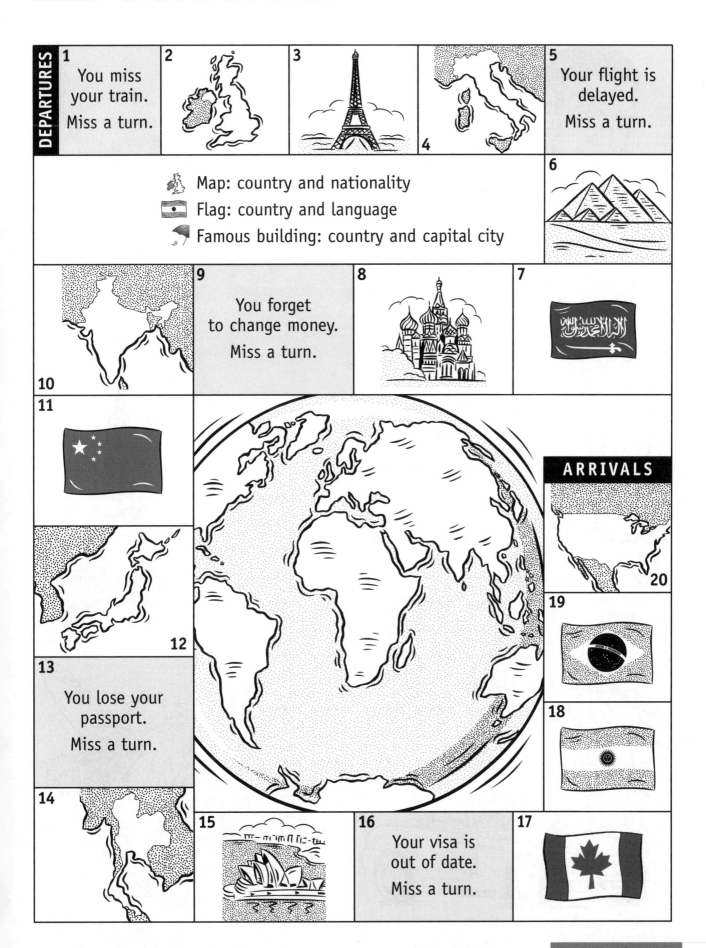

2 Grammar

True or false?

My favourite food is _____

My favourite drink is _____

My favourite car is _____

My favourite sport is _____

My favourite actor is _____

My favourite singer is _____

My favourite day of the week is _____

My favourite month is _____

My favourite city is _____

    New Inside Out **Elementary Teacher's Book**

2 **Vocabulary**

What's the job?

actor	IT technician	doctor
hairdresser	shop assistant	taxi driver
singer	nurse	writer
waiter	farmer	dancer
model	secretary	teacher
bus driver	artist	tennis player

thirteen

sixty
sixty
sixty
sixty
sixty
sixty

40

fifteen

thirty

14

30 30 30
30 30 30
30 **30** 30
30 30 30
30 30 30

sIXTEEn

16

50

forty

60

fourteen

fifty

15
15
15
15
15

13

3 Grammar

Who's who?

Student A

1 Look at Family tree A and complete these sentences with the correct names.

1) *Grace's* grandfather is Stan.
2) _____ wife is Liz.
3) _____ sister is Emily.
4) _____ mother is Julie.
5) _____ husband is Steve.
6) _____ brother is Paul.
7) _____ aunt is Sandra.
8) _____ nephew is Daniel.
9) _____ niece is Olivia.

2 Read your sentences to Student B. Student B writes the names.

3 Listen to Student B and write the names in Family tree B.

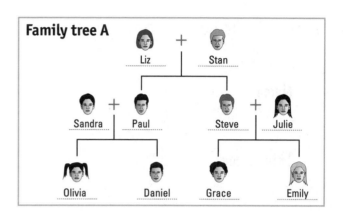

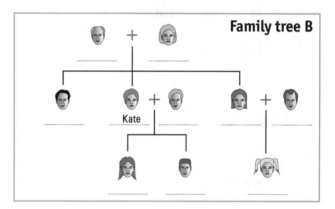

Student B

1 Look at Family tree B and complete these sentences with the correct names.

1) *Kate's* husband is Mike.
2) _____ sister-in-law is Vicky.
3) _____ brother is Alan.
4) _____ nephew is Ben.
5) _____ sister is Rose.
6) _____ grandfather is Richard.
7) _____ wife is Mary.
8) _____ granddaughter is Annie.
9) _____ father is Dave.

2 Listen to Student A and write the names in Family tree A.

3 Read your sentences to Student A. Student A writes the names.

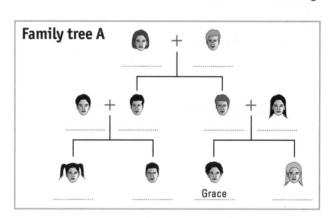

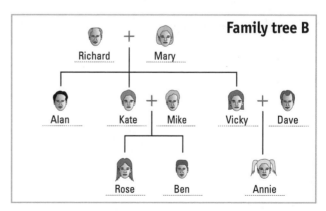

3 Vocabulary

Family photos

Write about someone in your family.

Name: _____

_____

This is my ... _____

_____

... is ... years old. _____

... lives ... _____

_____

_____

_____

... works ... _____

_____

... is married / single. _____

_____

I see him / her ... _____

_____

_____

_____

Other information _____

_____

_____

_____

_____

Attach photo here

3 Communication

Am I right?

Name		I think this is true (✓) / false (✗)	I'm right (✓) / wrong (✗)
	does the housework.		
	has two children.		
	goes to bed late.		
	lives in a big house.		
	has a brother.		
	watches TV in bed.		
	drinks beer.		
	goes to bed early.		
	knows someone famous.		
	plays football.		

4 Grammar

Find out

Who ...
- goes shopping every weekend?
- has a brother?

Find out

Who ...
- works outside?
- has a sister?

Find out

Who ...
- drives an expensive car?
- chats online?

Find out

Who ...
- eats three meals a day?
- does the housework?

Find out

Who ...
- likes cooking?
- has a motorbike?

Find out

Who ...
- reads the newspaper every day?
- smokes?

Find out

Who ...
- listens to hip-hop?
- goes swimming every week?

Find out

Who ...
- goes dancing at the weekend?
- doesn't have a mobile phone?

Find out

Who ...
- works in an office?
- studies at the weekend?

Find out

Who ...
- watches TV every day?
- plays a musical instrument?

Find out

4 Vocabulary

I love playing charades!

I love skiing.

I don't like writing letters.

I like playing the guitar.

I don't mind doing the washing up.

I like reading the newspaper.

I hate watching football.

I love listening to very loud music.

I hate ironing.

I don't like getting up before 10.00 a.m.

I love going to the beach.

I love reading magazines.

I don't mind Chinese food.

The group *The Killers*	The actor *George Clooney*	The actress *Nicole Kidman*	The film *Gladiator*
The group *The Sugababes*	The footballer *Ronaldinho*	The singer *Beyoncé*	The Frank Sinatra song *My Way*
The group *Radiohead*	The actor *Russell Crowe*	The actress *Angelina Jolie*	The film *Lord of the Rings*
The group *Oasis*	The singer *Justin Timberlake*	The singer *Avril Lavigne*	The Beatles song *Yesterday*
The group *U2*	The actor *Tom Cruise*	The actress *Cameron Diaz*	The film *Pirates of the Caribbean*

Tell the truth

Tell a lie

Review A

Song: *I Like The Way ...*

Kaz James and Dylan Burns are The BodyRockers: an Australian duo. They had a huge hit in 2005 with *I Like The Way ...* . They recorded the single in only four hours!

1 🔘 **1.60 Listen and match the two halves to complete the lines of the song.**

There's so many things I like about you, I ...
I just don't know where to begin,

a) I like the way you look ...   1 along.
b) I like the way you act ...   2 to dance.
c) I like the way you sing ...   3 your hands.
d) I like the way you always get ... 4 at me with those beautiful eyes.
e) I like the way you clap ...   5 it wrong.
f) I like the way you love ...   6 all surprised.

g) I like the way you put ...   7 so much.
h) I like the way you shake ...   8 your hands up in the air.
i) I like the way you like ...   9 your hair.
j) I like the way you stare ...   10 to touch.

But most of all, yeah, most of all ...

I like the way you move.

> *sing along* = sing at the same time
> *get it wrong* = sing the wrong words
> *stare* = look at someone for a long time

2 **What does the singer like most about the girl in the song?**

3 **What do you like and what don't you like about your friends and family? Write sentences.**

I like the way + [A PERSON] + [VERB]   *I like the way my wife sings.*
I don't like the way + [A PERSON] + [VERB] *I don't like the way my mother drives!*

Compare your sentences with a partner.

5 Grammar

Breakfast survey

Example:

Name	Time	Who with	Food	Drink
Me	7.30	alone	toast and jam	black coffee

Name	Time	Who with	Food	Drink
Me				

In our group ...

1 .... % of people don't eat anything for breakfast.

2 .... people have breakfast before 7.00 a.m.

3 .... % of people eat breakfast alone.

4 the most popular breakfast food is ....

5 the most popular breakfast drink is ....

 New Inside Out Elementary Teacher's Book   © Macmillan Publishers Limited 2007

5 Vocabulary

Daily routines

Complete each sentence with one of the verbs below.

| get go have read listen |

Find someone who ...	**Name**
gets up after ten on Sunday mornings.	
_____ shopping every weekend.	
_____ a shower every morning.	
_____ to work on Saturdays.	
_____ the newspaper every day.	
_____ to the radio every morning.	
_____ a bath every evening.	
never _____ breakfast.	
_____ on the internet every day.	
usually _____ to bed after midnight.	

Time dominoes

It's twenty-five to three.	(clock)	It's eight forty-five.	**8.55**	It's five to nine.	(clock)
It's twenty-five past three.	**4.30**	It's half past four.	(clock)	It's quarter to five.	**9.40**
It's twenty to ten.	(clock)	It's quarter past one.	**7.30**	It's seven thirty.	(clock)
It's half past five.	**5.50**	It's ten to six.	(clock)	It's five to ten.	**1.55**
It's five to two.	(clock)	It's twelve thirty-five.	**11.35**	It's twenty-five to twelve.	(clock)
It's five past two.	**10.05**	It's five past ten.	(clock)	It's six fifty.	**3.15**
It's three fifteen.	(clock)	It's ten twenty.	**12.45**	It's quarter to one.	(clock)
It's ten past seven.	**5.15**	It's quarter past five.	(clock)	It's eleven forty.	**2.35**

6 Grammar

A question of time

1 Write the words in the box under the correct preposition in the table.

> Saturday night   the autumn   the weekend
> 6:15   the evening   the spring   Friday
> February   quarter to six   24th April   night
> October   the afternoon   Sunday
> four thirty
> two o'clock   18th November   Monday morning

on	in	at
Saturday night	the autumn	the weekend

2 Ask and answer the questions with a partner. Use time prepositions.

Partner's name: _____

1   What time do you get up? _____

2   What time do you go to bed? _____

3   What time do you eat in the evening? _____

4   When is your birthday? _____

5   What do you do on your birthday? _____

6   What do you do at the weekend? _____

7   What's your favourite day of the week? Why? _____

8   What's your favourite time of year? Why? _____

6 Vocabulary

Make or *do*?

homework		a lot of noise	
dinner		the shopping	
a decision		the beds	
the washing		the washing up	
the housework		exercise	
a phone call		a mistake	

6 Communication

Snakes and ladders

| DATE | say the date | MONTH | name the month |
| ORDER | re-order the sentence | ? | answer the question |

FINISH

20
DATE
New Year's Day

19
?
What's the name of your favourite festival?

18
ORDER
hardly ever goes Anna out

15
?
Who do you usually make phone calls to?

16
MONTH
The tenth month

17
DATE
Your birthday

14
ORDER
cycle I often to work

13
DATE
Halloween

12
MONTH
The fourth month

8
MONTH
The eighth month

9
DATE
Valentine's Day

10
ORDER
John late school for never is

11
?
Who does the housework in your house?

7
?
How often do you do the washing up?

6
ORDER
home I'm at 8.00 p.m. always

5
DATE
Christmas Day

4
MONTH
The eleventh month

START

1
MONTH
The sixth month

2
ORDER
up get at 6.30 a.m. I usually

3
?
How often do you do homework?

New Inside Out Elementary Teacher's Book   © Macmillan Publishers Limited 2007   PHOTOCOPIABLE   169

7 Grammar

I did the same!

1 Complete the sentences to make them true for you.

1 I got up at _____ this morning.

2 I _____ yesterday evening.

3 I went to _____ for my last holiday.

4 The last time I travelled in a car was _____ .

5 I _____ last Sunday.

6 The last time I read a newspaper was _____ .

7 The last film I saw at the cinema was _____ .

8 The last time I played a game was _____ .

9 I was _____ (age) when I fell in love
for the first time.

10 When I was a child I couldn't _____
but I can now.

2 Walk around the class. Read your sentences to other students. Write the
name of the person who did the same as you next to each sentence.

 New Inside Out **Elementary Teacher's Book** © Macmillan Publishers Limited 2007

7 Vocabulary

Weather forecast

1 Find eight adjectives to describe the weather in this word snake and write them below.

w a r m w e t b a d c o l d d r y g o o d h o t l o v e l y

_____ _____ _____

_____ _____ _____

2 Now complete these adjectives which also describe the weather.

clo_ _y   f_g_ _   su_n_   w_nd_   r_i_y   sn_ _y   st_r_y

3 Read this weather forecast. Which of the picture slides does it describe?
Look in your dictionary or ask your teacher about any new words.

> Today will start foggy and cold. A light wind will clear the fog, but it will be cloudy and cold all afternoon. There will probably be some heavy rain. The rain will clear later and the early evening will be dry and sunny.

4 Choose one of the other picture slides and write your own weather forecast to describe it.
Then practise presenting your forecast to other students in the class.

7 Communication

What's the sport?

Student A

			¹F	O	O	²T	B	A	L	L			
		³C	Y	C	L	I	N	G					
	4					⁵S	⁶W	I	M	M	I	N	G
			7										
⁸S	U	R	F	I	N	G		9					
									10				
¹¹K	I	T	E	S	U	R	F	I	N	G			
				¹²J	O	G	G	I	N	G			

Student B

			1		²T						
					E						
					N						
		3			N						
					I						
	⁴S				⁵S	⁶W					
	C		⁷R			I					
8	U		I			N	⁹F				
	B		D			D	I				
	A		I			S	S	¹⁰S			
	D		N			U	H	A			
	I		G			R	I	I			
	V					F	N	L			
11	I					I	G	I			
	N					N		N			
	G		¹²			G		G			

 New Inside Out Elementary Teacher's Book © Macmillan Publishers Limited 2007

8 Grammar

I think …

I think …   ✓ or ✗

went to a last weekend.   ☐

sent an yesterday.   ☐

ate in a last week.   ☐

listened to some this morning.   ☐

watched last night.   ☐

sent a today.   ☐

spent a lot of last weekend.   ☐

came to school by today.   ☐

was late for this week.   ☐

did some yesterday.   ☐

stayed at last night.   ☐

didn't have any this morning.   ☐

cooked a last night.   ☐

didn't do any last night.   ☐

8 Vocabulary

How do you feel?

Team A

Five things that make you feel **frightened**	Five things that make you feel **happy**	Five things that make you feel **bored**	Five things that make you feel **worried**	Five things that make you feel **relaxed**

Team B

Five things that make you feel **excited**	Five things that make you feel **sad**	Five things that make you feel **angry**	Five things that make you feel **interested**	Five things that make you feel **embarrassed**

 New Inside Out Elementary Teacher's Book

8 Communication

Last summer, I …

Last summer, I went to Phuket in southern Thailand with my brother, Joe. We travelled by plane and stayed at a guesthouse at Kata Beach for five days. Every day, I swam and went jetskiing, but Joe didn't because he can't swim very well. He just sunbathed on the beach and slept! In the evenings, we drank cool drinks and watched the sunset, and then, after dinner, we went dancing at a nightclub. We both thought this holiday was fantastic, so we plan to go back to Phuket next year.

Put the words into the correct order to make the questions for these answers.

1 go when you did last on holiday
When did you last go on holiday?   Last summer.

2 you where go did
_____ Phuket.

3 with who you did go
_____ My brother, Joe.

4 did how go you
_____ By plane.

5 stay you did where
_____ At Kata Beach.

6 you what did do
_____ swam / went jetskiing / sunbathed / slept

7 it you enjoy did
_____ Yes, we did!

Now ask the same questions (1–7) to complete the table.

	Teacher	You	Student 1	Student 2
1				
2				
3				
4				
5				
6				
7				

Review B

Song: *Don't Worry, Be Happy*

Don't Worry, Be Happy was a massive hit in 1988 for
American singer, composer and conductor, Bobby McFerrin.

1 Match a word from list A with a word from list B to make
word pairs that rhyme.

A	B
wrote	bed
style	litigate
trouble	smile
head	note
frown	double
late	down

2 Complete the song with the word pairs from Exercise 1.

Here's a little song I (1) *wrote*.
You might want to sing it note for (2) *note*.
Don't worry, be happy.

In every life we have some (3) _____ .
When you worry you make it (4) _____ .
Don't worry, be happy.

Ain't got no place to lay your (5) _____ ?
Somebody came and took your (6) _____ ?
Don't worry, be happy.

The landlord says your rent is (7) _____ .
He may have to (8) _____ .
Don't worry, be happy.

Ain't got no cash, ain't got no (9) _____ ?
Ain't got no girl to make you (10) _____ ?
Don't worry, be happy.

'Cos when you worry your face will (11) _____ .
That will bring everybody (12) _____ .
Don't worry, be happy.

Ain't got = Don't have
lay your head = to sleep
landlord = the owner of a rented house
to litigate = to take someone to court

cash = money
style = fashionable clothes
frown = opposite of smile
bring everybody down = make everybody unhappy

🔊 2.28 **Listen and check your answers.**

3 What do these people worry about? Choose words from the box or your own ideas.

clothes	exams	friends	hairstyle	health	homework	looks	money	the future	work

a) *She worries about friends.*

4 How does this song make you feel? What sort of music makes you feel happy? Tell your partner.

 New Inside Out **Elementary Teacher's Book** © Macmillan Publishers Limited 2007

9 **Grammar**

Spot the difference

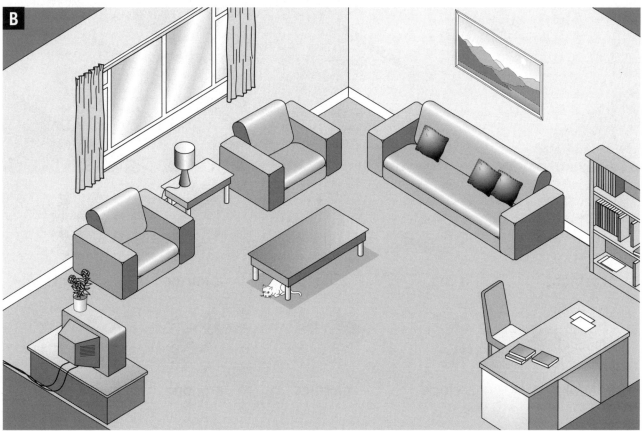

9 **Vocabulary**

Where are they?

Listen and draw the objects at the bottom of the page in the picture.

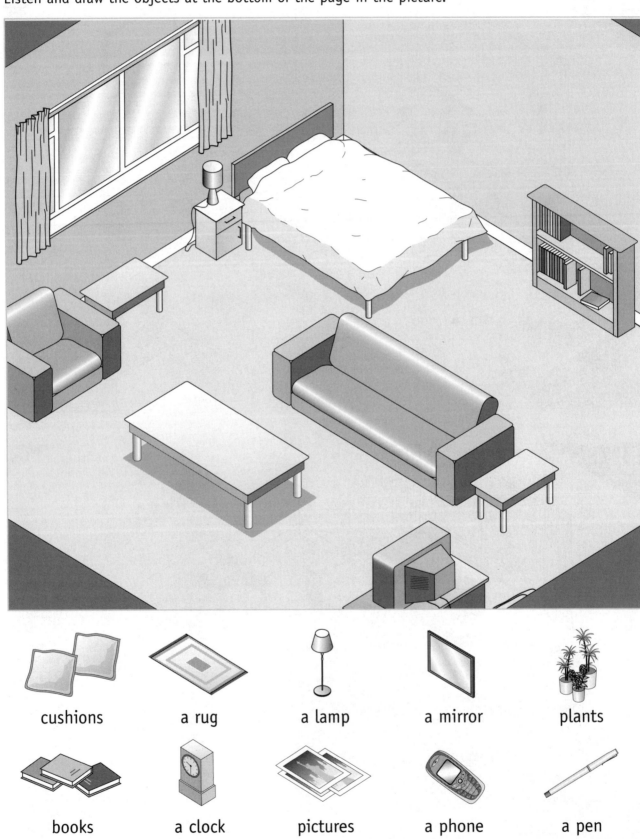

cushions	a rug	a lamp	a mirror	plants
books	a clock	pictures	a phone	a pen

  New Inside Out **Elementary Teacher's Book**   © **Macmillan Publishers Limited 2007**

9 Communication

In my room ...

10 Grammar

How much milk is there?

Student A

Ask Student B about the food and drink in the box and draw it in your picture.

| bread | rice | tea | bananas | tomatoes | apples |

Student B

Ask Student A about the food and drink in the box and draw it in your picture.

| pasta | milk | oranges | onions | steaks | coffee |

   New Inside Out Elementary Teacher's Book   © Macmillan Publishers Limited 2007

10 Vocabulary

Describe it!

apple	beans	cake	fish
cheese	garlic	banana	rice
onion	cereal	tomato	lemon
grape	bread	strawberry	carrot
potatoes	cauliflower	pear	steak
melon	chicken	pepper	pasta

QUESTIONNAIRE

Answer the questions to find out how good your diet is.

1 What's your favourite meal?

a Breakfast.
b Lunch.
c Dinner.

2 How many glasses of water do you drink every day?
a One.
b Three.
c Five or more.

3 How much fruit do you eat every day?
a One piece.
b Three pieces.
c Five or more pieces.

4 What's your favourite kind of tea?
a Black.
b Green.
c Herbal.
d I never drink tea.

5 How many cups of coffee do you drink every day?
a One.
b Three.
c Five or more.

6 What do you usually eat for breakfast?
a Fruit.
b Bread.
c Cereal.
d I never eat breakfast.
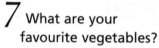

7 What are your favourite vegetables?
a Green vegetables like beans, cauliflower and lettuce.
b Red vegetables like tomatoes and red peppers.
c Potatoes – preferably chips.

8 How much chocolate do you eat?
a A lot.
b Not much.
c I never eat chocolate.

9 What's your favourite bread?
a Brown.
b White.
c I never eat bread.

10 How much sugar do you put in your coffee and tea?
a Two spoons or more.
b One spoon.
c None.
d I never drink coffee or tea.
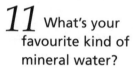

11 What's your favourite kind of mineral water?
a Still.
b Sparkling.
c I only drink coke.

12 How much meat do you eat?
a A lot.
b Not much.
c I never eat meat.

SCORE

1	a 4	b 3	c 2	
2	a 2	b 3	c 4	
3	a 2	b 3	c 4	
4	a 2	b 3	c 4	d 4
5	a 4	b 2	c 0	
6	a 4	b 3	c 3	d 0
7	a 4	b 3	c 1	
8	a 0	b 2	c 4	
9	a 3	b 2	c 2	
10	a 0	b 2	c 3	d 4
11	a 4	b 3	c 0	
12	a 1	b 3	c 4	

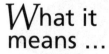

What it means …

You scored 13 to 25
OH DEAR! – You eat too many of the wrong things, and not enough of the right things.

You scored 26 to 35
BALANCED – You eat a good balanced diet but you don't think about food all the time.

You scored 36 or over
HEALTHY – Your diet is very good – are you sure you told the truth?

11 Grammar

What are they doing?

Student A

Ask Student B what these people are doing and write their names in the picture.

| Anna | Ben | Emily | Will | Cathy | Rob |

Useful verbs: dance, drink, eat, hold, play, sit, sleep, smile, stand, talk, watch, wear

Student B

Ask Student A what these people are doing and write their names in the picture.

| Ed | Nick | Olivia | Tom | Louisa | Carla |

Useful verbs: dance, drink, eat, hold, play, sit, sleep, smile, stand, talk, watch, wear

11 Vocabulary

Fashion and style

1 Use the words in the boxes to label the two pictures below.

1 _____

2 _____

3 _____

4 _____

5 _____

6 _____

7 _____

8 _____

9 _____

10 _____

11 _____

12 _____

13 _____

14 _____

15 _____

16 _____

17 _____

18 _____

top	bag	bracelet	skirt		belt	socks	jacket	glasses	T-shirt
scarf	boots	hat	coat	ring	jeans	trainers	shirt	cap	

2 Write five sentences to describe a classmate's clothes. Use the words from Exercise 1, the adjectives in the box below and the present continuous.

beautiful	dark	short	long	elegant	trendy	casual	formal	lovely	light

Ana is wearing a beautiful long skirt.

_____

_____

_____

_____

_____

11 Communication

Fashion show

START	What's she doing? 	Describe what you're wearing.	Fashion disaster! You're having a bad-hair day. **GO BACK 2**	**ORDER** you jeans wearing Are ?

KEY: **ORDER** = Put the words in the correct order to make a question.

What's he/she doing? = Describe the action you see in the picture.

What's he/she wearing? = Describe the clothes.

What's he wearing?

What's she wearing?

Describe today's weather.

Fashion triumph! Everyone loves your clothes! **GO FORWARD 4**

ORDER Are dancing they ?

What's he doing?

ORDER are you what doing ?

What's she doing?

Fashion disaster! You're wearing last year's colours. **GO BACK 3**

What's she wearing?

Describe what a member of your family is doing right now.

ORDER working isn't She today

Fashion triumph! You're having a good-hair day. **GO FORWARD 2**

What's she wearing?

Fashion disaster! Someone is wearing the same clothes as you! **GO BACK 2**

Describe what your teacher is wearing.

ORDER is going Jane Where ?

What's he doing?

What's he doing?

Fashion triumph! You're sitting with a top fashion editor. **GO FORWARD 2**

Describe what one of your classmates is wearing.

What's he wearing?

Fashion disaster! You spilled coffee on your white top. **GO BACK 4**

FINISH

12 Grammar

Quiz time

Put the alternatives into the correct order starting with the highest, biggest, most intelligent, etc. See Question 1 for an example.

1
a **Kilimanjaro**
b **Everest**   high
c **Fuji**

Answer *B, A, C*
Everest is the highest, and Kilimanjaro is higher than Mount Fuji.

2
a **Amazon**
b **Mississippi**   long
c **Nile**

Answer _____

3
a **cheetah**
b **rabbit**   fast
c **horse**

Answer _____

4
a **Mars**
b **Mercury**   near to Earth
c **Venus**

Answer _____

5
a **Frankfurt Airport**
b **Heathrow Airport**   busy
c **JFK Airport**

Answer _____

6
a **chimpanzee**
b **dolphin**   intelligent
c **gorilla**

Answer _____

7
a **Australia**
b **Russia**   big
c **Brazil**

Answer _____

8
a **I**   common in
b **it**   the English
c **the**   language

Answer _____

9
a **elephant**
b **rhinoceros**   heavy
c **hippopotamus**

Answer _____

 New Inside Out Elementary Teacher's Book   © Macmillan Publishers Limited 2007

12 Vocabulary

Ready, steady, search

Student A

1 Find eight more adjectives (➡ ⬇ ↘) and write them in the 'My words' column.

F	A	S	T	Q	U	G	L	Y	X
D	D	Y	S	W	Z	X	Y	O	Z
G	I	I	W	R	L	R	T	U	L
J	F	D	R	Y	K	I	R	N	K
P	F	H	K	T	J	C	W	G	J
L	I	K	M	P	Y	H	Q	P	H
W	C	H	E	A	P	C	M	S	G
Q	U	L	G	S	G	V	B	I	G
Y	L	O	N	G	R	B	N	D	F
N	T	Z	R	D	F	G	O	O	D

My words	Opposites
fast	
difficult	

2 Work with Student B and complete the table with his/her words to make ten pairs of opposites.

Student B

1 Find eight more adjectives (➡ ⬇ ↘) and write them in the 'My words' column.

S	M	A	L	L	Z	O	K	L	M
W	B	K	F	V	S	L	O	W	Q
C	L	E	A	N	D	D	J	R	S
R	J	W	A	C	V	S	H	T	H
B	A	D	F	U	T	W	G	Y	O
T	H	X	L	X	T	Q	D	P	R
E	X	P	E	N	S	I	V	E	T
Y	G	O	R	B	Y	Z	F	Q	R
P	F	O	H	G	P	V	X	U	D
S	D	R	M	E	A	S	Y	Z	L

My words	Opposites
small	
old	

2 Work with Student A and complete the table with his/her words to make ten pairs of opposites.

12 Communication

What is it?

Work in pairs.

Student A: Choose one of the objects below. Don't tell Student B what it is!

Student B: Ask questions to find out Student A's object. Use the language in the box at the bottom of the page. You may ask no more than ten questions.

Student A: Answer Student B's questions. You may answer only *Yes, it is. / No, it isn't.*, or *Yes, you do. / No, you don't.* to Student B's questions.

Is it made of ...	metal / plastic / cloth / paper / glass, *etc.* ?
Is it ...	round / square / rectangular / irregular-shaped / long / thin / wide, *etc.* ? black / white / grey / silver / multi-coloured *etc.* ?
Is it bigger/smaller than ...	a book / a television / a car *etc.* ?
Do you use it to ...	send messages / open things / play with / travel in / buy things, *etc.* ?

    New Inside Out **Elementary Teacher's Book**   © **Macmillan Publishers Limited 2007**

Review C

Song: *Sailing*

Sailing was a number 1 hit for Rod Stewart in 1975.

1 Work with a partner. Match the words in column A with their opposites in column B.

A		B	
a)	calm	1	free
b)	far	2	dark
c)	in prison	3	high
d)	low	4	stormy
e)	light	5	near

2 Complete the song with words from column B. You can use some words more than once.

I am sailing, I am sailing,
Home again, across the sea.
I am sailing, (1) *stormy* waters,
To be (2) _____ you, to be (3) _____ .

I am flying, I am flying,
Like a bird, across the sky.
I am flying, passing (4) _____ clouds,
To be near you, to be (5) _____ .

Can you hear me, can you hear me,
Through the (6) _____ night, far away?
I am dying, forever crying,
To be with you, who can say.

Can you hear me, can you hear me,
Through the (7) _____ night, far away?
I am dying, forever crying,
To be with you, who can say.

We are sailing, we are sailing,
Home again, across the sea.
We are sailing (8) _____ waters,
To be (9) _____ you, to be (10) _____ .

Oh Lord, to be near you, to be free.
Oh Lord, to be near you, to be free.
Oh Lord, to be near you, to be free.
Oh Lord.

🔊 3.04 **Listen and check your answers.**

3 Which sentence best summarises the song?

a) The singer is running away from his love because he wants to be free.
b) The singer wants to be with his love, but she lives far away.
c) The singer is on a boat with his love.

4 Think about a good friend who lives far away from you. Tell your partner about them.

13 Grammar

How do you do it?

Get dressed
fast

Play the
drums loudly

Do the ironing
angrily

Write your name
beautifully

Do your
homework happily

Drive the car
carefully

Play tennis
badly

Arrive for the
lesson late

Play the guitar
badly

Eat a banana
slowly

Do the washing
up unhappily

Play the piano
quietly

 New Inside Out Elementary Teacher's Book © Macmillan Publishers Limited 2007

13 Vocabulary

Character jumble

1 Complete the crossword by rearranging the jumbled character adjectives.

Across	**Down**
1 sflihse	1 syh
5 brgoni	2 ieenstitrgn
8 gnroeesu	3 sirueos
9 cideonftn	4 fynun
10 sbubotnr	6 fnilryed
11 qteiu	7 snseiebl

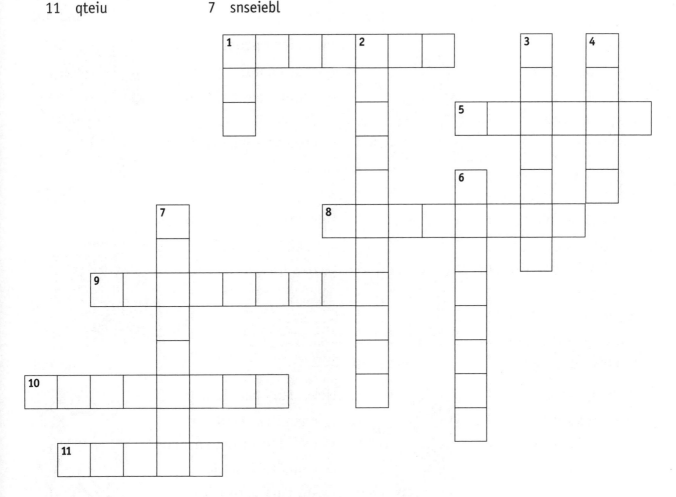

2 Work in pairs and for each of the adjectives:

a) decide which is the stressed syllable.

b) decide whether it has a positive, negative or neutral meaning.

c) think of a person, either famous or someone you know, who you can describe using the adjective.

13 Communication

How many people can do it?

How many people can...
- ride a horse?
- say the English alphabet without making a mistake?

Find out

How many people can...
- name five kinds of fruit in ten seconds?
- name five vegetables in ten seconds?

Find out

How many people can...
- say *I love you* in four languages?
- play a musical instrument?

Find out

How many people can...
- snowboard?
- count from 1–20 in English without making a mistake?

Find out

How many people can...
- say the months of the year in English without making a mistake?
- name five words starting with *s* in twenty seconds?

Find out

How many people can...
- spell *headache*?
- ride a motorbike?

Find out

How many people can...
- spell *beautiful*?
- name five sports in ten seconds?

Find out

How many people can...
- name five kinds of clothing in ten seconds?
- name five words starting with *t* in twenty seconds?

Find out

How many people can...
- spell *cousin*?
- name five words starting with *c* in twenty seconds?

Find out

How many people can...
- say the days of the week backwards in twenty seconds?
- stand on one leg for thirty seconds?

Find out

New Inside Out Elementary Teacher's Book   © Macmillan Publishers Limited 2007

14 Grammar

Make a sentence with ...

A Cards

A	A	A	A
would like to	want to	hope to	be going to
would like to	want to	hope to	be going to

B Cards

B	B	B	B
study	be	travel	have
play	make	meet	write

1 Read the statements and then choose the box that matches your own opinion / situation.

✓✓✓ = I strongly agree
✓ = I generally agree
? = I don't know
✗ = I generally disagree
✗✗✗ = I strongly disagree

		✓✓✓	✓	?	✗	✗✗✗
1	I'd prefer to have fewer television channels but better programmes – like it was before.					
2	I never watch more than two hours' of television a day.					
3	I think *The Simpsons* is the best cartoon on television.					
4	You can learn a lot about a person's true character when they appear on chat shows.					
5	There aren't many good documentaries on TV these days – it's all reality TV and quiz shows!					
6	I never watch soap operas – they're a total waste of time.					
7	The only reason I switch the TV on is to watch sport.					
8	The questions on game shows are too easy.					
9	There's too much opinion and not enough fact in news reporting these days.					
10	There's no future for TV. We'll soon watch everything on our computers.					

2 Discuss your answers in small groups.

14 Communication

What's your future?

1 Complete the questions with *would*, *do* or *are*.

2 Answer the questions for you. Then ask your partner.

	You	Your partner
1 What _____ you hope to study in the future?		
2 What job _____ you like to get?		
3 How many children _____ you like to have?		
4 Where _____ you going to go for your next holiday?		
5 What luxury item _____ you hope to buy one day?		
6 Where in the world _____ you like to live?		
7 Which famous person _____ you want to meet?		
8 What _____ you going to ask for on your next birthday?		
9 What _____ you going to watch on TV this evening?		
10 Where _____ you hope to be next summer?		

15 Grammar

Where have they been?

Student A

1 Ask Student B questions to complete the information on your card.

Amy		Joe		Karen		Andy		Eva	
Egypt	✓	Disneyland	✓	a Broadway play	✗	Australia	–	a Broadway play	✓
India	✗	a U2 concert	✓	India	✓	Mexico	–	Egypt	✗
The Olympics	✓	the UK	✓	Egypt	–	a U2 concert	–	Italy	✓
Italy	✓	Australia	✓	The Olympics	–	Thailand	–	The Olympics	✗
a Broadway play	✓	Thailand	✗	Italy	–	Disneyland	–	India	✓
Buenos Aires	✗	Mexico	✗	Buenos Aires	–	the UK	–	Buenos Aires	✓

Tom		Beth		Oliver		Darina		Bob	
Thailand	✓	Italy	–	Mexico	–	The Olympics	✓	a U2 concert	–
the UK	✓	Buenos Aires	–	Disneyland	–	a Broadway play	✗	Mexico	–
Mexico	✓	a Broadway play	–	Australia	–	Egypt	✓	Australia	–
Australia	✓	The Olympics	–	Thailand	–	Buenos Aires	✓	the UK	–
a U2 concert	✗	India	–	the UK	–	Italy	✓	Disneyland	–
Disneyland	✗	Egypt	–	a U2 concert	–	India	✗	Thailand	–

2 Choose one person from the card but don't tell Student B. Student B asks questions to find out who you chose. How many questions does Student B ask?

Student B

1 Ask Student A questions to complete the information on your card.

Amy		Joe		Karen		Andy		Eva	
Egypt	✓	Disneyland	–	a Broadway play	✗	Australia	✓	a Broadway play	–
India	✗	a U2 concert	–	India	✓	Mexico	✗	Egypt	–
The Olympics	–	the UK	–	Egypt	✓	a U2 concert	✓	Italy	–
Italy	–	Australia	–	The Olympics	✗	Thailand	✓	The Olympics	–
a Broadway play	–	Thailand	–	Italy	✓	Disneyland	✗	India	–
Buenos Aires	–	Mexico	–	Buenos Aires	✓	the UK	✓	Buenos Aires	–

Tom		Beth		Oliver		Darina		Bob	
Thailand	–	Italy	✗	Mexico	✓	The Olympics	✓	a U2 concert	✓
the UK	–	Buenos Aires	✓	Disneyland	✓	a Broadway play	–	Mexico	✓
Mexico	–	a Broadway play	✓	Australia	✓	Egypt	–	Australia	✗
Australia	–	The Olympics	✓	Thailand	✓	Buenos Aires	–	the UK	✓
a U2 concert	–	India	✓	the UK	✗	Italy	–	Disneyland	✓
Disneyland	–	Egypt	✗	a U2 concert	✗	India	–	Thailand	✗

2 Choose one person from the card but don't tell Student A. Student A asks questions to find out who you chose. How many questions does Student A ask?

 New Inside Out **Elementary Teacher's Book** © **Macmillan Publishers Limited 2007**

15 Vocabulary

Bingo!

visit New York	do a bungee jump	visit Australia	go surfing
break your leg	play the piano	have toothache	play the drums
lose a credit card	win a prize	eat octopus	find a wallet
visit London	go fishing	visit Paris	climb a mountain
have an accident	play the guitar	have an x-ray	play golf
meet a celebrity	lose your ID card	be on TV	fall in love
visit Russia	go scuba diving	visit Egypt	go skiing
have a tattoo	play basketball	break your arm	see a whale
ride a motorbike	break the law	win some money	have an operation

15 Communication

Life experience

Example: Student A: *Have you ever lost any money?*
Carlo: *Yes, I have.*
Student A: *When did you lose it?*
Carlo: *Last week.*
Student A: *Where did you lose it?*
Carlo: *In the city centre.*

Example:

Have you ever ...	Name	Details (Ask questions to find out where, when, who with, etc.)
lost *any money* ?	*Carlo*	*lost it last week in the city centre*

Have you ever ...	Name	Details (Ask questions to find out where, when, who with, etc.)
lost _____ ?		
been to _____ ?		
broken _____ ?		
eaten _____ ?		
seen _____ ?		
cooked _____ ?		
found _____ ?		
met _____ ?		

PHOTOCOPIABLE   *New Inside Out* Elementary Teacher's Book   © Macmillan Publishers Limited 2007

16 Grammar

Circuit training

Grammar

Team _____

Read the sentences below and
correct the mistakes.

1 She is a woman very intelligent.

2 Mary has the dinner at 8.00 p.m. always.

3 After dinner he see a film in TV.

4 David always cook and Phillipa does the wash up.

5 My mother gets to job at the 9.30 a.m.

6 He has for breakfast the toast and coffee every day.

7 Where you go on holiday next summer?

8 I like to buy a jeans tomorrow.

Vocabulary

Team _____

Write as many words as possible
related to these topics.

Things in a living room
Vegetables and fruit
Character adjectives

Pronunciation

Team _____

Match the words with the same vowel sounds
and put them into the correct box.

more word easy much four big
ship walk rich meet girl but three
first work seat door cut bit son

/ʌ/ e.g. come	/ɜː/ e.g. bird	/ɔː/ e.g. draw

/iː/ e.g. cheap	/ɪ/ e.g. trip

English in use

Team _____

Match each sentence with the best response.
Use each response once only.

Sentence	Response
1 Have a nice weekend.	a) How do you do.
2 How often do you go?	b) Here you are.
3 How are you?	c) What a pity!
4 I don't have any money.	d) I'm a waiter.
5 Italian food is the best.	e) Twice a week.
6 Where are you from?	f) Fine, thanks.
7 How do you do?	g) Certainly, madam.
8 I can't come tonight.	h) Thanks. You too.
9 What do you do?	i) Do you think so?
10 Can I try it on?	j) Italy.

1 _____ 2 _____ 3 _____ 4 _____ 5 _____

6 _____ 7 _____ 8 _____ 9 _____ 10 _____

16 Vocabulary

Challenge

Vocabulary	Grammar	Pronunciation	Speaking

✂   ✂

25 points VOCAB	**25 points** GRAM	**25 points** PRON	**25 points** SPEAK
Say these times in English: 08:40 21:30 17:15 10:45 06:05	Write the plurals of these nouns. **child** **family** **wife** **church** **bus**	Say these words with the correct pronunciation. **afternoon** **thirteen** **experience** **interesting** **hotel**	Talk non-stop for 30 seconds about your … **routine.**

✂

50 points VOCAB	**50 points** GRAM	**50 points** PRON	**50 points** SPEAK
Write on the board: **10 types of food** **and** **10 types of drink**	Divide the words into *countable* and *uncountable* nouns. **lemon potato** **bread egg** **pasta meat** **carrot rice** **grape oil**	<u>Underline</u> the stressed syllable in each word. **correct** **Chinese** **children** **visit** **interesting**	Talk non-stop for 45 seconds about your … **family.**

75 points VOCAB	**75 points** GRAM	**75 points** PRON	**75 points** SPEAK
Give the opposite of these words: **strong** **nephew** **like** **near** **go to sleep**	Write the past simple form of these irregular verbs. **go sleep** **hear can** **say fly** **buy see**	Put these words into the correct column. /s/ /z/ /ɪz/ **pages envelope** **roads stamps** **horses**	Talk non-stop for one minute about your … **free time.**

100 points VOCAB	**100 points** GRAM	**75 points** PRON	**100 points** SPEAK
Write on the board: **10 items of men's clothes** **and** **10 items of women's clothes**	Make adverbs from these adjectives. **unhappy** **fast** **careful** **good** **early** **loud**	Put these words into the correct column. /d/ /t/ /ɪd/ **divided enjoyed** **needed washed** **created**	Talk non-stop for one and a half minutes about your … **house.**

 New Inside Out Elementary Teacher's Book © Macmillan Publishers Limited 2007

16 Communication

It takes ages!

1 Draw lines to match the sentences in the two columns.

I go by car.   I walk by the canal.

I go by taxi.   I catch the 7.20 from platform 7.

I go on foot.   I ride my Kawasaki 600.

I go by bus.   I catch a cab.

I go by train.   I drive along the motorway.

I go by ferry.   I catch the number 49. It goes down the High Street.

I go by motorbike.   I take the 7.15 boat from Liberty Harbour.

2 Complete this table.

Name	Type of transport	Leave home	Arrive	How long does it take?
Ann	bus	8.10	8.55	
Ben	car / ferry	7.30		90 minutes
Chris	foot / train		8.45	one hour
You				

3 Now ask your classmates how they go to school or go to work.
Complete the table.

Name	Transport	How long ... ?

Review D

Song: *Get Here*

a ☐ by caravan   **b** ☐ on a carpet

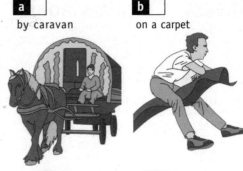

1 🌐 3.59 **Listen to the song and number the pictures (*a–h*) in the order you hear them mentioned.**

c ☐ by sled   **d** ☐ on an airplane   **e** ☐ in a balloon   **f** ☐ on a coach   **g** ☐ by railway   **h** ☐ by sail boat

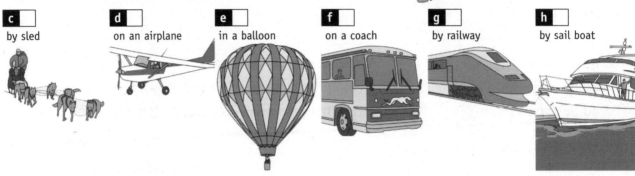

2 **Read and listen to the song again. Find at least two more ways of travelling.**

You can reach me by railway.
You can reach me by trail way.
You can reach me on an airplane.
You can reach me with your mind.
You can reach me by caravan,
Across the desert like an Arab man.
I don't care how you get here.
Just get here, if you can.

You can reach me by sail boat,
Find a tree and swing rope to rope.
Take a sled and slide down the slope,
Into these arms of mine.
You can jump on a speedy coach,
Across the border in a blaze of hope.
I don't care how you get here.
Just get here if you can.

There are hills and mountains between us,
Always something to get over.
If I had the way, surely you would be closer.
I need you closer.

You can windsurf into my life,
take me up on a carpet ride.
You can make it in a big balloon,
But you better make it soon.
You can reach me by caravan,
Across the desert like an Arab man.
I don't care how you get here.
Just get here if you can.
I don't care how you get here.
Just get here if you can.

reach = to arrive somewhere	*slope* = a piece of ground that has one side
trail = a path through the countryside	higher than the other.
swing = move from side to side	*speedy* = fast

3 **Complete the table with travel phrases from Exercise 1. Compare with a partner.**

I've travelled like this	I haven't travelled like this	I'd like to travel like this
on an airplane, *by train ...*	*on a flying carpet,* *on a coach ...*	*in a hot-air balloon,* *by sled ...*